GRAND DELUSION

Also by Steven Simon

The Sixth Crisis
(with Dana H. Allin)

Our Separate Ways
(with Dana H. Allin)

The Pragmatic Superpower
(with Ray Takeyh)

Iraq at the Crossroads
(with Toby Dodge)

The Next Attack
(with Daniel Benjamin)

The Age of Sacred Terror
(with Daniel Benjamin)

GRAND DELUSION

The Rise and Fall of
American Ambition
in the Middle East

STEVEN SIMON

PENGUIN PRESS
NEW YORK
2023

PENGUIN PRESS
An imprint of Penguin Random House LLC
penguinrandomhouse.com

LIBRARY OF CONGRESS CATALOGING-IN-PUBLICATION DATA
Names: Simon, Steven, author.
Title: Grand delusion : the rise and fall of American
ambition in the Middle East / Steven Simon.
Description: New York : Penguin Press, 2023. |
Includes bibliographical references and index.
Identifiers: LCCN 2022039041 (print) | LCCN 2022039042 (ebook) |
ISBN 9780735224247 (hardcover) | ISBN 9780735224254 (ebook)
Subjects: LCSH: United States—Foreign relations—Middle East. |
Middle East—Foreign relations—United States.
Classification: LCC DS63.2.U5 S574 2023 (print) | LCC DS63.2.U5 (ebook) |
DDC 327.73056—dc23/eng/20220822
LC record available at https://lccn.loc.gov/2022039041
LC ebook record available at https://lccn.loc.gov/2022039042

Printed in the United States of America
1st Printing

Book design by Daniel Lagin

For Virginia
Hinakh yafah ra'ayati

CONTENTS

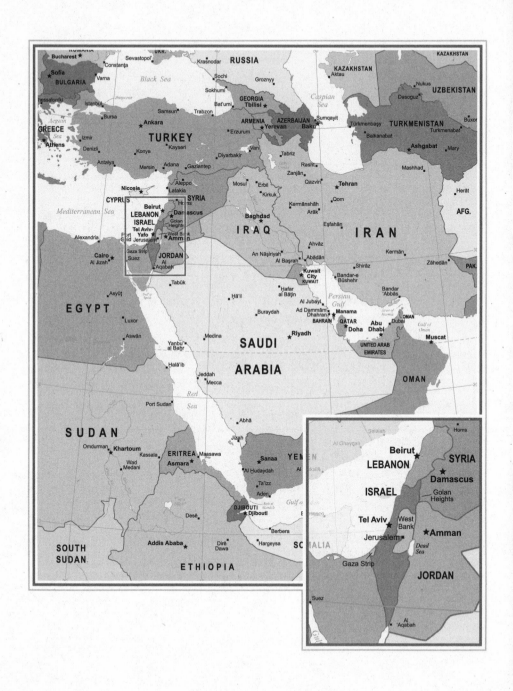

THE MIDDLE EAST
AND NORTH AFRICA

PREFACE

————

In addition to being an account of a forty-year span of U.S. entanglement in the Middle East, this book is a memoir, if one in which the
narrator is largely hidden from view. Although the book is not about
me, I was involved in much of the action from the middle of Ronald Reagan's first term, when I began at the State Department, through the early
part of Barack Obama's second term, when I was engaged in an unofficial
effort to reduce the level of violence in the Syrian conflict. Thus, the book
implicitly covers the trajectory of one participant's career that happens to
map neatly onto the arc of U.S. activism in the Middle East. My first assignment as a young civil servant was to game out a diplomatic strategy
to facilitate the Reagan administration's plans for military operations in
the Middle East; my last government post, as National Security Council
senior director for the Middle East and North Africa, ended at the White
House, witnessing Obama's refusal to attack Iran or to put boots on the
ground in Syria.

While this personal dimension is of little intrinsic interest, it was
important to the conception and execution of this book. The narrative

emerges from the imaginative space between the worldview of the author as witness and as historian. Although I am today far from the person I was as a government official, I remember that person, his perceptions, and emotions, and therefore the mood and aspirations that permeated the policy process over that span of three decades. In my view, the reconciliation of those recollections, and the historical understanding that evolved as the book was written, separate this book from others that have covered all or part of this epoch of war and diplomacy in the Middle East.

The book, therefore, reflects my experience as a civil servant and political appointee whose long engagement with the Middle East paralleled his country's blundering efforts to reshape it. As events unfolded, I favored the exercise of American power in the Middle East, more to secure strategic interests than to disseminate either values or material largesse. I favored the first Gulf War and helped negotiate U.S. base access agreements throughout the Arab states of the Persian Gulf in the months that followed. In the ensuing years at the White House as the senior director for counterterrorism, my role was to be, as my colleague Richard Clarke aptly described himself, against all enemies. And in the Obama administration, I participated in the planning and oversight of two ill-fated interventions in the Middle East. So the narrative arc of this book reflects a certain sober reassessment.

Indeed, this is not the book I set out to write, and it reflects a skepticism that surprised even me. Not unfairly, early readers have chalked up the negative judgments herein to the clarity of hindsight. They have noted that the decisions under review were made in the fog of war, under great uncertainty, by human beings subject to moral, intellectual, and cognitive limitations, and buffeted by political winds. This book takes no issue with these explanatory factors; it deploys them. Yet even when these conditions are taken into account, the frequent rejection of less costly alternative courses of action in favor of force of arms can still be mysterious and even breathtaking. One of the attributes of a great power is the freedom to act without regard to cost. "Lead us not into temptation" had long been expunged from the Beltway version of the Lord's Prayer. But the costs exist—they are cumulative and, over time, corrosive, particularly the cost of American actions to largely powerless Middle Eastern populations.

I've been asked whether the United States is singularly inept, cruel, solipsistic, or any of many other moral or intellectual defects. My answer is an emphatic no. America not only enjoys a great deal of company but is leagues ahead of other imperial powers that have trod the vanquished territories of the Middle East, Africa, and the Asia-Pacific region. The British, French, Portuguese, Dutch, Belgians, Germans, Russians, Japanese, and Turks were far crueler, greedier, and violent than the United States has been. The United States, moreover, has failed in distinctively American ways, rooted in a belief in its exceptionalism, frontier mythology, invulnerability as a continental power shielded by oceans on its flanks, and the inordinate might it wielded in the mid-twentieth century.

Another question readers have raised relates to my personal assessment of the policymakers involved in this story. Immanuel Kant, in his *Universal History*, wrote, "Out of the crooked timber of humanity no straight thing was ever made." He was onto something, going back to the doctrine of original sin or perhaps even further in time. I am a Kantian in this respect and deeply skeptical of the perfectibility of human beings. What I do believe, however, is that the policymakers depicted in this book believed they were acting in their country's best interests. They also projected these interests onto the states and populations of the Middle East. In the book, I frame this dynamic as a tension between the intentionalists who made and carried out U.S. policy and the consequentialists who were the objects of that policy. Yes, we meant well and our anger was righteous. But in this account, I try to link intentions and consequences and do justice to both. In any case, the book avoids moral judgments about the key players, although it should provide enough context for the reader to make up their own mind. Reading former defense secretary Robert McNamara's memoir and his son's recently published examination of his relationship with his father has reaffirmed my reluctance to go down that road.[1]

Was there was a grand delusion? There was, and it was multidimensional. If there is a consistent theme in this book, it is of the superimposition of grand ideas on antithetical Middle Eastern realities and American capacities. It is reflected in the rejection of intelligence community analyses and sober contemporary commentary. The delusion was rooted in the conviction that facts don't matter, just intentions; that we create and inhabit our own reality, our capacities are unconfined, and the objects of our policy have no agency. They are just avatars in our own metaverse.

So, against this understanding of events, the fact that the U.S. policymakers involved—including me—wanted, when at their best, to make the Middle East a better place for its peoples while advancing U.S. strategic interests amounts to a contributing factor; it is not exculpatory. Hence the reckoning that follows.

GRAND DELUSION

WHAT WENT WRONG?

I n September 1982, Ronald Reagan dispatched U.S. Marines to Lebanon, telling the American people, "We owe it to ourselves and to our children. The whole world will be a safer place when this region, which has known so much trouble, can begin to know peace instead."[1] His predecessor, Jimmy Carter, had declared that the United States would not tolerate any threats to "our" oil, as was commonly said at the time, but Reagan was not talking about warning off oil poachers in the Persian Gulf. By casting a local mash-up of ethnic and religious vendettas and Israeli and Syrian maneuvering for territorial advantage as a cause with global consequences and multigenerational importance to all Americans, Reagan had fired the starting gun of a U.S. race to dominate the Middle East.

Thirty-four years later, Barack Obama told a former Senate colleague, "There is no way we should commit to governing the Middle East and North Africa. That would be a basic, fundamental mistake."[2] Donald Trump, in the wake of a devastating Iranian air attack on two Arabia American Oil Company (Aramco) installations that took half of Saudi production offline, tweeted that "we don't need Middle Eastern Oil & Gas."[3] He then cast doubt on Iranian responsibility and declared that if the United States did intervene on the Kingdom's behalf, it would be purely on a fee-for-service basis.[4] How did we go from a belief that a regional tussle over a small patch of land was a historic battle that would affect the entire world to an apparent rejection of the Middle East as an arena for U.S. military intervention?

The aim of this book is to explore the reasons for the rise and fall of American engagement in the Middle East from 1979 to the present day. It is a tale of gross misunderstandings, appalling errors, and death and destruction on an epochal scale. According to Brown University's 2021 "Cost of Conflict" report, the United States incurred $8 trillion in costs to wage the post-9/11 wars in Iraq and Afghanistan, which claimed over 900,000 lives and displaced millions.[5] The number of Iraqis killed in the first Gulf War, and in the ensuing decade by sanctions, is estimated by demographers in the hundreds of thousands. This book describes the impact on the region of a great power whose policymakers—sophisticated, ethically inclined, superbly educated, certain of U.S. interests—took understandable pride in their intentions while discounting the disastrous consequences of their actions.

Cycles of foreign engagement and retrenchment have churned since the earliest years of the American republic. But none has been so prolonged and dramatic as that between the fall of the shah of Iran during the Carter presidency and the collapse of the U.S. position, or illusions about it, in the Middle East during Barack Obama's administration: the open contempt of Gulf states and Israel, the failure of a vast effort to arm and train Syrian rebels; the "shit show," as Obama described it, of intervention in Libya; the stalled attempts to foster democratic transitions during the Arab spring; the rise of the Islamic State; the inability to forge a durable constituency for a nuclear deal with Iran; and a bitter end to the Israeli-Palestinian peace process. Obama's successor, Donald J. Trump, acquiesced in this situation while denying it and, where he could, exploiting it for personal or political gains.

This paradigm of engagement and retrenchment began more than two centuries ago, when the United States—then a tiny country with almost no foreign presence—was forced to defend its sailors and trade against the hostage-taking privateers of North Africa's Barbary Coast. Those maritime campaigns, waged by the Adams, Jefferson, and Madison administrations, have little popular resonance today. But they shaped the way Americans thought of their country's role in the world, as well as their attitudes toward Muslims.

One of the causes of the war was the enslavement of captured American crews and passengers by rulers in Tripoli and Algiers. Abolitionists turned around slaveholders' patriotic denunciations of Arab enslavement of Americans to expose their hypocrisy and highlight the evil of chattel slavery at home. At the same time, images of Oriental despotism reinforced a belief in American exceptionalism and the superiority of democracy as a political system. These campaigns also boosted American self-confidence and pride in its military and, in particular, its naval prowess. The Marine Corps hymn refers to "the shores of Tripoli." After 9/11, these mostly forgotten battles were resurrected as America's first "war on terror."

Victory in the Barbary wars cost a great deal more than the demand for tribute that caused them. In the following decades, American involvement in the region settled into a largely commercial groove, trading rum for Turkish opium and selling ships, weapons, and military expertise to the Ottoman rulers of the Middle East. The United States pursued commercial and diplomatic relations despite the popular conviction that the Ottoman sultan was the Antichrist or the beast prophesied by the Book of Revelation. Values and interests stayed in their respective lanes. Protestant missionaries swarmed the region and, although they did establish durable institutions in the American universities of Beirut and Cairo, Robert College in Istanbul, and the American Colony in Jerusalem, they made few converts, focusing instead on an equally futile effort to reform the Catholic and Orthodox churches in the region.

American influence surged briefly toward the end of World War I and the postwar negotiations at Versailles and San Remo. Woodrow Wilson famously proposed "Fourteen Points" to regulate the postwar order. The twelfth stipulated that "the Turkish portion of the present Ottoman Empire should be assured a secure sovereignty, but the other nationalities which are now under Turkish rule should be assured an undoubted security of life and an absolutely unmolested opportunity of autonomous development."

This statement was, as they say in Washington, aspirational; but nationalist elites in the Arab parts of the Ottoman Empire took it as an American demand, not a mere whim. They fully expected Wilson to enforce British and French compliance with the Fourteen Points and to midwife the independence of Syria and Egypt. However, the burgeoning threat of communism and the possibility of German recovery and renewed aggression dictated the preservation of Western wartime alliances. Lloyd George, the British prime minister, and Georges Clemenceau, his French counterpart, ridiculed the Fourteen Points in private and insisted that Wilson support their national claims to Middle Eastern territory.

They had already divided it between them in 1916, as memorialized by the Sykes-Picot Agreement, which Russian revolutionaries had discovered in the czarist archive and revealed to the world. There was no way the Wilson administration would endanger transatlantic security by undermining British and French rule of the Middle East. Nor was it clear that Wilson himself cared very much. He did send a delegation of distinguished Americans to the Middle East to ascertain the mood of Arabs subject to British and French authority, but reportedly forgot having done so almost immediately.

The only self-determination movement that Wilson supported turned out to be Zionism, because the British asked him to do so both for wartime purposes and to ensure post-WWI British control of Palestine. London wanted to secure Jewish backing for the war effort, especially in revolutionary Russia, where the new government might sign a separate peace with Germany. Since Jews were prominent in the ascendant Bolshevik leadership, the British calculated a concession to a presumed Jewish interest would keep Russia in the war.[6] Others think the declaration had more to do with influencing American Jews, whose wealthy leadership was pro-German and whose poorer numbers had fled Russia and were eager to see its anti-Semitic regime defeated.[7] After the war, close ties between Zionists and the British government, secured by the Balfour Declaration in 1917, ensured a body of supportive subjects in Palestine. Palestine might have been the Holy Land, but it was also the right flank of the Suez Canal, an integral part of Britain's global security strategy. By the time Wilson died, hopeful Middle Eastern expectations of the United States were already dashed.

After World War II, however, the United States made its influence felt once again. Communist encroachment in western Europe made reconstruction there supremely urgent. The Marshall Plan, which brought to impoverished European countries essential food supplies, building material, machinery, and other equipment, was one response. But the redevelopment of industrial infrastructure, especially in Germany and France, needed one more ingredient: oil. This essential commodity had to come from the Middle East. The British could get theirs from Iran, which it controlled through the Anglo-Iranian Oil Company—otherwise known as BP, British Petroleum—and a pliable government in Tehran. The United States, UK, and USSR had occupied Iran during the war in light of the pro-Nazi leanings of the shah (and many Iranians), who hoped for Britain's defeat by Germany. Britain's thirst for oil and the Allies' need for a four-season route to Russia to resupply Soviet forces struggling against the Wehrmacht demanded that threats to Britain's control of Iran be removed. The rest of the oil for Europe had to come from the Arab side of the

Persian Gulf. The United States and Britain assumed that the Soviets were aware of this Western vulnerability and were prepared to exploit it by smashing through Iran and Iraq, seizing oil fields on the way to the Suez Canal, and choking off Western shipping.

In retrospect, the distances involved seem vast and the threat exaggerated. But a glance at the map shows that the route from Crimea, across the Black Sea and through Turkey down to the Arabian Peninsula, or along the coast of Palestine to Sinai and the Suez Canal, is not that long. Likewise, a Soviet army road march from Azerbaijan through Iran, across Iraq and Jordan to either the oil fields of northeastern Saudi Arabia or to the Suez Canal would have been a manageable task. As well, before the development of the B-52 bomber and then intercontinental ballistic missiles, the United States and UK needed Middle Eastern bases from which to launch nuclear attacks against the USSR.

The Second World War had also decimated European Jewry. Survivors, penned up in miserable camps and unable or unwilling to return to the countries where they had suffered so much, had to be settled somewhere. As the British pointed out at the time, Washington would much rather have them in Palestine than at American ports of entry. In November 1947, when a broke and bloodied Britain was eager to shed responsibility for Palestine, the United Nations, with U.S. and Soviet backing, split Palestine into Arab and Jewish territories, resulting in a new Jewish state, while the Arab parts were absorbed by Jordan and Egypt. Though the Zionists declared a state in May 1948, Arab Palestinians bet on its rapid extinction and swift end to the expropriation of Arab land by Jews. Inter-Arab rivalries combined with the unsettled politics within new independent Arab states to hamstring the ensuing Arab war effort. The Israelis, benefiting from interior lines of communications, access to the sea, an adequate supply of weapons and military gear, and well-developed organizational skills, turned back the Arab assault, albeit at great cost. By January 1949, combat operations had subsided, leaving Israel better off territorially than it had been at the time of partition. The United States at this point kept its distance from Israel, whose socialist politics raised suspicions about its alignment with the West and whose unpopularity in the Arab world rendered it a strategic liability.

The United States, at the same time, took on Saudi Arabia as its informal protectorate. American engineers had discovered a great deal of oil in the country in 1938, and a consortium of American companies formed an entity called Aramco to manage drilling, pumping, and transloading operations. Aramco profits were split between its American partners, which took the most revenue, and the ruling dynasty, the Al Saud. The Al Saud, which had expelled their British-backed Hashemite rivals from the Arabian Peninsula twenty years earlier, harbored deep suspicions of an allegedly vengeful Britain conniving to reinstate a Hashemite emir. From a Saudi perspective, the best defense was an American base at Dhahran, near the Saudi capital, opened in 1947, and a visibly close relationship with the United States symbolized by Aramco.

Overall, though, the U.S. military presence in the region remained quite small. Dwight Eisenhower kept the United States out, with the small exception of an easy-on-easy-off deployment of a marine contingent to influence the outcome of a political fracas in Beirut, and the not-so-small exception of backing a British coup against an Iranian nationalist in 1953. In 1956, he hammered Britain, France, and Israel for invading Egypt and pulled back from a coup against the Syrian government in 1957.

Both John F. Kennedy, who carried on a warm correspondence with Nasser and admired Israel while trying to halt its nuclear weapons program,[8] and Lyndon B. Johnson also largely steered clear of the region. The Johnson administration was so loath to get involved that it passed up the chance to prevent the Six-Day War of 1967 and thereby preserve the existing order in the Middle East, despite alternative options from the State Department and the national security adviser. But Johnson feared a congressional backlash, faced Pentagon foot-dragging, and was too preoccupied with

Vietnam to act. In the absence of tangible American support but with Johnson's apparent yellow light, Israel launched extremely effective pre-emptive attacks against its neighbors. The regional order dismantled by the war was far from perfect, but it was probably better than the one that emerged from its wreckage. We will never know. But the resulting insta-bility led to a devastating Arab-Israeli war six years later and shifts in the domestic politics of the regional states that are still playing out.

The British, meanwhile, maintained the only serious military presence in the region. With armies deployed to Korea, elsewhere in Asia, and Eu-rope, Washington was only too happy to play the free rider in the Middle East. Britain kept 100,000 troops in Palestine until 1947, and thousands of soldiers in Egypt until 1954 (and for a few months in 1956). In Iraq, British bases lasted until the 1958 revolution; in Aden, Yemen, until 1967; and around the Persian Gulf until 1971. That year, Great Britain struck its colors east of Suez for the last time, leaving Gulf security to an American administration tied down in Vietnam and coping with demonstrations and riots at home.

As the sun set on Britain's moment in the Middle East, Richard Nixon was settling into the White House. Rather than police the Gulf, he depu-tized Saudi Arabia and Iran to do so, arming and advising their militaries while keeping U.S. forces out of the picture. He stuck to this approach throughout his time in office, despite the Arab-Israeli conflict of 1973 and the ensuing Saudi oil embargo, which caused spiking oil prices and saturated the newspapers with political cartoons featuring hawk-nosed, bearded Arabs swathed in robes, choking the life out of the American economy.

Jimmy Carter's Middle Eastern interest lay in what became known as "the peace process." His intense focus produced a peace treaty between Israel and Egypt, forged in a marathon negotiation at Camp David in Sep-tember 1978 and finalized in March 1979. This was a significant achieve-ment. Whether it qualified as strategically vital for the United States is debatable. Carter's feat was driven by fear of renewed war that might trigger another Arab oil embargo, since the first was nominally to punish the United States for its support of Israel. With Cold War tensions rising and the effects of the first oil embargo still throttling the economy, the importance attached to Carter's peace process is easy to understand.

However, by 1978, both Egypt and Israel were in the American camp. The prospects of war between them were nil. The pathway to an eventual return of Israeli-held territory to Egyptian control had already been carved out by Henry Kissinger in 1974. As for an oil embargo, prices had been rising rapidly well before the 1973 war, largely thanks to the emergence of the Organization of the Petroleum Exporting Countries (OPEC) cartel, strong market demand, and tightening supply as U.S. domestic producers got out of the business. The 1973 embargo was in part a lofty pretext for a long-delayed price correction. In strategic terms, the Camp David Accords did not prevent another war between Israel and Egypt; rather, it ceremonially marked the eclipse six years earlier of the age of Israel-Egypt wars. Regrettably, Carter, perhaps distracted by the prospect of an Arab-Israeli peace, failed to anticipate an impending revolution in Iran. As such, he was unprepared to intervene to help a vital American ally, the shah of Iran, ride out the protests that eventually forced him to flee Tehran.

This was a case of intelligence failure to be sure, as the Central Intelligence Agency's own internal study has shown.[9] Carter did authorize planning for a countercoup, but it was too little too late.[10] The deployment of forces to the Persian Gulf, for example, as a signal of strong support for the shah despite domestic turmoil, might have stiffened his spine. However, hatred of the shah was volcanic, and even robust quasi-military support for his continued rule might not have saved him. And it would have been morally wrong to endorse, let alone abet, the massacre of unarmed protestors, which keeping a grip on power would likely have entailed. But the truth was that the overthrow of the shah was a profound reversal of fortune for the United States, plunging it into the maelstrom.

From the Reagan administration through Obama's first term, U.S. involvement in the Middle East followed a rising trajectory, cresting in Iraq after the September 11 attacks, descending through the grinding occupation of that troubled land, through the destruction of Libya and Syria, a brush war with the Islamic State, and the faintest possibility of rapprochement with Iran. This arc traced the loss of thousands of American lives, hundreds of thousands of Arab ones, and trillions of dollars that might otherwise have made lives at home more satisfying and productive. As these consequences loomed ever larger, Obama's second term in office and Donald Trump's presidency largely turned away from regional intervention. Joe Biden and his close advisers might have been tempted to reverse course by the conviction that this time the United States will get it right. But they could still be trapped by the dubious legacy of previous administrations that were once committed to the idea of the Middle East's strategic centrality. To avoid partisan criticism, policymakers will sometimes stick to outdated commitments they know to be strategically valueless in the present day. Old ideas die hard. And the White House will be distracted by the rise of China, the reverberations of conflict with Russia, challenges to the constitutional order at home, and, of course, climate change.

One could argue that the time frame for this history, beginning with a new era of intervention in 1979, is both artificial and at odds with what is widely known about American engagement in the Middle East. That it is artificial is undeniable. Even when a new era is thought to have been ushered in by a singular dramatic event—Caesar crossing the Rubicon in 49 BCE, the nuclear attacks on Hiroshima and Nagasaki in 1945, or the transmission of the first internet message in 1983—there is inevitably overlap between the old dispensation and the new one. Indications of what is to come can be detected before the event, while aspects of life prior to the pivotal moment carry on unchanged. But historians have to start somewhere. The alternative is Jorge Luis Borges's absurdity of a 1:1 map of the world: comprehensive, but useless as a navigational aid.

Of course, intervention takes many forms. It is tempting to resort to Justice Potter Stewart's 1964 definition of obscenity in *Jacobellis v. Ohio*: "I know it when I see it."[11] U.S. participation in the 1953 coup in Iran against Mohammad Mossadegh was an intervention; CIA support for the 1963 murder of President Abd al-Karim Qasim in Iraq was too, as was Eisenhower's deployment of 14,000 marines to Lebanon in 1958 to cow opponents of the Christian leader Camille Chamoun. Some would argue that Nixon's resupply of the Israeli military midway through the October War of 1973 qualified as intervention.

There was, however, a qualitative and quantitative difference between these episodes and post-1979 interventions, from Operation Eagle Claw, staged to free American hostages in Iran, to the Obama administration's actions in the region. None of the marines deployed by Eisenhower to Lebanon fired a shot during their short visit; Nixon's transfer of heavy weapons to Israel in 1973 did not entail the deployment of U.S. forces apart from air crews, let alone their direct involvement; the 1953 coup in Iran mostly entailed a flow of cash to pro-shah factions who were already so strong that even U.S. embassy reporting indicated that covert funding for incitement was unnecessary; in Iraq's 1963 coup, although one of the conspirators discussed riding to power "on the CIA train," there is still little evidence of the CIA's precise role beyond some contact with the plotters. It is really after 1979 that we first see America militarizing its Middle East policy.

The drafting phase of this project came to a close before the Biden administration had reached the midpoint of its first term. At that stage, the administration's instincts began to clarify, but the account of the new administration necessarily remains, to a degree, speculative. Biden has a bold domestic agenda that many compared with Roosevelt's New Deal owing to its scope and implications for the United States as a polity and the Democrats as a party. And he had only a brief window to push it through and seems to have largely succeeded despite obstacles within his own party and uncompromising Republican resistance. Given his razor-thin margin in Congress, anything that gets in the way, whether it relates to Israel or Iran, was likely be pushed aside. His foreign policy is focused on China and Russia. But in the shopworn phrase favored by Washington pundits, you can avoid visiting the Middle East, but it can always visit you. If it does so during Biden's term as president, it will be in the form of a confrontation between Israel and Iran, which will in turn depend on the fate of the 2015 Iran nuclear deal. As of this writing, the jury is out. If it is restored, the arc of American intervention in the Middle East will continue to decline; if not, it will remain suspended. But not, one suspects, for very long. The cumulative effect of the rise of China, decades of failed interventions, and political disarray at home will ultimately widen America's distance from the Middle East.

———————

CHAPTER ONE

JIMMY CARTER

Opening Act

I wish I had sent one more helicopter to get the hostages, and we would've rescued them, and I would've been reelected.[1]

—JIMMY CARTER, ASKED FOR THE ONE BIG REGRET OF HIS PRESIDENCY

Ronald Reagan began the great entanglement of the United States and Middle East, but his predecessor, Jimmy Carter, set the stage. Carter was the last of a dying breed, the southern Democrat. He's remembered now for the liberal temper of his administration, his self-consciously everyman cardigans, a maladroit speech blaming the country's dour mood on a crisis of confidence in itself rather than in his administration, inadvertently undermining the national morale by firing his cabinet, and in an exemplary gesture of thriftiness and prudence, keeping his thermostat turned down. There was of course much more to his agenda. Like his fellow southern Democrats, he was relatively conservative on economic and social issues, though his exceptionally deep commitment to civil rights linked him to the northern wing of his party. He was vocal about his Baptist faith, freely expressed himself in religious language, and was prone to stern moralizing. In the aftermath of Watergate, this priggishness was undoubtedly a relief to voters shocked by Gerald Ford's pardon of Richard Nixon.

The thrust of Carter's foreign policy initially repudiated the realpolitik of preceding administrations. Carter ushered in a multilateral approach, especially to the use of force, and a preoccupation with human rights as a criterion for foreign policymaking. In some ways, he was a Wilsonian, harking back to the Fourteen Points and Wilson's short-lived endorsement of self-determination for peoples colonized by France and Great Britain. There was something radical to Carter's approach in the Cold War context, but it was also deeply rooted in the American self-conception as a city on a hill.[2]

As hallowed as these concerns were, they were met by a skeptical foreign policy establishment that saw nothing but trouble emanating from Carter's advocacy of human rights, given that so many of America's allies and security partners were repressive and often brutal autocrats. From a realist standpoint, judging the value of allied governments on how nicely they treated their people would lead the United States into a cul-de-sac. The rulers in question would have too much to lose by slackening the reins at home, and the United States would have too much to lose in its global struggle with communism by forcing the issue. In the end, human rights would be no better protected in these countries, while perceptions of America's reliability as an ally would suffer. The only winner would be the Soviet Union. And as far as Carter's political opposition was concerned, the focus on human rights lapses on the part of America's friends, as opposed to those of its enemies, was absurdly misplaced.

Carter's push to grant Panama full sovereignty over the Canal Zone, which had been under exclusive U.S. control for a century, was just the sort of concession to liberty and self-determination that panicked his Republican critics. For them, Carter's move presaged strategic disaster by placing control over a crucial sea line of communication in the hands of a volatile anti-American banana republic. His administration's failure to anticipate the Soviet invasion of Afghanistan, react to the deployment of a Soviet brigade to Cuba, and foresee the 1979 revolution in Iran all contributed to a general impression of naivete and incompetence.

The Carter team's approach to the defense and intelligence arenas also drew his opponents' savage criticism. Carter had been a nuclear engineering officer in the navy and thought himself qualified to oversee defense programming and budgeting. Others saw this as micromanaging, a conviction fed by the secretary of defense appointment of Harold Brown, one of Robert McNamara's "whiz kids," during an era of civilian technocratic defense leadership that had left the military feeling bruised. Carter was determined to trim the defense budget, cancel expensive weapons systems, and reduce waste. At the very moment that the largely neoconservative Committee on the Present Danger, an organization whose membership ranged from Saul Bellow to retired generals, was resuscitated to warn of Soviet arms buildup, Carter was seen as eager to build down. The phrase "hollow army" was coined to describe the allegedly tragic fate of Carter's armed forces.

Carter appointed Stansfield Turner, a senior admiral with a reputation for intellectual independence, to head the CIA. This proved to be a grave affront to yet another powerful part of the government with strong supporters in Congress. Turner, who was skeptical of the value of espionage but gung ho on the virtues of electronic eavesdropping and photographic sensing, cut the clandestine side of the CIA. Turner's bias was rooted in reality: the payoff from technical intelligence collection was larger and more reliable than that of spies operating overseas. To this day, the budget for intercepting communications and photographing adversaries' activities and assets dwarfs the CIA's clandestine operations budget. National Security Advisor Zbigniew Brzezinski's abiding interest in Soviet-occupied eastern Europe ensured that our spies kept busy in Prague and

Warsaw, but the downgrading of the clandestine service—the bureau-cratic essence of the intelligence community—sowed the seeds of revolt within the agency and broader Republican outrage.

These were not the only burdens Carter had to bear. Like many presidents, he composed a dysfunctional inner circle by combining incompatible personalities. On the one side was Brzezinski, a Columbia professor and son of a prewar Polish diplomat who had witnessed the rise of Hitler and Stalin. On the other was his secretary of state, Cyrus Vance, a patrician, well-connected Yale Scroll and Key initiate, and partner at the white-shoe law firm of Simpson Thacher & Bartlett. They clashed over policy toward the Soviet Union, Iran, and arms control. Vance favored diplomacy and accommodation to resolve disputes between the United States and its adversaries, while Brzezinski was more combative, especially vis-à-vis the Soviet Union. Vance was committed to détente; Brzezinski, who later left the Democratic Party, was more inclined to confrontation. Brzezinski had the upper hand in this tug-of-war, not least because of his access to the president. The national security adviser's office is just down the hall from the Oval Office; the State Department is across town. Vance still remained at his post until nearly the end of the administration, his premature departure triggered by a showdown with Brzezinski over an ill-fated attempt to rescue the fifty-two American hostages seized by Iran the previous year.

This infamous hostage taking had a long backstory. Well before the United States came on the scene, outside powers had occupied and even dominated Iran. Russia had carved out a sphere of influence in the north, Britain in the southwest. Russia's interest was the security of the southern flank of the czar's empire; Britain's was the security of the Persian Gulf and its link to the route to India, its most important colony. The discovery of oil in Iran in 1909 and the subsequent conversion of the Royal Navy from a coal- to oil-fired fleet intensified Britain's interest. Two world wars and the advent of a Soviet blue-water navy only increased the centrality of Iran in Britain's security strategy, not to mention the profits to be extracted from the lopsided revenue-sharing arrangements that London imposed on a succession of weak and indebted Iranian governments.

During World War II, Russia, Britain, and the United States occupied Iran, the shah having unwisely backed Germany, and in 1946 the Truman administration demonstrated its own growing interest in Iran by forcing Stalin to withdraw its forces from the country. Surging nationalism, inflamed by resentment over the exploitation of Iran's resources by a predatory Britain, found a voice in Mohammad Mossadegh, a fixture on Iran's political scene for years and, in 1953, its prime minister. He demanded that the profit-sharing arrangement dictated by Britain earlier in the century be changed in Iran's favor. British resistance led Mossadegh to threaten to nationalize Iran's oil industry. For London, this was an intolerable threat. The question for Washington was whether open conflict between the United States and Britain was strategically more damaging than a regional perception of a bullying West ripping off a vulnerable society. Mossadegh inadvertently answered this question by threatening to form a coalition with Iran's Communist Party to strengthen his government in its dispute with Britain. Fear of a communist takeover in Iran induced Eisenhower to support a brewing British plot to unseat Mossadegh and restore the shah to power. He unleashed the buccaneering Kermit Roosevelt Jr., Teddy Roosevelt's grandson and FDR's cousin, and a CIA officer, to collaborate with the British on Operation Ajax, a coup against the Mossadegh government. It worked.

With the shah reinstated and in debt to the United States and the UK for his throne, he enjoyed a close relationship to foreign powers detested by many Iranians, and therefore became an object of popular loathing himself. There was something of the hapless fool about the shah. He genuinely sought to lift his country's quality of life but failed to find a way to circumvent the notorious "king's dilemma": the tragic reality that reform empowers opposition that can then only be suppressed by violence. You cannot do good without doing evil. And the shah's security services were evil indeed. His modernizing reforms, collectively known as the White Revolution, undermined and offended entrenched interests and often ran counter to the religious customs important to the more traditional segments of Iranian society.

One event was particularly indicative of the shah's tone-deafness. In 1971, he threw a grotesque party for hundreds of foreign leaders and a hodgepodge of minor celebrities to celebrate the 2,500-year anniversary of the rule of the Achaemenid king Cyrus at the desert ruin of Persepolis. He kicked off the celebration with an encomium to Cyrus and pre-Islamic Iranian history, implicitly denigrating the Islamic current of Iranian life as it had been lived for the past thousand years. He spent close to $200 million in 2018 dollars for the extravaganza at a time when large tracts of the capital city were still unpaved and much of the rural population endured grinding poverty. In a country whose culture was restrained, where life was hard, and where gluttony and drunkenness were frowned upon, the toast was raised with a Dom Pérignon Rosé 1959. The opening banquet was catered by Maxim's in Paris, which closed its doors for two weeks to manage the shah's bash. Menus included the following:

- Quail eggs stuffed with golden Imperial Caspian caviar [the shah, allergic to caviar, had artichokes], champagne, and Château de Saran
- Mousse of crayfish tails with Nantua sauce, Château Haut-Brion Blanc 1964
- Champagne sorbet, Moët et Chandon 1911
- Fifty roast peacocks—Iran's ancient national symbol—with restored tail feathers, stuffed with foie gras, accompanied by roast quails and a nut-and-truffle salad, Musigny Comte Georges de Vogüé 1945

As the shah was paving his personal road to Hell, both the United States and Israel were becoming increasingly reliant on him to secure their strategic interests. Israel's situation was complicated. Victory in the 1967 June War afforded it the strategic depth it had long coveted. Before the war, Israel's narrow geographic waist could easily be cut by an invading army, splitting the country in two. It now had the space of the West Bank within which to block an enemy's armored advance to the Mediterranean coast. But Israel was still surrounded by hostile Sunni Arab states, which were themselves more or less surrounded by antagonistic non-Arabs or non-Muslims. Ethiopian Christians were south of Egypt; Maronite Catholics and Greek Orthodox Christians populated Lebanon; Kurds occupied northern Iraq; Turks blanketed the border with Lebanon, Syria, and Iraq; and, most significantly, Shiite Persians were poised on the eastern flank of the Arab world. Israelis understood that this geographical distribution of states and ethnicities could alleviate Israel's regional isolation and inhibit Arab states from driving Israel into the sea. Hence Israel's so-called "strategy of the periphery." The big prize was the shah's Iran, which strategically competed with Iraq and Saudi Arabia, two of Israel's implacable foes, and had the military, diplomatic, and economic weight to counter both countries. From Washington's perspective, close security ties between Israel, Turkey—a NATO ally—and Iran were highly desirable.

During the 1970s, Iranian-Israeli military and intelligence ties flourished, though on the surface the shah generally joined the public Arab consensus in criticizing Israel. At the high point of the relationship, there were twenty thousand Israelis living and working in Iran, with their own housing compounds and schools. At a time when travel within the Middle East was largely impossible and Israel's neighbors radiated hostility, Israelis in Iran enjoyed a measure of acceptance.

Iran was equally important to the United States. The Nixon administration was focused on fostering détente with the Soviet Union. With Vietnam and a faltering economy on their plate, the last thing Richard Nixon and Henry Kissinger—and after Nixon's resignation in 1974, Gerald Ford

and Kissinger—wished to do was expend even greater resources on polic-
ing the Persian Gulf, which had become a more urgent U.S. priority in
1971 after Britain's departure from the region.

Nixon and Kissinger had solved the problem by declaring Iran and
Saudi Arabia to be the Twin Pillars, which together would ensure the security of the Persian Gulf. Both countries were armed by the United States
and pivotal suppliers of oil to its allies. Although the Nixon administration
was compelled to intervene in the 1973 Yom Kippur War between Israel
and the Arabs and unable to constrain OPEC from hiking up the price of
oil and knocking Western economies off-kilter, the Twin Pillars policy was
seen an effective device for avoiding more direct and costly U.S. involvement in the Persian Gulf.

In the spring and summer of 1979, as the deterioration of the shah's
position began to accelerate, the Carter administration, which had entered office in 1977, was focused on forging a peace treaty between Israel
and Egypt even though the likelihood of another war between Israel and
Egypt had greatly diminished. Carter managed to get the querulous and
deeply incompatible Egyptian and Israeli leaders to sign on the dotted line
at the end of a fraught eighteen-day bargaining session at Camp David,
the presidential retreat. On its own terms, it was a remarkable diplomatic
achievement. In broader regional terms, it was a major distraction at the
very moment that the president should have been concentrating on the
fate of the shah. Astonishingly, the United States was completely unprepared for the fall of the regime. The United States had very few Farsi
speakers at its embassy in Tehran and none at all in the CIA station. Intelligence was also crippled by the prohibition of the recruitment of sources
by U.S. case officers by SAVAK, Iran's intelligence and security service,
which made the United States entirely dependent on whatever intelligence
and analysis SAVAK chose to share. What it did share was intended to
portray a regime in control of its destiny. When the roof caved in on the
Pahlavi dynasty, it also crushed one of the two pillars securing U.S. in-

terests in the Persian Gulf. Iran opted to become an Islamic republic led by a charismatic anti-American cleric, Ayatollah Ruhollah Khomeini.

The Carter White House at first unrealistically believed that the situation could be salvaged. The United States had such close ties with the Iranian military and intelligence services and was such a crucial arms supplier that it seemed inconceivable that these institutional connections could simply evaporate. Indeed, the CIA continued to pump highly sensitive intelligence about Iraq to Iran for months following the shah's departure. In the political realm, despite Ayatollah Khomeini's extremism, two moderate prime ministers held office in succession, apparently validating residual optimism in the West Wing. The moderates soon lost their grip as the regime embarked on a frenzied purge, killing at least four thousand and imprisoning thousands more.

A way back to the status quo ante still might have been found but for Carter's disastrous decision to admit the shah, who had left Iran under duress in January 1979, into the United States. The president, supported by Vance, had initially refused on the basis of a cable from William H. Sullivan, the U.S. ambassador in Tehran, stating that admitting the shah "would almost certainly result in an immediate and violent reaction." But the broader establishment view was that the shah's position was salvageable—hard to believe in retrospect, given the massive anti-shah demonstrations in Tehran and other cities—and the foreign policy bulls of both parties pressured Carter to change his mind. In mid-October, after the shah's family had disclosed to U.S. officials that he had life-threatening cancer and would benefit from American medical care, Carter relented.

For Ayatollah Khomeini, the United States loyalty to the shah was the perfect pretext to discredit moderate factions. He unleashed militant students who stormed the U.S. embassy in Tehran on November 4 and took the remaining staff hostage. Failure to withdraw U.S. personnel in advance remains inexplicably foolish. After Khomeini authorized the release of the women and African Americans among the hostages and, as readers who saw the movie *Argo* would know, the Canadians spirited six diplomats out of Iran, fifty-two hostages remained in captivity. There they would stay for 444 days.

The Carter administration sought a negotiated settlement. The bargaining with Iran, facilitated by Algeria, revolved around what ransom the United States would be willing to pay without appearing to reward Iran for an atrocious breach of international law. For Iran, it was about getting even for twenty-seven years of American perfidy. The trade space was obviously limited. Hence Carter's order in the late fall of 1979 to the Pentagon to begin planning for a rescue mission. It was a daring and risky move, involving at least twenty aircraft that would execute landings and takeoffs at ten different sites on four continents.[3] The hostages were not only deep inside Iran but divided between two locations within the densely populated capital city. The population was violently anti-American and certain to respond aggressively to an armed intrusion. Per Carter's orders, the rescuers had to extract the fifty-two hostages with a minimal loss of Iranian lives, which meant that the U.S. soldiers involved were required to defend themselves in the first instance with nonlethal weapons, such as tear gas. Underscoring the planners' audacity, the mission would be the first foray of the Army's Delta Force, which had been cobbled together two years earlier by a visionary colonel, Charles Beckwith, and which the Pentagon considered of dubious utility. The Pentagon insisted that the services would decide what personnel and materiel he would get to carry out the mission, which was dubbed Eagle Claw.* Increasing the likelihood of failure inherent in such a daring mission was an understandable but misplaced concern for secrecy. Stovepiping was such that individual units

---

* Failure can occasionally lead to success. These flaws were eventually corrected with the formation of Joint Special Operations Command and enactment of the Goldwater-Nichols Defense Reorganization Act of 1986, which mandated interservice cooperation. In a sense, the fiasco at Desert One in 1979 led to the astonishing success at Abbottabad in 2011, where Osama bin Laden was trapped, shot, and killed by U.S. special operations forces.

participating simultaneously in the operation could not share vital information.

In addition to shooters, the plan called for the advance infiltration of undercover intelligence and military personnel into Iran to surveil the targets, establish safe houses, and obtain vehicles to ferry the hostages to the coast for exfiltration by the U.S. Navy. At zero hour, C-130 cargo planes would stage from Masirah Island in Oman, an old British air base, to a remote desert location within reach of Tehran. These planes would be packed with the shooters, their equipment, and huge rubber bags filled with thousands of gallons of aviation fuel. They were to rendezvous in the middle of the night with eight CH-53 Sea Stallion helicopters launched from an aircraft carrier off the Iranian coast. The gas loaded on the C-130s would be used to refuel the helicopters, which would then cover the remaining distance to Tehran. Once they had landed, the shooters would split up, enter the foreign ministry to recover the two hostages there and the U.S. embassy building to round up the fifty hostages there. After the shooters herded them into an unused sport stadium, they would be taken to a coastal exfiltration point by covert operatives who had previously entered Iran under Canadian and German cover. Hovering over the stadium would be two MC-130s, cargo planes converted into flying firebases wielding 40mm cannons and heavy machine guns, to discourage Iranians from getting too close to the rally point. Across the border in Turkey, a large marine long-range reconnaissance formation was poised to deploy to Tehran to bail out the rescue party should it find itself in a serious jam. The marine commander was one Major Oliver North, who within a few years would be an indicted key conspirator in the Iran-Contra scandal.

An essential ingredient that the rescuers lacked was luck. The landing zone in Iran, code-named Desert One, was chosen for three qualities. First, the ground, tested in advance by a covert team, could support the weight of the aircraft and was solid enough to permit takeoff and landing operations. Second, it was within range of the Sea Stallion helicopters that were to sortie from the aircraft carrier, and less than an hour's flight time to Tehran. Third, it was isolated, astride a road that was rarely traveled, especially at midnight. The chance that the rescuers would encounter any Iranians in the vicinity of Desert One was, in theory, a million to one. Yet within minutes of landing in the dead of night, April 24, 1980, a busload of migrant workers came chugging along the road. The ramshackle vehicle was promptly disabled by the raiders, the bewildered passengers and driver taken off and sequestered. Then a second vehicle came barreling down the road from the same direction. It was going too fast to intercept, so the U.S. forces fired on it with a shoulder-launched rocket. As it happened, the occupants were fuel smugglers, and the truck exploded in a jet of flame that shot upward hundreds of feet. One of them was seen running away.

There were eight Sea Stallion helicopters, with at least five required to complete the mission. They would need to fly through an unexpected haboob, a blinding sandstorm spiraling thousands of feet high. The C-130s avoided it, but their crews did not warn their counterparts on the Sea Stallions, which were designed to fly over water, not deserts where high winds would be blasting dirt into every aperture of the aircraft and reducing visibility to nearly zero. Extreme communications security prevented the crews on the first choppers to encounter the dust column from alerting those behind them. One of the helicopters turned back. When the seven remaining finally arrived at Desert One, an hour late, a fault in one of the helicopters' subsystems led its marine pilot to declare the unfamiliar navy helicopter grounded, unaware that it was in fact flyable under navy protocols. With two of the aircraft out of the picture, the mission commander was prepared, from a remote base in Egypt, to scrub the mission and authorize release of the bus passengers. Within twenty minutes, Carter had been informed and consented.

All the helicopters and C-130s had to do was reposition themselves for refueling and take off. But the swirling dust whipped up by propellers in the planes and choppers made it very difficult to see what was going on. As the lead helicopter ascended, it collided with one of the C-130s loaded with a full refueling bladder, which ignited. An enormous fireball killed eight crew members and injured several others. The rescue party kept its cool and completed the withdrawal from Desert One but left their dead behind without destroying the disabled helicopters. All the survivors returned to their respective launch points, and the covert operatives in Tehran were eventually able to leave the country undetected.[4] There were no prisoners for the regime to parade through the streets of Tehran as there would be in Mogadishu in 1993, yet the disaster was comprehensive. The clerical regime had scored a tremendous propaganda coup without firing a shot. The hostages were rapidly dispersed to hidden sites, impossibly complicating any second rescue attempt. Jimmy Carter, even in his own assessment, instantly became a one-term president.

The Reagan campaign running against him, however, was not convinced. The candidate himself, viewed through the rose-colored lens of nostalgia and manufactured Republican Party legend, is remembered as immensely popular. In April 1980, though, he was not. Many voters were suspicious of the belligerent tone of his foreign policy speeches, even if they were disappointed with Carter's performance. The Reagan campaign's polling seemed to show that the election was too close to call. Voters might find nobility in failure. The commission appointed to assess the debacle had not yet declared its findings.[5] Within Reagan's inner circle, there was a growing conviction that something had to be done. Carter's most recent biographer, Kai Bird, writes that a member of Reagan's team warned that "it's ours to throw away. . . . If [Carter] does something with the hostages, or pulls something else out of the hat, as only an incumbent president can, we're in big trouble."[6]

Reagan's team had just the man for the job. William Casey, his campaign manager, was a wealthy businessman with a cloak-and-dagger past. Born in 1913, he came from a modest background in Queens, New York, and worked his way through the undistinguished but serviceable local college and law school. By the time the United States entered the Second World War he had made a fortune writing, or perhaps in some cases plagiarizing, a series of handbooks for businessmen struggling to understand the implications of New Deal legislation for commercial firms. On the strength of his analytical talent, he found a billet in the Office of Strategic Services, the wartime predecessor of the CIA. The OSS chief, General William Donovan, liked him and assigned him to the OSS post in London, along with two other future heads of the CIA, where he was soon directing espionage operations against Germany in the European theater. He had a gift for clandestine work.

After the war, Casey entered Republican politics, running for Congress and losing. His failure to obtain a seat did not dent the growing influence he was developing by way of his wealth and formidable intellect. He served in Nixon's administration as the chairman of the Securities and Exchange Commission, where he was an unexpectedly tough enforcer of trading regulations. By the time the Nixon-Ford era was fading, he'd established himself as a key player. In the Republican 1980 campaign, all three leading contenders for the nomination—George H. W. Bush, John B. Connally, and Ronald Reagan—sought his backing. But he and Reagan really hit it off, sharing an extravagant anti-communism and a reverence for business as the essence of America's life and purpose. Casey became Reagan's campaign chairman.

Once Reagan had won the nomination—and at Casey's suggestion made Bush his running mate—Casey approached the job like the OSS program manager he had been in the war: as a combination of intelligence analysis, espionage, and covert action. One key move was the theft of Carter's briefing book for the presidential debates. Casey denied it; his rule was to lie under such circumstances, the same way a spy would. But even Bush conceded that Casey had arranged for it to be stolen and that he had seen the book on Casey's desk.

If Gary Sick, a naval intelligence officer who served on the National Security Council (NSC) staff under Brzezinski as Carter's adviser on Iranian affairs, is to be believed, the purloined briefing book was just the beginning. Casey's more consequential achievement, according to Sick, was stealing credit for the return of the American hostages in Iran. It took Sick two decades to come to this conclusion. He had always been bothered by Iran's sudden withdrawal in the fall of 1980 from ongoing hostage release negotiations. Though arduous, the talks had been proceeding for months, and the mediated, transactional approach to the crisis seemed to be working. Something seemed odd about the Iranians calling a complete halt to the process, rather than grinding on while signaling dissatisfaction. In January 1981, Iran abruptly reversed its position, agreeing to let the hostages go on January 19, Carter's next to last day in office, and releasing them to U.S. officials just after Reagan was inaugurated the next day. Although Carter did fly to Germany to greet them, Reagan reaped the applause.

Having retired from the navy and entered academia, Sick wrote what is still the best account of the Islamic Revolution from an American perspective, *All Fall Down*, deftly combining academic rigor and insider knowledge. As his research unfolded, he encountered several Iranians, Americans, and Israelis peddling a disturbing story of collusion between the Reagan campaign and Iran. The Reagan campaign was worried about an October surprise in the form of a Carter foreign policy triumph that would restore voter confidence in his administration, perhaps a second rescue attempt. Although the challenges involved in a renewed rescue attempt were thought to be insuperable by those in the know, Carter insisted that planning for it proceed, if only because the Iranians might at some point lash out against the United States by killing or injuring the hostages. Like the case officer he had been, Casey tapped sources within the U.S. intelligence community and Pentagon to keep the Reagan campaign informed of Carter's plans. He was able to exploit the accumulated disgust and suppressed rage within these bureaucracies to get a reliable flow of intelligence.

There was also an international dimension to Casey's covert operations. Beginning in the spring of 1980, he reached out to Cyrus and Jamshid Hashemi, Iranian brothers operating an import-export company that originally dealt in commodities such as rice, sugar, and oriental rugs but moved on to arms and items, such as aircraft parts, that were illegal to sell to Iran. The Hashemis used their connections to set up high-level meetings between Casey and Iranian officials in Madrid in July and August 1980, and in Paris in October. They struck a deal that reportedly entailed the transfer of military equipment from Israel and the United States to Iran in exchange for the release of the hostages. Although Iran was prepared to release the hostages immediately after the election in November, Casey appears to have insisted that they wait until after Reagan's inauguration. The implication that he consigned the hostages to an additional two months of imprisonment simply to gut Carter's reputation is difficult to dismiss. Casey played hardball.

In Iran, tensions had been building between the revolutionary government and the Baathist leadership of Iraq. Both sides were preparing for a war that each thought it would win. Saddam Hussein dreamed of annexing an oil-rich chunk of southwestern Iran and becoming a regional superpower; Ayatollah Khomeini hungered for the liberation of Iraq's Shia majority and the extension of Iran's Islamic Revolution to the oil-rich territories to the west. They were both deluded. But only Iran's armed forces had been purged by zealous revolutionaries. Moreover, its predominantly American equipment could not be kept operationally ready without the support of American contractors. The Reagan campaign's offer of weapons via the Israelis in the near term and continued transfers after Reagan's ascension to the presidency was an existential incentive for Tehran.

Sick's exploration of this Faustian bargain attracted attention when his book was released in 1991. Certainly, the claim that a presidential campaign had reached out to a hostile foreign country to undermine an incumbent president and implement an alternative foreign policy was shocking. But Sick himself was a very steady pair of hands: a nonpolitical military detailee to the Carter White House, specializing in assessing the significance of intelligence for U.S. military plans and operations. The media were all over Sick's accusation, as were both Democrats and Republicans in Congress. Each held hearings with the political objectives, respectively, of criminalizing the Reagan administration or exonerating it. There was no special prosecutor, however, so there was no systematic investigation of Sick's allegations and no power to compel the cooperation of witnesses. The controversy broke out a dozen years after the fact; the Iran-Contra scandal (discussed later) and the first Gulf War took place in between. Neither party had a strong incentive to scorch the earth over the scandal. And Sick's sources were not model citizens. Like the parade of indictees in the 2018 investigation of collusion between the Trump campaign and Russian secret service, Sick's sources were by turns self-promoters, hucksters, and fixers, corrupt and mendacious. It was easy for Reagan's defenders to dismiss their character and provenance. Yet their key claims were largely corroborated; liars do occasionally tell the truth. That said, there will never be a smoking gun because, astonishingly, Casey's passport and travel records mysteriously disappeared in the course of the congressional hearings.

Thus did the American plunge into the Middle East begin: with a secret deal between an unscrupulous incoming administration and the Middle Eastern state that would come to define regional opposition to U.S. encroachment. The terms of the deal would be revived within a few years as the Reagan administration sought a solution to its own Iranian hostage crisis, which arrived in the form of Hizballah's kidnapping of Americans in Lebanon, some of whom were tortured and killed. Hizballah was—and still is—a hybrid political and military organization that emerged in Lebanon, with Iran's help, to push Israeli forces out of the country after Israel's 1982 invasion. In the interim, the administration would make its official Middle Eastern debut by intervening militarily in Lebanon, with disastrous results.

CHAPTER TWO

RONALD REAGAN

Empathy and Indecision

Perhaps we didn't appreciate fully enough the depth of the hatred and the complexity of the problems that made the Middle East such a jungle. . . . The irrationality of Middle Eastern politics forced us to rethink our policy there.[1]

—RONALD REAGAN, LOOKING BACK ON HIS INTERVENTION IN LEBANON

What began as a strategic opening to Iran deteriorated in its implementation into trading arms for hostages. This runs counter to my own beliefs, to administration policy, and to the original strategy we had in mind.[2]

—RONALD REAGAN

Lost in the Levant

There is a marvelous 1960s promotional video, still available on YouTube, that depicts the sophisticated pleasures awaiting visitors to Lebanon: glamorous women wrapped in Chanel, champagne flutes aloft; dashing couples speeding through hairpin curves in convertible sports cars; water-skiers waving at partygoers on the corniche, all with cedar-clad mountains in the background. Beirut was in fact an international city buoyed by its patina of French culture, status as a regional banking center, hedonistic reputation, and Mediterranean climate. All good things come to an end, however, and Lebanon's Europeanized postwar frolic was no exception.

Lebanon's politics after attaining independence from France were complicated by religious rivalries. Christians vied with Druze, Sunni, and Shiite Lebanese for control of the state and access to its resources. A deal struck in 1943, called the National Pact, stabilized the situation by stipulating that henceforth the presidency would go to the Maronite Catholics, the premiership to the Sunnis, and the leadership of the Chamber of Deputies—the parliament—to the Shiites. The basis for this hierarchical distribution of government posts was a 1932 census indicating that the Christians were in the majority, with the other religious groups coming in second and third. However, by the 1960s, it was increasingly obvious that the Maronite population was shrinking compared with Sunni and Shiite numbers. Under assault, the established political elites tried to perpetuate the demographic fiction underlying the allocation of key posts.

Unfortunately for them, Gamal Abdel Nasser had seized power in Egypt in the fifties. He was charismatic, blessed with the looks of a Middle Eastern movie star, and a gifted orator. Owing to the new medium of transistor radio, his influence radiated throughout the region. His was the voice of anti-colonialism, political independence, and economic egalitarianism. In an age of monarchs enthroned by imperial powers within borders set by those powers, of vast disparities in wealth, and the emergence of a Jewish state in the heart of the Arab world, Nasser's radicalism galvanized the public. It signified salvation.

For the old elites in Lebanon, it signified something else entirely: upheaval. Their fear was justified. The Lebanese whose political influence was hemmed in by the old order learned from Nasser's broadcasts that there was another, revolutionary order on offer. The authority and legitimacy of the zuama, the notables who controlled politics within a framework of patronage and bribery, was beginning to slip. The spur to civil conflict, however, turned out not to be indigenous to Lebanon. It was Palestinian, and it arrived via Jordan, beginning in 1970 in the backwash of the June 1967 Arab-Israeli war.

When Israel conquered and occupied the West Bank of the Jordan River in 1967, Palestinian refugees who fled across the river into the Hashemite Kingdom of Jordan fielded an army under the Palestine Liberation Organization (PLO), which had been founded by Ahmad Shuqairy in 1964 by an Arab summit meeting. Fatah, organized by Yasir Arafat a few years before, took over the PLO in 1969 in the wake of the Arab defeat in 1967. It seemed at the time that the Palestinians were intent on forming a state within a state and ultimately overthrowing the ruling Hashemite dynasty. The Hashemites were a legitimate target from the perspective of militant Palestinians. Not only did they rule by virtue of British favor after World War I but, since the 1940s, had worked hand in glove with the Zionists in Palestine and then Israel to preserve their own position within Jordan at the expense of displaced Palestinians. In 1970, egged on by Syria, the PLO decided to strike. A combination of Hashemite resolve and Israeli military maneuvering held off Syrian intervention and eventually delivered a crushing blow to Palestinian fighters. With the defeat of the PLO and the lethal hunt for lingering militia members ongoing, Arafat was ejected from Jordan in 1971 with his surviving combatants and their families. Their destination was Lebanon, already home to 400,000 Palestinian refugees jammed into a cluster of barrios, where armed groups held sway in defiance of Lebanese authorities. Weakened by the breakdown of political consensus, Lebanon was too fragile to keep them out.

The influx of armed Palestinians had two related effects on Lebanon's politics. First was the injection of a new cohort of radicalized population of bitter, battle-hardened brawlers into an already brittle situation. Nasser had laid the groundwork for opposition to Lebanon's entrenched elites. The Palestinians united imported firepower with incendiary local resentment of the old order. Second was the demographic impact. In a system in which political power was apportioned on the basis of demographics, the sudden entry of thousands of Sunnis into Lebanon's body politic undermined whatever residual credibility there was to the status quo.

Civil war broke out in 1975, transforming the Edenic Lebanon of promotional tourism videos into a battlefield. The Palestinians sided with Sunni militias against the Maronite government. The Maronites found support in Damascus, where Lebanon was viewed as an extension of Syria; Palestinian claims to independent action challenged Syria's control and had to be suppressed. Syria's leader, Hafiz al-Assad, got the blessing of the Arab League, an important diplomatic group of Arab countries, to deploy a 30,000-strong "Arab Deterrent Force." The Palestinians exploited their freedom of maneuver in Lebanon to use it as a base from which to attack Israel, until prime minister Menachem Begin launched a military operation to establish a buffer zone within Lebanon that would push Palestinian forces northward, rendering their relatively short-range artillery useless against towns in the north of Israel.

The political terrain in Lebanon began to shift at the same time. By 1981, the alliance between the Maronites and Syrians against the PLO was beginning to fray. The Maronite leaders wanted to assert a degree of independence from Syria, while Damascus was looking at restoring relations with the PLO. The Maronites had a notable tendency to bite the hand that fed them. In looking for a way to repudiate Syria's claim to de facto sovereignty over Lebanon, the Maronites overestimated their reach by setting up a base at Zahle, a pleasant mountainside town overlooking the Beirut-Damascus highway and well outside their recognized sphere of influence. For Assad in Damascus, this was both an affront and a strategic challenge. His ensuing invasion of historically Maronite territory got Syria in a wrangle with Israel, which could not tolerate Syria's boot on the Maronites' neck.

In 1981, the United States entered the fray by brokering a short-lived truce between Israel and the Palestinians in Lebanon. Both sides chafed under their respective constraints. Israel felt it had been making progress with its air strikes, despite collateral damage to which Washington objected. Begin was in no mood for American moralizing on this score, declaring, "I don't want to hear anything from the Americans about hitting civilian targets. I know exactly what Americans did in Vietnam."[3]

The view from Jerusalem during this period was scarcely comforting. The pullback of Israeli forces under U.S. pressure led to renewed attacks by Palestinian splinter groups eager to outbid the PLO for recognition, recruits, and funding. How numerous the Palestinian provocations actually were is open to debate. The United Nations force along the border, acting as a referee, judged that most of the cross-border infiltrations were carried out by Israeli forces.

However, by the summer of 1982, Israel had waited long enough. The shooting of Israel's ambassador to the United Kingdom by an Iraqi agent was used as a pretext to push 60,000 troops and 800 tanks into Lebanon with objectives of destroying the PLO, expelling Syria's forces, buttressing Christian rule, and extracting a peace treaty from the Lebanese government. According to Israel, U.S. Secretary of State Alexander Haig gave the invasion a green light.

Although the official Israeli name for the invasion was Operation Shlom HaGalil ("Peace for Galilee"), at the U.S. embassy in Tel Aviv, where I was at the time, the war was dubbed Vietnamowitz. The analogy was inescapable. No one had any confidence in Israel's ability to achieve its objectives, and all were sure that Israel would come out of the war worse for the wear. The size of the Israel Defense Forces (IDF) presence in Lebanon eventually doubled and, as we now know, would last for twenty years.

One Israeli force made it up the coast to the outskirts of Beirut expeditiously. Two other columns churned through central Lebanon and farther east along the Syrian border. Begin explained to Reagan that "[he felt] as a prime minister empowered to instruct a valiant army facing 'Berlin' where, amongst innocent civilians, Hitler and his henchmen hide in a bunker deep beneath the surface."[4] Begin was clearly determined to kill Arafat, in whatever dark Beirut cellar he was holed up. He authorized a seven-week siege, cutting the city off from food, fuel, and communications, essentially trapping its residents. When the PLO still held out, he gave the go-ahead for a terrible air and artillery bombardment of Beirut. By mid-August, it was so intense the Israeli cabinet stripped Defense Minister Ariel Sharon of his authority to order the use of airpower without permission, while one IDF armored brigade commander refused to obey an order to move his unit into Beirut for fear of killing even more civilians. Policymakers in Washington could scarcely believe what was happening. Reagan, ever averse to confrontation, was so appalled he agreed to call Begin to insist that the shelling be stopped. The conversation had an absurd edge, with Reagan describing the bombing as a "holocaust" and Begin archly asserting in response, "Mr. President, I know what a Holocaust is."[5] Nevertheless, Begin did order a halt to the attacks, while the White House tried to figure out what to do next.

The plan that emerged called for the evacuation of the PLO leadership and about 11,000 Palestinian fighters from Beirut to Tunisia, Yemen, and other locations, and the deployment of a multinational force of U.S., French, and Italian soldiers to ensure that the disarmed Palestinian population left behind in Lebanon would not be victimized.[6] It was a good plan, skillfully negotiated and well executed. During the evacuation, all the players were on their best behavior. Even the Israelis, who, it was later revealed, had Arafat targeted by snipers as he took his leave from Beirut, did not take their shot. But that moment of restraint was as good as it got.

On September 14, Lebanese president Bashir Gemayel, the Christian leader and CIA asset collaborating with Israel, was killed along with twenty-six others in a large blast.[7] He was the scion of an important Maronite clan; his father, Pierre, whose cause was a Christian Lebanon, was still a major influence among radical Maronites. Both were central to the Phalange Party, which emulated prewar European fascist organizations. The U.S. government blamed the murder on the Syrian Socialist Nationalist Party, to which the assassin belonged, and concluded that the regime in Damascus was behind it.[8] Hafiz al-Assad certainly had ample motivation to take out Israel's man in Beirut. The heavy death toll, in addition to the intense emotional attachment the Phalangists felt for the Gemayels, all but guaranteed an awful response.

It came at nightfall two days later to Sabra and Shatila, Palestinian refugee camps near Beirut. Led by Elie Hobeika, a fanatical Phalangist whose family had been massacred by Palestinians earlier in the civil war, a militia gang occupied the camps for thirty-six hours, killing men, women, and children. At least seven hundred were slain, but the actual toll will never be known. The atrocity was carried out with the full knowledge of Israeli forces surrounding the camps, who kept the area lit by flares throughout the night so the intruders would not be impeded by darkness.

Apart from its disastrous effect on the camps, the violence held serious implications for both Israel and the United States. The Begin government had justified its initial invasion as an act of self-defense; Israeli complicity in the massacre of noncombatants now made that a difficult claim. UN and Israeli investigative commissions were unsparing in their condemnation.[9] Begin, demoralized, went into seclusion.

In Washington, there was alarm, confusion, and shame. The deal that Philip Habib, Reagan's envoy, had crafted to get the PLO fighters on ships to foreign shores included assurances that the vulnerable Palestinians remaining in Lebanon would not suffer the vengeance of their enemies. This pledge might have meant something to Habib, who negotiated it, the State Department, and possibly even the White House. But the Reagan administration was not structured in a way that yielded crisp decisions enforced by a tough national security adviser. It was more a clutch of baronies run by thin-skinned, devious, recalcitrant antagonists. There was no authoritative center.

As a result, as soon as the PLO fighters had embarked, the secretary of defense, Caspar Weinberger, had unilaterally ordered the withdrawal of the U.S. Marines based in Beirut back to their vessels in the Mediterranean. With no troops on the ground, there was no way the United States could honor its pledge to protect the Palestinians in the camps. For Robert McFarlane, this was "criminally irresponsible."[10] Weinberger's resistance to backing the administration's diplomatic efforts by deploying even small numbers of troops was a constant factor in the bloodily slapstick intervention that followed. As Geoff Kemp, an NSC staffer at the time, later summed up the situation, "We had promised to protect the Palestinian civilians, [but] it was our allies, the Israelis, who permitted the massacre to happen, and it was our boy Bashir Gemayel's troops that did the killing."[11]

After the Sabra and Shatila massacres, Reagan attempted to explain the rationale for the redeployment of marines in an address to the nation on September 21. In retrospect, it was barely comprehensible. According to the president, two battalions headquartered at Beirut International Airport, less than 2,000 soldiers, were going to "[enable] the Lebanese government to resume full sovereignty over its capital." This goal would be accomplished even though the deployment would continue for only a "limited time" and "was not going to act as a police force, but [to] make it possible for the lawful authorities of Lebanon to do so themselves." Reagan explained that, "by working for peace in the Middle East, we serve the cause of world peace and the future of mankind."

Universal salvation, however, had to begin with the more mundane step of removing Syrian and Israeli troops from Lebanon. "Israel," Reagan intoned, "must have learned that there is no way it can impose its own solutions on hatreds as deep and bitter as those that produced this tragedy. If it seeks to do so, it will only sink more deeply into the quagmire that looms before it."[12] This was good, even prescient advice, but unlikely to impress Israelis, who had invested a great deal of blood and treasure getting to Beirut, only to see their prey slip through their fingers, thanks to American meddling.

At the Pentagon, eyeballs were rolling. No one could work out how the marines would translate the goals outlined by the president into missions, let alone accomplish them. The stated tasks at hand could not really be captured in the highly stylized and idiosyncratic vocabulary of military "alert" and "execute" orders. Meanwhile, the State Department could not believe that its military counterpart could possibly be so dense as to not comprehend its role in the administration's overall strategy.

Strictly speaking, the diplomatic notes authorizing the deployment did spell out what the marines were supposed to do: "The mandate of the [Multinational Force in Lebanon (MNF)] will be to provide an interposition force at agreed locations and thereby provide the multinational presence requested by the Lebanese government to assist it and the LAF [Lebanese army] in the Beirut area."[13] Yet from the Pentagon's standpoint, this was unhelpful because it failed to define the parties between which the marines would be sandwiched, and how specifically the marines would assist the Lebanese government by their mere presence. Matters were confused further by public U.S., French, and Italian squabbling over the nature of the mission and the differing agreements each contributor had signed with the new Lebanese government headed by the late Bashir's older brother and Lebanon's playboy-in-chief, Amin Gemayel.

The Peace Process Resurfaces

Gorged on self-congratulation after orchestrating the safe departure of the PLO fighters and ending Israel's siege of Beirut, Reagan announced a Middle East peace plan on September 1.[14] He declared it to be a strategic interest, but also a moral one. Reagan went on to dismiss the notion that Israeli settlement activity in disputed territories was, as Israel maintained, legitimate: "Further settlement activity is in no way necessary for the security of Israel and only diminishes the confidence of the Arabs that a final outcome can be freely and fairly negotiated."

Reagan also spoke of Palestinian aspirations for self-determination with evidently sincere compassion.

Though he argued without explanation that Palestinian statehood was not a solution to Palestinian statelessness and, with better justification, that indefinite occupation was in neither Israeli nor Palestinian interest, Reagan then did what no U.S. president has done since. He laid out a U.S. plan for what he called a "third way" that would entail the confederation of the Hashemite Kingdom of Jordan with the Palestinian territories of the West Bank of the Jordan River and Gaza, a strip of land on the Mediterranean coast between Israel and Egypt. This confederation would include an Israeli-Jordanian peace treaty.

Getting a grip on the situation in Lebanon, which meant inducing Israel's withdrawal, was seen as the essential precondition for the negotiation of Reagan's plan. For one, the Camp David agreement between Israel and Egypt had not yet been fully executed. Both sides would have a convenient excuse to stall if the situation in Lebanon remained unresolved. And if Camp David obligations went unfulfilled, the administration could hardly embark on another highly consequential treaty negotiation. And then there were the Jordanians and Palestinians, who would view the U.S. intervention in Lebanon as a litmus test of the administration's will to stay the course in the face of Israeli resistance.

Thus, the Reagan Plan flowed from the U.S. intervention in Lebanon and, at the same time, greatly increased the perceived stake in achieving the administration's grandiose goals there. It was very nearly perfectly silly. The Israelis opposed the plan because it would return the West Bank to Jordan, and since Israel had already set up a large number of settlements on the West Bank, these communities would have to be removed or submit to Jordanian rule. The administration's miscalculation was compounded by the linkage between the Reagan Plan and Lebanon, which provided a strong incentive to Israel *not* to withdraw. After all, if implementation of the Reagan Plan was predicated on Israel's withdrawal from Lebanon, then the simplest way to avoid dealing with the plan would be to stay in Lebanon. Administration officials later said that they never really expected Begin to agree to the initiative; they just felt they had to do something positive after the implosion of Reagan's intervention in Lebanon.

Mission Creep

While the administration struggled to persuade Israel to discuss the Reagan Plan, it was also trying to figure out how Lebanese sovereignty could be restored. In the cover note to Reagan's National Security Decision Directive (NSDD) 64 to this effect, Bill Clark, the national security adviser, proposed that accomplishing his objectives would probably require "the expansion of the MNF and that it may have to be deployed into any of several areas of Lebanon (northern, central or southern). While we should generally seek to broaden international participation, we must accept that the measure of U.S. leadership relies on our own willingness to contribute."[15]

There are three foreshadowing elements in Clark's gloss on Reagan's directive. The first is mission creep. Within a month, the MNF has morphed from a limited-duration small-scale deployment confined to Beirut into an open-ended countrywide deployment. The second is the absence of an exit strategy. The MNF was a hostage to fortune, its departure pegged to conditions over which the United States had no real control, namely the ability of the LAF to sustain operations outside of Beirut and the readiness of Syria and Israel to withdraw. Third was Clark's warning that there should be no expectation of international assistance. The United States had to plan on carrying the can alone.

These drawbacks should have led to the conclusion that further involvement was not a very good idea. That was certainly the view at the Pentagon, which would shoulder the burden. Why then head toward the precipice with such determination? The answer, in Reagan's words, was "the opportunity which now exists to further the cause of peace between Israel and all its neighbors, we cannot let this historic moment pass."[16] Somehow, the executive branch had gotten the idea that Lebanon's woes constituted a "historic moment" for the United States and the world.

For those involved in the melodrama, the perception was disconnected from the facts on the ground. Even before the NSDD, the intelligence community warned that withdrawal was not in the cards, with the analysts ending their gloomy assessment with an unusually strong warning. "In this context," they wrote, "avoiding an open-ended MNF presence in Lebanon requires a decision to withdraw the MNF before the situation is finally resolved in all its dimensions."[17] In other words, get out while you still can.

The Lion of Syria Roars

Efforts to implement NSDD 64 throughout the exceptionally cold Lebanese winter failed to yield much progress, despite an uneasy truce that offset the impression of complete failure. The administration mistook Assad's apparent calm for fear of American power. On April 18, that belief was tested by the destruction of the U.S. embassy in Beirut by a truck loaded with 500 pounds of high explosive.[18] The collapse of one wing of the building killed 17 Americans, including most of the senior CIA officers in the Middle East, who had gathered in Beirut to confer with the national intelligence officer for the Middle East, Robert Ames. (Ames was among the dead.) Thirty-two Lebanese also died, along with 14 visitors. At least 120 others were wounded.[19]

The White House was shaken by the attack and took ten days to articulate a policy response. It emerged as another NSDD, "Accelerating the

Withdrawal of Foreign Forces from Lebanon."[20] Expressing "grave concern" that foreign forces were still in Lebanon, it instructed Secretary of State George Shultz to travel to the region and quickly nail down an Israeli-Lebanese agreement that would facilitate an Israeli withdrawal. The NSDD linked this increasingly urgent imperative to the Soviet presence in Syria. As Syria's Cold War backer, Moscow had replaced the aircraft and ground equipment that Israel had destroyed in a violent clash there the previous summer. Both sides understood the crisis as a test of their commitments to regional allies. With the collapse of détente under Nixon and Ford, there was a resurgence of Cold War tension. It was the Russians, however, who were expecting a U.S. attack while bemoaning their worldwide reverses. In Afghanistan, the Soviet army was caught in its own version of America's Vietnam quagmire; Cuba, Moscow's foothold in the Western Hemisphere, was foundering economically and draining Soviet funds; the pro-Soviet regime in Angola was struggling to contain a potent insurgency supported on and off by Washington; and Nicaragua's Marxist government faced a growing challenge from U.S.-equipped opposition forces.[21] In Washington, however, policymakers saw the USSR as on a roll and a threat to America's position in the Middle East. The intelligence community took a countervailing line, suggesting that Soviet maneuvering room was limited and that their broader regional opportunities were foreclosed by their close association with Assad, a pariah, especially in the Arab Gulf countries, owing to his reliance on Iran and the Soviets.[22] Outside of the U.S. government, the view was that the Syrians, not the Soviets, were calling the shots. As *The New York Times* then framed the relationship, the Syrian tail was unmistakably wagging the Russian dog.[23] Yet, there was little doubt that the extravagant display of Soviet support and its restorative effect on Syria's combat capability hardened Syria's resistance to any deal that would equate Syria's presence in Lebanon with Israel's.

Sounding like an Old Testament covenant, "Do this and ye shall live;

Do that and ye shall perish!," the NSDD laid down two possibilities for the U.S.-Israel relationship: "One is to restore and enhance the relationship and that is a very high priority of this Administration. The other course leads inevitably to a fundamental reappraisal of the entire U.S.-Israeli relationship." The president affirmed, "We clearly prefer the former course, but we are also committed to obtaining the withdrawal of foreign forces from Lebanon." And this was no joke, because "U.S. leadership and our credibility as a world power is at stake." Shifting from cosmic to microcosmic, the NSDD went on to declare that the United States "commitment to the sovereignty of the state of Lebanon as outlined in NSDD-64 is also at stake." In sum, Reagan appears to be saying that Israel's continued presence was imperiling U.S. credibility as both a world power and savior of Lebanon.

Shultz's Salvage Operation

Armed with these instructions, Shultz left for the region. His first task was to walk back Israel's sweeping demands, such as Israeli prior approval for the deployment of any other countries' forces in Lebanon; the deployment of Israeli observations posts wherever Israel wished; and a 45-kilometer (27-mile) buffer zone within Lebanon that would be patrolled by Israeli forces and their South Lebanon army, Christian proxies under Major Saad Haddad.

There was more. Israel wanted "normalization," that is, an exchange of embassies, diplomatic relations, and free travel for Israelis in Lebanon and vice versa. By May 6, Shultz had gotten the Gemayel government and the Israelis to agree on a set of border security measures, a list of conditions for normalization that might happen at some undefined future time, and a side letter between the United States and Israel saying that Israel would not be obligated to withdraw if the Syrians did not. Shultz reckoned that this would be a foolproof concession to Israel, on the assumption that Syrian withdrawal would be virtually automatic once Israel was on its way out. Intelligence analysis disputed this assumption in fairly strong terms, but Habib and now Shultz were on the ground conducting the diplomacy and it was their judgment that mattered.

The next day, Shultz was in Damascus asking Assad for Syrian concurrence. He did not get it. Assad endeavored to explain to Shultz Syria's rationale for staying in Lebanon by pointing out that just as the United States had no embassy in Chicago, Syria had none in Beirut. The message was that there was no more of a distinction between Lebanon and Greater Syria than there was between Illinois and the United States.

The U.S. team proceeded on two parallel tracks. The one was to get moderate Arab states with deep pockets, such as Saudi Arabia, to persuade Assad to reverse his position on withdrawal through threats of isolation and the promise of financial aid. This proved fruitless. The other track was to finalize the Israeli-Lebanese agreement on an IDF withdrawal, despite the fact that according to the U.S.-Israel side letter, Syria's recalcitrance relieved Israel of its obligation to withdraw from Lebanon. As soon as the agreement was signed, Assad condemned it and declared Philip Habib persona non grata, effectively ending his utility as a presidential envoy. He then set in motion a plan that would ultimately remove the United States from Lebanon.

It is par for the course for policymakers to dismiss intelligence analysis. They generally think they know more than the analysts and believe that the CIA has a strong incentive to play Cassandra. Even worse, the analysts eat up decision makers' time with expositions of the weaknesses in their policy proposals but never offer any ideas about how to make them better. In this case, however, the analysts' pessimism was more than equaled by the intense skepticism of professional diplomats. Geoff Kemp, the NSC staffer, recalls a "very, very acrimonious" meeting in Cairo between Shultz and a gathering of regional U.S. ambassadors that "reflected the judgment of the top professionals in the foreign service that [the policy] wasn't going anywhere. But the professionals were overridden by Shultz [and the political appointees], and there was very little they could do about it."[24] This indifference to professional advice was in a different category of carelessness.

McFarlane Takes Charge as the Fighting Heats Up

With Habib out of the picture, Reagan appointed Robert McFarlane as his envoy. In McFarlane's view, it was about time. In his memoir, he offers a withering critique of Habib and his professional ability. He refers sarcastically to Habib's "giant reputation as a skilled diplomat" while underlining the fact that "he had no experience dealing with Arabs or Israelis, nor had he ever been a man with strategic breadth, able to analyze American issues regionally, not just in Lebanon." Per McFarlane, Habib had just been "dithering" for eight months during which "Syria [was] so vulnerable to external pressure. . . . Habib should have stepped aside and given us a chance to get someone else in there to talk to Assad."[25]

McFarlane's critique of Habib makes for uncomfortable reading because it draws attention to his own deficiencies. His deep involvement in the U.S. intervention in Lebanon and subsequently in the Iran-Contra scandal was defined by an inability to grasp regional power dynamics and the motivations of key players. In strategic terms, he appeared to have had no realistic conception of Lebanon's place in the hierarchy of U.S. interests, which, as national security adviser, he might have examined more closely.

Be that as it may, at the time, he faced a strong Syrian challenge on one hand and a weak Gemayel government on the other. The geography of Beirut made it vulnerable from the northeast, where it was overlooked by the Metn ridge, and from the southeast, where the Shouf mountain range loomed above it. The Shouf had been populated for centuries by two minority populations, Druze and Maronites, that naturally sought the isolation and security of a mountainous habitat. The two communities fought a bloody war in the 1860s and since then had coexisted uneasily. In 1983, Druze were galvanized by their young leader, Walid Jumblatt, and came into intense conflict with Maronites radicalized by Phalangist ideology. The Druze were determined to strip the Maronites of the privileges they enjoyed under the old political order; the Maronites were bent on a Christian Lebanon. Druze fighters were joined by Palestinians who had remained behind after the evacuation of the PLO from Lebanon the summer before. Atrocities were commonplace. Assad saw an opportunity and took it, and Syria threw its support behind the Druze, who began to shell the capital that lay below in the shadow of the Shouf ridgeline. Their target was the marine battalion landing team bivouacked at the airport in south Beirut.

The only barrier between the Druze and Palestinians on the Shouf, and Beirut below, was an Israeli force dug in on the slope to which they withdrew from Beirut the previous year. They were taking casualties, however, for no apparent Israeli gain. The United States was now in the strange situation of pleading with Israel not to withdraw. The Israelis were not unsympathetic, but they were not going to incur losses just to serve as an outer defensive perimeter for U.S. Marines. After the IDF pulled out, the MNF began losing marines to Druze artillery, mortar, and rocket fire.

McFarlane's "Worst Case Scenario"; Reagan Brings Out the Big Guns

On September 5, Jumblatt launched an offensive along the Shouf that quickly swamped scores of Christian villages. There were dozens of local massacres. As the carnage was taking place, McFarlane, who was in the region, fired off a brief cable to Washington with the subject line "Worst Case Scenario for Lebanon."[26] He wrote that he had discovered that the "central factor in the Lebanon conflict is Syria's determination to maintain an enduring influence over Lebanese policy."

Recognition of Syrian commitment to Lebanon a full year after the U.S. decision to intervene could not really qualify as snappy strategic insight. McFarlane went on to propose rounding up British, French, and Italian military and diplomatic support for Syrian withdrawal while mobilizing Saudi pressure on Syria to back off. The United States, he wrote, would have to expand the scope of MNF operations to within Syria, to signal Damascus that Washington was prepared for "strategic escalation in both political and military terms." In the meantime, the United States would jump-start a Lebanese national dialogue. He wrote that the "strategic stakes were enormous." Reagan's written comment on the margin of his copy indicated that he concurred in this assessment.

His cable spurred policymakers back in Washington to think things through. The outcome was a memorandum dubbed "Worst Case Strategies for Lebanon."[27] The document conformed to the classic DC menu of three options: nuke 'em; surrender; or my option. The nuke 'em option was McFarlane's strategic escalation; the surrender option was to maintain the goal of getting the Syrians and Israelis out but stop trying to make it happen; the prudent "my option" was to "Modify our objectives for Lebanon and realign our strategy to what is feasible and doable without incurring the risk of direct confrontation with Syria." As one might expect, this emerged as the preferred course of action. Not that it mattered.

On the Shouf, the Maronite Lebanese Forces (LF), supported by the Lebanese army (LAF), was locked in a desperate struggle to hold the strategic town of Suq al Gharb, a mountain resort for well-heeled Beirutis that overlooked Baabda, the seat of government, and the Defense Ministry at Yarze. At one point, McFarlane and his party were at the U.S. ambassador's residence as mortar fire from a nearby skirmish could be heard near the compound. Despite his experience as a combat veteran, McFarlane was rattled. As he relates in his memoir, he cabled Washington to warn of "uncivilized forces" posing "a serious threat of a decisive military defeat which could involve the government of Lebanon within the next twenty-four hours," and to urge the White House to immediately authorize U.S. forces "to fire in support of the Lebanese army."

This had a predictably seismic effect at the White House. Shaking off Weinberger, who derided McFarlane's urgent message as "the sky-is-falling cable," Reagan put his thumb on the scales in favor of the embattled LAF. He had no illusions about the policy departure he was authorizing and the risk it entailed. He confided to his diary that the "N.S.C. [National Security Council] is meeting . . . on Lebanon re a new cable from Bud MacFarlane [sic]. Troops obviously PLO and Syrian have launched a new attack against the Lebanese Army. Our problem is do we expand our mission to aid the Lebanese Army with artillery and air support? This could be seen as putting U.S. in the war." This diary entry leaves little room to question Reagan's acumen. But he believes the risk is merited because "it might signal the Syrians to pull back."[28]

In a subsequent passage, he shifts into a more political mode, indicating that the public rationale for escalation was going to emphasize protection of vulnerable marines rather than an American offensive. "Our Navy guns," he wrote, "turned loose in support of the Lebanese Army fighting to hold a position on a hill overlooking our Marines at the Beirut airport. This still comes under the head of defense."[29]

Thus, on Reagan's command, four U.S. Navy vessels, a cruiser, a frigate, and two destroyers, unleashed a storm of shell fire as a fifth vessel, the gigantic World War II–era battleship USS *New Jersey*—mounting 16-inch guns compared with the 5-inch guns of the smaller ships—arrived on the scene.

The Other Guy Has Big Guns Too

The good news for Washington was that the navy's entry into the fray quickly produced an informal cease-fire, negotiated by McFarlane in Damascus, that provided the breathing room for his attempt to organize a national reconciliation process. The bad news was the Druze leader Walid Jumblatt's October 1 call for the Druze brigade in the LAF to desert, and for the formation of a parallel government. At that moment, the LAF ceased to exist as a multiconfessional national entity. Henceforth, it would be just another Christian militia and client of the United States and Israel. National reconciliation failed to gain traction; Amin Gemayel could deliver neither the concessions demanded by Sunnis and Shiites or show that he could lever the IDF from Lebanese territory. In his memoir, Karim Pakradouni, a senior Phalange member, had good reason to characterize McFarlane's mission as "a disastrous tragicomedy."[30]

Fighting in the vicinity of the Shouf intensified with the incremental breakdown of the truce and the growing Lebanese perception of the marines as just another Christian militia. By early October the marines and the Druze were trading fire. The United States kept up its offshore bombardment, but now the marines had 155mm howitzers—heavy artillery—to hammer the Druze batteries on the mountain.

Disaster struck on October 23. At 6:22 a.m., a Mercedes truck smashed through the flimsy razor wire and chain link barriers and a guard shack between the marine barracks in Beirut and the parking lot on the perimeter. Because the marines' rules of engagement required that rifles be set on safety with chambers empty, only one marine was able to fire on the truck before it penetrated the lobby of the barrack structure. When detonated, multiple canisters of compressed butane combined with 21,000 pounds of pentaerythritol tetranitrate (PETN) to create a fuel-air explosion that literally lifted the entire building from its foundation, severing all its 15-foot-diameter structural concrete pillars. The building then fell back to earth and pancaked, crushing nearly all the marines, sailors, and other personnel who had been sleeping within it. The U.S. military death toll was 241; 6 civilians died as well. Minutes after the attack on the marine barrack, the French compound was also attacked, killing 58 paratroopers.[31]

Reagan Fires Off a Decision Directive, Heavy Artillery, and Jesse Jackson

The immediate U.S. response was a brief statement by Reagan at the south portico of the White House after disembarking from Marine One. He described the attack as "despicable" and perpetrators as "bestial." Another NSDD, number 111, on October 28, loosened the rules of engagement and restarted "strategic cooperation" with Israel.[32] This program had been initiated earlier in the Reagan administration but suspended in 1981 because Israel used U.S. weapons against civilians and annexed the Golan Heights. It included aid for the acquisition of weapons and equipment made in the United States, now increased by $500 million by the NSDD. Moreover, Reagan directed that the Defense and State Departments "enhance our deterrence of possible Soviet-Syrian activities in the Middle East and eastern Mediterranean, [by undertaking] joint military planning and exercises with the Israel Defense Force." This was, in part, a restatement of previously articulated objectives and lines of effort that made no reference to the attack on the marine barracks. But it was also a significant watershed in U.S.-Israeli strategic cooperation.

Combat accelerated after the Beirut barracks attack. On November 9, the marines had to abandon their southernmost position due to heavy fire from the Shouf. The next day, two U.S. carrier jets were downed by antiaircraft fire. On December 4, naval aircraft were ordered to attack Syrian positions on Mount Lebanon for the first time. It was a regrettable decision. Syria's Soviet-supplied air defense systems destroyed both planes.[33] A prominent African American cleric, civil rights activist, and presidential hopeful, Jesse Jackson, won the release of the sole surviving crew member by appealing directly to Assad.[34]

In what seemed to some observers at the time as a symbolic eruption of grief, rage, and frustration, the USS *New Jersey* fired its big guns in

action for the first time since the Vietnam War. By the time it was redeployed from Lebanon's coast early in 1984, it had launched 338 16-inch
shells at the high ground around Beirut, each round, as Reagan liked to
say, "as big as a Volkswagen!"[35] Although the bombardments discouraged
shelling of the marines ashore, it made no strategic difference. Army chief
of staff "Shy" Meyer later observed, "When Bud McFarlane directed that
those 16-inch guns fire at villages, that merely created more anti-Marine,
anti-American sentiment. . . . It just increased the level of threat to the
forces who were already in a non-tactical and non-strategic position."

NSDD 117, issued the day after the USS *New Jersey*'s guns roared,
tried to square the circle of "vigorous defense" and the effect of U.S. gun-
fire on Lebanese opinion. The resulting guidance was so tortured, commanders could not figure out when they could fire their weapons.*

The Bad Guys Get Away with It

In the meantime, there had still been no direct retaliation for the attack
on the marines. Earlier, on September 3, the National Security Planning
Group at the White House had considered the need to deter attacks and,
in somewhat melodramatic terms, recorded for posterity that the United
States had "now delivered a strong demarche putting Syria on notice that
the United States intends to defend its personnel against attacks from any
quarter. . . . The line has been drawn."[36] And as the barrack rubble was
still smoldering, the president issued NSDD 109, which requested, "The
Director of Central Intelligence [will] prepare an urgent summary of all

---

* The instructions were as follows: "The U.S. contingent of the MNF supported by naval
surface and tactical air forces will pursue a policy of vigorous self-defense against all attacks from any hostile quarter. Responsive attacks will be used to destroy targets originat-
ing fire if this can be done with minimum collateral damage. . . . In the event the above
action cannot be carried out due to risk of collateral damage or lack of precise information
on the source of fire, destructive fire will be directed against discrete military targets in
unpopulated areas which are organizationally associated with the firing units."[37]

source intelligence; the Department of Defense [will] submit options for overt military retaliation against identifiable sources of terrorist activity against our forces; [and] . . . the Department of State [will] provide a policy review of the costs and benefits of such retaliation."[38]

Within four days, National Intelligence Officer Graham Fuller, the successor to Robert Ames, who had perished in the April attack on the U.S. embassy in Beirut, circulated a response. Fuller was typically straightforward, writing, "The evidence of guilt in the Beirut bombing of the Marine Headquarters falls somewhat short of the smoking gun we would all like. This parallels the situation following the bombing of our embassy in Beirut last April. In all likelihood we will never get the smoking gun, and we legalistically-minded Americans tend to want to have the kind of evidence that would hold up in court before taking lethal action."[39]

This said, he laid the blame squarely on Iran, which had the means, motive, and opportunity. In the back of his mind must have been a step that Assad had taken during the summer of 1982 as part of a larger scheme to make life difficult for the United States and Israel in Lebanon. He allowed Islamic Revolutionary Guard Corps (IRGC) fighters into Lebanon, where they established a headquarters, housing complex, and training facility they called the Sheikh Abdullah barracks. These Iranian militants had reached out to Shia combatants around Beirut and in south Lebanon, extending aid and military training that paid off early in 1982 and then in 1983 with destructive attacks on the Israeli military headquarters in Tyre, which killed 103 Israelis and injured many more. In the CIA's view, they had now turned their Lebanese Shia allies against the United States with devastating success. Fuller's recommendation was that the United States hit the Sheikh Abdullah barracks—hard.[40]

The administration was inclined to follow through but could not muster the internal cohesion and focus to do so. Although most agreed that the Sheikh Abdullah barracks was the logical target, concerns about collateral damage and confusion about the best weapon to use slowed the process. Revenge is supposed to be a dish best served cold, but political and diplomatic realities demand a hot meal. The longer the gap between provocation and response, the greater the number of complications arise. Allies weigh in to urge restraint, the adversary muddies the water with denials, government agencies squabble over whether and how to counterattack, tempers cool, and, ironically, the longer the delay, the more observers are likely to conclude that the identity of the attacker remains unknown, or that reprisal would make a bad situation worse.

In this case, the evidence of Iranian and Syrian complicity was comically abundant. U.S. intelligence had intercepted an Iranian government instruction to its ambassador in Damascus to launch a major attack against the United States. Just before the bombing, another intercept documented an order from the Iranian ambassador in Damascus to Abu Haydar al Musawi to "undertake an extraordinary attack against the U.S. Marines."[41] In the immediate aftermath, the Mossad informed the CIA that the Iranian embassy in Damascus had supplied a Lebanese contact with $50,000 to finance an attack and further identified a Syrian intelligence officer and Hizballah's "spiritual leader" Sheikh Muhammad Hussein Fadlallah as the organizers of the bombing. There was also evidence that the Syrian proconsul in Lebanon, Ghazi Kanaan, had given the go-ahead for the attack.

According to intelligence analysts, the Islamic Revolutionary Guard Corps had checked in with the Iranian embassy in Damascus before the attack, apparently to request permission to go ahead. U.S. intelligence also had evidence linking Imad Mughniyah, the presumed perpetrator of the attack on the U.S. embassy in Beirut earlier in the year, with the barracks bombing. Mughniyah was closely associated with the IRGC in Lebanon and was a frequent visitor to Damascus and, apparently, Tehran. Both the French military, who were virtually next-door neighbors to the Iranian embassy in Beirut, and Lebanese intelligence reported that the embassy emptied out just before the bombing. And then there was the nature of the explosives used against the U.S. Marines and the French compound. The material was not the poor man's mixture of fertilizer and propane; it was PETN and hexogen, high-energy chemical explosives that, at the time, would have been readily available to governments, but not to lone wolves.

Still, for the Defense Department and to a lesser degree the uniformed services, retaliation was not a great idea. Weinberger's assistant secretary for international security affairs, Richard Armitage, thought it would be a "feel good" exercise that would not yield any tangible benefit.[42] The record of the internal debate suggests that civilian leadership in the Pentagon thought retaliation would put the United States on a slippery slope to more intensive involvement in Lebanon, precisely the opposite outcome they were hoping for. Using the likelihood of collateral damage to a hospital and school near the Sheikh Abdullah barracks as a bureaucratic smoke screen, the Pentagon killed the first proposal to emerge, which was to launch Tomahawk cruise missiles from an offshore vessel. This move bought time to sow additional obstacles to a military response.

Ground force commanders pointed out that retaliation would ultimately kill more marines, since the enemy would almost certainly respond to a U.S. attack and the marines at the airport were easy targets for assault or shelling from the high ground overlooking their forlorn bunkers. Protecting the marines would require additional forces and the elimination of the mortar and artillery fire tormenting the existing garrison. Retaliation would lead ineluctably to a radical transformation of the U.S. commitment, more mission leap than mission creep.

The navy, which had no forces on the ground, was busy developing an attack plan for White House approval. In addition to destroying the Sheikh Abdullah barracks in a large-scale raid, the plan called for the use of smart munitions to take out the floor used by Syrian and Iranian operatives in a nearby hotel. Television news footage had been used creatively by targeteers to pinpoint the exact location, and very precise missiles promised minimal collateral damage. Reagan approved the plan, but nothing happened.

There is no agreed-upon explanation of why nothing happened. Shultz, McFarlane, and Vice Admiral John Poindexter all thought that the president had explicitly told Weinberger to begin the attack. Weinberger, according to one version of events, responded to the president in the affirmative, while suggesting that conditions could yet change in a way that might preclude an attack. As the hours passed without the launch of any aircraft, an anxious White House staff learned that Weinberger had told the navy to stand down, or perhaps even that no execute order had even been given. In his memoir, McFarlane writes that when he informed the president of Weinberger's disregard for his order to carry out the attack, Reagan responded, "Gosh, that's really disappointing. That's terrible. We should have blown the daylights out of them. I just don't understand."[43] Reagan's unwillingness to rebuke Weinberger was typical of his timid approach to his old buddy and of his anarchic approach to management.

Reagan himself, however, remembers it differently. In his memoir, he recalls that "our intelligence experts found it difficult to establish conclusively who was responsible for the attack on the barracks. Although several air strikes were planned against possible culprits, I cancelled them because our experts said they were not absolutely sure they were the right targets. I didn't want to kill innocent people."[44] Weinberger, predictably, denied that the president had ever ordered an attack, recalling only a vague discussion of a pinprick strike on targets in Baalbek.

A New Role for Israel

In looking for ways to put strategic cooperation with Israel into practice, strategic planners in the Pentagon proposed that the United States and Israel agree on a set of tasks that would facilitate the U.S. defense of the Persian Gulf should war with the Soviet Union break out. Initially, plans were limited to prepositioning of U.S. medical gear in Israel for treatment of American casualties in the Persian Gulf; Israel was closer than Germany and speed of surgical attention can mean the difference between life and death for victims of traumatic injury.

The Israelis were more ambitious. Jolted by the rapid rate of their losses in opening days of the 1973 War, they were looking for the prepositioning of U.S. armor and munitions in Israel that would eliminate the need to formally request replenishment, wait for a decision from the White House, and then wait longer for gear to be shipped from Germany or even the United States. Israel's objective was to short-circuit the diplomatic, bureaucratic, and logistical obstacles to instantaneous reinforcement. With U.S. munitions and equipment stored in Israel, it would, in effect, be reserved for Israel's use. And who, after all, would be in a position to prevent the IDF from raiding the cupboard?

The work begun under Carter finally emerged in a formal Memorandum of Understanding in 1981. It covered a number of topics. The United States and Israel would form a committee to arrange for joint military exercises and provide for the use of Israeli ports by the U.S. Sixth Fleet; Israel would to agree to the prepositioning on its territory of military supplies for use by the U.S. rapid deployment force but available to Israel in a crisis; the U.S. would resume the delivery to Israel of the American cluster bombs that the IDF had used against civilians; Israel would use U.S. funds to build its own fighter aircraft for the export market (a project eventually abandoned by Israel); U.S. aid to Israel for military purposes would be increased by $425 million per year; and Israel and the United States would conclude a trade agreement that would allow duty-free and tax-free imports and exports for both countries, giving Israel a preferential treatment in comparison with other U.S. trading partners at that time.

The Pentagon, which saw the Persian Gulf as the regional center of gravity, considered Israel to be a burden, as one chairman of the Joint Chiefs of Staff summarized the situation. As a practical diplomatic matter, the

United States could not project power from Israel into the Persian Gulf and, in the words of another senior officer, the eastern Mediterranean would be a "sideshow" in a war with the Soviet Union. But the more open-minded and enthusiastic White House and State Department wanted a formal agreement to enmesh the Pentagon into a strategic relationship with Israel, despite the reluctance of both civilian and military defense officials.

The committee enjoined by the agreement to set up exercises and execute other cooperative programs became known as the Joint Political Military Group, or JPMG. Some referred to it, perhaps inevitably, as the "Jew-PMG." The group met every six months, alternating between Israel and the United States. Procedurally it was an odd arrangement, in that it was chaired on the U.S. side by the State Department and on the Israeli side by the Ministry of Defense. Even stranger was that the State Department delegation was not led by the Near Eastern Affairs Bureau, then still populated by Arabists whose outlook limited their eagerness for U.S.-Israeli military cooperation. As "Arabists"—foreign service officers who specialized in the Arab world and empathized with Arab hostility to Israel—were displaced by a new generation that recognized Israel's importance in American domestic politics and the growing centrality of peace process diplomacy to U.S. foreign policy, such perceptions waned, but at the time they were strongly held.

Initially, a subset of the group produced a "Combined Operational Contingency Plan." In my experience, it was a remarkable document, in that it spelled out how the United States and Israel would work together in a war with the Soviet Union. This was nothing if not strategic cooperation; allies fighting shoulder-to-shoulder in what would certainly have been a desperate struggle against a totalitarian adversary. I had always wondered why it never led to closer cooperation in other areas.

An illuminating insight into this question finally arrived in a recent conversation I had in Israel with Major General (Ret.) David Ivry, a former air force chief of staff who was the director general of Israel's defense ministry in the mid-1980s and head of its JPMG delegation.[45] I noted that the combined operational contingency plan signed by the United States and Israel in 1984 signified a depth of strategic cooperation that never seemed to gain traction. He replied that he had no recollection of such an agreement.

Taken aback, I asked how it was that an agreement obligating Israeli cooperation with the United States in a global conflict could have faded from his memory. He reiterated he had no recollection of such an agreement, but in a conciliatory tone, offered that if the United States had asked Israel to take certain actions on its behalf in a war with Soviets, surely the Israeli government would have given the American request at least some consideration. I then asked how the process he was describing, one in which Israel brushed off a wartime contingency plan with the United States, counted as strategic cooperation. He responded that the IDF needed the assurance of U.S. equipment located on its territory for rapid and un-fettered access in an emergency. If his predecessor as the Israeli head of the JPMG signed a combined operational contingency plan in order to get the prepositioned equipment Israel needed, then he did what he thought he had to do. To Israel, strategic cooperation, he concluded, was nothing more—and nothing less—than U.S. agreement to preposition crucial war materiel in country. U.S. officials from that era recall thinking that strategic cooperation in its early stages was indeed one-sided, but the global Cold War context, which dictated that the U.S. be seen to secure the interests of its allies, and a pro-Israeli Congress tilted in Israel's favor.

The focus of the JPMG on the Soviet threat, from the point of view of American advocates of strategic cooperation, was intended to seduce Weinberger into a more accommodating posture toward Israel. But he never bought this idea. The State Department was split between the Arabists who believed that a U.S. military relationship with Israel would disrupt U.S. ties to Arab states, and political-military professionals who perceived a strategic advantage in closer military links. Even the services were split. The army was accustomed to working with Israelis, but the air force, which was closely tied to the Saudis, feared that cooperation with Israel would reduce its access to Persian Gulf bases.

The United States, Israel, and Strategic Ambivalence

So, a deeper strategic relationship never really came to pass. By the end of the Reagan administration, the Soviet Union was on the verge of collapse and the danger of the Cold War turning hot had faded. As the prospect of superpower rivalry receded, so did the rationale for strategic cooperation.

Moral hazard was baked into the dynamics of the strategic relationship. The closer the cooperation, the greater the Israeli temptation to exploit the trust it engendered. The most colorful example of this structural dynamic was the discovery in 1985 that Israel had recruited a Jewish American, Jonathan Jay Pollard, to spy on the United States. In the eighteen months before his arrest, Pollard used his access as a naval counterintelligence analyst to hand over thousands of top secret documents to his Israeli handlers, including a handbook on decrypting ciphers. The sheer quantity of material was staggering. So was the incompetence of his employers in Naval Intelligence, who let Pollard have access to material he was not cleared to read and supplied him with a courier pass he used to remove scores of documents at a time from his office.

The Israelis brushed off their recruitment of Pollard and exploitation of material he stole as a consequence of the United States failing to hand over the information voluntarily. As an ally whose security concerns related to the intelligence transferred by Pollard, they argued that they had a right to it. Moreover, as an ally, Israel by definition could not have used the stolen material to damage U.S. interests. This being the case, what harm could there possibly be to Pollard's theft?

Pollard fleshed out this argument by blaming anti-Semitism within the U.S. government for its decision to withhold certain information from Israel. He also argued that as a loyal American, he would never have proffered to Israel any intelligence that might harm his country. This was a problematic line of debate. Even if Pollard had the technical competence to decide what might or might not endanger U.S. interests, he could not possibly have had the time to read through the thousands of documents he handed over to the Israelis in order to make the determination. Pollard was ultimately convicted under 18 U.S. Code § 794, "Gathering or delivering defense information to aid foreign government," and was sentenced to life, despite a plea bargain struck with prosecutors.[46]

A small encounter I had at the State Department, where I managed the day-to-day implementation of strategic cooperation at that time, typified Israel's perspective on the spy scandal. After a wrenching deliberative process, the United States decided to go through with a JPMG meeting that had been scheduled before Pollard's arrest. Prior to the meeting, I drafted an agenda for the Israelis to review and combine with their own ideas for topics to discuss. My Israeli counterpart, who later ascended to Israel's supreme court, arrived to pick up the agenda I'd drafted. After sliding it into his pocket, he removed a thick packet from his briefcase, which he handed to me, saying, "I assume the usual amount will suffice, Mr. Simon?" (For the record, the packet contained invitations to a concert hosted by the Israeli embassy.)

For the Israeli diplomat, this was hilarious not just because it made light of Pollard's espionage, but also because I am Jewish, which made the joke all the more piquant. It was also unapologetically public. In the wake of Pollard's treachery, Israelis were banned from State and Defense Department office spaces where they might be able to get their hands, or eyes, on classified documents. My encounter with the Israeli embassy's standup comedian therefore took place in a corridor, where colleagues were beetling between offices with ears wide open. Not long thereafter, a military colleague asked me whether the Israelis had bought me a kibbutz for my retirement. This was atypical; the genteel anti-Semitism that might have been perceptible at the State Department in an earlier era had long since dissipated. Jewish officers in my experience enjoyed the same prospects as their peers. But the Pollard affair and some of its quirkier ramifications raised the question of dual loyalty among some colleagues and observers.

Reagan's presidency reinforced the trend toward U.S.-Israeli strategic partnership despite the tense and periodically unproductive state of relations during his administration. The U.S. commitment to Israel on the basis of its ability to contribute to U.S. strategic goals supplemented and arguably supplanted the American urge to keep a cool, liberal country afloat in the wake of the terrors of the Holocaust.

In a sense, this path was the more difficult one to take. For Israel to be accepted as a legitimate security consumer—because Americans thought it deserved protection as a democracy, had a right to self-determination, was unjustly attacked by its neighbors, and because the Jewish people had, in effect, suffered enough—was an easy call.

But redefining Israel as a strategic asset that merited American protection by virtue of its security cooperation burdened Israel with an obligation it could not possibly meet. Israel, after all, was a tiny country with purely local interests, while the United States was a superpower with global commitments. As an object of popular resentment throughout the region, Israel could not be used as a platform for American power projection. Although Israel had a large conscript army, it was not big enough to defend Israel's borders and deploy alongside U.S. forces at the same time, even if a situation arose in which this might have made sense.

Moreover, Israel, for its part, was unwilling to enter any arrangement with the United States that might have given Washington a say over Israeli strategic decisions or military operations. Though it was unable to materially contribute as a strategic partner, Israel leveraged its status of "major non-NATO ally" to extract increasingly hefty rents from the United States, in the form of incremental but lucrative technical concessions that were barely understood by Congress and the media. These measures enabled Israel to use U.S. aid to buy military goods from its own contractors, instead of American ones; compel U.S. suppliers to spend part of their profits in Israel; and front load the disbursement of U.S. aid to Israel so that the Israeli treasury could capture interest revenue that would otherwise have accrued to the United States. But the big prizes were the prepositioning of U.S. equipment on Israeli soil and the opportunity to forge closer ties to the U.S. military, which would chip away the Pentagon's reluctance to work with Israel.

Reagan and Iran

Do I ice her? Do I marry her?

—JACK NICHOLSON, HITMAN IN *PRIZZI'S HONOR*,
MUSING ABOUT HIS RIVAL, KATHLEEN TURNER

If strategic cooperation is thought of as bilateral coordination of high-level security strategies in pursuit of shared objectives—especially where cooperation is expected to produce better results than either party could achieve on its own—then the Iran-Contra scandal that blighted Reagan's second term serves as a perverse example of how such a joint venture could go wrong.

Iran-Contra consisted of two intertwined covert operations that played out during 1985–86. The Iranian part entailed the sale of weapons to the clerical regime in Tehran by Israel and the United States; the Contra piece involved using revenue from these sales to fund U.S.-backed insurgents fighting the socialist Sandinista regime ruling Nicaragua. It was scandalous because weapons transfers to Iran were banned under U.S. law and ran counter to established U.S. policy; and U.S. support for the Contras was also illegal.* When these operations were revealed in November 1986, they sparked a firestorm that led to a special investigation, the indictment of most of the participants, and a weakened administration.

According to the investigative record and the recollection of key conspirators, including Reagan, the notion of supplying U.S. weapons to Iran came from David Kimche, director general of Israel's foreign ministry and Israeli Prime Minister Shimon Peres's point man on this gambit. Kimche was an extraordinary, even legendary, individual. Born in the London district of Hampstead, which he left at age eighteen to fight in Israel's War of Independence, he emulated the posh accent and demeanor of Britain's ruling class. During the war he was wounded at the battle of Abu Tor, a crucial stage in the fight for Jerusalem in 1948. (He died in 2010 with a bullet still in his leg.) He then went on to shape, along with a small number of other founding fathers, the Mossad, where he went on to run three of the major directorates, including foreign penetration operations. In addition to running agents in the Arab world, he himself operated in challenging environments, particularly in Africa and the Middle East, under diplomatic and nonofficial cover as a journalist and businessman. Eventually, he reached the number two slot in Mossad and appeared destined for the top, but clashes with his boss curtailed his intelligence career. His appointment to the foreign ministry was a consolation prize. Kimche's collegiality, elegant English accent, and extraordinary operational record made him the ideal salesman for an audacious proposal: the sale of weapons to the revolutionary regime in Iran that had been complicit in attacks on the United States in Lebanon.

Kimche met with McFarlane in early February 1985 to gauge the administration's backing for Israeli "political discourse" with Iran and pro-

---

* The Boland amendment to the 1982 Defense Appropriations Act prohibited support for the Contras and was renewed every year through 1985.

pose the sale of arms to pave the way. Within a week, McFarlane, in the presence of White House chief of staff Donald Regan, presented the president with a version of Kimche's proposal. In the aftermath, none of the parties remembered the meeting in the same way, especially regarding the key element of the proposal, which was to sell weapons to Iran. But there is little question that McFarlane left the hospital room where Reagan was recovering from surgery believing that the president had signed off on the initiative.

Reagan and McFarlane's interest in this project was not as eccentric as it might appear in retrospect. From the earliest days of the new Iranian regime, the United States fretted about the potential for an alliance of convenience between the Soviet Union and Iran. Officials tortured themselves with visions of these two adversaries making common cause, either voluntarily in a collaborative mode, or because Iran would fracture under the pressures of its ongoing war with Iraq and the Soviets would hasten to annex territory near its borders, or because the Iranian communist Tudeh Party would stage a coup d'état with secret Soviet support and join the Soviet camp (a similar scenario had led to the Soviet invasion of Afghanistan in 1979).[47]

There was little if any evidence to suggest that any of these were taking shape, or even plausible, except in the most general, speculative sense. But evidence in the U.S. policymaking process is often superfluous in a system where preconceived notions and conceptual frameworks derived from ideological conviction are what really matter. Confirmation bias, a preference for data that can be seen as supporting one's preexisting perceptions and a disregard for information that does not, can propel policy in bizarre directions.

In this instance, the fact that the Tudeh Party had been persecuted by the shah's secret police and then savaged by the Islamic regime was discounted in favor of detailed, fantastical assessments of its possible pathways to power. Similarly, the vast difference in worldview between an

Islamist revolutionary regime led by clerics and the materialist, secular, and communist Soviet regime was disregarded, as was the fact that Iranian nationalism had been boosted in part by czarist and Soviet aggression. There was moreover little evidence that the Soviets themselves harbored the hope, let alone expectation, of a close relationship with the clerical Iranian regime. Soviet disdain for the ideology of revolutionary Iran was deep. And Moscow was well aware of the contempt the clerics held for the USSR. The Russians were under no illusion that even a tacit anti-American alliance was in the cards.

Still, U.S. regional strategy was pegged to fear Soviet influence and aggression. In 1983, after a prolonged gestation, the administration had issued NSDD 99—United States Security Strategy for the Near East and South Asia—which directed government agencies to prepare to deny the Middle East to the Soviet Union.[48]

By the mid-1980s, these threat perceptions were still very much in play. The reason was the Iran-Iraq War, which had started in 1980 with Iraq's invasion of Iran. As is true of most leaders who start wars, Saddam expected this one to end with swift victory. But wars generally do not proceed according to plan. Iran turned out to be tougher and more resilient than Saddam expected. The revolutionary regime pushed back hard, eventually conquering parts of southern Iraq. But it was a brutal seesaw battle. Although Iran had few friends and Iraq had many on the Arab side of the Gulf and in the West, there was no telling which country would crack first.

This uncertainty played into fears that the Soviet Union might exploit the weakness or defeat of Iran to move south toward the Persian Gulf. In the early summer of 1985, the CIA distributed a national intelligence estimate that asked whether and how the Soviets might invade Iran on the margins of a major war between NATO and the Warsaw Pact in Europe.[49] The implication for readers was that if the intelligence community thought the Soviets might invade Iran even while battling NATO in

Europe, then what might they be tempted to do if they were not otherwise engaged?

These underlying anxieties motivated a search for U.S. basing options in the Persian Gulf. U.S. blandishments failed to induce any of the local states to provide basing for American ships or planes except for Oman, which then as now marched to the beat of its own diplomatic drum, and Bahrain, which permitted a navy "administrative support unit" to set up shop at the port near Manama. For the Saudis, at the time, the domestic political repercussions of hosting U.S. forces far outweighed their fear of either Russians or Iranians hopping across the Shatt al-Arab waterway to occupy the Arabian Peninsula.

The CIA Rethinks U.S. Policy toward Iran;
the Fuller Memorandum

At about the time that the intelligence community produced its analysis of Soviet military options in Iran, the national intelligence officer for the Middle East, Graham Fuller, wrote a memorandum that proved to be pivotal. Fuller, who came from the operational side of the CIA and served in the Middle East and Afghanistan, began by unleashing a remarkable set of propositions:

> The U.S. faces a grim situation in developing a new policy toward Iran. . . . The Khomeini regime is facing growing Internal problems. . . . The U.S. has almost no cards to play; the USSR has many; . . . the USSR can both hurt and help Iran more than the U.S. can. Our urgent need is . . . for leverage in the race for influence in Tehran . . . The U.S. and the USSR . . . are both on Iraq's side because we lack our preferred access to Iran. Whoever gets there first is in a strong position to work toward the exclusion of the other. . . .

We also already know where Moscow wants to go and that it will devote major resources to claiming this important prize.[50]

Let us unpack these claims. The first, that U.S. policy toward Iran had reached a dead end, is unchallengeable. It is as true now as it was then.

The second proved inaccurate. Iran was capable of ejecting Iraqi forces from Iranian territory and carried the fight to Iraqi territory, even if it was unable to defeat Iraq in detail and achieve its objective of regime change. The tide was eventually turned against Iran by Iraqi access to U.S. targeting data—after news of Iran-Contra broke, the United States installed a data downlink in Baghdad so that the Iraqi army could get real-time satellite imagery of Iranian forces. Operation Staunch, the U.S.-led effort to deny Iran access to the supplies it needed to defend itself, also aided Iraq, even as the United States scoured the globe for weapons and munitions that were illegal to supply itself to sustain Baghdad's war effort. Finally, Saddam's use of ballistic missiles and nerve gas to demoralize Iran's home front and blunt its offensives did much to secure Iraq's victory. The Iraqi spokesman commented, "The invaders should know that for every harmful insect there is an insecticide capable of annihilating it whatever their number, and Iraq possesses this annihilation insecticide." The hideous humor of this Iraqi's joke lay in the fact that nerve gas is chemically indistinguishable from agricultural insecticides.

An NSDD issued around this time declared that an Iraqi defeat would be a strategic setback for the West. The U.S. effort to ensure Iraqi victory, while panicking about the prospect of Iranian defeat, was perhaps the strangest feature of U.S. policymaking at that moment. However, the United States was not alone in its confusion. The Israelis, nervous about Iranian gains in Lebanon, asked the United States to convey an offer of Israeli arms to Baghdad. The United States did pass on the offer, but it was rejected by Saddam's close aide Tariq Aziz, who pointed out that Saddam would "shoot me on the spot"[51] if he raised the subject.

The fact was that Iran was headed neither to defeat nor collapse, as feared by Fuller and his counterparts at the White House. Whether their judgment regarding Iran's viability represented a U.S. intelligence failure is a fair question. It is also an important one, since the belief in Iran's fragility was the premise for selling arms to Iran, a dramatic policy departure.

The third premise was that the United States had no cards to play, while the Soviets could help or hurt Iran in ways the United States could not—and that Iran understood this hard truth. Yet the facts were otherwise. The Soviets were stretched thin in Afghanistan and on a glide path to defeat. Iran was already boxed in internationally, and the Soviets could not have helped or hurt the regime diplomatically. Iran did reach out to Moscow. During this period there were two Iranian delegations to Moscow, where they met with the Soviet foreign minister Andrei Gromyko. But his message was a warning that Iran should drop its crusade to topple Saddam and negotiate an end to hostilities. And while it is true that the Soviets could have supplied weapons to Tehran, and that some items did reach Iran from the USSR, Iran's military was geared largely to U.S. weapons systems.

Equally jarring is the idea that both the United States and Soviet Union were supporting Iraq only because the prom queen—Iran—had spurned them, and that Moscow and the United States were both maneuvering to place on a ring on her finger. In retrospect, the muddled policy of the Reagan administration highlights the prevailing nostalgia for Nixon's Twin Pillars strategy, when the U.S. and Iranian militaries were joined at the hip. This was true too of the Israelis involved in Iran-Contra, who longed for the time when they and their Iranian allies comingled, concluded profitable business deals, cooperated on intelligence and military matters, and a beleaguered Israel found relief from its regional isolation. Iran, with its long history as an independent nation, large population, diverse economy, oil wealth, experience with parliamentary government, and an erstwhile Western ally, rather than Iraq, was the strategic prize.

What we now know is that nearly every assertion in Fuller's influential memo was inaccurate. The strength of the argument, though, was greater than the sum of its parts. The fact was Iran's strategic weight made it impossible to ignore or relate to solely through pressure.

The memo went further, outlining a range of policy options that might rationalize and stabilize the U.S. position in the Persian Gulf and, if possible, restore some comity to relations with Iran. Fuller's option would avoid the need for direct U.S. contact with Iran by enlisting friendly countries to open channels to Tehran, which would relieve Iran's diplomatic isolation while affording access to the international arms market. Israel was close to the top of Fuller's list of countries that could be deputized for these purposes. Although there seemed to be no hope that the revolutionary leadership would seek an accommodation with the West, there was the hope that moderates who delivered Western weapons at a crucial moment to the beleaguered regime would be strengthened within the Iranian political system. With their credibility boosted, the moderates would be able to nudge the regime over time toward a less hostile posture toward the United States.

Putting the Fuller Memo into Action

Fuller's memo reflected thinking at the White House that had been spurred by Kimche's encounter with McFarlane and subsequently by Michael Ledeen, an NSC consultant who'd been dispatched to Israel to meet with officials to discuss Iran and told McFarlane that "the situation has fundamentally changed for the better."[52] In June, two NSC staffers, Don Fortier and a young passionately pro-Israeli political appointee, Howie Teicher, drafted an NSDD for McFarlane to distribute to Weinberger and Shultz for comment. Describing the contents as "provocative," the drafters summarized the message in their cover note in blunt terms:

It basically calls for a vigorous policy designed to block Soviet advances in the short-term while building our leverage in Iran and
trying to restore the U.S. position which existed under the shah
over the longer-term. This would require a sharp departure from
ongoing overt and covert measures, most notably the supply of
Western military hardware, U.S. initiative to dialogue with Iranian leaders, and activist covert actions.[53]

Shultz and Weinberger both disparaged the proposal. Weinberger
compared it to inviting Muammar Qaddafi, the Libyan dictator and one
of the administration's bêtes noires, to the White House for a "cozy chat."
Shultz, who did not like the idea, nonetheless told McFarlane that he'd go
along with a noncommittal show of interest to the Israelis. Even at this
early stage, McFarlane could anticipate how the initiative might go wrong,
conceding that the Iranians could pocket successive gifts from the United
States and Israel without delivering anything in return, namely U.S. hostages that had been seized in Lebanon by Shiite groups aligned with Iran.
As McFarlane framed the plan, "The short-term dimension concerns the
seven hostages; the long-term dimension involves the establishment of a
private dialogue with Iranian officials on the broader relations."[54]

Bill Casey, whom Reagan had made director of Central Intelligence,
was particularly enamored of McFarlane's idea—it was just the sort of
caper Casey liked—and no doubt encouraged Fuller to make a compelling strategic case for it. Harking back to the Reagan presidential campaign, when Casey was alleged to have traded arms sales to Iran in return
for the release of the embassy hostages, one can imagine Casey picking
up where he left off.

Once Reagan had signed off on the plan in August, a cinematic cast of
private sector characters was assembled to make it happen. On the American side, there was a retired air force major general, Richard Secord. New

to the world of business, he had left military service under a cloud, despite an amazing record. He had been involved in covert operations, in Vietnam and Laos—where he organized proprietary air transport for secret missions—and in two tours in Iran, where he was involved in aerial reconnaissance of the Soviet Union. The secret transfer of weapons to Iran would put him back in the game he had played exceedingly well.

Secord worked with Albert Hakim, a Lebanese-American businessman with Iranian roots, who had lived in California in the 1950s on a student visa that was later revoked. His unique gift was an ability to circumvent U.S. export controls on sensitive equipment by slicing and dicing the systems into unregulated subcomponents. It was an art he had perfected on behalf of the shah's regime. In 1983, he and Secord cofounded Stanford Technology Trading Group International. Known as the Enterprise, their company managed the covert arms sales through secret Swiss bank accounts.

For the two of them, this was a get-rich-quick scheme. According to the special prosecutor who would come later, "In 1986 the Enterprise received $30.3 million from the sale of this U.S. Government property to Iran. [. . .] Only $12.2 million was returned to the United States. Direct expenses of the Enterprise were approximately $2.1 million. Thus, the amount of U.S. Government funds illegally held by the Enterprise as its own was approximately $16 million."[55] While much of this taxpayer money was illegally diverted to the Contras, Hakim and Secord kept a piece of it.

On the Iranian side, there was Manucher Ghorbanifar. Before the Islamic Revolution, Ghorbanifar was a dealmaker, possibly linked to the shah's secret police. During this period, he had formed close business ties to an Israeli who also figured in the Iran-Contra deals, Yaakov Nimrodi. Nimrodi had been born in Baghdad; his family immigrated to Palestine in time for him to join the Palmach, a paramilitary organization that was ultimately absorbed by the IDF. He fought in the 1948 war and eventually migrated to the Mossad.

In 1956, Nimrodi was appointed as the Israeli defense attaché and Ministry of Defense representative in Tehran, in which capacity he oversaw large arms transfers as well as training for the shah's secret police. Ghorbanifar and Nimrodi were natural middlemen, entrepreneurial, worldly-wise, and greedy. Shortly after the revolution, as Iran was reeling from Iraq's invasion, the two men became quite wealthy by engineering a massive sale of Israeli weapons to the embattled clerics. (After the Iran-Iraq War, these weapons wound up in the arsenal of Lebanese Hizballah.)

Ghorbanifar offered his services to the CIA, which polygraphed him four times; he failed on each occasion. The CIA brushed aside the results, insisting that there was little choice in these conspiracies but to deal with shady figures—or in Ghorbanifar's case, to put it in McFarlane's words, "the most despicable character I've ever seen."

Ghorbanifar, who had plenty of money, was not interested in the Agency's cash, let alone its control. He saw himself as a businessman, not a spy. (In the latter role, he was clearly a liar, having told the CIA in a prior instance—to make the Israelis happy—that Libyans were plotting to kill Reagan. This invention lit a fuse in the U.S.-Libya relationship that would detonate with terrible results toward the end of Reagan's second term, in an attack on Libya that led to a retaliatory attack against Americans; the CIA issued a "burn notice" labeling Ghorbanifar as a fabricator.)

On the U.S. government side of things, there was of course McFarlane and a protégé, Oliver North, a lieutenant colonel in the Marine Corps, whom we met during Operation Eagle Claw, when he commanded a detachment of marines tasked to rescue the extraction force should things go wrong within Tehran. North was now on the NSC staff, which he reconceived as the covert operations arm of the White House. He commandeered one of the grand, high-ceilinged suites in the Old Executive Office Building adjacent to the West Wing of the White House and installed a second floor, connected to the first by a spiral staircase, to accommodate a burgeoning crew of selected buccaneers. This was an act of architectural vandalism I can attest to first hand, since I inherited his office at the NSC in 1994; he would apply the same wrecking ball to the structure of U.S. foreign policy.

Together this group pulled off a sequence of weapons transfers that yielded the return of three hostages and the kidnaping of three others in Lebanon by Shiite militants. (All the hostages were ultimately freed.) The first iteration was the neatest; 100 anti-tank missiles for the immediate release of an American, Benjamin Weir. Thereafter, the system the parties had worked out began to deteriorate. Mistrust was sown by the hugely inflated prices the conspirators charged for the weapons and spare parts being traded. The Iranians well knew that they were being ripped off.

North's Plan Goes South

Iran's perception of bad faith was reinforced when antiaircraft missiles they received from the Israelis on behalf of the United States did not pack the technology that the Iranians had made clear they needed. And when they finally got the right missiles, the quantity was a fraction of what they had expected. On the other hand, internal disarray, the controversial nature of this arrangement within policy circles in Tehran, and questionable authority of Iran over its unruly Lebanese allies essentially ruled out the possibility of a systematic release of hostages, either in one go or as phased transfers.

On the U.S. side, misjudgments or snafus were seen as understandable procedural glitches that in no way reflected the seriousness of purpose and basic integrity of the Washington players. Confusion and apparent noncompliance on the Iranian side, however, was perceived in Washington as evidence of bad faith. Nonetheless, thousands of anti-armor rockets and a vast tonnage of spare parts changed hands by the time the deal fell apart.

The shambolic nature of Reagan's policy process was further underlined by his failure to formally authorize the U.S. government to carry out the weapons transfers until December 1985, when he finally called the key players to a meeting in the White House residence. The group included the vice president, the secretaries of state and defense, the deputy director of the CIA (in lieu of Casey, who was traveling), the White House chief of staff, and the national security adviser and his deputy. Weinberger's notes record that the "President wants to free hostages. . . . I argued strongly that we have an embargo that makes arms sales to Iran illegal + President couldn't violate it + that 'washing' transaction thru Israel wouldn't make it legal—Shultz, Don Regan agreed." But Reagan was adamant. Weinberger's notes go on: "President sd. he could answer charges of illegality but he couldn't answer charge that 'big strong President Reagan passed up a chance to free hostages.'" In response, Weinberger wrote that he told Reagan that in prison "visiting hours are Thursday."[56]

The emotional roller coaster continued throughout 1986. Deliveries would be made, expectations overturned, hopes dashed by the catch-and-release pattern whereby new hostages would be taken following the liberation of those in captivity. McFarlane had resigned in December 1985 to spend more time with his family but remained the administration's point man on the Iran initiative; in early 1986, he told his successor, John Poindexter, not to do any more deals. The Iranians just couldn't be trusted.

Yet the process continued to lurch forward. By this time, the freelancing shysters who had been handling the transactions were replaced by government officials in Israel and the United States. As Hunter Thompson prophesied in *Rolling Stone* magazine, "When the going gets weird, the weird turn pro."[57] The Washington team included Poindexter, McFarlane, North, Tom Twetten, the CIA operations chief, and George Cave, a Farsi-speaking retired CIA operative. In Jerusalem the baton was grasped by the prime minister's rugged-looking counterterrorism adviser, Amiram Nir.

Still working with Ghorbanifar despite their misgivings, the group resolved to travel secretly to Tehran, where they would meet representatives of the regime's leadership, arrange, once and for all, the release of the hostages, and embark on a broader discussion of strategic matters of mutual concern. This was to be the breakthrough. Think Nixon's opening to China, only smaller. The visit fizzled. No Iranians of any importance would meet with them, the celebratory cake picked up at a Tel Aviv bake shop before their departure for Tehran was gobbled up by hungry Revolutionary Guard recruits at the airport, and four days after their arrival, they were wheels up, never to return.

On the mission to Tehran, McFarlane wrote to Poindexter, describing the Iranian government this way: "It may be best for U.S. to try to picture what it would be like if after nuclear attack, a surviving Tartar became Vice President, a recent grad student became Secretary of State, and a bookie became the interlocutor for all discourse with foreign countries."[58]

Fiasco though it was, the visit did not put an end to the arms-for-hostages wheeling and dealing. But on November 3, seemingly out of the blue, a small Lebanese magazine, *al-Shiraa*, broke the story of U.S. and Israeli arms sales to Iran to embarrass the faction in Tehran involved in the transaction in the context of an intramural power struggle. The fact that the story was unpublicized until then has always mystified me. Either the Iranian participants were better at keeping secrets from their colleagues, or opponents of the deal took time to decide that it might actually succeed. Even as a junior officer at the State Department, I was aware that something was going on, if only because I had to draft letters from Shultz to the Iraqi ambassador to the United States, Nizar Hamdoon, denying Iraqi allegations of the transfer of anti-tank missiles to Iran.

The sheer quantity of material, the complex logistics, the number of personnel involved in executing the transfers, and the size of the Defense and State Department staff components who were aware of the internal debate about the deals, all made disclosure at some point inevitable. The very next day, during his speech to Iran's parliament on the anniversary of the seizure of the embassy hostages in 1979, Iranian president Ali Akbar Hashemi Rafsanjani confirmed the *al-Shiraa* story.

Was Reagan Right?

After an interval punctuated by futile denials, Reagan spoke to the nation, justifying the initiative as an attempt to restore relations with a strategically significant Gulf state; seek an end to the Iran-Iraq conflict; eliminate state-sponsored terrorism in the region; and secure the release of American hostages held in Lebanon. The president confirmed that "modest deliveries" of "defensive weapons and spare parts"[59] had been made to Iran as a signal of U.S. preparedness for a new relationship. There was, he contended, ample precedent for such secret and highly sensitive diplomacy, that no federal laws had been violated, and that no concessions had been made to terrorists. He also explained official silence on the initiative as essential to the release of Americans still held in Lebanon.

Reagan again defended his actions at a nationally televised news conference on November 19, rejecting critics' claims that the secret arms transfers to Iran had been a mistake. He said that they were intended to signal American good faith to moderates in Iran who might succeed the radical regime of Ayatollah Khomeini. The president described the shipments as "minuscule" and again denied they were ransom payments for American hostages. With respect to the Iran operations, the president declared that the responsibility for the decision was "mine and mine alone."

And it was. Yet he managed to evade the consequences. Others, on the U.S. side of the deal, were punished but subsequently pardoned. Their transgressions, however, had more to do with the diversion of funds to the Contras and lying about it than selling weapons to Iran. A shamed

McFarlane attempted suicide in February 1987 by overdosing on Valium. The Iranian cleric who exposed the arms-for-hostages arrangement via the article in *al-Shiraa* was executed that same year, convicted of "being at war with God."

Amiram Nir, who accompanied McFarlane to Tehran, left government, opened up a security business office in London, and, in 1988, was killed in mysterious circumstances in Mexico on a mission to procure a large quantity of "avocados." Oliver North went into politics. Poindexter continued to circulate within the national security establishment, but descended into obscurity by pushing an Orwellian government domestic surveillance program he dubbed TINA, "total informational awareness." He was clearly a man ahead of his time.

Iraq, ironically, was the main beneficiary of the administration's secret sales to Iran. The disclosure of the deals and of McFarlane's screwy trip to Tehran generated outrage not just in Baghdad, but in Riyadh, in allied capitals, and on Capitol Hill. Damage limitation required a decisive tilt toward Iraq. Not that there hadn't been such a tilt even as the Iran deal was gestating in Washington and Jerusalem; the administration was already stacking the deck in Iraq's favor, not least by whitewashing Iraq's massive use of deadly toxins against Iran, an inexcusable war crime. The big tilt ultimately led to U.S. combat operations against Iran itself.

Before turning to these direct U.S.-Iranian hostilities, it is worth asking whether the prevailing narrative of the Iran arms sales—as a pathetic, even desperate, gambit by a president whose personal sympathy for the hostages swamped his less-well-developed grasp of statecraft—really holds water. McFarlane, who was not necessarily the most articulate of strategic thinkers, grappled with this question in the weeks following his suicide attempt. He explained to *The New York Times* that "it was the right policy to try to open lines of communication with Iran. . . . Think of how much respect this country has now for Japan and Germany compared to the way people felt in the early 1940's," he said. "The Iranian leaders may have to make extravagant statements denouncing the U.S. to local audiences, but that Government is going to change. And many Iranian leaders are conscious of their own vulnerability to Soviet pressure. They want a relationship with the West, particularly with the U.S."[60]

One could well see how this reasoning would resonate with Reagan. In fact, the impulse motivating the approach to Iran is very much like the one that motivated Reagan to seek a dialogue with Moscow. He had tried to open a channel during his first term, but the turnover in Moscow following the death of Leonid Brezhnev, when his successors Chernenko and Andropov both expired shortly after taking power, made this impossible. "They keep dying on me," complained a frustrated Reagan. Finally, in 1985, just when the administration decided to reach out to Iran, a young dynamic Mikhail Gorbachev took the helm in Moscow and immediately made clear his interest in a dialogue with Reagan.

Reagan was not seeking a relationship with Gorbachev to perpetuate Soviet power. He thought that the Soviet Union and its communist ideology were headed for the dustbin of history. But he did consider that a working relationship with the USSR would hasten that outcome while reducing the prospect of conflict in the interim. Most historians think that this strategy succeeded. My impression of Reagan's approach to Iran is of a parallel attempt to speed the collapse of an ideologically repugnant regime by dealing with it. Failure, regrettably, was overdetermined. Reagan's inability to manage his own staff, the infighting within the cabinet, incompetence and villainy among the National Security Council staff, reliance on unscrupulous and money-grubbing middlemen, nonexistent intelligence regarding Iranian decision-making and domestic politics, vulnerability to manipulation by Israel—any one of these factors would have made success unlikely. But more important than any of them was the fact that there was no Gorbachev in Tehran.

The Iran-Iraq War Begets the Tanker War

The administration's abandonment of the Iran arms deal coincided with intensified attacks by Iran and Iraq on oil shipping and transloading facilities. Saddam, as we have seen, expected this war to be short, the natural expectation of aggressors, and to profit from captured Iranian oil fields. But owing to Iraqi incompetence and Iranian will to survive, Saddam's blitzkrieg turned into a war of attrition fought on his own territory. It was a war of attrition for the Iranians as well, despite their success in expelling Iraqi forces from Iranian soil and taking the war to the enemy. Wars of attrition devolve to demography and economics. The side with the bigger population and larger GDP is probably going to win. Both sides were running into manpower problems by 1987. Thus, destroying the basis of the enemy's finances by depriving him of access to the oil market became the goal of both antagonists.

Iraq began the so-called tanker war by launching air strikes against Kharg Island, a huge pumping and loading complex used by Iran to fill tankers queued up around the terminal. Like rail marshaling yards, such installations are hard to knock out because they incorporate so many redundant elements. At Kharg Island, the enormous welter of pipelines had enough excess capacity to keep oil flowing despite the Iraqi pilots' best efforts, which were generally lackluster. Crews were afraid to fly low and tended to miss even broad targets. With newly acquired French Super Etendard aircraft and Exocet missiles, however, Iraq could attack Iranian shipping with greater success as well as immunity to Iranian retaliation. Crew competence was less a factor with precision-guided missiles. Nonetheless, an Iraqi pilot managed to misidentify the USS *Stark*, an American frigate patrolling the upper Gulf, for an Iranian tanker and destroyed it with two Exocet missiles, killing thirty-seven sailors and wounding twenty-one. It took two years of wrangling with Iraq to extract $27.3 million in compensation for the families of those killed.

Although Iraq had two reliable pipeline routes to bring its oil to market, Iranians targeted Kuwaiti tankers loading Iraqi oil at Kuwaiti terminals. From Tehran's perspective these vessels were fair game: Kuwait, after all, was breaking the Iranian blockade of Iraq and undermining Iran's war effort. As Iran stepped up its attacks, Iraq did likewise, partly in the hope that Iran would overreact and attempt to close the Gulf to shipping by blocking passage through the Strait of Hormuz, the narrow body of water that forms the gateway to the Gulf from the northern Arabian Sea. Threats to block the Gulf were an Iranian mantra, but Iran had more to lose than gain by taking such a dramatic step. Iraq nonetheless calculated that aggressive attacks on Iranian shipping might yet push Tehran over the edge. And if Iran did indeed escalate, then the United States would surely enter the war as a combatant on Iraq's side.

Kuwait's agitation for international cover peaked in the spring of 1987. They began by leasing three Soviet tankers in the hope that Iran would refrain from attacking them lest they alienate the Soviets. For Moscow, an opportunity beckoned. Washington, which had already refused a Kuwaiti request to protect their tankers, was unnerved by the Soviets' nimble reaction to Kuwait's plea for help. The fact remained, though, that the U.S. Navy could not legally protect the vessels of other countries. Fortunately for Kuwait, administration lawyers came to the rescue. They determined that Kuwait could legally reflag its own vessels with the Stars and Stripes, thereby rendering the vessels eligible for U.S. defense against Iranian attacks. Kuwait then turned down Moscow's help and Operation Earnest Will, the U.S. protective effort, began on July 24, 1987.

The very first convoy escorted by the navy ran into trouble that same day. The MV *Bridgeton*, a reflagged Kuwaiti oil tanker, hit an Iranian mine. Big tankers like the *Bridgeton* were constructed with double hulls, one inside the other, so the mine did not cause catastrophic damage. The difference in the specific gravities of seawater and crude oil also tended to minimize flooding of the tanker's holds.

The notable aspect of this event was the navy's failure to anticipate the problem of mines. There were no minesweeper ships in the Gulf, and very few in the navy's possession worldwide. Minesweeping in the anticipated great war with the Soviet Union was supposed to be carried out by lesser NATO allies incapable of deploying big ships but with the resources and organizational ability to handle more quotidian tasks with correspondingly modest equipment. Once the navy understood that mines would be Iran's weapon of choice against Kuwaiti tankers, it scrambled to find the tools necessary to do the job, such as minesweeping surface vessels and Sea Stallion helicopters as well as the specialized sensors and mechanical devices to detect underwater mines and destroy them.

After the delay imposed by the attack on the *Bridgeton*, Earnest Will spawned three further operations, Prime Chance, Nimble Archer, and Praying Mantis. Prime Chance was a cleverly planned and executed operation designed to hobble Iran's mine-laying effort in intelligence-led, more or less precisely targeted actions.[61] It marshaled army helicopters operating from navy vessels, used barges as offshore staging bases, deployed highly trained commandos, and used then-new technologies such as Forward Looking Infrared (FLIR) sensors and night vision goggles. Operating in darkness, the team caught the Iranian ship *Iran Ajr* laying mines in the channel used by tankers to approach oil-loading terminals. U.S. forces attacked the vessel, killing several crew members, and boarded the ship, capturing the rest. The boarding party also found documents that revealed considerable detail about Iran's mine-laying campaign. Armed with this information, the navy had the edge going forward.

Knowledge of Iranian operational patterns came into play in October, when an Iranian Silkworm anti-ship missile struck the MV *Sea Isle City* just outside the Kuwaiti port. No deaths resulted, but seventeen crew members were hurt, including the U.S. skipper. The navy counterattacked in Operation Nimble Archer by destroying the oil platforms used by the Revolutionary Guard as bases in the Gulf. The zone remained relatively quiet until April 1988, when the guided missile frigate USS *Samuel Roberts*, steaming near Bahrain, detonated a mine that blew a huge hole in its side. There were no fatalities, but ten crew members were injured. The navy unleashed an assault on a few oil platforms and a handful of Iranian naval vessels, sinking one frigate and damaging another, which is still in service with the Iranian navy.

Reagan's Restraint Riles the Navy

The striking thing about this engagement was the restraint exercised by the U.S. side. Iranian mines had taken a U.S. warship completely out of action and wounded dozens of sailors, followed by an aggressive defense against the U.S. response, and yet no Iranian shore facilities were attacked. The U.S. action, although condemned by the International Court of Justice as unnecessary for the defense of vital U.S. interests, was narrow in both conception and execution, clearly designed to minimize the possibility of escalation. Whatever else the Reagan administration was trying to achieve, it did not want to end up in a spiraling confrontation with the Islamic Republic.

This was a sensible stance to take under the circumstances, but not universally shared within the navy. Admiral James "Ace" Lyons, commander of the Pacific Fleet, believed that the tanker war had fortuitously built up the U.S. naval presence in the Persian Gulf region to a level where it could inflict decisive damage on Iran's military capability. He envisaged a short, sharp coordinated assault on a range of Iranian military assets, which would plunge the Iranian regime into chaos and create the conditions for its overthrow or collapse.

Lyons's thinking had been evolving since the fall of 1986, as the deployment schedule for the Pacific Fleet under his immediate command began to jell. According to this timetable, the United States would have three aircraft carriers in the theater, along with the powerful flotilla of frigates, destroyers, and submarines that form the battle group around each carrier. These floating airfields each embarked an aviation wing of as many as ninety fighter-bombers.

In addition to the carrier battle groups, the USS *Missouri*—"Mighty Mo," on whose deck the Japanese surrendered in August 1945—would also be in Gulf waters, with its array of 16-inch guns and a hull constructed to immunize the ship against torpedoes and large-caliber projectiles and, it was thought, Silkworm anti-ship missiles. The simultaneous arrival of another ship loaded with marines would add a ground attack element to this extraordinary conglomeration of floating firepower.

In early summer the following year, Weinberger was on a swing through Asia, stopping in Honolulu en route. He called on Lyons, who took the opportunity to brief him on Operation Window of Opportunity, Lyons's fifteen-page plan for exploiting the unusual convergence of so many warships in the same time and place. He explained that the execution of the plan would destroy 70 percent of Iran's military capability and choke off its main source of revenue.

According to the plan, in a forty-eight-hour avalanche of U.S. explosives, Lyons's force would destroy the Kharg Island oil terminal; all shore-based installations capable of threatening ships in Gulf waters or the coast along the Arab side of the Gulf; wreck the port facilities all along the Iran coast both inside the Gulf and east of the Strait of Hormuz, mining the two most important ports; and deposit marines of the 13th Expeditionary Unit to storm the island of Abu Musa, which the shah had wrested from the United Arab Emirates in the 1970s.

Lyons underscored the historic nature of this opportunity. As his spiel unfurled at the conference table, Weinberger said nothing and repeatedly tried to get up and leave, each time detained by Lyons, who rushed to get through the entire plan before losing his personal window of opportunity with the secretary of defense. By the time Weinberger pried himself loose, he had still not broken his silence. His body language, however, suggested that he was not a convert.[62]

Working with Admiral William Crowe, the chairman of the Joint Chiefs of Staff and his mentor and patron, Lyons continued to refine his plan. Crowe understood the sensitivity of Lyons's objectives and proposed that the plan be sent to him as a hand-carried letter and not through the navy's communication system, where it would be seen by others. Crowe thought that the scale of the attacks was more than the president was likely to approve, but Lyons argued that given the fallout from Iran-Contra, such a bold move would rescue the president's position.

The two admirals then addressed the challenge of getting the marines into place to carry out their part in the larger, still hypothetical plan. The force was embarked on the USS *Guadalcanal*, a utility vessel used as a hospital, troopship, and for other logistical purposes. It was en route from the remote U.S./UK base at Diego Garcia in the Indian Ocean. Lyons had it rigged with camouflage so that it would appear as though it was a normal cargo vessel, and, in Operation Slipper, it slipped into Gulf waters under the cover of darkness. Knowledge of this deployment was withheld from Lyons's two bosses: CINCPAC (Commander-in-Chief Pacific Command), and the chief of naval operations, Carlisle Trost, back in Washington.

It could not, however, be kept secret forever. As awareness spread of Lyons's intention to bring down the Iranian regime by imposing a humiliating military defeat on the Mullahs, two key Pentagon players, Weinberger's military assistant Colin Powell and the assistant secretary Rich Armitage, recommended to Weinberger that Lyons be removed. In view of Reagan's reluctance to get involved in a bigger fight with Iran than was necessary to regain balance following the vertiginous effects of Iran-Contra, Lyons's departure was a foregone conclusion. In a matter of weeks he retired, turning to consulting and far-right politics.

Earnest Will culminated in a disaster attributable in part to the navy's local commanders' urge to deliver a beating to the Iranians. On the morning of July 3, a navy cruiser, USS *Vincennes*, was engaged in a fight with Iranian gunboats that had broken off from the engagement to shelter in their home waters.

Although the captain of the *Vincennes* was ordered to disengage and steam in the opposite direction, he decided to pursue the gunboats and destroy them. He left international waters for Iran's territorial zone, where he was located at 10:47 a.m. when his ship launched two surface-to-air missiles at an Iranian civilian aircraft headed for Dubai from Bandar Abbas. The missiles found their target, killing 290 passengers, including 60 children. A clumsy cover-up ensued. The United States asserted that the *Vincennes* had been in international waters, and that the plane, which had taken off from an airport that handled both military and civilian aviation, had been descending at high speed toward the ship. U.S. communicators had tried to contact the Iranian crew on an emergency frequency, but there had been no response.

In the dance of seven veils that often trails a cover-up, it soon became known that the Iranian Airbus 300 had been ascending at the time of impact and apparently at a steady speed; that the airframe that was said to be the target was actually a fraction of the size of the Airbus and that a nearby U.S. vessel correctly identified the plane as an Iranian civilian aircraft; that the Iranian crew was in constant contact with two air control towers and would not have been expected to monitor the particular emergency frequency used by the *Vincennes*; and that the *Vincennes* was not in fact in international waters but had shot the airplane down within Iranian airspace. For the United States, the incident soon blew over. The *Vincennes*'s commander was awarded the navy's Legion of Merit for his "outstanding service" in the Persian Gulf, and the United States—compelled by the International Court of Justice—paid $61.8 million to compensate the victims.[63] Whether it blew over for the Iranians is a separate question.

It's often said that the combination of U.S. attacks on the Iranian navy and, in Iran's perception, the deliberate targeting of a civilian aircraft, were the developments that finally persuaded Ayatollah Khomeini to accept UN Security Council Resolution 598, which called for a cease-fire between Iran and Iraq.[64]

In Khomeini's words, "Taking this decision was more deadly than taking poison. I submitted myself to God's will and drank this drink for his satisfaction," even though "I had promised to fight to the last drop of my blood and to my last breath." To this he added the enigmatic phrase "thanks to some incidents and factors that I do not mention at this moment, and God willing, will become clear in the future." Perhaps he was alluding to U.S. intervention. We will likely never know unless the Islamic Republic or its successor opens its archives. Nonetheless, the war did draw to a close soon thereafter, Earnest Will was discontinued, and the international relations of the Persian Gulf seemed at long last to settle into an uneasy equilibrium. The illusory nature of this state of affairs will be explored in the chapters on the two Bush administrations.

The United States and Saudi Arabia

U.S. involvement in the Middle East has been rooted in two policy priorities: the security of Israel and Saudi Arabia. The driving factors differ, of course. In Israel's case the driver has been domestic politics and, during the Cold War, rivalry with the Soviet Union. In the Saudi case, access to oil, which was a strategic and economic priority. During the Reagan administration, the Saudi Arabia relationship went through two phases. In the first phase, ties were quite close. Iran was threatening both Saudi and American interests. The clerical regime in Tehran challenged the legitimacy of the Al Saud, accusing it of original sin: failing to take on Israel. Iranian propaganda showcased the facts that the Kingdom bordered Israel, had a big army, great wealth, and advanced weapons. Yet despite these geographic, economic, and military advantages, what was it doing?

This was clever geopolitical gamesmanship. The population of the Arab Middle East is only 10 percent Shiite, and of course Iran itself was not ethnically Arab. The only way that Iran could outflank the Al Saud—the self-proclaimed guardians of the two holy mosques—was by demonstrating that Iran was more authentically Muslim than the corrupt and flaccid Saudi royal court, whose princes were cavorting in the fleshpots of Europe while Palestinians suffered. Even worse, the Shiite 10 percent of the Kingdom's population was concentrated in the northeast, where much of Saudi oil production took place. The risk of Iran's vitriolic criticism striking a nerve with Saudi Shiites intensified the Royal Court's fear and loathing of the clerics on the other side of the Gulf.

The United States and Saudi Arabia in Reagan's first term also bonded over the peace process. The Reagan administration's rescue of Arafat from death at the Israeli hands in Beirut and pressure on Begin regarding Palestinian self-determination was popular in Riyadh. The Saudis and Americans were also on the same side in the Iran-Iraq War, both working behind the scenes to ensure Iraqi victory, and had a joint effort to push the Soviets out of Afghanistan. This effort moved slowly at first. Aid to the Mujahideen—Afghan opponents of the Soviet intervention—was limited, consisting mostly of Korean War–vintage Chinese weapons.* This only produced a stalemate, though, which both the U.S. administration, pressed by several gung ho congressmen, and the USSR sought to break. The Russians stepped up their helicopter operations, deployed vans equipped with eavesdropping gear to monitor the mostly unencrypted Mujahideen communications, and inserted 7,000 special operations soldiers to go on the offensive. The U.S. intelligence community reluctantly responded by arranging for Mujahideen to get missiles to shoot down helicopters and destroy the mobile surveillance vans, as well as secure communications

---

* The Chinese were eager to inflict pain on Moscow ever since the Sino-Soviet split in the 1960s and the subsequent formation under President Nixon and Chairman Mao of an informal U.S.-China coalition aimed at containing Russian power.

equipment. All this cost a lot of money. The Al Saud agreed to match every dollar spent by the United States, ultimately contributing hundreds of millions to the war effort.

Unfortunately, by arrangement with Riyadh, the Saudi contribution was channeled to Afghan recipients selected by Pakistan's intelligence service, which backed anti-American Pashtun warlords. These were the chieftains who sheltered al Qaeda in the years leading up to 9/11. Individual wealthy Saudis, including Osama bin Laden, also injected large sums, while many young Saudis traveled to Afghanistan as combatants. These fighters would come back to haunt both the Kingdom and the United States.

The close U.S.-Saudi relationship ran aground when news broke of Reagan's behind-the-scenes arms sales to Iran. The Saudis were thunderstruck by the deal with Iran. For them it signified two intolerable developments. The first was the fact of American duplicity. For a regime that counted on the United States for its protection from external threats, the notion that its security guarantor would sell weapons to the Saudis' worst enemy behind their back was a profound shock. The second was Israeli involvement. The Saudis, like many Arabs, were convinced that the White House and Congress, owing to Jewish influence, followed Jerusalem's instructions. The Iran arms deal seemed to confirm what the Saudis had long suspected.

Though the Reagan administration did its best to reassure the Saudis, in the mid-1980s, Prince Bandar pitched the Chinese ambassador in Washington on the proposition that China sell its intermediate-range ballistic missiles to the Kingdom. The Saudis apparently felt owning the missiles would deter Iran and Israel from attacking, even though they lacked nuclear warheads to use with them. By the time the CIA got wind of the deal, the missiles were already deployed and ready for use. The administration was infuriated by the Saudi maneuver and insisted that U.S. personnel be deployed to the launch installations, but the Saudis, unrepentant, refused and, as far as known publicly, still maintain the missiles, albeit without nuclear warheads.

The Shores of Tripoli

Before turning to the Bush dynasty, there remains one last Reagan intervention in the greater Middle East; this took place in Libya, where it unfolded slowly and confusingly from 1981 through U.S. attacks in 1988, and culminated in Libya's horrific retribution in the last year of Reagan's presidency. In the years following the attacks endured by the United States in Lebanon, the Reagan administration was confronted with five terrorist crises produced by the toxic combination of resentment, weakness, cynicism, desperation, and the rediscovery of terrorism as potent theater in a media-driven age: the hijackings of TWA 847 on June 14, 1985, and the *Achille Lauro*, a cruise ship, on October 7 through 10, 1985; the Rome and Vienna airport massacres in December 1985; the bombing of the La Belle disco in Berlin in April 1986; and, between the election of George H. W. Bush and his inauguration, the destruction of Pan Am 103 in December 1988.

As these events drew American attention to the challenge of terrorism, Libya's leader, Colonel Muammar Qaddafi, was publicly embracing it. Qaddafi had been presiding over an increasingly ramshackle country for sixteen years. He had entered leadership as a typical postcolonial Middle Eastern military academy graduate, the kind of soldier that American Middle East experts thought of as technocratically inclined and dedicated to modernization. He soon showed that he did not fit the mold. Although fervently anti-colonial, like his counterparts throughout the region, he was not secular, having devised an idiosyncratic reading of Islam incorporating his own socioeconomic and political philosophies.

Qaddafi wielded ultimate authority in Libya, using a large domestic intelligence apparatus to enforce his will. He was, until his death in 2012, a megalomaniac. Libya's oil wealth afforded him the opportunity to pursue grandiose fantasies of dominance in Africa. Unable to confront the United States directly despite the enormous arsenal of weaponry he purchased from the Soviet Union, Qaddafi relied on terrorism to further his various radical causes.

It was a sensible strategy. The United States had shown, since 1979, that it had no effective capacity to respond to terrorism, whether in the form of hostage taking, plane or ship hijackings, bombings, kidnappings, or murder. This was not for want of effort. The first organizational steps to cope with the terrorist threat were underway. The administration had formed a terrorist incident working group to manage crises and an emergency response team, led by a State Department official, to deploy to countries where an attack was underway to coordinate U.S. actions with the host government.[65]

These were positive developments. But bureaucratic and cultural barriers between agencies were still in place, and a White House–led "whole-of-government" approach was still a decade away. Terrorism-related intelligence derived mostly from friendly regional governments that nonetheless had their own agendas and whose own intelligence gathering was flawed. And an overall strategy had yet to be developed to ward off a threat against innumerable civilian targets—transportation systems, hotels, tourist attractions, gathering spots, and myriad others—that could not even be catalogued, let alone defended.

Libya also had friends to shield it from a U.S. response. European business ties to Libya were strong, especially in the energy sector, and governments did not want to expose themselves to Libyan attacks that they were unable to block. And the Soviet Union had emerged as Libya's informal ally, arming Qaddafi's forces in return for desperately needed hard currency, establishing an air base on Libyan territory and gaining access to the port at Tobruk.

Many in Washington believed that Libya's position was reinforced by membership in what the State Department derisively labeled "the triple entente" of Iran-Syria-Libya in an ironic reference to the Russian-British-French alliance of 1907. The fear of an axis of evil, as a later administration expressed the concept, lay in the belief that countries opposed to the United States would naturally cooperate in mutually beneficial ways, posing a collective challenge that was greater than the sum of its parts.

From 1981 onward, the administration struggled to find a way to subdue Qaddafi's Libya without getting embroiled in a conflict more violent than the underlying provocations, which included Libyan meddling in Chad, which held large uranium deposits, and Sudan, a U.S. friend in the early 1980s; Qaddafi's designation of the entire Gulf of Sidra in the southern Mediterranean as Libyan territory, contrary to international law; an assassination campaign against dissidents abroad, including in the United States; and funding of a grab bag of terrorist groups, especially the Abu Nidal Organization, which broke away from the PLO in 1974 to pursue Palestinian independence exclusively through terror.

The Chad problem was dealt with by throwing money at it, mostly to fund a peacekeeping force that could neutralize and eventually expel the Libyan presence. The administration thought to use Qaddafi's interest in Sudan to lure him into a trap that would result in a serious beating, but Sudan proved to be less a lure than had been thought. Libya's assertion of sovereignty over the Gulf of Sidra was countered by U.S. "freedom of navigation" exercises, which consisted of sending warships across Qaddafi's "line of death" and destroying Libyan air or naval forces that rose to the challenge. Assassination of dissidents and support for terrorism, on the other hand, appeared to be beyond remedy.

By 1984, the administration had at least three studies underway to assess Qaddafi's vulnerabilities and devise policies to box him in. State came up with options stretching from doing nothing to regime change, but leaning toward the use of force. Robert M. Gates, who was Bill Casey's deputy, sent Casey a briefing on Iranian, Syrian, and Libyan support for terrorism. It concluded that deterring or punishing Iran and Syria would be "too hard. . . . So the process of elimination brought CIA to Libya."

Casey issued a Special National Intelligence Estimate titled "Libya's Qaddafi: The Challenge to the United States and Western Interest," which judged that Qaddafi would directly target U.S. personnel or installations if he "(1) could get away with the attack without U.S. retaliation, or (2) believed the United States was engaging in a direct threat to his person or was actively trying to overthrow his regime." The document purported to show that Qaddafi had meddled in twenty-five states around the world.[66]

Much of this activity was trivial or simply ineffectual. Graham Fuller, the national intelligence officer for the Near East, searched for chinks in Qaddafi's armor, while other CIA analysts downplayed the threat that Qaddafi could pose to U.S. interests, except perhaps in Sudan. They noted that Libya had only a limited capability to operate within the United States, where there were allegedly two hundred "fanatical" pro-Qaddafi students. Strategically, Libya was hemmed in to the east by Egypt, a mortal enemy. Fuller's review, which accounted for the views of the intelligence community as a whole, judged that "no course of action short of stimulating Qaddafi's fall will bring any significant and enduring change in Libyan policies."

The inescapable conclusion was that the feckless Libyan opposition-in-exile would have to be bucked up and that "a broad program in cooperation with key countries [i.e., Egypt and Algeria] combining political, economic and paramilitary action" be put into effect.[67] These measures were very much in the CIA's wheelhouse. The Pentagon was fine with whatever other agencies and departments proposed as long as it did not involve military participation.

The NSC was pessimistic, concluding in an internal assessment that "Qaddafi's adventurism is accelerating and the constraints of his international behavior are fewer. NATO allies, despite Qaddafi's demonstrated capacity for mischief-making, compete with each other for profitable Libyan contracts while pronouncing the convenient rationale that it is better to collaborate with Qaddafi than to isolate him."[68]

A Bouquet for Qaddafi

By July 1985, the National Security Planning Group (NSPG) at the White House had reached a dead end, with no consensus regarding how to solve the Qaddafi problem. The NSC, with Casey's support, was pushing Operation Flower, the umbrella term for two overlapping operations named Tulip and Rose.

Under Tulip, the CIA would work with Libyan exiles on coup planning and preparation; under Rose, Egypt would invade Libya from the east, while the United States bombed Tripoli and an array of other targets that underpinned Qaddafi's control and the Libyan military's ability to respond effectively to intruding Egyptian forces. Apart from Casey at the CIA and, initially, George Shultz, no one liked the idea. Weinberger tried to kill it using a time-honored Pentagon custom, which is to say yes of course, we are gung ho, sir, and then produce a plan that is laughably impractical. In this case, the Pentagon planners insisted that the United States could crack Qaddafi's defenses only by redeploying about one third of the U.S. ground forces in Europe, during the tensest period in U.S.-Soviet relations in thirty years. Gates remarked that it looked like the invasion of Normandy.[69]

Admiral Poindexter, the national security adviser, was in thrall to Operation Flower and, against the advice of the State Department, traveled secretly to Cairo to meet with Hosni Mubarak and brief him on the plan. In the room with the Egyptian president, Poindexter proceeded to read a four-page briefing memorandum. The U.S. ambassador, Nick Veliotes, had tried to discourage Poindexter from this sort of mind-numbing presentation, but without success. Mubarak rejected the proposal, or rather as much of it as he had heard before terminating the meeting. Shultz, by this time, had been convinced by Veliotes that Operation Flower, at least insofar as it involved Egypt, was a nonstarter. For Mubarak, removing the best part of his army from the Nile delta, where it was essential to protect his regime from domestic threats, for the purpose of toppling Libya's lunatic leader made little sense.

The summer and fall of 1985 were consumed by the TWA 847 and *Achille Lauro* crises, so when Qaddafi actually did strike in December, using the Abu Nidal gunmen to massacre travelers gathered at the El Al counters in the Rome and Vienna airports, the United States had no ready military options. Shultz and Weinberger sparred over whether the time had come.

The president authorized Tulip, the plan to work with Libyan exiles to overthrow Qaddafi, and coordination with Egypt on Rose, the plan to invade Libya that Mubarak had already rejected. Economic sanctions were the preferred path. Reagan intensified existing sanctions by executive order, invoking the International Emergency Economic Powers Act (IEEPA). None of Libya's European trading partners was interested in joining in sanctions, however, so the executive order was largely futile.

The Pentagon formalized the process of identifying targets, which had begun informally in the immediate aftermath of the airport attacks. The navy was ordered to conduct a large freedom of navigation exercise in the Gulf of Sidra. Reagan was satisfied with these actions. He confided to his diary, "If Mr. Qaddafi decides not to push another terrorist act, okay, we've been successful with our implied threat. If on the other hand he takes this for weakness and does loose another one, we will have targets in mind and instantly respond with a hell of a punch."

On April 5, 1986, Qaddafi did launch another attack, dispatching agents to plant a bomb in the La Belle disco in Berlin, killing two Americans and a Turkish woman. Intercepted communications between Tripoli and the Libyan embassy in East Germany conveying instructions for the operatives were quickly passed by the UK to the United States. The Libyans had been caught red-handed.

On April 14, U.S. aircraft hit the Tripoli Military Airfield, Tripoli Naval Base, Benghazi Naval Base, Benina Airfield in Benghazi, a terrorist training facility at Murat Sidi Bilal, Libyan Intelligence Service HQ in Tripoli, Qaddafi's desert camp and his bunker at the Bab al-Azizia barracks in Tripoli, and Jamahiriya Guard barracks at Benghazi. Including the al-Azizia barracks on the list had been touch and go because it raised the possibility that Qaddafi would be killed in the strike.

This would look a lot like an assassination of the kind prohibited by Executive Order 12333 that Reagan had signed earlier, not for humanitarian or rule of law reasons, but because to do otherwise would be to invite assassination attempts against U.S. or allied leaders. Reagan, however, was willing to make an exception in Qaddafi's case and told advisers that "he would take the heat." In the event, the strike killed Qaddafi's adopted daughter and left the villain himself alive to swear vengeance.

On December 21, 1988, vengeance was his when a bomb planted by two Libyan agents on board Pan Am flight 103 en route from London to New York detonated over Lockerbie, Scotland, killing all 243 passengers and 11 people on the ground. On the aircraft were dozens of Syracuse University students heading home for the holidays. Qaddafi's accounts with the Reagan administration were closed. As Rand Beers, the U.S. government official responsible for managing the response to this atrocity, recalled, there was the sense that it had been "tit for tat."

Paradigm Lost

The Reagan administration immersed the United States in Middle Eastern military commitments that Washington had avoided since World War II, when U.S. and British forces landed in Morocco and Algeria and had taken

Tunisia, and 20,000 U.S. troops were sent to Iran in 1942 to secure the supply of equipment to the Soviet Union.

Throughout the intervening period, the United States had relied on local powers or the British to maintain the regional order so the United States could focus on Europe and Asia. Successive administrations had defined U.S. interest in the region as narrowly as possible, making no defense commitments to friends in the region, while signaling that if push came to shove, the United States would help them get out of a jam.

Washington had had to follow through on this implicit obligation only twice: in 1958, when Eisenhower sent a small contingent of marines to Lebanon for four months to reassure a nervous clique of pro-American politicians, and in 1973, when over the course of three days, Nixon replenished Israeli armor losses on the Golan Heights. The United States did participate in the coup planning that secured the throne of Reza Pahlavi's son, Mohammad, in 1953, but deployed no military force to affect the outcome.

This paradigm was discarded by Reagan. He jettisoned the cautious restraint of the preceding quarter century by plunging the United States into the Lebanese civil war. By the time he left office, he had used force against Iran and Libya. The administration set in motion a quest for military bases in the region that made two subsequent major wars feasible.

The administration also set a new pattern of large investments of prestige and resources for puny or negative returns. There was nothing the administration attempted in the Middle East in its two terms that left the United States better off. Lebanon descended into civil war and never returned to the American sphere; Qaddafi's policies were even more radical after the air strikes, contributing to more terrorism, then Libya's decline and its disastrous Arab Spring; Washington lost whatever capacity it had to affect either Iraqi or Iranian actions and earned a reputation for confusion, untrustworthiness, and ineffectuality; and it injected a great deal of energy and money into its relationship with Israel while mostly failing to turn its largesse into influence.

Reagan's rhetoric exaggerated the U.S. stake in the region, while simultaneously overestimating U.S. capacity to secure these occasionally absurdly inflated interests. Conversely, the administration consistently underestimated the capacity of local players to secure their parochial interests either by defying Washington or by manipulating it, sometimes with comical ease.

On Reagan's watch, the State Department and National Security Council staff were prone to applying military solutions to fundamentally political and diplomatic problems. During the Reagan years, the line against the casual use of force was held—ironically, perhaps, by the defense secretary—but just barely. Yet this push-pull dynamic sometimes yielded questionable, even bizarre results, most obviously in the U.S. failure to respond to the attacks against the embassy and marine barracks in Beirut.

Reagan cast the die for future U.S. interaction with Iran, which then as now reflects a tacit recognition that the Islamic Republic is not a country one wants to go to war with. His administration typified the aversion–attraction posture of his successors, each of whom either entered into office seeking a rapprochement with Iran and departed in a frustrated, punitive mood, or the other way around. Looking back at Reagan's record, it is astonishing that Republicans have criticized Democratic presidents for their search for a modus vivendi and, for that matter, Democratic self-flagellation over the Iran nuclear deal of 2015. If Reagan is the archetypal tough patriot, deals with Iran should be regarded as American as motherhood and apple pie.

The Reagan administration was the first in a long line of administrations that could not quite work out how to balance powerful regional countries against one another to prevent them from challenging U.S. interests, unable to decide whether to put its thumb on the Iranian or Iraqi side of the scales. By the end of its second term, it had sided with the stronger against the weaker, contributing to an imbalance that encouraged Saddam's aggression against Kuwait, triggering Desert Storm and a consequent entanglement with Iraq that cost the United States dearly in the decades that followed.

Until Reagan's presidency, the source and justification for U.S. support for Israel was a moral commitment to a liberal peace-seeking democracy and national home for a people savagely persecuted during World War II. Under his administration, the relationship became transactional, justified by Israel's contribution to U.S. strategic success in the Cold War. The husk of the old relationship was never discarded, but the shift in its basis from shared values to strategic justification facilitated an Israeli policy shift to the right, especially toward the Palestinians.

The Reagan administration turned repeatedly to allies for help both within the region and outside it. These attempts to elicit cooperation generally failed, despite America's leading role in NATO, its one-third share of global trade, the absence of an Asian competitor except perhaps Japan, and no troublesome European Union. Reagan's record underscores the vacuousness of the perennial debate about "leadership." The United States in the 1980s might have been the leader of the free world, but allies still went their own way on profound strategic issues.

Reagan's team also demonstrated how hard it is to construct a coherent policy when the underlying strategy is disconnected from reality. With respect to the Middle East, the administration was unalterably convinced that the Soviets were a clear and present danger to the regional order, when observable realities pointed in the opposite direction. Virtually the entire thrust of the administration's actions in the region was in response to a nonexistent threat. Thus, the vastness of U.S. power was harnessed to a mirage. Such strategic hallucinations continued to regulate U.S. policy—with a few exceptions—through the years between then and now.

The relationship between the intelligence and policy communities conformed to a pattern whereby an early phase of tell-it-like-it-is intelligence reporting devolves to what later became known, without irony, as opportunity analysis. In this mode, the intelligence community, relevant only to the extent that it has the president's ear, finds a way to tell the administration what it wants to hear and proffers, directly or by implication, policy recommendations of exactly the kind the intelligence community is supposed to avoid. The White House does not want to hear why its preconceptions are inaccurate or its policies destined to fail. The president needs cover for his actions—or someone to blame for their failure—and the intelligence community is meant to serve both these requirements. The community walks a tightrope. Speak truth to power and get excluded from the policy process; play along and get blamed when policies fail. On balance, the prospect of exclusion is seen to be more dangerous than taking the blame for failure. If the community is thrown under the bus by the White House, it can fight back through leaks to the press or by exploiting partisan politics. If the community is left out in the cold, there's no easy way to get back to the warmth of the Oval Office. This dynamic does not solely affect Middle East policymaking, but it is an especially prominent feature of it, certainly since the Reagan administration managed U.S. interests in the region.

Both Republicans and Democrats are clearly troubled by the lack of "moral clarity" in foreign policy. There has always been a tension between the strategic imperative and the impulse to draw a bright line between good and evil in the conduct of American foreign policy; it was evident in the Reagan period as it was for every administration that followed. Reagan was a person of deep if not universal compassion, yet he nevertheless endorsed or acquiesced to the massive and continuous Iraqi use of chemical weapons both on the battlefield and in cruel attacks on Iraqi civilians. The lesson, if there is one here, is that even an administration remembered as the avatar of moral clarity in foreign policy was perfectly prepared to subordinate principle to strategic necessity. The irony in this instance was that the strategic need to which moral interest was subordinated was illusory. No administration following Reagan was any more or less attentive to moral demands in the strategic environment of their time.

Reagan's administration was not the first to demonstrate that a coherent policy is elusive where the structure of government is itself incoherent. But Reagan's team, with its strong but anarchic cabinet and weak National Security Council, was the example par excellence. As McFarlane later complained, the president respected wealthy self-made men and enjoyed their company, whereas mid-level military officers and career staffers—like himself—could not command his attention. This meant that the president rarely got the neutral advice he needed as the four incompatible pachyderms of the administration—the chief of staff, secretaries of state and defense, and director of central intelligence—slugged it out. McFarlane was just the dwarfish peasant waving his stick at the elephant trampling the crops. Occasionally the NSC staff won: when Oliver North really wanted to run with Iran-Contra, he was able to hold just enough sway over Reagan to keep Weinberger and Shultz at bay. The result was not a happy one.

The Reagan administration was the first to confront Middle Eastern terrorism. In that long-ago moment, the violence was state sponsored. Adversaries of the United States lacking the military power to challenge it on the battlefield used terrorism as the weapon of the weak it has always been. With the advent of terrorism carried out not by states but by ideologically motivated groups unlinked to government patrons, state-sponsored terrorism has now begun to look like a relatively simple problem from a simpler time. Yet the record shows that the Reagan team, like the Clinton administration, found state-sponsored terrorism to be virtually insoluble. They discovered that even towering military capability could not deter terrorist attacks or even meaningfully avenge them. The failure to learn this lesson would come to haunt Reagan's successors.

CHAPTER THREE

GEORGE H. W. BUSH

The Old New World Order

Since Bush, Scowcroft, and Baker, no Administration has had both the opportunities and the wisdom, prudence, and will to know what to do with them. The combination of their ability to marry ends with means; the judgment to know how to stay out of trouble and not over-reach; the political smarts to build consensus at home; and above all to define and focus on the national interest has been unmatched ever since.[1]

—AARON DAVID MILLER, MIDDLE EAST ADVISER TO JAMES A. BAKER

This is clearly policy being made on the run. . . . We didn't have a grand design going in, and we don't have a grand design coming out.[2]

—WILLIAM B. QUANDT, MIDDLE EAST ADVISER TO PRESIDENT CARTER,
REFERRING TO OPERATION DESERT STORM

We never did have a plan to terminate the war.[3]

—GORDON BROWN, POLITICAL ADVISER TO GENERAL NORMAN SCHWARZKOPF,
REFERRING TO OPERATION DESERT STORM

The administration of George H. W. Bush represents the pivot in American strategy in the Middle East, embracing Reagan's interventionism and locking the United States into a posture of imperial overreach. In so doing, Bush trapped succeeding administrations into ever deeper military commitments to the region. The first Gulf

War, made up of operations Desert Shield and Desert Storm, is little re-membered now. The events that it engendered—the 9/11 attacks, the second Gulf War and invasion of Afghanistan, the grim antics of the Arab regimes that underwrote U.S. policy—have all overshadowed the first Bush administration and its war against Iraq.

Although the Reagan administration's forays into the Middle East broke new ground and established patterns of thought and action that have since become second nature to U.S. policymakers, it was George H. W. Bush who entwined the United States with Iraq in a dance of death that lasted for thirty years. The American obsession with Iraq has killed hundreds of thousands, including over 4,000 U.S. military personnel and wounded thousands of others. Demographers estimate that from the Gulf War launched by the first Bush administration to the aftermath of the invasion by his son's administration, between 687,000 and 878,000 Iraqi children under five years of age died as a result of U.S. actions. The combination of war and sanctions destroyed Iraq's health-care system, stripped the country of nutrients that children need to survive—let alone develop properly—blanketed the country with cluster munitions that are not magically deactivated by cease-fire declarations, and left a legacy of childhood traumatic stress syndrome from which recovery is highly unlikely. The financial cost of the Iraq War borne by the United States is over $2 trillion, a sum that will fluctuate with interest rates since the war was fought with borrowed money.

Many observers would contend that this assessment of George H. W. Bush is unfair. After all, a large portion of the civilian and financial tolls were paid during later administrations. In this narrative, George H. W. Bush and his team were serious, prudent, and responsible, steeped in the strategic wisdom developed by civilian experts at prominent universities and think tanks in the postwar years, students of history and shrewd interpreters of its implications for the United States at a pivotal moment. They presided over the most powerful nation on earth by every relevant measure: gross domestic product, overall federal budget, size and techno-logical sophistication of armed forces. They saw themselves as wise stew-ards of a fragile international system. They were not a whimsical group. As one of them, Richard Haass, observed, under George H. W. Bush's lead-ership, the United States fought a war of necessity against Iraq, whereas Bush's son (for whom Haass also worked) fought a war of choice. The comparison was meant to be invidious. In Haass's conception, the United States under Bush I was "the reluctant sheriff." It was charged, largely but not solely as a matter of self-interest, with responsibility for keeping the global peace; but like Gary Cooper in *High Noon*, the lawman's duty is an unsolicited, inescapable burden, embraced more in sorrow than in hubris.

Yet the "Vulcans" of the first Bush administration, as they later styled themselves, committed the original sin of armed conflict by acting on the assumption that victory would be swift and decisive. Unfortunately, nearly all long wars are begun in the misbegotten belief that they will be short. And since many of these intellectual policymakers rematerialized in the George W. Bush administration, it is perhaps unsurprising that they made the same mistake in 2003. In retrospect, the United States did not fight two separate Gulf wars. Rather, the nation engaged in a single long war punctuated by a truce, during which economic warfare substituted, with a couple of minor exceptions, for high explosives. It was a truce that could not last, for reasons that were unseen by the team that launched the war, blinded as they were by the glare of U.S. power and comforts of wishful thinking.

This is not to deny that Iraq's invasion and occupation of Kuwait in August 1991—the predicate for the U.S.-Iraq war that followed—was an outrageous act of aggression. Most just-war theorists would agree that reversing Iraq's victimization of Kuwait would be ethical, particularly if the minimum necessary force was used. They would also concede that Iraq's transgression posed a threat to international peace and security, as the UN Security Council affirmed. And from a realpolitik perspective, there was no question that U.S. interests were threatened by a hostile power acquiring a very large share of regional oil production. As one of my superiors once explained to me, "It was our oil," and we were entitled to safeguard it. The royal families who happened to rule the oil-producing countries were de facto U.S. allies because of the accidental colocation of their palaces and the oil deposits underneath them. Washington naturally believed that access to oil would be more secure if these families relied on the United States for their protection.

By this time, there was a powerful constituency that took this view a step further, arguing that regime change in any or all of the oil-producing states on the Arab side of the Gulf, particularly Saudi Arabia, would be a terrible calamity. These advocates included the region's oil companies, large banks that handled Arab oil wealth, infrastructure and construction companies, and manufacturers of tactical systems, especially big-ticket items like aircraft (both military and civilian), armor, and technology, which they also maintained. It wasn't just commercial interest; there was a commonsensical aspect to the notion that it would be better to have friendly regimes sitting on large regional oil deposits than rancorous powers.

This combination of apparently simple logic and vast business interest was so potent it even outweighed the power of Israel's lobby in Washington and outlasted the Soviet Union, the only outside threat to U.S. access to regional oil. The relative weight of the Saudi lobby was considerable and well matched to its Israeli rival. This was tested at least three times, with the Saudis emerging on top. The first two involved the sale of fighter jets and combat management aircraft, both of which were ferociously contested by Israel, and the third was the relegation of day-to-day U.S. military ties to Israel to the U.S. European command rather than Central Command, which managed Middle Eastern operations. This was a cumbersome arrangement and would have complicated coordination of

U.S. military operations in the event of a regional war, but the Arabs would not countenance sharing links with a U.S. military command with Israel. And the Pentagon complied.

America and Iraq after the Iran-Iraq War: A Match, but Not Made in Heaven

The Reagan administration had asserted neutrality in the Iran-Iraq War, but gradually tilted toward Iraq, while hedging its bets by secretly transferring desperately needed weapons to Iran. As we have seen, these transactions were ultimately leaked, embarrassing the administration and propelling it into an informal military alliance with Iraq. The optics of the relationship were politically inconvenient because Saddam was such an avid user of chemical weapons against Iran and unruly Iraqi citizens, whose use was banned under the Geneva Protocol of 1925.

The depravity of the chemical attacks, unfortunately for the Reagan administration, was all too public, since refugees displaying symptoms of exposure to chemical weapons made it to Turkey, where the Western press could question them, and to Iran, which had its own media operation optimized to vilify the eminently villainous Iraqi foe.

Congressional anger, fueled by press reporting, led to demands that the United States impose sanctions on Iraq for its use of chemical weapons. As a member of the State Department's political military affairs bureau monitoring the Iran-Iraq War, I drafted an options paper for Secretary Shultz outlining alternatives. I recommended two actions that were intended to show serious displeasure without crippling Iraq's gasping wartime economy. The one was to suspend work on a Ford auto plant; the other was to suspend $500 million in agricultural commodity credits that Iraq was using to get wheat for public consumption.[4] Both approaches would step on the toes of important constituencies, automakers, and farmers, which would stand to lose money.

In a meeting to review the options before submitting them to Shultz, the chief Middle East diplomat at the State Department chuckled while chewing on his unlit stogie, amused that there was anyone within the Beltway naive enough to believe that the administration would actually levy sanctions on Iraq, given the gamut of opposing strategic, commercial, and political interests.[5]

This of course was not a unique situation. Allies and security partners of the United States frequently misbehave, but when they do, the U.S. interests that impelled the partnership to begin with generally dictate inaction, if not silence. In recommending sanctions, I was a minority of one; the prevailing view was that sanctions would be counterproductive because they would leave both the United States and Iraq worse off. Baghdad's stability in an ongoing conflict with Iran would be jeopardized, a development that would benefit Washington's Iranian adversary, while Iraqi decisions regarding the use of chemical weapons would be unaffected. In fact, it was hard to disregard this assessment. The counterargument that it would set a precedent the United States might eventually regret was exactly the sort of long-run case that policymakers tend to dismiss as both speculative and dismissive of the more urgent needs of the moment.

With the end of the Iran-Iraq War in August 1988, Saddam appeared more secure, or so it was thought on the basis of his more moderate tone regarding the Arab-Israeli conflict and interest in links to the United States that would facilitate Iraq's recovery from the war with Iran. Iraq had bought huge quantities of weapons to sustain its war effort, much of it consisting of top-shelf French and Soviet systems as well as quantities of U.S. so-called dual use materiel—civilian items, like heavy trucks, that can be used for military purposes. Iraq's total procurement expenditures between 1980 and 1988 were about $47 billion, a gargantuan sum in then-year dollars, especially during a period of sharply diminished oil revenues. The country was in a deep hole and even reconstituted oil sales were not going to rescue it from a debt crisis. The very influx of weapons that had enabled Saddam to force Iran to quit while maintaining control over a restive populace had saddled the regime with a financial ball and chain that now threatened its survival. Saddam, therefore, needed all the help he could get.

With the election of George H. W. Bush in November 1988, the administration determined, following a policy review, that the United States would seek improved relations with Iraq, while strengthening ties to the states of the lower Gulf and Saudi Arabia. The latter relationships would be served by large-scale arms sales, limited only by Israel's ability, through its friends in Congress, to block them. Iraq would get loan guarantees and commodity credits to help it recover from the Iran war. These objectives were summed up in National Security Decision Directive 26 on October 2, 1989:

> Normal relations between the United States and Iraq would serve our longer-term interests and promote stability in both the Gulf and the Middle East. The United States Government should propose economic and political incentives for Iraq to moderate its behavior and to increase our influence with Iraq. At the same time, the Iraqi leadership must understand that any illegal use of chemical and/or biological weapons will lead to economic and political sanctions. . . . Human rights considerations should continue to be an important element in our policy toward Iraq. . . .
>
> We should pursue, and seek to facilitate, opportunities for U.S. firms to participate in the reconstruction of the Iraqi economy, particularly in the energy area, where they do not conflict with our non-proliferation and other significant objectives.

All this turned out to be too hard to do. In the first place, in August 1989, a federal investigation of a small Atlanta branch of Banco Nazionale del Lavoro, an Italian multinational bank based in Rome, revealed that

Iraq had received illegal loans, including $1 billion underwritten by agricultural credits but used for weapons purchases. It was a complex case and there was some evidence that the CIA knew of the transactions but did not report them. Democrats in Congress, already upset by what they saw as Republican coddling of a tyrant, held hearings that put the administration on the defensive. But the White House was determined to block congressional attempts to sanction Iraq, knowing that Saddam would not react well.[6]

NSDD 26 reflected the administration's conception of a post Iran-Iraq War Middle East, from which the Soviets were rapidly fading.[7] The specified threat to U.S. interests was now solely Iran. The corresponding strategy was to boost Arab military capabilities and deepen U.S. influence by inculcating greater reliance on Washington as their security guarantor. Arms sales entail the penetration of the buyer's defense establishment by the seller. The buyer's military personnel must be trained to operate the equipment either in the United States or in their own country by teams of U.S. instructors. The equipment also needs to be assembled and maintained by technical representatives of the manufacturers, which expands the American presence to include industry executives and hordes of engineers. Hence the connection made by the NSDD between arms and influence.

But there was more than just geopolitics at work. Participation in the reconstruction of Iraq meant contracts for major U.S. infrastructure companies—Brown and Root, Halliburton, the Bechtel Group. Internal U.S. deliberations went beyond the NSDD, insisting that bureaucratic and legislative opposition to loan guarantees "should be kept under close policy review because the stakes are big. We need export markets, and Iraq is a potential market."

Revealingly, internal U.S. documents about this issue cite the perception and reality of corruption in the context of the recent scandal, rather than the Iraqi regime's brutal management of domestic opponents or its dabbling in weapons of mass destruction. No one was oblivious to these problems; one administration official conceded that Saddam was unlikely to be "admitted to the Kiwanis Club." But there seemed to be a feeling that the best the United States could do was moderate Saddam's criminal instincts through admonition and inducement.

America and Iraq: Sometimes You Just Can't Love the One You're With

By February 1990, however, the administration was losing control of the situation. The Voice of America was a quasi-governmental radio station originally focused on Warsaw Pact publics, beaming anti-Soviet propaganda. With the end of the Cold War its programming covered other issues, including the malevolent nature of Saddam's regime. A broadcast on this topic irritated Saddam; when it was followed by a *Frontline* segment on network television that covered more or less the same ground, his conviction that the United States was out to get him reignited. A succession of other incidents roiled the waters. The United States and UK carried out sting operations that caught Iraq trying to smuggle krytrons, electronic triggers for nuclear weapons, and then components for a gigantic cannon that Saddam had hired a British engineer named Gerald Bull to design. Bull had already been assassinated, apparently by Israeli agents, at his home in Brussels, which only reinforced Saddam's fears. While the effects of these incidents rippled through both Washington and Baghdad, Saddam had a British journalist, Farzad Bazoft, executed for spying, despite international pleas for clemency.

On April 2, an increasingly paranoid Saddam gave a long speech in which he threatened to "burn half of Israel"[8] with chemical weapons, should Israel attack Iraq. Even though the threat was framed as a deterrent to an

Israeli strike, like the one that had destroyed Iraq's nuclear reactor in 1981, the allusion to chemical weapons in the context of an attack on Jews could not have been better calculated to offend American sentiment.

The administration still hoped to salvage its ties to the regime, despite Saddam's conviction of American malign intent. Acting on instructions from the State Department, U.S. ambassador April Glaspie wrote to Iraqi foreign minister Tariq Aziz to reassure him that "it is absolutely not United States policy to question the legitimacy of the government of Iraq, nor to interfere in any way with the domestic concerns of the Iraqi people and government."[9] But in the flurry of mixed signals emanating from Washington, Saddam was going to recognize only those confirming his perception of the administration's malign intent.

A congressional delegation led by Robert J. Dole of Kansas, a farm state that would greatly benefit from a deal with Saddam that enabled Iraq to buy large amounts of American grain, tried to reassure Saddam by blaming criticism of his regime on irresponsible media reporting that did not reflect America's true feelings of friendship. One member of the delegation praised Saddam for his rough handling of Iraqi reporters who dared to oppose him.[10]

By mid-April, the administration's ability to provide additional loan guarantees was exhausted. Balancing the demands of the export sector, oil companies, and midwestern farmers against the impact of Saddam's weird and violent behavior on congressional and public opinion proved to be too trying. Yet Bush's instruction to his cabinet to mesh these incompatible factors remained in effect.

The survival of Saddam's regime hinged on its ability to provide a peace dividend for Iraqis after the hardships of the Iran-Iraq War, which had destroyed Iraq economically. The country was $80 billion deep in foreign debt after the war, unable to make good on payments owed to trade partners, and facing reconstruction costs of an estimated $230 billion.[11]

Believing that the war had substantially benefited the states on the

Arab side of the Gulf, Saddam continued to demand that Iraq's export quota and OPEC prices be adjusted to compensate Iraq for its sacrifices. He also became interested in Kuwaiti oil, which raised the question, in his mind, of the legitimacy of the Iraq-Kuwait border as determined by the British after World War I. The correct border, according to Iraq, would incorporate Kuwaiti oil fields into Iraqi territory. There was much inter-Arab diplomatic maneuvering around Saddam's demand, but little give on the part of other exporters. As the pace of diplomacy accelerated, Saddam summoned April Glaspie to his palace on twenty-four hours' notice for a meeting on July 25. Glaspie was an experienced hand in the Arab world, but had not met with Saddam in the two years that she had been posted to Iraq. Given the time difference between Baghdad and Washington and the short interval between the invitation to the palace and the meeting, there was no chance for the State Department bureaucracy to supply authoritative instructions for the meeting. Glaspie was going to have to wing it.

The U.S. and Iraqi records of the meeting largely agree. In the version reported by *The New York Times*, Saddam vented about the ungrateful and uncooperative attitudes of his Arab brothers regarding oil revenues and chastised the United States for its criticism of the regime and controls on exports to Iraq. He then paused to allow Glaspie to respond.

> GLASPIE: I think I understand this. I have lived here for years. I admire your extraordinary efforts to rebuild your country. I know you need funds. We understand that and our opinion is that you should have the opportunity to rebuild your country. *But we have no opinion on the Arab-Arab conflicts, like your border disagreement with Kuwait.* (Italics added.)[12]

When Iraq released the transcript, complete with references to an interpreter and notetaker breaking down in tears as Saddam described

Iraqi suffering, it set off a firestorm. Glaspie had apparently assured Saddam that the United States would not oppose an invasion of Kuwait. Even though she was relying on standard talking points in the absence of updated instructions, Glaspie was hung out to dry by the State Department.

This would have been cruelly unfair under any circumstances, but the fact was that Saddam had already decided on the seizure of Kuwait, fearing a coup if he failed to act. Glaspie's disavowal of a U.S. interest in the border dispute might have reinforced his determination to go to war, but it did not flip the switch.

Saddam, after all, had what he thought were good reasons to believe he would get away with it. Military resistance from within the Arab world was inconceivable. The only other large Arab armies were in Egypt, which was incapable of deploying outside its own borders, and Syria, which relied on its army to fend off Israel and safeguard the Assad regime. Neither of these states would be a factor in a war against Kuwait; nor would European countries lift a finger to defend it.

Kuwait, an oil state ruled by an old merchant family, had no defensive capability and few friends. Perceived as arrogant by Arabs elsewhere, there would only be schadenfreude on the streets of Arab capitals when the Kuwaitis got what was coming to them. Kuwait had also alienated Washington by, among other things, refusing to accept a career diplomat as ambassador because of U.S. support for Israel. And the United States, as far as Iraq was concerned, had never actively involved itself in the Iran-Iraq War when the stakes were presumably higher, so there was no compelling reason to think it would attack Iraq in defense of Kuwait. Besides, in Saddam's mind the United States was soft; it had lost the Vietnam War to a smaller, much less developed country. Saddam also believed that Kuwait was not really an independent country but rather part of Iraq. The unification of the two states under Iraqi rule would right a historic wrong committed by British colonial power. Since Saddam believed he had the right to absolute rule over Iraq, he therefore had the right to rule over Kuwait as well.

The United States and Iraq at the Brink: Character, Mindset, Misperception

The United States, of course, had ideological fixations too. Ironically, defeat in Vietnam led many Americans to internalize precisely the image that Saddam held of the United States. But the humiliation of loss drove the United States to welcome an opportunity to demonstrate that the country still had the right stuff. The Republican Party's Vietnam narrative held that the United States fought with one hand tied behind its back because Democrats, backed by liberal media, were afraid to let the military take the ruthless actions needed to win. This time, the war would not be constrained by timid politicians and a reluctance to use whatever means necessary to ensure victory.

The Bush administration asserted a new doctrine to suit the mood: the United States would use force only to protect vital interests, only with solid public backing, and only with the determination to win. Nothing would be held back once the decision to fight was made. In this case, oil was the vital interest, but on a grander scale, so was an orderly post–Cold War world run along Western lines. The administration went out of its way to clarify for voters that unlike Vietnam, where impenetrable jungles gave the enemy an advantage, Iraq was trackless desert. The enemy had nowhere to hide, and the battlefield was perfectly tailored to the combined use of American airpower and armor. In addition, the war would be fought by a highly professional, volunteer army. The racial tensions, drug use, and morale problems that had plagued a conscript army in Vietnam were safely in the past.

The other fixation was Munich, the German metropolis where British prime minister Neville Chamberlain met Adolf Hitler in 1938, concurred in the seizure of Czech Sudetenland by Nazi Germany, and returned home to declare that he had secured "peace in our time." This concession to German ambition was dubbed appeasement, a word that evolved from a neutral verbal noun to an epithet as it became clear that Hitler had been emboldened, rather than mollified, by British conciliation. Bush and his national security adviser, Lieutenant General Brent Scowcroft, had matured in this era and thoroughly internalized the idea of appeasement as strategically disastrous and morally repugnant. Munich, appeasement, and the meme of Chamberlain's tightly furled umbrella had come to represent foreign policy in its most self-deceptive and pitifully naive form.

Bush was the scion of a monied, politically connected family that could have served as the heraldic crest of the white Anglo-Saxon ascendancy in New England. Whether despite the privileged entitlement of his upbringing or because of it, he had dropped out of school during World War II to serve as a combat pilot in the Pacific theater, where he was shot down and rescued. He was a person of demonstrable physical courage and moral commitment. His personal inclinations were distinctly liberal. Yet he could be cold-blooded in the pursuit of his political ambition, the presidency. This grail led him to Texas and the embrace of the right wing of the Republican Party, whose values were alien to the centrist tradition in which he was raised, but were essential to his credibility as a Republican in the Reagan era. On his way up the political ladder, he served as the U.S. permanent representative to the United Nations, envoy in Beijing, and director of the Central Intelligence Agency. He had viewed the latter appointment as the kiss of death for his quest for the presidency and is said to have wept on being notified of the appointment. But he did his duty, nonetheless. In sum, he was probably the best-prepared wartime president in American history.

Brent Scowcroft, Bush's foreign policy soulmate, was a few years younger, graduating from West Point just after World War II. While training to be a fighter pilot, his P-51 aircraft malfunctioned; he survived the crash but broke his back, putting a permanent end to his flight status. He nonetheless stayed in the air force and got a doctorate at Columbia University in international relations just when this academic discipline was taking off. His academic work injected a systematic logic into his policy analysis and recommendations in government. He had already served in positions at the White House in previous administrations, so by the time Bush chose him to be the national security adviser, his academic, bureaucratic, and military credentials were about as good as could be.

Although the two men's worldviews and policy preferences largely overlapped, their age gap and Scowcroft's scholarly work yielded somewhat different perspectives. For Bush, Saddam Hussein was Hitler: a monstrous dictator bent on conquest, undeterrable, incapable of compromise, untrustworthy, and certain to interpret concessions as a sign of weakness to be exploited. Any leader seeking to negotiate with Saddam might as well bring an umbrella, because he would be no better than Neville Chamberlain. Both Colin Powell, then chairman of the Joint Chiefs of Staff, and Scowcroft urged Bush to tone down his rhetoric about Saddam because it risked boxing in the administration if feasible alternatives to war emerged, or if war aims were limited to chasing Iraq out of Kuwait in deference to UN resolutions and coalition wishes. Saddam, though genuinely hideous, was also no Hitler, as any informed observer would be quick to point out. And Iraq was no 1940s Germany, demographically, technologically, or militarily.

Apart from his ideological blinders, Saddam's thinking was hampered by two major misconceptions. The first was his failure to grasp the "new world order" impulse of the administration and the policy direction it would dictate. Whether the concept of a new world order was an ex post facto justification for a policy that was arrived at instinctually, or decision makers were indeed thinking in these terms since the collapse of the Berlin Wall, is still debated. Bush and Scowcroft, in their fascinating coauthored book, *A World Transformed*, contend that they both perceived the fall of the wall as a historic break with the past and the beginning of a new era. It is clear that as the first year of the Bush term sped by, this idea constituted the larger frame in which the White House thought about international affairs and foreign policy.

Saddam displayed astonishing gaps in his understanding of the United States and Europe. He got the Vietnam effect, for example, precisely backward. It had indeed been a disgraceful loss, but it had galvanized the administration to demonstrate, at the first opportunity, that the United States had the will and the capacity to win a major war. And Saddam's invasion of Kuwait provided just this opportunity.

Saddam also mistook the diplomatic and military freedom of action the collapse of the Wall afforded the United States. In the diplomatic arena, the United States was perceived globally to have won a colossal battle with the USSR, and to be a superpower without a single strategic challenger. In most capitals, the instinct therefore was to cater to American desires. The overall posture of the United States since World War II had been to build and support multilateral rules-based arrangements and institutions and to avoid the overt trappings of imperialism. And with the demise of the Soviet bloc, there were no countervailing pressures.

Saddam did not realize that these truths, and the dismantling of Warsaw Pact forces in Europe and the unification of Germany, left a massive U.S. Army in Europe with no obvious mission. This was true as well for the French and British militaries. These forces were well equipped and had a martial tradition that included the defeat of Nazi Germany within living memory. NATO formations trained to fight precisely the sort of battle that a war with Iraq would entail, including reliance on heavy armor and artillery, opposing a professionalized enemy, and maneuvering on more or less flat terrain. And it was an army that was already halfway to the Middle East. Moreover, in the U.S. case, it was an army that had been rebuilt from scratch in the decade following the Vietnam War, and was now well led and determined to expunge the shame of Vietnam. Saddam's fear of a coup or popular unrest blinded him to the imperative of patience. Had he waited, two things would have made the situation dramatically different relatively quickly: he would have had a nuclear weapon, which might have changed the U.S. calculus, while the armored forces that the United States ultimately wielded against him would have been back in the States.

By the spring of 1990, the United States had largely given up on a productive relationship with Iraq. It was unpopular with Congress, bellicose, and Saddam was a paranoid bastard; yet Iran was still a threat best contained by Iraqi power. Thus, in policy terms, the administration had nowhere to go, especially since it had rejected sanctions as ineffective. But as frustrating as the situation was, there did not seem to be reason for despair. Arab leaders told Washington that Iraq would not go beyond the boundaries of intimidation and that a deal would ultimately be done with Kuwait.

Among diplomats, the possibility of invasion was not a prevailing concern because there was no clear precedent for it. There were unclear ones, however, like the Egyptian and Saudi invasions of Yemen in the 1960s, Syria's threat to Jordan in 1971, or even Iraq's invasion of the West Bank in 1948 in an attempt to grab it from Jordanian and Syrian hands. But the mantra in the State Department's Bureau of Near Eastern Affairs was that no Arab state had ever attacked another Arab state. Essentially, it was an argument based on historical inference where both the history and the inference were wrong. The obtuseness could be funny at times. A State Department Middle East intelligence analyst explained to me at the time that "it was too hot to fight," so invasion by Saddam was not in the cards.

My colleagues in the political-military bureau, unimpeded by complacent regional expertise, looked at Iraq's rhetoric, force deployments, and incentives, against Kuwait's combination of arrogance and weakness, and assumed correctly that Iraq would go for it. So did the Defense Intelligence Agency, which looked at the satellite imagery of Iraqi forces deployed north of the Kuwait border and saw, essentially, the exact pattern that Soviet forces were trained to take before invading West Germany.

The U.S. military also saw which way the wind was blowing. On July 19, Powell called Schwarzkopf to tell him to begin planning for the defense of Kuwait and Saudi Arabia. The next day, with Iraqi news outlets reporting the buildup of Iraqi troops on the Kuwait border, CENTCOM (Central Command) placed a mobile tactical air operations center in the UAE and, on July 24, held an air force exercise with the Emirati air force. As these measures were getting underway, the commander of Schwarzkopf's air assets staged a desktop exercise, "Internal Look," based on the notional invasion of Kuwait by a "country to the north."

On July 25, the very day Ambassador Glaspie had her fateful meeting with Saddam, the intelligence community's national intelligence officer for warning, Charlie Allen, a deeply experienced, legendary analyst, issued a warning of war and briefed the NSC staff on the impending Iraqi attack. But he was a lone voice. Moreover, there is a tendency for warning officers to be dismissed because they have a strong incentive to cry wolf. Allen's warning did not spur the administration to intervene diplomatically. Kuwait, in contrast, had gotten the hint and agreed on July 26 to meet Iraq's demands for compensation, but it was too little too late.

War Begins

Saddam launched the invasion on August 2, 1990. That morning the vanguard of an army of 140,000, including a tank armada and hundreds of artillery tubes, brushed aside Kuwait's 16,000-man ground force and seized the capital and oil fields. In the coming months, Iraqi units would dig in on the Saudi border, construct a defensive system of berms, trenches, minefields, and other obstacles and, to all appearances, settle in for the long haul.

The White House mobilized quickly, scheduling back-to-back Principals Committee and NSC meetings. The first disappointed Scowcroft because cabinet members appeared not to take the situation seriously. He suggested to Bush that the stakes were too high for experimentation with policies short of war. There was no way to be sure that the large force Saddam had inserted into Kuwait, far beyond what was necessary to overwhelm Kuwait's meager defenses, was going to stay there. Saudi Arabia was an even bigger prize, and an army that size could have taken Saudi oil fields. On the other hand, Iraqi forces did not, in fact, keep going once they had taken Kuwaiti territory, which might have suggested that Saudi Arabia was not on Saddam's dance card.

One can see, however, that the thought of an out-of-control hostile power commandeering nearly all Gulf oil deposits, deploying the world's fifth-largest army, and known to be developing weapons of mass destruction might be disorienting. Bush himself stated twice in this early phase of the crisis that Iraq's seizure of Kuwait could "not stand," a fairly clear summary of his assessment of the policy options. This reaction helps explain why no alternatives to war were seriously considered.

In addition to pushing the Pentagon for a war plan, the White House set the State Department in motion. The UN Security Council would have to issue resolutions condemning Iraqi aggression and demanding the withdrawal of its forces from Kuwait. Foreign capitals would have to be put on notice that that the United States considered the invasion of Kuwait to be a matter of strategic importance. The diplomatic support of key countries would have to be harnessed and directed. A unified international response was going to be key to convincing Saddam that he had bitten off more than he could chew and in preparing the ground for a military response. This would mean keeping freelancing by interested states to a minimum. A coordinated diplomatic campaign required leadership and discipline, which Washington would provide. Saddam would attempt to exploit divisions within the international community, drive wedges, widen differences, and force the diffusion and collapse of a campaign to oust his forces from Kuwait. This could not be permitted.

Less than a week after the invasion, Bush sent Vice President Dick Cheney and Powell to Saudi Arabia to request approval for the deployment of U.S. forces to the Kingdom to block an Iraqi advance from Kuwait toward Saudi oil fields. Agreement was not automatic, but debate among the senior princes was settled by the king's stark warning that without U.S. troops, the Al Saud would rule their kingdom from hotel rooms in Paris. Upon the delegation's return to Washington, Bush announced the deployment of a brigade of the 82nd Airborne Division and an unspecified number of combat aircraft to Saudi Arabia.[13] Over the next three months, the rest of the 82nd arrived in Saudi Arabia, along with the 101st Air Assault Division, the 24th Mechanized Infantry Division, the 3rd Armored Cavalry Regiment, and a division of marines. On August 20, Bush signed National Security Decision Memorandum (NSDM) 45 authorizing an array of diplomatic, economic, and military measures, including the formation of a multinational force. At this point, an Iraqi invasion of Saudi Arabia had effectively been ruled out by U.S. deployments.

The administration understood that the use of force would have to be multilateralized and blessed by the UN Security Council as well as the Arab League, if at all possible. Arab political cover would in any case be essential, whether it was purchased wholesale via the Arab League or retail, in individual capitals. The Gulf countries would not be enough; the big players, Egypt and Syria, would be essential. Although for historical reasons both countries would be overjoyed by Saddam's defeat in a terrible war, neither would have been naturally inclined to participate militarily in a U.S.-run coalition effort against Iraq. But Hosni Mubarak,

Egypt's president, had been trying to get talks going between Iraq and Kuwait and thought he was making progress; he had actually called Saddam to report on his progress while Saddam was meeting with Glaspie. Mubarak felt angry and abused. As for the Gulf, Saudi king Fahd concluded that Saddam had been lying to him all along, and the Saudis used their wealth to induce both Egypt and Syria to contribute troops to the anti-Saddam coalition force. Saddam's treatment of Mubarak and Fahd illustrated what people mean when they talk about burning bridges.

On the other hand, Saddam understood that he was probably more popular in Egypt than Mubarak. His threat to burn half of Israel was widely admired, particularly in Egypt and Jordan. Market alleys were overflowing with Saddam memorabilia, many depicting his face superimposed on the image of the al Aqsa Mosque in Jerusalem. (Somewhere in my house, there is a box of old tchotchkes containing a Saddam wristwatch bought at a street stall in Amman in this era.) In Jordan, the position of King Hussein of Jordan was precarious; the many Jordanians of Palestinian origin were rooting for Saddam, expecting to see him teach their tormenters— snooty Kuwaitis, oppressive Israelis, an imperious America—a lesson. On the condition that the king block Iraqi forces from entering his territory, Jordan was permitted by Washington to sit out the war.

In the five weeks following the entry of Iraqi forces into Kuwait, the administration shepherded five resolutions through the UN Security Council condemning Iraqi aggression, the annexation of Kuwait by Iraq, and Saddam's use of hostages to deter counterattacks, as well as demanding Iraqi withdrawal from Kuwaiti territory and imposing an economic blockade. Ambassador Thomas Pickering was the permanent U.S. representative to the UN. A person of determination, focus, diplomatic skill, and crisp delivery, he navigated the complex and often cumbersome process of transforming U.S. national objectives into international ones, framing them as United Nations Security Council resolutions, and winning a consensus of the permanent members of the Security Council in U.S. favor.

Pickering's labors were facilitated by a cordial relationship between Mikhail Gorbachev and Bush and, in China's case, Bush's readiness to overlook Chinese government atrocities against unarmed demonstrators in Tiananmen Square in return for Beijing's cooperation at the UN. The international Rolodex Bush compiled in his years as ambassador to the UN, head of CIA, chief of the U.S. mission in Beijing, and Reagan's vice president made direct diplomacy among heads of government possible and streamlined the process of assembling a broad coalition.

The Situation on the Ground

In the interim, Kuwait under Iraqi rule was becoming a violent, lawless place. Iraqi archives show that Saddam entrusted Kuwait to his cousin, Ali Majid, who had been responsible for the use of chemical weapons against Iraqi Kurds. Governance was in the hands of intelligence and security personnel, ordinary soldiers, and sketchily trained, undisciplined militia units, since the occupying force did not include experienced administrators. Essential ministries stopped functioning and vital services were no longer available. Due process was obviously not a feature of the occupier's judicial system. Audiotapes of conversations between Ali Majid and Saddam make it clear that Iraq wanted Kuwaiti territory and resources, but not Kuwaitis.

A key objective of occupation policy was to force the departure of Kuwaitis who had not already been out of the country, as was customary in the summer months for the country's elite. Oppressive rule and shortages of important goods were seen as the way to foster the replacement of Kuwaitis by Iraqis. Ultimately about 300,000 of about 2 million Kuwaitis fled.

Although Kuwait's public relations consultants in Washington were busily inventing atrocities to make the case for American intervention, there were enough real crimes against humanity to grasp the nature of

Iraqi occupation. Based on Saddam's approach to rule at home, it is possible, maybe even likely, that having made his point through terror he would shift to bribery.[14] But the U.S.-led intervention shifted history in a different direction.

Bush Comes to Shove

By September, the administration's thinking had jelled sufficiently for Bush to convene a joint session of Congress. After enumerating four UN-authorized objectives—unconditional withdrawal of Iraqi forces, return of Kuwait's government, the security and stability of the Persian Gulf, and protection of American citizens abroad—Bush's rhetoric took wing.

> Out of these troubled times, our fifth objective—a new world order—can emerge: A new era—freer from the threat of terror, stronger in the pursuit of justice and more secure in the quest for peace. . . . A world in which nations recognize the shared responsibility for freedom and justice. A world where the strong respect the rights of the weak.[15]

The phrase "new world order" was widely noted. Some cynics observed the similarity to Hitler's *Neue Ordnung,* or new order for Europe under German rule. Others recalled that as the "new order for the ages," or *novus ordo seclorum,* the phrase was on the reverse of the 1782 Great Seal of the United States, on the dollar bill, and on the crest of the Yale School of Management. In Bush's language, it comes across as utopian, conjuring up images of swords beaten into ploughshares and lions lying down with lambs. His speechwriter was clearly aiming for a biblical, mythic tone. For someone who had derided the "vision thing" earlier in his presidency, this was quite a departure.

Scowcroft apparently used the term in private discussions with Bush, but with a narrower meaning. From 1945 to 1989, the world order had been bipolar. Power—and much of the world—was divided between the United States and Soviet Union in a stalemate reinforced by nuclear weapons and the threat of mutual destruction. The sudden collapse of the Soviet empire left the United States as the sole remaining superpower, a global hegemon. This was nothing if not a new world order, although the one Bush imparted in his speech to Congress was really the liberal order FDR had put in place. The emergence of bipolarity had limited the space in which this order could prevail, but the regions where it could be imposed or be embraced were not insignificant. The world order was new, therefore, insofar as the spread of the American post–World War II order was no longer bounded by the alternative of the USSR. It would emerge that alternatives still existed and that some societies did not like being told that there were none. But the blowback was yet to come.

The United States Readies for Combat while Working Out War Aims

With a large force capable of blocking an Iraqi advance into Saudi territory in place—removing at a stroke the strategic threat of an Iraqi invasion of Saudi Arabia—Schwarzkopf and his subordinates at CENTCOM began to compose air and ground plans for a war to liberate Kuwait. The air campaign plan, which underwent important shifts during the war, was greeted enthusiastically back in Washington. The concept for the ground campaign, which called for an assault on the Iraqi front line, met with sarcastic derision. Cheney dubbed it "hey diddle-diddle, up the middle." But Schwarzkopf, working from guidelines he got from Powell and the White House, did not see other feasible options. Powell had offered him a single corps, or roughly three divisions plus an assortment of independent artillery, aviation, and logistics units, which was not enough to compensate for Iraq's advantage as an entrenched defender. And the president and UN had limited the military objective to expelling Iraq from Kuwait. Given this limited objective and relatively modest force, Schwarzkopf's initial plan to concentrate his firepower, punch through the center of the Iraqi line, and drive toward Kuwait City was the best bad option.

But thinking was evolving in Washington toward more ambitious goals. Iraq would be thrown out of Kuwait, but now, in addition, the Republican Guard divisions that ensured the survival of Saddam's regime were to be destroyed in the process. This in turn would trigger the fall of the regime itself. As this concept solidified, Powell and Schwarzkopf came to a meeting of the minds. Powell would authorize a second corps and Schwarzkopf would come up with a plan to crush the Republican Guard while liberating Kuwait from Iraqi occupation.

This left unresolved the question of the regional military balance. If the Republican Guard was destroyed and Saddam's military capacity fatally weakened, and if his regime fell, what would remain to rein in Iranian power? In Scowcroft's words, "The trick here was to damage [Saddam's] offensive capability without weakening Iraq to the point that a vacuum was created, and destroying the balance between Iraq and Iran."[16]

Whether this kind of fine-tuning was possible remained open to debate. Saddam committed only three of his eight Republican Guard divisions to the conquest and occupation of Kuwait. The other five units would be kept close to home to ensure the security of the regime. If Schwarzkopf was to accomplish the goal of destroying them, he would have to plunge into the Iraqi heartland and get into a serious, possibly prolonged fight. The coalition would fall apart, UN backing would dissolve, and in the worst case, the United States would end up running a defeated Iraq. Bush himself acknowledged the problem, saying that he "firmly believed that we should not march into Baghdad. . . . Our stated mission . . . was a simple one—end the aggression, knock Iraq's forces out of Kuwait, and restore Kuwait's leaders."[17] Yet he very much wanted to see severe damage inflicted on Iraqi forces. Powell got the message and ensured that

Schwarzkopf got it too, telling him in early November, "We need to destroy—not attack, not damage, not surround—to destroy the Republican Guard." In Powell's presentation to the media on the U.S. plan, he declared, "Our strategy to go after this army is very, very simple. First we're going to cut it off, and then we're going to kill it," plus "rip up the [Iraqi] air force in its entirety."[18]

The plan that emerged from these conflicting and partially hidden objectives consisted of two main thrusts. The first would be executed by a marine division under General Walt Boomer; it would penetrate Kuwait more or less in the middle of its border with Saudi Arabia and drive northeast to Kuwait City. On either side of it, various Arab and other coalition forces would enter Kuwait as well. As a diversion, a large marine contingent at sea would move toward the Kuwaiti coast but without actually landing any troops. The marines punching through Iraqi defenses and the threat of an amphibious attack would suck Republican Guard divisions southward into Kuwait. In the desert, hundreds of miles to the west, VII Corps under General Fred Franks—with the XVIII Airborne Corps protecting its left flank and a British division on its right—would be waiting. This was a large, heavy armored force including 1,584 tanks, 1,442 Bradley Fighting Vehicles, 238 attack helicopters, 521 artillery pieces, and 129 multiple rocket launchers.

As the Medina, Hammurabi, and Tawakalna Republican Guard divisions moved to blunt the marine attack, VII Corps would charge up the Wadi al-Batin, a riverbed running north-south along Kuwait's western border. As it advanced north of Kuwait into Iraq, it would pivot to the right, driving eastward, cutting off the highway running from Kuwait into Iraq, and then drilling down into Kuwait, enveloping the three Republican Guard divisions and destroying them in detail.

The ground plan would be set in motion once the preceding air campaign had destroyed half of Iraq's combat power within the Kuwait theater of operations—a standard that all admitted would be hard to verify—

while wrecking other so-called "centers of gravity," such as command and control installations, lines of communications, and the country's administrative capacity. This would require thousands of sorties from a range of bases and aircraft carriers. It was meant to be a devastating campaign, and for the most part, it was.

By late October, sanctions imposed by the UN on Iraq were beginning to bite. The CIA assessed that imports had been reduced by 90 percent; virtually all of Iraq's assets in foreign banks were frozen, so Iraq could not pay for anything even if a seller could be found; oil exports were at a standstill, costing Iraq about $1.5 billion per month; and development projects had been shut down. The 42,000 tractors and other farm machinery necessary for the winter harvest lacked fuel and could not be repaired. Rationing reduced Iraqis' food intake to 1,250 calories per day, as access to flour, bread, cooking oil, and other commodities diminished. Food prices increased astronomically. The lack of chemicals for water purification, according to CIA, would soon result in an increase in waterborne diseases, in addition to malnutrition caused by food shortages.[19]

With Saddam feeling the pain, and with coalition building begun, the administration turned to next steps. These included building a justification for war, blocking efforts by other countries to broker deals that would undercut Washington's insistence on unconditional withdrawal, and building up Schwarzkopf's army in Saudi Arabia.

Diplomatic, Political, and Military Developments as Hostilities Draw Closer; Showdown in Geneva; Congress Gives the Green Light

Although justification would seem to have been easy, given Iraq's predation in Kuwait, Saddam's hostage taking, use of weapons of mass destruction, threat to destroy Kuwait's oil fields if Iraq were "strangled," and clear violation of international rules and norms, there was resistance at home and abroad to war as an appropriate response. The Soviets and the French launched diplomatic initiatives designed to induce an Iraqi withdrawal in return for face-saving concessions. The Iraqis came up with their own bargaining chip, offering to withdraw if Israel agreed to pull out of territories occupied in the 1967 war. Linking the occupation of Kuwait to the occupation of Palestinian (and Syrian) territory was a clever move. It boosted Saddam's popularity in the Arab world via "what-about-ism." The U.S. response was to counteroffer with "deferred linkage," parrying Iraq's gambit by acknowledging the injustice done to Palestinians and offering to do something about it immediately *after* the reversal of Iraq's subjugation of Kuwait. This maneuver probably failed to sway the Arab street, but it provided governments something to point to in justifying their participation in the coalition.

French diplomacy was swatted aside by the administration, but Russian meddling was a more complicated problem. The Bush administration had come late to the end of the Cold War party. Bush viewed Reagan's partnership with Gorbachev as overly eager and oblivious to the possibility that Gorbachev's reforms and talk of a common European home were deceptive, or easily reversed. A U.S.-Soviet summit meeting in Helsinki, where Gorbachev joined Bush in condemning Iraqi aggression despite a long-standing Soviet treaty with Iraq, helped convince Bush that Gorbachev was genuinely committed.

With the peaceful unification of Germany hanging in the balance, a cooperative relationship with Moscow emerged as a priority for the White House. Running roughshod over Gorbachev's attempt to avert a war would humiliate the Soviet leader, endanger his position during a hazardous political transition in Moscow, and weaken an essential collaborative relationship. Allowing the Soviet leader to pursue his diplomatic initiative, on the other hand, would legitimize the Iraqi occupation; provide Iraq time to consolidate its position in Kuwait; exploit anti-war sentiment in the Arab world and Western capitals; and force the United States to maintain a huge army in Saudi Arabia for months, possibly through the summer of 1991 and beyond.

And it was certainly huge. On November 8, Bush announced a large increase to the 230,000 troops that had already descended on regional bases. This surge was widely and correctly interpreted as a commitment to war. American military personnel in the region numbered 532,000. They were accompanied by 2,000 tanks, over 1,800 aircraft, and 120 ships. Combined with other coalition units, the total number of troops was 737,000 with 190 ships. The care and feeding of this army in a desert was a gargantuan task. Every day, along a 3,000-mile network of roads, logisticians had to deliver 62,500 cases of food rations, 9 million gallons of water, 450 tractor trailer loads including 95,000 tons of ammunition, and 1.7 billion gallons of fuel. No one in the administration, let alone the Pentagon, wanted to keep this up for months, especially as the weather turned with the onset of summer. The United States was going to have to fish or cut bait.

To manage Gorbachev's maneuvering and Saddam's own cascade of vague, conditional peace feelers before the ground war began, the administration had little choice but to engage with Baghdad directly. Engagement was not to be mistaken for negotiation. From Bush's perspective, there was nothing to talk about, except the timetable for Iraq's compliance. The key feature of U.S. diplomacy was therefore an ultimatum for Iraq's evacuation by a certain date, after which the coalition would militarily act to force the outcome. This ultimatum was expressed on November 29 by UN Security Council Resolution 678, passed unanimously but for China's abstention. It offered Iraq "one final opportunity, as a pause of goodwill," to get out of Kuwait.[20]

With this resolution in hand, Bush offered to send Secretary of State James A. Baker to Baghdad to eliminate any expectation that war could be stopped by anything short of full Iraqi withdrawal by January 15, 1991. Not ready to withdraw, Saddam demurred. Given the situation, a tongue lashing by an imperious American diplomat was not something for which he could make time.

The two sides finally agreed to a meeting between Tariq Aziz, the Iraqi foreign minister, and Baker in Geneva on January 9. The purpose of the meeting for both sides was to demonstrate to the world, including their respective domestic audiences, that each had gone the extra mile in pursuit of peace but were disappointed by the other's recalcitrance. Baker handed Aziz a letter from Bush to Saddam, stressing several themes: war guilt was Saddam's alone; the war would end in Iraq's costly defeat; and the use of unconventional weapons would unleash the whirlwind. The letter concluded that the "American people would demand the strongest possible response [to the use of unconventional weapons]. You and your country will pay a terrible price if you order unconscionable actions of this sort."[21]

The encounter itself was strangely cordial. Aziz left the letter in its 10 x 12 manila envelope on the table throughout the six-and-a-half hour meeting. He declined to speak about Kuwait, talking instead about the Iraqi view of the world, its encirclement by enemies, unfriendly acts taken by the United States, and, in general, the victimization of Iraq by others. There were even moments of levity. Baker gave Aziz high marks for playing a bad hand well. Then, having briefed Bush and Eduard Shevardnadze, the Soviet foreign minister, Baker and his team headed for home, and the United States headed for war.[22]

The mood in Congress at this late stage was unsettled. Not everyone was convinced that the war was a good idea. Fear of terrible losses fueled these doubts. An array of impressive analysts within and outside government predicted high casualties. Estimates ranged from 20,000 to 40,000, or even higher. These calculations were based on historical data, the immense firepower available to Iraqi forces, and the formidable physical obstacles erected by Iraqi forces, from earthworks and minefields to battlefields flooded by lakes of crude oil. Compounding the prevailing pessimism was the possibility that Iraq would use chemical or biological weapons. U.S. forces were equipped to fight on a toxic battlefield, but the protective gear was cumbersome and, for obvious reasons, not breathable. Temperatures inside the suits on a hot day could be dangerous and impair the ability of soldiers to fight. The Pentagon backed these high estimates, whether to amplify an eventual victory by being able to portray it as against the odds, or because senior officers really believed that Iraq could deliver a serious beating to the U.S. military.

The office I ran at the State Department was asked to provide an independent estimate to Baker. Using standard quantitative methods informed by the best available intelligence assessments of Iraqi capabilities, we determined that U.S. casualties would be on the low side. An important factor was the damage we expected the air campaign to inflict on Iraqi forces as well as the formidable capabilities of U.S., British, and French ground forces. During this study, I traveled to Maxwell Air Force Base in Alabama to meet with Colonel John Warden and his team, who were developing the air campaign plan. I returned to Washington with strengthened confidence in our own estimates. Prying Iraqi forces out of Kuwait would involve hard fighting, to be sure, but they did not stand a chance.[23]

Yet the never-ending debate about airpower was in full flow. Was the role of airpower to facilitate the ground campaign, or to degrade "centers of gravity"? Carpet bombing of entire cities was no longer acceptable; its utility and morality were both lacking. In the case of Iraq, the more infrastructure destroyed, the more that has to be rebuilt. Certain classes of targets, especially if their destruction would create public health hazards, were out of bounds. But command and control targets could also be controversial if they verged on assassination of government leaders.

In September 1990, the new air force chief of staff, General Michael Dugan, had been fired by Cheney for implying in an interview with the *Los Angeles Times* that the air force could win the war on its own.[24] Cheney's arch response was, "Statements in the article to the effect that the Army and the Marines would provide for diversionary activities while basically the Air Force carried the ball were inappropriate." Cheney also deplored Dugan's speculation about the effect that targeting Saddam's mistress would have on the viability of the Iraqi regime, not to mention the impact of killing Saddam himself from the air.[25]

Saddam's mistress no doubt breathed a sigh of relief upon Dugan's premature departure. But so did Schwarzkopf, who was trying hard to keep the air component of his campaign reined in and working in tandem with the ground commanders. Dugan's view had been that the Vietnam War could have been won by airpower alone, thanks to the inexorability of strategic bombing, but for the interference of politicians. His understanding of warfare was unsophisticated and expressed with reckless disdain, but probably reflected the mood in the higher echelons of the air force. Their confidence was reinforced by the U.S. ability to neutralize Iraqi air defenses using advanced electronic warfare capabilities developed to ensure American air superiority in a war with the Warsaw Pact.

None of this resolved congressional concerns about casualties in a ground war. The debate, which began January 10, was serious, thoughtful, and responsible.[26] Looking back from the present, it seems surreally eloquent and dignified. Members against the war argued that sanctions should be given time to work their magic before putting American lives at risk. Two former chairmen of the Joint Chiefs of Staff, both of whom had served under Reagan, testified before the Senate Armed Services Committee. Admiral William Crowe told senators, "If in fact the sanctions will work in 12 to 18 months instead of six months, the trade-off of avoiding war with its attendant sacrifices and uncertainties would, in my view, be worth it. . . . It would be a sad commentary if Saddam Hussein, a two-bit tyrant who sits on 17 million people and possesses a gross national product of $40 billion, proved to be more patient than the United States, the world's most affluent and powerful nation."

Crowe and his supporters also responded to pro-war claims that the

American army could not be expected to dig into Saudi Arabia while sanctions took effect because difficult conditions in the desert would breed morale problems and degrade readiness to fight. Crowe was sardonic: "It's curious that some expect our military to train soldiers to stand up to hostile fire but doubt its ability to train them to occupy ground and wait patiently." His predecessor, General David Jones, depicted Bush's decision on November 8 to double the size of the U.S. force in the Gulf as a ploy to force an early war. He told the committee, "As we build to 400,000 troops, however, the support, morale, training, cultural and readiness problems rise sharply the longer the troops remain in forward garrisons. . . . My main concern . . . isn't that we might choose to fight, but rather that the deployment might cause U.S. to fight—perhaps prematurely and perhaps unnecessarily."

Henry Kissinger, who also testified, insisted that Crowe and Jones missed the point. He argued that "the issue in Arabia is not American staying power but the host country's domestic stability." This analysis led him to conclude, "By the time it is evident that sanctions alone cannot succeed, a credible military option will probably no longer exist," presumably because the Al Saud would have thrown out U.S. forces, or been thrown out themselves by Saudis who opposed the presence of U.S. forces. The fierce reaction within CENTCOM to troops wearing T-shirts emblazoned with a picture of Bush and the phrase "protector of the two Holy Mosques"—an honorific title reserved for the Al Saud—suggested that Kissinger's anxiety was shared by others. Crowe's view was that anti-Americanism would be a much bigger problem in the region beyond Saudi Arabia if the United States was perceived as having rushed into a war with Iraq.[27] The intelligence community, supporting the White House, briefed congressional members that sanctions, although painful, would not force Iraq to surrender Kuwait in the near term, a conclusion already shared by both sides in the debate.

With the end of the debate, Congress voted on January 12 to authorize military action against Iraq. The vote in the House, 250–183, reflected both a partisan divide but also widespread unease with the prospect of war, if sanctions might eventually get the job done. Republicans tended to focus more on the need to support the president in a crisis, while Democrats, with significant exceptions, believed the costs of the war would hurt Americans at home and that the anticipated casualties made sanctions preferable to a fight. The Senate vote was closer, 52–47. Members talked about their votes as a matter of conscience and the product of solemn reflection. Judging by the quality of the debate, their self-presentation was sincere.

Once the vote was taken, Americans rallied around the flag. The specter of forty thousand casualties was outweighed by a shared belief in the importance of the stakes involved—oil, congressional and media support of the war, and the fact that it looked like a sure win. Bush said at the time and afterward that he would have ordered an attack even if Congress had not authorized it. As he put it in a speech after the war, "I didn't have to get permission from some old goat in the United States Congress to kick Saddam Hussein out of Kuwait."[28] This was a pretty good sound bite and was substantially correct. But Bush knew he would get congressional authorization, so the charade was risk free. Even better, Congress had now implicated itself in the adventure. If things went south, the White House could credibly spread the blame.

The next day, the UN secretary general, Javier Pérez de Cuéllar, journeyed to Baghdad to persuade Saddam to leave Kuwait before the storm broke. He was unsuccessful. When the January 15 UN deadline for Iraqi withdrawal passed, the Defense Department confirmed that the 425,000 troops then in the region were preparing to challenge the 545,000 Iraqi troops defending Kuwait. In addition to U.S. troops and strategic bombers, there were ground forces from nineteen coalition countries and naval units from fourteen.

Bombs Away!

At 4:00 a.m. on January 17, coalition aircraft attacked an array of targets in Iraq in 978 sorties. The war had finally begun. The very next day, Saddam launched Scud missiles at Israel and Saudi Arabia. The strikes against Israel were significant. If Saddam were able to draw Israel into the conflict, he would be able to portray the coalition as battling against Iraq on Israel's behalf, which would have created serious problems for the Arab governments in the coalition and disrupted the war effort. The Israeli view was that it had the right to defend against threats regardless, but the United States argued that Israel's interests would be best served by Saddam's defeat and that the key to this outcome was the success of the coalition effort. Restraint, the United States argued, was in Israel's best interest.

The administration sent a small delegation led by the deputy secretary of state, Lawrence Eagleburger, to Israel twice, both before the war and as the Scud strikes were underway. I was a member of the team; we were supplied with chemical weapons protective gear and atropine injectors and instructed to keep Israel focused on the long game. There was already agreement on the installation of a special communications link, code-named "Hammer Rick," between the Pentagon and the office of Moshe Arens, the Israeli defense minister.[29] The United States would also deploy Patriot antimissile batteries to Israel. These proved to be ineffective, but despite their poor performance, the deployment was a vivid symbol of U.S. support for Israel, especially since they were operated by U.S. personnel who were themselves at risk of a successful Scud strike. In addition, the administration offered instantaneous notification of Iraqi missile launches detected by our Defense Special Missile and Aeronautics Center, so that Israel's civil defense agency could have at least a few minutes to sound the alarm and get people into shelters.[30]

Most consequentially, the coalition would recast the air campaign to allocate as much as 40 percent of the combat sorties to locating and destroying mobile Scud launchers in the western desert of Iraq. The Israeli prime minister, Yitzhak Shamir, defined inertia and was predisposed to stay out of the war; he got his way. But it was always clear that if any of the dozens of Scuds that descended on Israel had resulted in mass casualties or contained chemical weapons, the Israelis would go after Iraq with all the means at their disposal. There were rumors that Israel had prepared nuclear-tipped missiles for launch if Iraq used weapons of mass destruction.

Israel also made persistent requests for coalition IFF, or Identify Friend or Foe, codes. These are encrypted signals transmitted by combat aircraft to alert their compatriots that they are friendly and not to be fired upon. The Israeli air force wanted these codes so its aircraft could penetrate Iraqi airspace without risk of getting shot down by coalition forces.[31] The administration refused to provide the codes, in effect warning Israel that any aircraft it inserted into Iraqi skies risked destruction.[32]

This was a dramatic, behind-the-scenes development. It illustrates an important truth, namely that however much influence Israel wields in Washington, no administration would subordinate a truly strategic U.S. interest to conflicting Israeli priorities. The myth that Israel calls the shots is not just an anti-Semitic meme. It is disconnected from geopolitical realities.

The air campaign against Iraqi infrastructure and regime targets was relatively discriminating, killing "only" about 1,600 Iraqi civilians. The new class of remotely guided weapons were effective, despite prewar skepticism that had reduced the number of them supplied to the air force. Major Iraqi units were worn down by air strikes.

Iraq tried to disrupt coalition preparations for the assault on Kuwait by attacking the Saudi town of Khafji, near the Iraqi border, with several armored divisions. Coalition forces counterattacked as American airpower tore the Iraqi invaders apart. Iraq's losses were severe, while coalition casualties were low. Within a day Khafji was back under Saudi control. The speed with which the Iraqis were beaten back was apparently Schwarzkopf's first inkling that estimates of Iraqi combat power had been grossly inflated. This was good news in a way, but the phasing of the campaign plan was based on those inflated estimates. If the dismal fate of Iraqi intruders at Khafji had not been a fluke, then assumptions about how long it would take coalition forces to meet their objectives were mistaken. The precise synchronicity built into the plan would be thrown off.

Unexpected Developments on the Ground; Marines Too Fast, Army Too Slow

The ground campaign began in the early hours of February 24 with the marines' breach of enemy defenses and entry into Kuwait. Iraqi forces had been hammered from the air and were already in disarray. The marines' advance was far swifter than anticipated. Instead of a slow slog that would draw in Republican Guard divisions, the marines were in a sprint. As one analyst explained, the marine assault functioned as a piston pushing Iraqi divisions out of Kuwait, rather than as a vacuum sucking them in, where they could be trapped and destroyed as had been planned by U.S. heavy divisions coming in behind them.

As these developments were becoming clear to Schwarzkopf, he asked his ground commander whether General Franks—whose powerful armored corps was meant to block the Republican Guard divisions in Kuwait from escaping, and then to crush them—could begin the swing into Iraq a day earlier than planned. Franks unleashed a part of his force, but needed more time to get the bulk of his corps in motion. Thousands of vehicles, 100,000 troops, and tons of fuel, ammunition, and water could not be organized for a march at the snap of a finger.

The sun was already setting. Moving out in darkness through channels carved in minefields, where some units would have to make way for others to pass between them, was a nightmarish scenario. Formations could get lost, blunder into minefields, inadvertently bypass Iraqi units, or mistake one another for the enemy. Franks's VII Corps had come from Europe, where it had trained for years to fight a brutal battle, outnumbered by a wily and technologically advanced foe. He was not going to risk disaster by an ill-prepared advance in the desert night.

Franks got an early start on February 25, figuring that he still had enough time to surround the Republican Guard divisions in Kuwait. Maneuvering and fighting occupied VII Corps all day on the twenty-sixth. It wasn't until the morning of the twenty-seventh that Franks was prepared to send a division south into Kuwait to envelop Iraqi forces from the west and south, while he propelled a cavalry division eastward to shut the door on Iraqi forces trying to get back to Iraq. As instructed by Powell, he was still going to surround the Republican Guard and kill it.

Misfire

But by that point, Powell and the White House were already thinking about winding down the war. The battle was so violently lopsided, Powell feared that U.S. forces would look like they were slaughtering Iraqis without any tactical purpose. Iraqi soldiers were on the run and Saddam's army was no longer capable of fending off the U.S. offensive. The trail of wrecked vehicles along Highway 6, the road from Kuwait City to Basra, was featured prominently on news networks. Although there seemed to be no demand from coalition partners, the United Nations, or American observers for a halt to the fighting, Powell was nonetheless concerned about perceptions of U.S. forces "piling on" and the appearance of a "massacre." At a meeting of the Gang of Eight—Bush, Scowcroft, Vice President Dan Quayle, Baker, Cheney, Powell, White House Chief of Staff John Sununu, and CIA director Robert Gates—on the twenty-seventh, the decision was made to stop the shooting at 8:00 a.m. Riyadh time the next day. Powell included Schwarzkopf in the discussion, asking for his view on whether combat objectives had been met and for his agreement on timing for the cease-fire.

In the fog of war, however, Schwarzkopf could not be entirely sure where his forces were. Specifically, he had no way of knowing in the moment that Frank's VII Corp had not yet trapped the three Republican Guard divisions it was supposed to have eliminated. In fact, although all three had been severely mauled by a combination of marines, soldiers of the VII and XVIII corps, and the British 1st Armoured Division, they were no longer in Kuwait. They were on their way home with 700–800 tanks and other gear. French and British commanders were aghast at the cease-fire order. When Scowcroft learned of it, he was allegedly "livid." Douglas Hurd, the British foreign secretary, saw Bush on the twenty-seventh and questioned the timing of the proposed cease-fire, but Bush silenced him by attributing the idea to the talismanic Powell, whose calm and matter-of-fact delivery made him highly credible. By the time the actual situation on the ground was fully understood, the cease-fire order had already been issued. Powell could have appealed to Bush to rescind the order, but this would have raised the question of his own competence as a commander and, more broadly, U.S. control of events. And it was clear that Bush wanted to wrap things up. There was no going back.

The blame game for this perverse outcome continues. Schwarzkopf put the onus on Franks. In his view, Franks was supposed to be carrying out an exploitation maneuver. This refers to a sudden breakthrough in the battle, when the enemy's line is breached, or he turns tail. In that situation, Franks's job was to exploit Iraqi disarray and keep advancing despite the risk of friendly fire, confusion, or outrunning his supply lines. Franks insisted that he was not in an exploitation scenario at all; the Republican Guard divisions were still fighting, and he wanted to hit them with his most powerful units at once, like a mailed fist. Stringing out his forces, as the faster units in front raced to exploit a supposed collapse of Iraqi discipline, made no sense. Schwarzkopf's critics point to his isolation from the battlefield and highlight the overestimation of Iraqi capabilities that had led to Franks's slow start. They also say that if Schwarzkopf wanted an exploitation maneuver, he should have fired Franks on the spot and replaced him with a more aggressive commander. Shortly after the war, Powell said that he had not concurred in the timing of the cease-fire and had asked for another day.

At the taping of an interview with David Frost on March 27, Schwarzkopf went public. "Frankly, my recommendation had been . . . continue the march. . . . We could have continued to, you know, reap great destruction on them. We could have completely closed the door and made it in fact a battle of annihilation." Having it both ways, he added that Bush "made the decision . . . we should stop at a given time, at a given place, that did leave some escape routes open for them to get back out, and I think that was a very humane decision and a very courageous decision on his part, also. . . . There were obviously a lot of people who escaped who wouldn't have escaped, if the decision hadn't been made, you know, to stop U.S. where we were at that time." After a conversation with Powell, Schwarzkopf said he had been misunderstood. Bush, Scowcroft, and Powell then closed ranks. When asked to respond to Schwarzkopf's account, Bush remarked that he did not "think there was any difference between any of us—me, Cheney, Powell, Schwarzkopf. . . . There was total agreement in terms of when this war should end."[33]

Cease-fire, but Continuing Confusion over Objectives

Despite some mishaps, as when a large Iraqi unit that had not gotten the cease-fire order opened fire on U.S. forces with suicidal results, the two sides met on March 3, in a tent at Safwan in southern Iraq, to sign the cease-fire agreement. It was there that Schwarzkopf gave Iraq the permission it had requested to use helicopters in the skies over southern Iraq.[34] He thought the request was reasonable. His Iraqi counterpart pointed out that with roads cratered and bridges blown, government officials had no other way to get around. The U.S. view was that as long as the aircraft did not fly over coalition forces, or were properly marked if they did, they could fly.

At the same time that Schwarzkopf was telling Iraq it could fly gunships, Bush was proclaiming that the Saddam regime was doomed and that its enemies now had an opportunity to kill it off. This, after all, had been the purpose of the order to destroy Saddam's three best Republican Guard divisions. As we have seen, though, they were not annihilated and had escaped with hundreds of tanks and headquarters elements.

The White House–imposed cease-fire at the 100-hour mark was consistent with the narrow, UN-mandated aim of liberating Kuwait. The overthrow of Saddam and occupation of Iraq, entailing the conquest of Baghdad, would not be tacked on as explicit aims. This was clear early on in the war, when I was told to stand down my team at the State Department doing post-invasion planning. There were good reasons for this decision: coalition allies did not want it; the UNSC would not support it; Congress would likely object; and, crucially, there were those in the administration who still wanted Saddam around as a barrier to Iranian power. Others, however, did not regard a limited UN mandate as ruling out regime change. For them, including the president, regime change would be accomplished on the cheap, by stripping Saddam of his defenses against a rebellion by trapping and "killing" the Republican Guard in Kuwait, and then calling on Iraqi Shiites and Kurds to revolt. In part because of the conflicting views and goals, no one seems to have thought too much about what exactly would transpire following the cease-fire. At State, we were still working on our draft of the cease-fire terms as Schwarzkopf was sitting down with Iraqi generals to hash out the surrender document. The absence of careful thinking was reflected in Schwarzkopf's off-the-cuff permission for Iraqi helicopter operations in southern Iraq. It is obvious from the transcript of the talks that the Iraqis were dumbfounded that this request was granted.

On February 15, 1991, Bush was broadcast by Voice of America saying: "There is another way for the bloodshed to stop: and that is, for the Iraqi military and the Iraqi people to take matters into their own hands and force Saddam Hussein, the dictator, to step aside and then comply with the United Nations' resolutions and rejoin the family of peace-loving nations."[35]

Revolts duly broke out in both the Kurdish regions of northern Iraq and the Shiite areas in the south. The Shiites had been seduced as well by Iran. Despite rapid rebel gains in the opening days of the insurrection, the regime kept its nerve. Marshaling its Republican Guard units and making effective use of helicopter gunships, the regime suppressed the uprising and held on to power. There was no support from Washington. Powell conceded in his memoir that the administration did indeed encourage a revolt in Iraq, but argued that to support the resulting insurrections would have benefited Iran, a bitter enemy of the United States.[36] Cheney sidestepped the issue of U.S. incitement by arguing that since the rebels were no better than the Saddam regime, he "was not sure which side you'd want to be on."[37] Scowcroft "frankly wished [the uprisings] hadn't happened. . . . We clearly would have preferred a coup."[38] This was wishful thinking at its worst. The United States had participated in a successful coup in Iran in 1953, engineered another in 1954 in Guatemala, but was never able to do it again despite attempts in Cuba, Panama, and Libya.

As the controversy became more heated, Margaret Tutwiler, Baker's right hand, took hairsplitting to a new level in an April 2 statement, insisting that "we never, ever, stated as either a military or a political goal of the coalition or the international community the removal of Saddam

Hussein."[39] Bush himself insisted three days later, just as the opposition was being decimated:

> I made clear from the very beginning that it was not an objective of the coalition or the United States to overthrow Saddam Hussein. So, I don't think the Shiites in the south, those who are unhappy with Saddam in Baghdad, or the Kurds in the north ever felt that the United States would come to their assistance to overthrow this man. . . . I have not misled anybody about the intentions of the United States of America, or has any other coalition partner, all of whom to my knowledge agree with me in this position.[40]

The administration had had differing public and private positions on regime change from the beginning of the crisis. For Bush, Saddam was Hitler. One does not launch a war on Hitler with the aim of forcing him out of Czechoslovakia but leaving him in power. The administration clearly believed that opposition forces in Iraq would remove Saddam if he was deprived of his defenses, which was why Schwarzkopf was not ordered just to push Iraqi forces out of Kuwait, but to carry out "a war of annihilation." In public, talk about Saddam as Hitler gave way, under Powell's influence, to talk about reversing Saddam's aggression. Privately, the objective of fatally weakening Saddam continued to drive strategy.

But there was yet another, conflicting, driver, which was to preserve Iraq as an effective foe of Iran. The administration never truly reconciled these incompatible objectives, though Scowcroft and Powell might have imagined that they had somehow braided them by fine-tuning the use of force so precisely that Saddam's hold on power could be threatened, but Iran would still somehow be cowed by him. This is why Scowcroft wished so fervently, if unrealistically, for a palace coup, which would have substituted another Sunni warlord with a mustache for Saddam, thereby preserving an Iraqi wall opposite Iran while removing "Hitler" from the stage.

See You Later!

The administration, meanwhile, was removing U.S. forces from the region as quickly as possible. The first to go were the tactical fighter and bomber wings that had been the backbone of the air campaign, as well as two special operations squadrons.* Ground forces followed as of March 19. By the end of June, the 545,000 troops in the area were down to 65,000, nearly 18,000 of whom were aboard ships; 5,000 were holding nervous Kuwaiti hands and the rest were at Saudi ports loading equipment onto cargo vessels for the long voyage home.[41]

As troops were redeployed to U.S. bases at home and in Germany, the U.S. mission to the United Nations was framing what became UNSCR 687. This omnibus resolution, dubbed "the mother of all resolutions" in homage to Saddam's moniker for the Gulf War, "the mother of all battles," wrapped up the preceding eight resolutions into a unified program aimed at disarming Iraq's weapons of mass destruction programs and weakening its capability to project military force beyond its borders. These objectives would be achieved through intrusive UN inspections of Iraqi facilities, limits on the weapons Iraq could produce domestically, and comprehensive economic sanctions to compel Iraq to comply.

This resolution embodied yet another expansion of war aims. Oddly, though, it was a war aim articulated after the cease-fire and the withdrawal of U.S. combat power from the region; UNSCR 687 was exactly the sort of resolution you can enforce if you occupy the country, control its territory, and exercise legal authority either as an occupying power or through a puppet government. If you don't have this leverage—and the existing regime understands that you cannot do Desert Storm all over again—you are reduced to asking if we can please rummage through your country, looking for contraband.

---

* 1st TFW, 42nd Bomb Wing, and 55th and 9th Special Operations Squadrons.

Sanctions, moreover, do not constitute effective leverage against an authoritarian ruler with a ruthless secret police capable of controlling the population while channeling available resources to the regime to maintain its patronage networks. A sanctions regime represents a marvelous arbitrage opportunity to organizations that can open and maintain smuggling routes. These entrepreneurs are empowered by the military and intelligence services to keep oil moving out and goods for the regime coming in. Thus, UNSCR 687 set requirements that simply couldn't be fully met without occupying the country and toppling the Saddam regime, both conditions the Bush administration had rejected. Sanctions in the meantime were experienced really only by ordinary Iraqis, who were impoverished, immiserated, and completely disempowered—a situation that would make Bush 43's Iraq adventure much more difficult than it might have been.

To sum up this fiasco, the administration changed war aims in midstream. The original war aim was to eject Saddam from Kuwait. From the administration's perspective, the job of pushing Saddam from Kuwait, if done as planned, would also strip him of the elite armored forces that were his praetorian guard. He would need these units to stay in power after the war; without them he was vulnerable to a coup or rebellion. This implicit war aim—regime change—was not mandated by the UN and was therefore not openly discussed. In due course, Saddam was pried out of Kuwait, but his elite armored forces, though badly hurt, were not destroyed, owing to a combination of military and intelligence mistakes, the fog of war, and a confused decision-making process in Washington regarding timing of the cease-fire. This succession of blunders took the administration's implicit plan for regime change off the table. Yet, even as the fight reached its climax, the formal U.S. war aim expanded from ejecting Saddam from Kuwait to the enforcement of a new, sweeping set of requirements. This was an unfortunate development, since Saddam remained recalcitrant and retained much of his combat power. Any effort to enforce UNSCR 687 would therefore require the military might to compel Saddam to comply. Yet, for primarily domestic political reasons, but also for the Pentagon's practical military purposes, Bush pulled U.S. forces out of the theater of operations almost immediately after the cease-fire. Arguably, this was inevitable, given that his initial war aim—the official one—had been achieved. However, with the shift in war aims from ejecting Saddam from Kuwait and hoping for the best to the enforcement of 687, Bush no longer had the force he needed in place. And as one might have expected of a well-armed Saddam, he did not just roll over. He refused to cooperate with the UN and moved to destroy his Shiite and Kurdish opponents, who, incidentally, had been encouraged by Bush to revolt. This tragedy of errors led to a ten-year U.S. standoff with Saddam and, eventually, a second U.S.-Iraq war.

Could Things Have Gone Differently?

The lingering question is what the Bush administration should have done to deter Iraq from invading Kuwait. The question hinges on the assumption that the administration could not have done nothing post-invasion. Kuwait was being ransacked and its population brutally suppressed. In any scenario, the United States would have wanted to buttress Saudi defenses. This could have been done fairly easily and sustainably by setting up bases, keeping a minimal force in place, and rotating air and naval units through these bases. Indeed, by the end of November 1990, the forces were already in place to do this. And not long after the guns fell silent, the United States acquired access to bases from which to operate not just in Saudi Arabia but in other Arab Gulf countries as well.

Admittedly, this was not an easy process, despite the demonstration of American might and fortitude in Desert Storm. For example, as one of the negotiators, I encountered pushback from my high-level counterpart in the UAE foreign ministry, who denied that the UAE and United States had common interests to defend and insisted that the United States engineered the war with Saddam's connivance to control the Persian Gulf. Kuwait, whose government had just been reinstated thanks to American intervention, initially rejected the U.S. draft agreement because the defense minister thought it was a ploy to bring Jews into Kuwait. (To his credit, he backed off when we explained that in the United States, discrimination on the basis of race and religion was prohibited.) The Saudis refused to sign an agreement with the United States for continued access, perhaps because they sensed that it would be unpopular, given growing unhappiness with the Kingdom's reliance on foreign forces for its defense. The negotiating team was quietly ushered out of the Kingdom after a particularly tense meeting with Prince Sultan, then the minister for defense and aviation. Despite these difficulties, by the mid-1990s the United States had military access to facilities in Kuwait, Saudi Arabia, and the UAE; agreements with Oman and Bahrain were already in place, while access to Qatar was yet to come.

What were the alternatives to the war as it was fought? The United States could have led a sanctions initiative that deprived Saddam of the resources he was hoping to get from Kuwait by blocking oil sales, while preventing the export of weapons or weapons technology to Iraq. As became obvious later on, these measures would not have gotten Saddam overthrown, but they might well have gotten him out of Kuwait and weakened his military. It would, however, have taken an indeterminate amount of time to do so.

Alternatively, the United States could have pushed Iraqi forces out of Kuwait militarily and then established the kind of defensive arrangement envisaged for Saudi Arabia along with sanctions and export controls. In this scenario, there would be no UN Security Council Resolution 687 that would require the United States to regulate Iraq's internal affairs in pursuit of weapons of mass destruction. The burden on the United States would have been lighter, but Saddam's ability to hurt Israel or the Gulf Arabs would still have been greatly diminished.

Finally, the Bush administration could have risked the cohesion of the coalition, driven to Baghdad, found Saddam, and replaced him, for example, with an Iraqi corps commander who would inherit Saddam's security apparatus but not his foreign policy instincts or lack of strategic judgment. This of course is speculative. But given the number of unsuccessful coup attempts that followed the war, there would have been no shortage of takers. In the hypothetical scenario explored here, the preexisting power structure would have been left intact, but defanged, and still subject to sanctions that would have made renewed Iraqi aggression infeasible. With that transition completed, the United States could withdraw its forces and reintegrate Iraq into the international order, subject to export controls that would make reconstitution of Saddam's weapons of mass destruction programs impossible.

Which of these options would have best met the administration's multiple objectives: Liberate Kuwait, get rid of Saddam, keep Iraqi power to block Iran's, and not have to police Iraq for decades? None was perfect, but on balance, a quick war to pry Iraq out of Kuwait in which an air campaign covered likely WMD-related installations, followed by sanctions tailored to prevent Saddam from invading his neighbors, would have been the better route over the long term. But of course, such counterfactuals cannot be proved, and moreover, we cannot know how Bush would have adjusted his strategy in a second term. We can say, though, that if the United States is going to go to war, it's a good idea to think about what happens afterward.

Unexpected Consequences

Having set the stage for the Clinton administration's eight-year struggle with Iraq and his own son's ill-starred Operation Iraqi Freedom, George H. W. Bush's Operation Desert Storm accomplished one other thing. It was to inspire Osama bin Laden to attack the United States.[42] In his *Jihad against Jews and Crusaders*, issued by the "World Islamic Front" in February 1998, bin Laden and his cosignatories levied a series of charges against the United States.[43]

In 1990, bin Laden had unrealistically urged the Al Saud to entrust him with setting up an Islamic army that would protect the Kingdom from attack by Saddam's forces. Bin Laden seems to have overestimated his role in the jihad that contributed to Soviet defeat in Afghanistan; he thought he was offering the king a credible alternative to an American/Christian military presence on the Arabian Peninsula, the "Isle of Muhammad." The occupation of Saudi Arabia by American forces instead was cosmically transgressive and the Saudi invitation blasphemous. Bin Laden wrote:

> For over seven years the United States has been occupying the lands of Islam in the holiest of places, the Arabian Peninsula, plundering its riches, dictating to its rulers, humiliating its people, terrorizing its neighbors, and turning its bases in the Peninsula into a spearhead through which to fight the neighboring Muslim peoples.[44]

The Prophet had been clear in decreeing, "Let there be no two religions in Arabia." In bin Laden's view, King Fahd's violation of this edict was the height of apostasy.

These sins were compounded by the destruction of Iraq, "the most powerful neighboring Arab state." The humiliation of Iraq, the murder-by-sanctions of one million Iraqis, according to bin Laden, was the keystone of a larger strategy to subjugate the Muslim world.[45] The ongoing U.S. occupation was part of an overall U.S. plan to occupy the entire Muslim world. For this reason, the West, led by the United States, intended to "keep Muslims weak and incapable of defending themselves."[46]

The administration had no way of knowing that its actions would spur a transformational attack against the United States ten years in the future. And the conviction that the truly transformational event had been the ejection of Iraq from Kuwait would have prevented them from imagining such a development. The euphoria sparked by the collapse of the Soviet Union was supercharged by the rapid victory over Iraq. The day the cease-fire was agreed at Safwan, I was preparing to leave for the Gulf as part of the team to negotiate long-term basing for U.S. forces in the region. I was stopped in a seventh-floor corridor by a jubilant senior Middle East adviser to Baker, who told me, "Steve, the last radical alternative has been eliminated from the Middle East."

As the air war was underway, President Bush gave his State of the Union address to an anxious country. He was grave, but hopeful.

> I come to this house of the people to speak to you and all Americans, certain that we stand at a defining hour.
>
> Halfway around the world we are engaged in a great struggle in the skies and on the seas and sands. We know why we're there. We are Americans, part of something larger than ourselves.
>
> For two centuries, we've done the hard work of freedom. And tonight we lead the world in facing down a threat to decency and humanity.
>
> What is at stake is more than one small country, it is a big idea—a new world order where diverse nations are drawn together in common cause to achieve the universal aspirations of mankind. . . .
>
> Together, together, we have resisted the trap of appeasement, cynicism and isolation that gives temptation to tyrants.[47]

Like Reagan before him, Bush viewed the U.S. war effort as having universal significance, with the additional impulse to see himself as a modern Churchill. Bush was not wrong to imagine a new world order, but he was incapable of conceiving the one that was taking shape; the one he saw was the one proclaimed forty-six years before at the founding of the United Nations. Bin Laden, as it turned out, had a different new world order in mind.

War and Peace

As a postscript, Bush, like his predecessors, also tried to sort out Arab-Israeli relations. Before Desert Storm, the effort involved wrangling with Israel over settlements and trying to draw the Likud prime minister, Yitzhak Shamir, into a deal with Syria and the Palestinians. After the war, the administration sought to fulfill its pledge to do something on behalf of the Palestinians, since the Arab states had come through for Washington by joining the coalition against Saddam. This phase produced a multinational peace conference staged by the administration but hosted by the Spanish government in Madrid.

In his first year in office, Bush, along with Baker sounded out Shamir on the state of the peace process. The team they assembled included Dennis Ross, Richard Haass, Daniel Kurtzer, and Aaron Miller. Ross and Haass were political appointees; Kurtzer was a foreign service officer, and Miller a State Department intelligence analyst. All had served in the Reagan administration. When "the last radical alternative" was gone from the Middle East, they reckoned that Israel's security concerns would be mitigated, which would make concessions more likely. The Palestinians would realize that with Saddam's defeat and a peace treaty between Israel and Egypt, they could no longer avoid the compromises necessary to get a deal with Israel. And the collapse of the Soviet Union meant that Syria no longer had a great power backer, armorer, and bankroller. Damascus too would be forced into dealmaking mode.

The team was not, however, wholly unrealistic. Ross believed the key to progress in the peace process, even under the prevailing favorable conditions, was an incremental approach. The parties were far apart and there was no shared history of negotiations to fall back on. This view was nicely aligned with Haass's mantra about "ripeness." According to this theory of negotiation, active mediation by Washington would work only when issues under negotiation by the parties were "ripe," meaning close to resolution. But as William Quandt, a political scientist and NSC veteran, noted, in an incremental process, ripe fruit can rot before it's picked.

Shamir and Baker had gotten off on the wrong foot during Shamir's April 1989 visit to Washington. During their meeting, Baker had asked Shamir to halt settlement activity while the administration tried to restart a diplomatic process between Israel and the Arabs. Shamir replied that settlements should not be a problem. A relieved Baker took that to mean that Israel would refrain from settlement activity. What Shamir meant was that settlement activity should be regarded as irrelevant to peace talks. With the continuation of construction, Baker concluded that Shamir had lied to his face.

Tensions increased with Baker's speech to the annual American Israel Political Affairs Committee conference in Washington in May 1989. He called on Shamir "to lay aside, once and for all, the unrealistic vision of a Greater Israel. . . . Forswear annexation. Stop settlement activity. Reach out to the Palestinians as neighbors who deserve political rights."[48] Although Baker was also critical of Palestinians, his words were undoubtedly pointed. Benjamin Netanyahu, then a deputy foreign minister, told television outlets the United States was "building its policy on a foundation of distortion and lies."[49] This sound bite ended Netanyahu's access to senior State Department officials for the rest of Bush's term.

Although Shamir indicated a readiness to engage in talks, the conditions he imposed seemed too hard to satisfy, given the positions of the other parties. Shamir believed that Israel should retain the territories it conquered in the 1967 war. He felt he already had a promise from the Ford administration that a peace agreement with Syria would not necessitate the departure of Israelis from the Golan Heights. No doubt the United States had a different interpretation as to what that might mean in practice. Shamir was, however, willing to accept Palestinians as part of a negotiating process, but not if they were members of the Palestine Liberation Organization (PLO). Since the PLO was by then recognized as "the sole legitimate representative of the Palestinian people," this was clearly an obstacle. Shamir would also not accept Palestinian negotiators who hailed from East Jerusalem, which Israel had annexed as part of the unified city serving as Israel's capital. U.S. policy, based on international law, regarded East Jerusalem as part of the West Bank. Jerusalem was also where many Palestinian leaders lived, so Shamir's condition had the practical effect of excluding key players from the process.

There was not enough time to work through these conditions and make diplomatic progress before the administration's focus was diverted by Iraq's invasion of Kuwait and the war that followed. As U.S. troops departed the Persian Gulf, the revolts in Iraq ended, and the UN began the inspection program for weapons of mass destruction, the administration had the space to turn back to the peace process.

This time, Bush and Baker enjoyed some leverage. In September 1991, Shamir reiterated an Israeli request for a $10 billion loan guarantee to enable Israel to finance the costs of absorbing the many Soviet Jews seeking residence in Israel as the USSR ceased to exist. The administration, however, held off on bringing this request to Congress for four months, pending a show of flexibility in Jerusalem on settlement activity and renewed negotiations. Bush was concerned by the transfer of Russian immigrants to settlements on the West Bank. Given the U.S. opposition to settlements, there was little appetite to subsidize their construction and increase the size of the Israeli population on the West Bank.

It was important to Bush and Baker to put the dispute over loan guarantees on the shelf while they were preparing for the Madrid Conference. The event, which began on October 30, 1991, was a remarkable success, insofar as the invitees all accepted, including Syria and Saudi Arabia. The Bush and Baker staffers who orchestrated it remember it even now as a crowning moment in their careers. Palestinians selected by the PLO but not of it were at the conference in speaking roles, and Palestinian leaders from Jerusalem were included as observers. The Saudis sat at a conference table with Israelis. Although, as expected, there was no agreement reached on any substantive issue, the gathering had a momentous aspect. It was as though—despite the strong inducements needed to bring reluctant parties to the table—anything was possible. The road ahead would be hard, thought the U.S. team, there would be reversals, but the indispensable first steps had been taken.

Baker went to the Hill in February 1992 at the end of the 120-day waiting period for congressional approval of the loan guarantees, with steep expectations of Israeli policy changes. The guarantees would be doled out in tranches geared to Israeli compliance with U.S. conditions. Israel would have to freeze all new settlement activity in the territories. Baker warned that "the United States should have the right to end, terminate or suspend any provision for absorption assistance" should the administration judge that new settlement building was underway.[50]

In that bygone era, members of Congress of both parties did not see settlement construction as defensible. And then as now, foreign aid was not a popular cause. The administration therefore got no pushback from Congress, which strengthened its diplomatic hand in dealing with Shamir. The Israeli prime minister was in an untenable position. His political base valued settlements and favored settlers' interests. Jewish control over Greater Israel, in the view of these voters, was divinely ordained as well as strategically useful. On the other hand, the influx of Russian Jews was a demographic game changer. It would ensure a Jewish majority in Israel for a long time even if Arab birth rates outpaced Jewish ones. But the absorption of all these newcomers required funds that Israel had to borrow. Lenders, however, demanded guarantees by the United States and that meant alienating pro-settlement Likud voters by submitting to Baker's conditions.

The timing was significant. There would be legislative elections in June 1992. Shamir's inability to forge a relationship with the Bush administration and secure the loan guarantees deprived him of cover on the left. When the elections were held in June, Shamir and the Likud Party were battered by Labor, which formed a government more amenable to working with the United States. In early November, Bush lost in an electoral landslide to an obscure governor of Arkansas, William J. Clinton. His Middle East legacy for Clinton was the twin illusions of victory in the Gulf and an apparent breakthrough in the peace process.

—————

CHAPTER FOUR

WILLIAM J. CLINTON

Enlargement and Containment

Who's the fucking superpower around here?

—BILL CLINTON, AFTER HIS FIRST MEETING
WITH BENJAMIN NETANYAHU IN 1996

Georg H. W. Bush's swift departure left the incoming Clinton administration with a legacy of unfinished business. The new president was very different from his predecessor. Their upbringings could scarcely have been more unalike. Bush had been born into great wealth, a scion of the Protestant ascendancy. His values had been an awkward mix of heroism and liberalism, apparent humility and tolerance, glazed by ruthless ambition for high office unhampered by principle. Clinton, on the other hand, grew up in a broken home that just got by, financially. He was a Protestant, but distinctly low church. He was a striver, though, an ambitious youth looking to make his mark. When he came of age, the war raging in Southeast Asia consumed other poor whites and Blacks, but unlike Bush, who dropped out of school at his first opportunity to train as a combat pilot, Clinton gamed the system and manipulated mentors to escape the draft. Like Bush, Clinton was prepared to compromise on his liberal principles; his flexibility on this score earned the scorn of the left wing of the Democratic Party. He sought welfare reform rather than its expansion, endorsed the death penalty, favored international trade, and courted Wall Street.

Thus, the unfinished business left by Bush was to be dealt with by a president not only of a different party, one that had been out of office for twelve years following Carter's single term, but also of very different character and priorities. Clinton's heart was in the realm of domestic policy rather than foreign affairs. During his only experience living overseas, as a Rhodes Scholar at Oxford University, he had been eager to get home. He had lived in Arkansas nearly his whole adult life, much of it as governor of the small, poor state. He did not partake in the kind of internationalism that imbued the Greatest Generation and was perpetuated by a global competition with a rival empire. He was born after World War II and took office after the Cold War. For Clinton, it was blue skies. Internationalism in the new era was more about capital mobility than military alliances and preparedness for war.

At this remove, it is hard to recapture the moment. As Bush and Scowcroft had declared, the collapse of the Soviet Union had ushered in a new world order. For them, the new order manifested in America's status as the sole remaining superpower, which had used its preponderance of power to liberate Kuwait without having to worry about Soviet interference, fulfilling the promise of the League of Nations in 1920 and United Nations in 1945 of a world where the big fish eat the little fish. There was something of a fading era about Desert Storm and its mélange of rationales. Munich hearkened back to 1938. The terms used to characterize the Saddam regime were rooted in an earlier time; the army deployed to fight it had been created to fight Soviet tanks on the north German plain. Even the victory parade down Constitution Avenue following the war was more reminiscent of celebrations of V-E and V-J days than anything since. In some ways, the new world order was infused by the symbols of titanic struggle that predated it. It was new, but not really.

Clinton and his team were focused on a future that was palpably different from any that their parents' generation could have imagined. The euphoria triggered by the defeat of Germany and Japan had been quickly submerged by the rising tide of the Cold War and Soviet acquisition of nuclear weapons. A new discipline had been required, even if its hard edge was softened by rising wages and exuberant consumerism. For the Clinton administration, there was to be a peace dividend, rather than renewed mobilization.

Clinton had a clear idea of how to seize this opportunity. He would stitch together a broad political coalition through "triangulation," or a third way, as Tony Blair, his British soulmate and Labour Party leader, referred to the same process of compromise with their ideological opponents. This would entail moving their respective parties to the center. Clinton, as a son of the South and an essentially conservative Democrat yet brimming with empathy and comfortable with Black constituencies, was built for just this sort of politics.

He saw the future in economic terms, but not just in a domestic context. He wove America's economic destiny into a narrative of global growth. Washington's friends and allies in the developing or less-developed world were urged through the International Monetary Fund to reform their economies, opting for free movement of capital, deregulation, privatization, reversal of subsidies for basic goods, shrunken public sectors and floating exchange rates, and other measures to facilitate foreign direct investment. At home he presided over deregulation of the financial sector, privatization of public services, and trimming the social safety net. He established a National Economic Council, brought in the head of Citibank, and shook the reins from United States and global banking and credit markets. Nowadays this would be labeled capitalism with a conscience, but both at home and abroad it led to extreme income inequality, creating a transnational billionaire class astride majority populations who would watch their jobs and earnings evaporate. Clinton was not the sole purveyor of these consequential policies. It would be as unfair to blame him for their adverse long-term effects as it would be to give him sole credit for the economic growth and geopolitical stability during his presidency. But as the leader of a victorious superpower, his policy preferences had a disproportionate impact.

On entering the White House, Clinton did not give much thought to foreign policy outside of the diplomacy entailed by the negotiation of trade and other agreements essential to his economic program, which had to be arranged internationally and then sold domestically to Democrats in Congress who were anti-trade and pro-union and could foresee their effects on key constituencies. Clinton's was a demanding policy and legislative agenda; coupled with the White House push for health-care reform, it left little air in the room for discussion of foreign policy in general and the Middle East in particular. Given the nature of the challenges bequeathed by the Bush administration, this was destined to be the source of problems down the road.

Foreign Policy

I was still at the State Department when Anthony K. Lake was selected to untangle these inherited challenges as national security adviser. As Bill Clinton emerged, somewhat improbably, as the likely Democratic nominee in 1992, his good friend and political adviser Samuel (Sandy) R. Berger was also his foreign policy handler. As Clinton's campaign gained momentum, Berger suggested Lake as a foreign policy tutor for Clinton, and a good candidate for his national security adviser. Berger had been Lake's deputy as a policy planning adviser in the Carter State Department, where they had bonded. Clinton would have been content with Berger as his national security adviser, but Berger felt he needed more seasoning before taking on this responsibility and proceeded to secure Lake's position with the campaign. Clinton, the freewheeling, Baptist good old boy, domestic policy wonk, and Lake, the straitlaced Episcopal Brahmin, foreign policy expert, made something of an awkward match, yet they held each other in high regard, even if Clinton did welcome Berger's replacement of Lake as national security adviser in 1997.

In this new dispensation, without a strategic competitor, what precisely was the purpose of American power? What would replace the doctrine of containment that had guided U.S. foreign policy to victory over the Soviet Union? To the task of imagining a new doctrine, Lake brought experience as a diplomat, an academic, and a State Department planner. He had seen the most distorted aspects of American foreign policy up close in Vietnam and while on Kissinger's staff at the White House. Lake was less preoccupied by the clash of empires and the European balance of power than he was by regions of the world that had long been perceived as marginal to U.S. interest outside of the framework of the Cold War. Kissinger, in what might be an apocryphal story, was once asked if there had ever been a Principals Committee meeting at the White House concerning Africa while he was national security adviser. He is said to have replied drily, "Not that I remember." Lake was cut from different cloth and, as it happened, was an academic authority on U.S. policy toward the states of Africa.

The Search for a Bumper Sticker

A new foreign policy approach required a concise, punchy moniker. Lake and his team experimented with several possibilities, finally settling on "enlargement" as the successor to containment and as the administration's foreign policy pennant. The process had been grueling—containment was a hard act to follow. The team had even consulted with George Kennan, the storied originator of containment, on the best "bumper sticker" for a new policy, but Kennan, somewhat embittered by the misuse of containment as a strategic formula, refused to abet the search for a catchy phrase. The concept of enlargement was essentially that now that market democracies had defeated the authoritarian, centrally planned economies of the Communist bloc, the United States was to use its hegemony to bring the former Soviet allies and client states into the circle of market democracies. This would be in the U.S. interest because it would create new opportunities for U.S. exports, it being understood that export-led economies were superior to alternatives, while stabilizing international relations, because democracies, it was believed, did not make war against each other. Thus, the political shocks that so often upset the apple cart of economic growth would dissipate, removing another barrier to prosperity.

Post–Cold War literature exemplified and reinforced the zeitgeist. In 1989, about six months after the fall of the Soviet Union, a political scientist at the RAND Corporation—a quasigovernmental think tank—who had been selected to serve as Dennis Ross's deputy on the secretary of state policy planning staff, published an article titled "The End of History."[1] Although the smug exuberance of Western commentators about the demolition of the communist state, combined with an insalubrious dose of schadenfreude, had already enveloped politicians, policymakers and journalists, Francis Fukuyama transformed triumphalism into eschatology. The fall of the Soviet Union was not the result of the workings of geopolitics and of poor economic management. It was, in fact, the culmination of a grand historical process anticipated by the German philosopher Georg Wilhelm Friedrich Hegel. According to Fukuyama, Hegel "had written of a moment when a perfectly rational form of society and the state would become victorious. Now, with Communism vanquished and the major powers converging on a single political and economic model, Hegel's prediction had finally been fulfilled. There would be a 'Common Marketization' of international relations and the world would achieve homeostasis." A titanic struggle of contending forces had been resolved in "the end point of mankind's ideological evolution and the universalization of Western liberal democracy." There would obviously be laggards, dead-enders, and trivial outliers, but for Fukuyama, "it matter[ed] very little what strange thoughts occur to people in Albania or Burkina Faso, for we are interested in what one could in some sense call the common ideological heritage of mankind." According to a *New York Times* interview with a Washington bookseller, Fukuyama's essay was "outselling everything, even the pornography."

When this sort of obscure and dense self-congratulation, inspired by a Continental thinker born in 1770, outsells smut, the pressure on policymakers to meet the moment has really reached a boiling point. "Enlargement," however, failed to match the cosmic import of the end of history. In the real world, the concept made sense, but critics on both the right and left savaged the new doctrine and Fukuyama's old boss, who they tagged "Lake Inferior."[2] The situation was fraught even within the administration. In his first major speech, the new secretary of state, a dour West Coast lawyer, Warren Christopher, did not deign to refer to enlargement or any overarching strategy, instead presenting America's diplomatic priorities as a case-by-case to-do list. Within the NSC, Lake told the staff that foreign policy was not the president's focus, so new initiatives that would require presidential time and attention should be carefully considered before being run up the flagpole.

The administration was swiftly overwhelmed by teapot tempests that appeared to mock its vision. In early 1992, a war broke out between Serbia and Bosnia-Herzegovina that would eventually draw U.S. forces into the Balkans. In 1993, a Special Forces assault in Mogadishu on the headquarters of a defiant local landlord led to the massacre of all but one of the raiders and a rescue mission that killed hundreds, if not thousands, of Somalis. Days afterward, a crisis in Haiti that led to a mob preventing a U.S. naval vessel, the USS *Harlan County*, from mooring at the port created an impression of weakness and indecision. When a genocidal wave of violence engulfed Rwandan Tutsis six months later, the military leadership informed Lake that nothing could be done, leaving the White House isolated as the only institutional advocate of intervention and Rwandan killers unconstrained by outside powers.

From the beginning, the incoming administration found it hard to work effectively with the military. In part, this was due to the continued presence of General Colin Powell as chairman of the Joint Chiefs of Staff. He had meshed nicely with the tough Republicans in the Bush administration but was an awkward fit for left-leaning Democrats working for the more centrist Clinton, who were suspicious of the uniformed military for its right-ish politics and post-Vietnam reluctance to commit to combat if the mission was not clear and decisive victory was not the objective. Powell personified these traits. An early and admirable push from the White House to win equal treatment for gay military personnel ran into a buzz saw at the Pentagon and deepened distrust in the White House. The situation would not improve until Powell was replaced by General John Shalikashvili, who was on the same wavelength as the West Wing when it came to the deployment of U.S. forces in scenarios where their role was ill-defined and rules of engagement necessarily murky.

The Middle East looked relatively easy compared with challenges in southeastern Europe and on the strategic periphery of the United States. Friends and enemies could be clearly identified. The administration's homework assignment had been clearly laid out by the outgoing Bush administration. And the Clinton team had a doctrine, "dual containment," that was specific to the region. Clinton himself had no prior knowledge of the Middle East and neither did Lake, whose work during the Carter administration and as an academic had not focused on the region. The gap was filled by Australian academic turned polemicist Martin Indyk, for whom volunteer work on a kibbutz in Israel in 1973 was, in his own telling, the turning point in his life. There was nothing intrinsically wrong with this; I was a war volunteer in Israel at the same time and knew others for whom it had been an epiphany. But Indyk came to see protecting the vulnerable state of Israel from danger as his purpose in life. (His subsequent high-level responsibilities, especially in Obama's second term, changed these views.) He migrated to the United States after getting a doctorate in political science from an Australian university, finding a home at AIPAC (American Israel Public Affairs Committee) and then the Washington Institute for Near East Policy. This institute worked primarily to foster a pro-Israeli understanding of regional conflict within the Washington foreign policy network of congressional staffers, lobbyists, government officials, and sympathetic journalists.

Foreigners working on behalf of the interests of third countries would not normally, or perhaps ever, be chosen to oversee a policy-making process at the White House. Indyk's advancement owed to an exceptional combination of circumstances. Wealthy trustees on his think tank's board were also donors to the Democratic National Committee and supporters of Clinton's candidacy. As a group, they were inclined to see the Bush administration's policy toward Israel as adversarial; Indyk himself believed the Bush White House had been out-and-out anti-Israeli. Within the administration, Dennis Ross, a former leader of the Washington Institute, was in a position to endorse his former colleague for a job on the NSC staff. There was of course the problem of Indyk not being an American citizen, but his citizenship application was approved in time for him to begin work without undue delay.

An Organizing Principle Unveiled

Dual containment was Indyk's contribution to a new administration looking for big, bumper-sticker ideas that were in tune with the spirit of the times and appeared to have few moving parts. The gist of dual containment was a departure from the old era of superpower competition, in which the United States had had to engage in the game of balancing one adversary against the other. When Iraq was up, U.S. pressure on Iran was relaxed; when Iran had the upper hand, Baghdad got a boost. This sort of balancing was a venerable game, intuitively appealing in its own way and with a distinguished pedigree. The long peace between the Napoleonic Wars of the early nineteenth century and the First World War was secured by European statesmen skillfully balancing their potential foes against one another by backing the weaker party to create rough power parity. The result was that neither would become strong enough to launch a war against the state that engineered the equilibrium between them. It was a game perfected by Great Britain to prevent any single Continental power from isolating and defeating it. Balancing had worked, at least until it failed with the rise of Germany under Kaiser Wilhelm II. But it had worked for a long time.

In Indyk's view, balancing was a stratagem pursued by the weak. The United States was the greatest power on earth and had no need for it, especially when it required Washington to tip the scales in the direction of one or another obnoxious, oppositional state. At a conference staged by his alma mater, the pro-Israeli Washington Institute, Indyk unveiled his doctrine:

> The Clinton administration's policy of "dual containment" of Iraq and Iran derives in the first instance from an assessment that the current Iraqi and Iranian regimes are both hostile to American interests in the region. Accordingly, we do not accept the argument that we should continue the old balance of power game, building up one to balance the other. . . . And we reject it because we don't need to rely on one to balance the other.[3]

To be fair to Indyk, Iraq's invasion of Kuwait did seem to call into question the utility of balancing. But as we saw in the last chapter, it was a case of balancing done ineptly. As Reagan and the National Intelligence Council both realized, the United States should have been doing more to help Iran during the 1980s to maintain a balance of power between Baghdad and Tehran. Instead, Washington backed Iraq to the hilt, which in turn left Saddam feeling sufficiently empowered to invade Kuwait in 1990. In the flush of Cold War victory, Indyk overlooked the key virtue of balancing; using one's enemies to neutralize one another was cheap and therefore sustainable.

But few observers within the Beltway disputed Indyk's argument. The jubilation permeating Washington following the twin victories over Soviet tyranny and the reversal of Saddam's rampage in Kuwait seemed to hobble capacity for systematic thinking. Academics, however, were on the case. Within months, F. Gregory Gause, a specialist in the international relations of the Persian Gulf, published "The Illogic of Dual Containment" in *Foreign Affairs*, which demolished Indyk's conceptual contribution to American strategy. With remarkable prescience, he concluded that "Iran could play a very destabilizing role in a post-Saddam Iraq. . . . While the idea of containing both Iraq and Iran has a facile geopolitical appeal, it is fraught with difficulties."

The U.S. allies who were supposed to help implement the new policy were disconcerted by it and generally declined to cooperate. The Sunni monarchies on the Arab side of the Gulf, whose main worry was Iran, were alarmed by the administration's commitment to weakening Iraq and removing Saddam. Countries in the lower Gulf, physically closer to Iran and for which trade with Iran—and fear of Iranian subversion—were paramount concerns, were reluctant to antagonize Tehran. The only country that welcomed dual containment was Israel, which had bad relationships with both Iran and Iraq.

The Lake View

The following year, in the Spring 1994 issue of *Foreign Affairs*, Tony Lake made a game attempt at reconciling the language of balancing, the doctrine of dual containment, and the administration's overall strategy of enlarge-ment.[4] Lake began by labeling Iran and Iraq as "backlash" states (the "rogue state" epithet was already taken by a previous administration). The phrase worked well because it suggested states that had not gotten the memo about how history had ended. They were acting out, not ac-cepting the conclusive ascendancy of democratic market economies. Un-like "Albania and Burkina Faso," which, in Fukuyama's narrative, could safely be ignored, Iran and Iraq (as well as Cuba, Libya, and North Korea), were in a position to make trouble that could not be overlooked. As the community of enlightened states expanded, Lake wrote,

> Our policy must face the reality of recalcitrant and outlaw states
> that not only choose to remain outside the family but also assault
> its basic values. . . . Their behavior is often aggressive and defiant.
> The ties between them are growing as they seek to thwart or quar-
> antine themselves from a global trend to which they seem inca-
> pable of adapting.

According to Lake, "As the sole superpower, the United States has a special responsibility for developing a strategy to neutralize, contain and, through selective pressure, perhaps eventually transform these backlash states into constructive members of the international community."

This was a ringing, if misplaced, endorsement of American exception-alism, grafted onto the *mission civilisatrice* of the French Third Republic. Aware of the costs involved, he redefined dual containment, writing that "we are not oblivious to the need for a balance of power in this vital re-gion. Rather, we seek with our regional allies to maintain a favorable balance without depending on either Iraq or Iran."

The problem was that none of the Arab Gulf states was capable of balancing against its two neighboring giants; the best they could do was to serve as stationary aircraft carriers for the U.S. military. Thus, there would still be balancing, but owing to the special responsibility of the United States, Washington would absorb all the costs and risk of maintaining a balance—maintaining a large military presence in the region and courting direct conflict with unpredictable states—instead of outsourcing them.

The peculiar thing about the formulation of dual containment and the bigger framework of enlargement is that both were produced by a speechwriting process rather than the formal procedure of interagency deliberations, which often yields lowest common denominator but generally safe policy options. A scheduled speech forces an administration to articulate its policy. Unlike the arenas of arms control and non-proliferation, or even Arctic policy, the Clinton administration never issued a presidential decision directive on Middle East policy. There was, therefore, no coordinated strategy or plan signed by the president directing policy toward a volatile region that had been declared a vital national interest by every administration since Jimmy Carter. The medium was now the message, even for the architects of America's national security strategy.

Iraqi Realities

Meanwhile, back in the real world, the intelligence community was closely studying the situation in Iraq. Several major reports, beginning several months after hostilities ended in 1991, while Bush was still in office, and carrying through the last year of Clinton's first term, scrutinized Iraq's ground forces, Saddam's staying power, prospects for Iraq down the road, and the effect of increased pressure on the regime due to sanctions. It was clear that U.S. attempts to compel Saddam's regime to comply fully with the raft of UN resolutions would have to contend with Iraq's ability to resist militarily.[5]

These analyses arrived at interesting conclusions. The first, dating back to May 1991, concluded that, despite the thrashing inflicted by the United

States, Saddam still had formidable combat power. There remained 300,000–500,000 soldiers still under arms, 2,000–2,200 tanks, 900–1,200 artillery pieces, and 3,600 armored personnel carriers. All eight of Iraq's original Republican Guard divisions had survived the war, although under-strength and under-equipped. During the confrontation with the United States, Saddam had managed to form four additional Guards divisions consisting of about fifteen newly formed brigades. These troops did not engage within the Kuwait theater of operations and were therefore more or less intact after the cease-fire, able to crush rebellious activity in the south while the original eight Guards divisions licked their wounds.

The analysis was firm on several points. The most important was that the military remained faithful to Saddam despite his disastrous leadership, maladroit handling of prewar diplomacy, and feeding of tens of thousands of recruits into Schwarzkopf's meat grinder. Senior officers still held an elite status and enjoyed access to material privileges; Saddam made no attempt to scapegoat the generals for Iraq's terrible defeat. On the contrary, he heaped praise and awards on the military brass.

In addition to Saddam's careful cultivation of the army's loyalty, the intelligence community expected him to do his utmost, even under ongoing sanctions, to try to replace his losses of manpower and equipment. Saddam at that point had not yet relinquished Iraq's claim to Kuwait or recognized the international border, and he was killing off rebels among the Shiite towns and villages of the south and in the Kurdish regions of northern Iraq.

The analysts judged that "Iraq's ground forces could successfully defend Iraqi territorial integrity against a single regional opponent but would be severely strained by an attack involving more than one state. The Iraqi military remains capable of suppressing internal opposition, even simultaneous rebellions by the Kurds and the Shia following Desert Storm." They concluded that "Iraqi ground forces already have begun to regain some of their lost capabilities and will recover more through reorganization and repair activities. Even after the UN embargoes are lifted, however, the devastation inflicted on the Iraqi economy and the drain of reparations make it unlikely that Baghdad would be able to rebuild its ground forces' combat power to prewar levels until the latter half of the decade at the earliest."[6]

The crucial points here are, first, that U.S. attempts to compel Saddam's regime to comply fully with the raft of UN resolutions would have to contend with Saddam's substantial, if residual, military capacity. There would be no question who would come out on top if the United States pushed back, but this would entail another Desert Storm, which no one in the administration or Congress was prepared to undertake. Second, intelligence analysts judged that it would be years, perhaps a decade, before Iraq could rebuild the army it had used to invade Kuwait, even assuming sanctions were dropped.

Saddam: The Guest Who Wouldn't Leave

The next major intelligence assessment hit desks in the West Wing in June 1992, also while George H. W. Bush was still in office. The title spoke for itself: "Saddam Likely to Hang On." The bottom line was that "Saddam Husayn is likely to survive the political and economic challenges of the next year. Although he is significantly weaker than he was before the Gulf war, he appears stronger than he was a year ago. The only real threat to Saddam remaining in power over the next year is from a sudden violent effort to remove him by one or more people with access to him. . . . Economic sanctions are not likely to bring about Saddam's removal but will contribute to public disaffection with his leadership. . . . Despite sanctions Saddam has managed to maintain his core support group by providing goods and services not available to the masses."

A violent effort to remove him, however, was not in the cards. "To maintain his personal security, Saddam will continue to isolate himself from all but his most trusted colleagues and family members. Saddam has reorganized the military and security services to provide additional protection for him, his family, and his regime. Significant Republican Guard and other key security services still surround Baghdad, posing as a formidable barrier to disgruntled military or other foes of the regime." The threat from within his inner circle, or in CIA parlance, "those who have access to him," had been nipped in the bud.

"Saddam's policy of generously rewarding relatives and cronies along with fierce and swift punishment of those with suspected loyalties is likely to ensure the continued support of his inner circle. They probably have also accepted his argument that only he can keep Iraq together and are fearful of retribution from the population" in his absence, the report explained. Overall, it was an example of what experts call "coup proofing," a process that sultans like Saddam have honed to a sharp edge.[7]

The Regime Adjusts while Bystanders Are Caught in the CrossFire

In December 1993, at the end of Clinton's first year in office, the intelligence community released National Intelligence Estimate 93-42, "Prospects for Iraq: Saddam and Beyond." Like many such documents, it was carefully structured. The first half seemed to validate the administration's commitment to sanctions by observing that worsening conditions in Iraq would necessarily weaken Saddam's position. The Iraqi dinar, for example, had fallen by 85 percent in the previous year, price increases had exceeded wage gains, and the price of a month's worth of basic foods had risen by 450 percent. Government rations were so limited in variety and quantity, Iraqis had no choice but to buy expensive food; they were selling their belongings on the street to make ends meet and delaying medical care. The latter half of the report then introduced a mass of data suggesting that Saddam was trying to adapt the Iraqi economy to the sanctions imposed by the UN. Yet his economic policy was just making things worse; oil revenues had declined from $15 billion to $500 million. He was down to executing merchants—forty-two in July 1992—for price gouging.

Some of Saddam's economic adjustments, according to the intelligence estimate, were working. "Iraq has utilized all its procurement tools, both front companies and financial networks, to maintain a considerable industrial capacity. . . . In addition to importing goods, the regime has cannibalized and drawn from large inventories of materials on hand to rebuild and sustain key industries, especially in the oil sector." Iraq was still selling future oil deliveries at a discount, while selling oil directly to Jordan, borrowing against frozen funds, selling off gold reserves, receiving funds from other countries, and other ploys. Analysts estimated that Saddam had managed to squirrel away $1.8 billion over the preceding year.

The authors of the estimate also pointed out that despite some shortfalls in financial or other rewards to important regime supporters, the burden of sanctions was falling mostly on ordinary Iraqis. The tone of the assessment was dismissive of these tribulations, arguing that Saddam was exaggerating them to elicit international sympathy and undermine support for sanctions. But these claims were not mutually exclusive. The burden was in fact weighing on what the CIA called "the masses" and was increasingly awful, and Saddam was also trying to use their plight to get sanctions relief.[8] Still, in assessing the threats that might take Saddam down, "popular revolt" was listed in the estimate among the "non-starters," which also included opposition by exiled enemies of Saddam.

Both forecasts proved accurate, but the frank assessment that destroying Iraqi lives through sanctions would not get rid of Saddam was revealing. The administration was now on notice that its strategy was not going to work. There was of course the possibility of an insider coup, but as the NIE wryly observed, "We do not anticipate receiving significant intelligence indicators that a successful coup is imminent. Any group of anti-Saddam conspirators that cannot keep their plot secret from U.S. intelligence is also not likely to keep it secret from Saddam's intelligence services."[9]

A year later, the intelligence community checked in again to update the score card. The key finding was straightforward:

> Economic sanctions alone are not likely to bring about Saddam's removal, but they will contribute to public disaffection with his leadership. Sanctions may also be increasing popular resentment toward the West.[10]

The phrasing was careful, the intelligence community being averse to declaring the administration's policy intended to weaken the regime as ineffective. But the sentiment between the lines is clear. Yes, of course, the more miserable people are, the more skeptical they'll be of a regime they are powerless to change, but they are also likely to blame the United States. The implication was that Washington was sowing animosities it would one day reap. The analysts also warned that sanctions would have to be coupled with the use of force, or negotiation and incentives. But sanctions alone were like a hammer without an anvil.

Ordinary Iraqis were already in trouble. The U.S. air campaign plan, executed during Desert Storm, had been aimed in part at destroying or incapacitating Iraq's electrical grid and power generation capability. Though Pentagon lawyers had declared the destruction legitimate, it crippled systems that turned out to be essential to public health. Without electrical power, sewage treatment plants could not function, pumps essential to the water supply stopped working, hospitals were taken out of operation, street lighting and other public necessities were knocked out, and communications were cut off. By the time postwar sanctions were implemented, the population, especially children, had already been hit hard by a range of pulmonary and intestinal ailments, while the breakdown in health care disrupted the inoculation of schoolchildren and triggered outbreaks of childhood diseases—from measles to polio—that were difficult to manage due to the very crisis that caused them.

Once sanctions were in place, these hazards were compounded by sheer hunger. In 1996, after five years of embargo, the World Health Organization estimated that the "vast majority of Iraqis continued to survive on a semi-starvation diet." A World Food Program representative concluded that "alarming food shortages are causing irreparable damage to an entire generation of children."[11] The well-to-do and well connected had few problems putting food on the table, but the poor, of which there were many, and the newly pauperized bourgeoisie, which was mushrooming, could not afford to fill the 50 percent gap in a healthy diet left open by the shortfall in government-issued rations. Without fundamental nutrients and vitamins, or clean water, stunted growth and child mortality rose.

A succession of task forces, study groups, and UN agency delegations trooped through Iraq, evaluating the state of Iraqi society, scrutinizing access to basic goods, the effects of rapid inflation, sinking quality of medical care, and other indicators. Youths were increasingly uneducated because of school closures and departure of teachers, and the robust middle class that had emerged in Iraq after the revolution of 1958 was steadily being pulverized.

These findings were naturally contested. First, there was the question of culpability. Whose fault was it that Iraqis were suffering? The answer, from a U.S. perspective, was Saddam Hussein. By complying fully with the gamut of UNSC resolutions, Saddam could get sanctions relief instantaneously. Here Washington's propensity for intentionalism over consequentialism was on display. The intent of sanctions was to compel Saddam to bend to the will of the international community as expressed through the UN Security Council. The intentions therefore were both legal and ethical, even if the consequences were suffered by the wrong party.

Second, there was the question of causality. Could anyone prove that sanctions alone wreaked such havoc? Iraq, after all, had been through the wringer of its war with Iran, strategic bombing by the United States necessitated by its aggression against Kuwait, and comprehensively inept economic management, on top of blatant corruption and scarcities resulting from the regime's diversion of resources to feed its patronage networks. Against this background, it was not really possible to discern the precise role of sanctions, let alone quantify it. There was also the problem of the quality of the data and eager misrepresentation of the data by sanctions opponents, including the regime itself.

To further snarl the debate, a team dispatched by the UN Food and Agriculture Office in 1995 surveyed twenty-five neighborhood clusters, finding that 29 percent of children were underweight and infant mortality rates had increased. The team extrapolated from its very small sample that, nationwide, sanctions had killed 567,000 Iraqi children.[12] When broadcast by the media, the fact that the number was derived from a small-scale survey raised questions about the agenda of breast-beating do-gooders decrying the savagery of UN sanctions. The controversy ultimately produced a new UN Security Council resolution in April 1995 that would permit Iraq to sell oil in order to buy "humanitarian" goods, the first attempt to counter the growing impatience of the international community with the sanctions program.

Saddam held out until early the following summer before agreeing to the terms of the oil-for-food arrangement. It swiftly deteriorated into a bonanza of graft for UN officials and the Saddam regime. Companies wanting to cash in on exports, Iraqi grifters and regime cronies anxious to cash in on imports, and energy exporters looking for a cheap source of fuel found UN personnel administering the program eager to arrange permits in return for generous bribes. The regime benefited, while Western powers sacrificed leverage.

The Search for Weapons of Mass Destruction

The West's primary objective was Iraq's disarmament. The previous chapter discussed UNSCR 687, the catchall resolution demanding that Iraq account for and surrender all its weapons of mass destruction. Sanctions were also designed to make it as hard as possible for Iraq to rebuild its conventional weapons capability. These were the strategic justifications for tormenting the Iraqi population. Sadism was not the issue; indeed, the repeated mantra of Saddam's guilt, minimizing the humanitarian price of sanctions, and sensitivity to criticism were features of American subliminal awareness of the pain being inflicted as much as of diplomatic tactics.

It was beyond dispute that Saddam had been developing nuclear weapons; in 1981, Iraq had lost its brand-new nuclear reactor to an Israeli air strike for this very reason. And the United States—as well as UN inspectors and the IAEA (International Atomic Energy Agency)—had found extensive preparations for a nuclear arsenal. The Iraqis had experimented with different pathways to enrich fissile material to weapons grade, had searched for uranium to use as bomb fuel, and had designed missiles to deliver warheads throughout the Middle East. Aside from Iraq's strategic reasons for becoming a nuclear state, perceptions of Saddam as recklessly violent and lacking judgment stirred fears of a Saddam-scale blunder involving nuclear explosives.

Saddam was also unstinting in his use of chemical weapons against Iranians and Kurds during the 1980s. It was reasonable to assume that because they had worked so very well—and had not elicited punishment by the West—Saddam would still view them as a useful arrow in his quiver. It was also believed that he was hard at work on developing bio-logical weapons, an assumption reinforced by the discovery of documents indicating the regime's purchase of tons of biological growth medium, which implied industrial-scale production of gruesome pathogens.

The UN assembled a large, professional apparatus, the United Nations Special Commission, or UNSCOM, to carry out the inspection of Iraqi weapons, research, and production and storage facilities and analyze the thousands of pages of documents related to Iraq's military programs. This was a mammoth undertaking. And until 1998, when Saddam blocked fur-ther inspections, it was extremely successful, as the U.S. occupation fol-lowing the 2003 invasion of Iraq would prove. Between 1991 and 1998, UNSCOM uncovered and destroyed all of Iraq's chemical and biological warfare stocks and completely dismantled the vast production system that had been built over the years by Saddam to research, develop, and fabricate these lethal weapons.

By 1997, IAEA and UNSCOM reported no "indications that any weapons-useable nuclear materials remain[ed] in Iraq" and no "evidence in Iraq of prohibited materials, equipment or activities." Of the 819 Scud missiles that U.S. intelligence believed were in Iraq's armory before Des-ert Storm, only two could not be found, whether because they were in-credibly well hidden, misplaced, or simply did not exist. Although Iraq made attempts to acquire some civilian items that could be used for mis-sile development and tried to get a Russian ballistic missile guidance sys-tem, no missile was ever tested. In the chemical weapons arena, UN teams destroyed nearly a half million liters of chemical agents and 3,000 tons of chemicals used to make much more. All the associated facilities were shut-tered, equipment destroyed, and subsequently monitored by UNSCOM.

Iraq's biological weapons stockpile, including anthrax, botulinum toxin, and aflatoxin, which had been disclosed by Saddam's son-in-law Hussein Kamel, was destroyed in 1996 along with the labs and factories that produced them. (Hussein Kamel inexplicably returned to Iraq, perhaps believing his temporary defection would be forgiven, but was massacred with his family shortly after his reappearance.) The UN left no stone unturned. Its Ongoing Monitoring and Verification (OMV) system incorporated "radiological and chemical sensors, cameras, ground-penetrating radar, and other detection systems bolstered by aerial surveillance and no-notice visits to weapons facilities by inspectors."[13]

Despite Saddam's tantrum in 1998, this system was in operation virtually through the 2003 Gulf War, after which Hans Blix, the IAEA chief, rather belatedly judged that "inspection and monitoring by the IAEA, UNMOVIC and its predecessor UNSCOM, backed by military, political and economic pressure, had indeed worked for years, achieving Iraqi disarmament and deterring Saddam from rearming."[14]

The lingering question, of course, is whether the danger posed by Saddam to U.S. interests warranted these measures. Lake, the first-term national security adviser, does not recall being told about the impact of sanctions but said that if he had known, he would have acted; Berger, his successor, has died, so we do not have a West Wing perspective for Clinton's second term. Secretary of State Madeleine Albright made it clear that she knew (even if the White House somehow did not) when challenged by Leslie Stahl in a 1996 *60 Minutes* interview. Stahl said, "We have heard that half a million [Iraqi] children have died. I mean, that is more children than died in Hiroshima and, you know, is the price worth it?" Albright replied, "We think that is a very hard choice, but the price, we think, the price is worth it."[15]

Policymakers judged the cost to be necessary. From a moral perspective, however, the trade-off was problematic. On that score, "If the aim of sanctions is to communicate a message or punish wrongdoing, then sanctions are on weak ethical ground because they create situations in which 'human suffering becomes merely a device of communication' and 'a wrongdoer remains untouched, and an innocent person is gratuitously harmed.'"[16]

The Beginning of the End

In the fall of 1998, Saddam indulged his instinct for defiance and expelled UN inspectors from Iraq. It was a mistake—he won in the short term but signed his own death warrant over the longer run. Still, one could see why Saddam and his supporters took this path. The goalposts for sanctions relief had already been moved as early as 1993, when Martin Indyk proclaimed that "it should be clear that we seek full compliance for all Iraqi regimes. We will not be satisfied with Saddam's overthrow before we agree to lift sanctions. Rather we will want to be satisfied that any successor government complies fully with all UN resolutions."[17] In other words, the U.S. commitment to sanctions was effectively permanent. Moreover, in the U.S. view, suspension of oil sanctions would depend on Iraqi compliance with the UN resolutions on human rights and respect for Kuwait's border, although neither invoked sanctions overtly.

For their part, the United States and UNSCOM were caught in a cognitive loop. Iraq's WMD and missile capability had been methodically eliminated by the UN, and Saddam had no realistic ability to re-create it. Every discovery of contraband, however, strengthened the suspicion that there must be even more squirreled away elsewhere. Success bred the conviction of failure. So when Saddam demanded that inspections end, instead of concluding that there was little risk at that point to acquiescing and perhaps even using this development to segue from comprehensive sanctions, the United States and UNSCOM elected to postpone the inevitable and bomb Saddam into compliance.

Operation Desert Fox, perversely if unintentionally named after a Nazi general who killed many Americans, was announced by Clinton as designed "to degrade Saddam's weapons of mass destruction program and related delivery systems, as well as his capacity to attack his neighbors."[18] The air strikes, which included 425 cruise missiles and over 1,000 sorties, were directed at 83 targets including WMD and missile-related facilities, air defenses, Republican Guard divisions, and intelligence headquarters.[19] Republicans mocked the seventy-hour air operation—conducted alongside UK forces—as "pin pricks." Partisan critics fed the rumor mill casting the strikes as "wagging the dog," that is, an operation staged to deflect attention from impeachment hearings about Clinton's affair with a White House intern. But this was a significant, large-scale attack that inflicted serious damage on Iraq.[20]

Clinton was pleased by the result, telling French president Jacques Chirac, UK prime minister Tony Blair, and Israel's Benjamin Netanyahu in separate phone calls that the attacks had been successful and would help dislodge Saddam. The combination of this display of resolve and the military effectiveness of the operation with an expansion of the oil-for-food deal "to make it look like we have no problem with the Iraqi people" would pave the way for the return of inspectors.[21] This was not to be.

Charlie Duelfer, the deputy head of UNSCOM and later chief of the Iraq Study Group following the second Gulf War, considered that the flaw in the administration's strategy was an unwillingness to use force, a view seconded by Martin Indyk, according to his memoir, *An Innocent Abroad*. Referring to a January 1993 strike against Iraq to clear the way for UNSCOM surveillance aircraft—compared with Desert Fox in 1998, which Duelfer pegged as "the high-water mark for the [UN security] council in its collective demands on Iraq to comply"—he wrote that "what Baghdad saw in this [1993] episode was the Security Council's lack of will to recommence military action—it had blocked inspectors and only been sanctioned with words. No enforcement action had been taken. Moreover, it was quite apparent that U.S. forces in the region were being withdrawn. . . . Thus, it became clear to Baghdad early on that the risk of noncompliance was limited."[22]

Duelfer was no fool; he was describing here what almost everyone without a stake in the situation knew to be true. Operation Desert Fox was no pinprick, but it was a one-off rather than part of a sustained air campaign that might have compelled Saddam's total submission to un-limited intrusive inspections. It was an insight eventually adopted by the second Bush administration, which drew the conclusion that the only way to be sure Iraq was free of WMD—and free of Saddam—was to invade the country, occupy, and rule it.

Cloak and Dagger

In October 1998, Clinton signed the Iraq Liberation Act, which stipulated, "It should be the policy of the United States to support efforts to remove the regime headed by Saddam Hussein from power in Iraq and to pro-mote the emergence of a democratic government to replace that regime." The act authorized the appropriation of up to $97 million to fund anti-Saddam broadcasting, military training, and nonlethal assistance, and humanitarian aid for Iraqis who had fled from Saddam-controlled Iraq to the Kurdish areas in the north under U.S. protection.

The main beneficiary was Ahmed Chalabi, an extraordinary charac-ter reminiscent of Signor Ferrari, the wily merchant played by Sydney Greenstreet in the classic movie *Casablanca*, and the Iraqi National Con-gress he founded in 1991, headquartered in London with an office in Irbil. Chalabi, a Shiite, came from a wealthy family and was schooled alongside other privileged Iraqis who grew up under American tutelage, including Ayad Allawi and Adel Abdel Mahdi. When the British were expelled from Iraq by the 1958 revolution, his family emigrated to the United States, where Chalabi earned a doctorate in mathematics at the University of Chicago. Soon after Desert Storm, Chalabi, who had acquired a fortune through shady business deals—caught embezzling from a Jordanian bank, he fled from Amman in the trunk of a car—showed up in northern Iraq. In addition to jump-starting the Iraqi National Congress, he got onto the CIA payroll. It was a good move for him, if not for the United States.[23]

In 1995, he conspired with a group of Iraqi army officers to assassinate Saddam, against the guidance of his CIA handlers, but the plot was compromised, and the Iraqi participants were tortured and put to death. Just a year later, the CIA launched its own coup attempt. This too was compromised, with blood-soaked results. The CIA operative, Bob Baer, who had choreographed the action, blamed Chalabi's interference for the blown operation, which killed 150 anti-Saddam Iraqi officers. Tony Lake had to call Baer from the White House to alert him to Chalabi's disastrous meddling and instruct him, too late, to call off the coup.[24] Chalabi, as we will see, played a similarly mischievous role in the second Bush administration, parlaying friendships he'd cultivated during the 1990s with neocon hustlers, including Paul Wolfowitz and Richard Perle, who spearheaded the 2003 invasion of Iraq.

The failed plots of the 1990s were notable for their obstinate perversity. After all, the coordinated judgment of the intelligence community had been clearly and emphatically expressed—literally in boldface type in the original documents—to the effect that reliance on exiles was a "nonstarter" and that coup attempts would be very unlikely to succeed, given the structure of the Saddam regime and the multilayered security apparatus Saddam had built up over time.

If there is a theme here, it is something like this: Intelligence agencies are the orphans of the executive branch. Their analysis can be first-rate, even if only to the degree that it subjects common sense to organized scrutiny and confirms its validity. But policy frequently defies common sense because it is constructed from dubious material, including political imperatives, ideological fixations, emotional impulses, and a coordination process that necessitates some sort of interagency consensus on the part of cabinet members whose priorities are often incompatible. In this case, as in other episodes already reviewed here and others to come, the intelligence community had laid out in lucid terms the parameters within which U.S. policy would ideally be formulated: Saddam won't be dislodged by the impact of sanctions or by popular revolt, nor would an internal coup be likely to work; working with exile groups would end in tears; the Iraqi military combined with Saddam's resolve would make it very hard for the United States to force its will on the regime, and a second invasion for this purpose would not garner international support; Iraqis blamed the baleful impact of sanctions on the West as much as on Saddam. The administration pursued a policy that was resolutely oblivious to this cavalcade of bad news. And the one thing the Clinton administration really wanted to know—had all Saddam's WMD been catalogued and destroyed?—was the one question the intelligence community could not answer.

The Other Half of Dual Containment

Then there was Iran. Indyk, the framer of dual containment, had distinguished between Iraq and Iran, the former irredeemable, the latter perhaps salvageable. Tony Lake adopted Indyk's distinction between the countries in his *Foreign Affairs* article "Backlash States."

Unlike with Iraq, there was a sense that the relationship with the Islamic Republic could be put on sounder footing. Conflict was not inevitable. Reagan had thought so too, in both terms; George H. W. Bush likewise declared in his inaugural address, "There are today Americans who are held against their will in foreign lands. Assistance can be shown here and will be long remembered. Good will begets good will. Good faith can be a spiral that endlessly moves on." This overture appeared to produce the liberation of the remaining Americans held captive by Iran's allies. Clinton's forbearance toward the clerical regime hewed to this pattern.

The Iranians were difficult dance partners. The revolutionary regime was still led by Ayatollah Ali Khamenei, a conservative cleric with strong anti-colonial convictions who drew on a deep well of resentment of the United States. The Iranian power broker thought to have gotten Khamenei the job was Ali Akbar Rafsanjani, also a cleric but a lower-ranking hojatolislam and a fixture of Iranian politics from the revolution until his death in 2017 at the age of eighty-two. Rafsanjani is typically referred to as a pragmatist in contrast to leftists, who urged a radically redistributive economy, on one side, and ideological heirs of the revolution, on the other side, who were dedicated to the propagation of Islam as the basis for public policy and were imbued with suspicion of the outside world. Political categories in Iran have long been difficult to construct, in part because there are no political parties and in part because the individual constituents gravitate around a variety of cross-cutting views.

Rafsanjani favored a liberalized economy and therefore an opening to the West, while insisting on the supremacy of clerical rule. He was not only a hardy perennial—one of my colleagues described him rather nicely as the Dick Cheney of Iran—but exceedingly shrewd. He probably backed Khamenei in the belief that he would be pliable, which turned out to be the case at least until the mid-1990s, by which time Khamenei had consolidated his own power base. During Rafsanjani's presidency, he authorized assassinations of Iranian dissidents in Europe as well as devastating terrorist attacks.

One such attack took place in 1994, when Iranian operatives blew up a Jewish community center in Buenos Aires, killing eighty-five, including children, and wounding countless others. This repulsive act disclosed the powerful current of anti-Semitism in the Iranian regime; the victims were massacred just because they were Jews. The provocation, from Iran's standpoint, was Israel's kidnapping of an Hizballah cleric, Abbas Musawi. For Iran, the kidnappers were not agents of an Israeli state ministry carrying out a covert operation against an enemy in disputed territory. Rather, they were Jews. And Jews could be attacked wherever they could be killed in large numbers at little or no cost to Tehran.

During his first three years in office, Clinton's approach to Iran was to do no harm. Iran had already been subject to a comprehensive trade embargo since 1984, when it was placed on the U.S. list of state sponsors of terror. Despite these sanctions, trade between the United States and

Iran still took place, mainly in oil services and farm and construction equipment with a total value of $326 million in 1994. Of greater significance were multibillions of dollars in Iranian oil purchased by American companies for sale in markets outside the United States through intermediaries. While these purchases amounted to a quarter of Iran's oil exports, they made up only about 2 percent of the world's total oil exports. These manufacturers and oil companies had sufficient influence in Congress and the White House to get the licenses required for these transactions, and sale of Iranian oil to third countries was not technically prohibited by existing sanctions law. Other exports were facilitated by waiver provisions normally written into sanctions law to allow the executive branch to override the ban when necessary. Iran's stance was essentially that contact with official Washington was undesirable, but the presence of U.S. companies in Iran was warmly welcomed.

From the standpoint of many in Congress and in the Israel lobby, the administration's tolerance for economic relations with Iran when it was facilitating Hizballah's hold on power in Lebanon, fomenting Palestinian terrorism, and working on its nuclear fuel cycle was troubling. In their estimation, coming down hard on Iran would deprive the regime of the funds needed to carry out its dangerous activities. In October 1993, the German trial of the Iranian hit squad dispatched by Rafsanjani to Berlin to kill Iranian-Kurdish dissidents showcased clear evidence of state support for terrorism, at the very moment when pressure was beginning to form on Clinton to bear down on Iran. The Iranian stance seemed to be that economic relations with the United States could be sustained despite rejection of diplomatic relations and while pursuing a bloody vendetta against Jews worldwide. While the American history of solipsism was impressive, Iranian narcissism in this period probably set a new Olympic record.

But it was a tense moment. Congressional dissatisfaction with Clinton's apparently blasé attitude toward sanctions enforcement impelled the administration to try to get foreign countries with high-value trade relations with Iran to seek other partners. Teams were sent to capitals worldwide, carrying intelligence information about Iran's disruptive behavior and the damning proof that violent acts, far from being rogue operations, had been ordered by leading decision makers in Tehran. This outreach effort proved fruitless. I participated in some of these missions and experienced polite but somewhat bored responses, suggesting that Washington should take a deep breath and move on. In western Europe, U.S. preachers of containment eventually bred a European response that diplomats referred to as "critical dialogue." The gist of this idea was that the best way to moderate Iran's behavior would be through talk therapy. The American pundit Robert Kagan likened the United States and Europe to parents with a problem child named Iran. The United States was the stern father who sent the wayward son to bed without supper, while Europe was the compassionate mom who sneaked upstairs afterward with milk and cookies.

Convinced that persuasion was not going to bring the Europeans on board, AIPAC officials drafted two bills that if enacted would allow the U.S. government to punish other countries who refused to punish Iran. They shared these with Republican senator Alfonse D'Amato of New York, heir to the seat of the late Democratic statesman Jacob Javits, and vigorous critic of Clinton. He was also the chairman of the Senate Banking Committee. Extending the territoriality of sanctions legislation was a sharp departure from existing practice, especially when the countries likeliest to face consequences were America's closest allies.[25] But these were not Israel's closest allies; indeed, Israel's relations with Europe in this period were burdened by a range of policy differences. From Israel's standpoint, and therefore AIPAC's, the proposed extension of sanctions to other countries was cost free.

The view from the White House was less sanguine. The states that would be targeted by the AIPAC plan were treaty allies with which the administration was working on issues of greater strategic salience. NATO expansion, relations with Russia, and war in the Balkans were all in play and required close coordination on contentious issues with allied capitals. Iran's regime was violent and self-righteous, a troubling mix, to be sure, but Iran was incapable at that point of imperiling core U.S. interests. Clinton recognized that he would have to move quickly to hip check D'Amato by taking action against Iran himself by executive order.

On April 30, 1995, Clinton gave the keynote address at the World Jewish Congress to announce his intention to halt all United States trade and investment with Iran, including the purchases by American companies that accounted for more than 20 percent of Iran's oil exports. This would put an end to American companies' purchases of Iranian oil for resale on the world market. Moreover, it would eliminate virtually all remaining United States exports to Iran. Japan and European countries couldn't be persuaded to join in the embargo. "This is not a step I take lightly," Clinton explained to the pro-Israeli gathering, "but I am convinced that instituting a trade embargo with Iran is the most effective way our nation can help to curb that nation's drive to acquire devastating weapons and its continued support for terrorism." Two weeks later, Clinton's proposal was published in the *Federal Register* as Executive Order 12959.[26]

During that intervening fortnight, Clinton took the dramatic step of blocking a billion-dollar deal between Iran and Conoco, an oil firm owned by E. I. du Pont de Nemours & Company, in which the head of the World Jewish Congress, Edgar M. Bronfman, the heir to the Seagram fortune, held a controlling stake. Bronfman had pressed Clinton hard to intervene and had the leverage within the Conoco board to ensure that there would be no pushback from the company.[27] There was still considerable controversy to be heard at Senate hearings on killing the Conoco deal. The oil company noted that it had kept the State Department informed during the long gestation of the deal and had never been told it violated any rules, which were "vague" in any event. Senator D'Amato came out swinging, with a crisp statement of what he saw as a stark choice for the administration: "Either we have an embargo on dealing with and taking—particularly in this case, Iranian oil—or we should call it off, it's a myth."

In defense of the U.S. policy that had permitted the deal to progress only to be turned off just before it was to be signed, a senior State Department representative "suggested that a ban on dealings with American companies would not deprive Iran of revenue, it would only deprive American companies of profit."[28] As it turned out, Total and Gulf Aquitaine, two of Conoco's competitors, swooped in for the prize.

Tehran was as surprised as everyone else by Clinton's move.[29] Just after the decision was made public, Rafsanjani, who assiduously avoided contact with Americans and the U.S. media, gave a seventy-five-minute interview to Peter Jennings, the ABC News anchor. Rafsanjani said the Clinton administration owed Iran "a thousand apologies" because of the "lies" and "bullying" Iran had been subjected to. He also raised the long-standing irritant of the United States withholding large amounts of Iranian money that had been deposited by Iran in American banks before the revolution. He was seemingly incredulous regarding the administration's accusations of Iranian use of terrorism and its ambition to build nuclear weapons, repeatedly asking Jennings whether he thought that these claims were true. He summed up the situation saying, "We invited an American firm and entered into a deal for $1 billion. . . . This was a message to the United States, which was not correctly understood. We had a lot of difficulty in this country [i.e., Iran] by inviting an American company to come here with such a project because of public opinion."[30]

This petulant whine had the ring of truth. Conoco had been the first firm Iran approached, and Rafsanjani had likely thought of it in terms of a conciliatory move. And his reference to opposition within the regime, which he carefully attributed to "public opinion," was almost certainly accurate. There were obviously powerful elements in both countries that saw no possibility of rapprochement and believed that any concession would be perceived as a sign of weakness and reward for bad behavior.

The problem with signaling—taking actions meant to send a message of intent to an adversary in the absence of an explicit diplomatic overture—is that such signals are almost always misunderstood, or simply missed, by the recipient.[31] And even where they are perceived correctly, the very ambiguity of the message fails to provide the recipient the political cover needed to counter domestic opponents. It is true that Clinton could have told D'Amato that Iran's choice of Conoco was a deliberately conciliatory message by Iran, but without a clear Iranian statement to that effect, the Conoco deal could still be dismissed as a dividend for its appalling behavior. On the Iranian side, of course, there was not much chance that Rafsanjani could have sold the Conoco deal to his own opponents, who would have argued that it was clearly a terrific bonus for an American administration trying to strangle the revolution.

United States-Iran: Neither Peace nor War

As these events were unfolding in the public eye, undercover agents of the Islamic Revolutionary Guard Corps had been deployed to multiple Iranian embassies around the world to case American installations. This reconnaissance was thought to be "pre-operational"; in other words, the Iranian operatives were mere tourists, except that they were gathering information that would be needed to plan and execute attacks. U.S. agents kept tabs on these activities using a variety of methods, including counter-surveillance teams skilled in the art of spotting enemy agents trained to escape detection, while remaining invisible themselves.[32] The hair-raising cat and mouse game escalated as Washington intensified its efforts to starve Iran of the cash it needed to survive.

The culmination of this campaign arrived in the form of the Iran and

Libya Sanction Act. On March 19, 1996, Ben Gilman, a Republican representative from New York, introduced a bill in the House of Representatives that would sanction countries that refused to join in the American bid to throttle Iran's economy. Specifically, the bill mandated sanctions against any entity anywhere that conducted more than $40 million in business with Iran's oil sector. The core of the legislation was the draft that AIPAC had written the year before and supplied to Senator D'Amato. The actual bill would not be approved in a floor vote and reach Clinton's desk until August, but there was no question that it would pass with strong bipartisan support.

As the bill wound its way through committees in both chambers to a floor vote, Iranian preparations to strike the United States were advancing. A senior IRGC officer responsible for liaison with regional terrorist groups relocated to Damascus, where he would oversee planning for a strike against the United States in Saudi Arabia, meeting with his crew at the Sayyida Zaynab mosque in the southern suburbs of the capital.

The evolving conspiracy required careful coordination between Lebanese Hizballah, which would supply the explosives, and Saudi Hizballah, which would execute the attack. About 10 percent of Saudi Arabia's population is Shiite. They are mainly located in the northeast, coincidentally where much of the Kingdom's oil is extracted. The Shiite community has long been subordinated to the Sunni majority, which disdains Shiism and fears that Iran will use Saudi Shiites as a fifth column to undermine Al Saud rule. The Shiite role in this Iranian plot would suggest such fears were not groundless. The reciprocal role that Sunni repression may have played in turning Shiite Saudis into terrorists was unfortunately not a topic of polite conversation.

The attack finally came at Khobar, a coastal city in Saudi Arabia's Eastern Province, near the King Abdul Aziz air base at Dhahran. On June 25, 1996, the explosives smuggled in from Lebanon were packed into a sewage tanker, which rammed through the gate of Khobar Towers, hurtling toward a cluster of air force housing units within a fenced compound. It detonated with stupendous force, erasing the facades of buildings 131 and 133, killing nineteen, some through overpressure, slicing to ribbons others who'd been near windows, and wounding hundreds more. How the United States determined that Iran had been responsible, rather than al Qaeda, which had bombed the headquarters of a U.S. military contractor working for the Saudi National Guard just a year earlier, remains a closely guarded secret. But the indictments released publicly by U.S. courts meticulously reconstruct the event and its links to Iran.[33] The key bits of evidence were declassified two decades ago and left little room for doubt regarding Iran's patronage of the attack.[34] A separate judicial process involving an individual captured by Canadian intelligence and extradited to the United States disclosed corroborating information.[35] The suspect ultimately withdrew his statement and was deported to Saudi Arabia.[36]

Iran has consistently rejected culpability over the years, so its motivation in staging the atrocity remains a matter for speculation, though it seems to fit well into the pattern of preoperational activity in Europe and elsewhere. A best guess is that Iran perceived correctly that it was under attack, but without examining why, and concluded that the best way to get the United States to back off was to draw blood. Looked at as an outsider to Iran's decision-making process, the move was a dangerous gamble. Attacking a U.S. base and killing Americans—military personnel off duty, not engaged in combat with Iranian forces—was about as clear an invitation to war as one could imagine. No gain commensurate with this risk leaps to mind. It is not impossible that Iran believed its role could be concealed, but it seems unlikely. Evidently, Iran saw the risk in a different light.

Ray Takeyh, an academic and former Obama administration official, believes that Iranian planners looked back to Tehran's devastatingly effective 1983 attacks on the United States in Beirut as a paradigm. As we have seen, the Reagan administration did not retaliate for the attacks against the Beirut embassy and marine barracks, but rather withdrew from Lebanon the following spring. Takeyh argues that Iran therefore assessed the risk to be low and the benefit to be strategically vital.

Others, including Trita Parsi and Ali Ansari, also Iran specialists, believe that the perpetrators calculated the risks more realistically but considered the goal to be worth it. Even in the era of the shah, Iran was uncomfortable with a permanent U.S. military presence in the region. After the revolution, Tehran's wish to see a Persian Gulf free of the U.S. Navy was all the more urgent. It is probable that Iran attacked Khobar to drive a wedge between the United States and Saudi Arabia and precipitate the withdrawal of the U.S. Air Force from the Arabian Peninsula. Yet there are pieces of the puzzle that do not quite fit. For example, the tactical air assets based in Dhahran were there to keep Saddam confined to central Iraq, which would seem to have served Iran's interest. But to Iran, ridding the region of the U.S. military would have outweighed the advantage of keeping Saddam fenced in by air. Iraq had, after all, been substantially weakened already by Desert Storm and the ensuing sanctions. In any case, the air operations against Saddam never stopped.

Over the long run, Iran's gambit failed to dislodge the United States from the region, even if it did provide the nudge that set U.S. military departure from the Saudi Kingdom in motion. What the aftermath of the attack did reveal, however, was Saudi determination to prevent the United States from following the trail of evidence to Tehran. The last thing the Al Saud desired was to be caught in the middle of a war between the United States and Iran that would be fought, at least partially, on Saudi soil. This episode reflected a long-standing pattern of Saudi behavior, which has been to spur the United States toward confrontation with Iran but withdraw their support for U.S. action as soon as the prospect of escalation hove into view. Ultimately, Washington tired of this game and moved both the Combined Air Operations Center and its forward deployed aircraft to

Qatar, which, like Bahrain, was a small country with its own reasons to se-cure the investment of a great power in the longevity of its ruling family.

The Khobar attack further drove congressional action on Iran. On August 5, 1996, Clinton signed into law the Iran and Libya Sanctions Act (ILSA) that had been working its way through Congress. European coun-tries understandably went berserk over this infringement of their sover-eignty, notwithstanding the administration's ability to waive sanctions under specific circumstances.[37] The EU was always fractious when it came to Middle East policy, but ILSA united them against Washington. A se-nior administration official made matters worse by characterizing the pur-pose of secondary sanctions not as aimed at Iran, but rather to prevent European firms from gaining market share while Congress took U.S. com-panies out of the game. This reinforced European suspicions that the Iran and Libya Sanctions Act was more about economic interest than strategic necessity. As we will see in the Trump administration, the precedent was there to be used again, but to greater effect.

Back to the Drawing Board

The Clinton administration's effort to tame Iran ended with a whimper, not a bang. In March 1997, while the administration was still trying to build a case it could bring to the public against Iran for its role in the Khobar attack, Iranians went to the polls to elect Mohammad Khatami as president of the Islamic Republic. Among other objectives, Khatami sought to turn the heat down under Iran's relations with Europe, Saudi Arabia, and the United States. His flexibility, however, was limited to largely rhe-torical declarations regarding a "dialogue of civilizations" that would reduce tensions through people-to-people contact.

He also pledged to carry out reforms within Iran, including greater oversight of the Ministry of Intelligence and Security (MOIS). For Washington, this carried little weight, since the IRGC had managed operations against the United States. If Khatami was going to get a grip on MOIS, that was all good and well for oppressed Iranians, but it didn't relieve the United States of the need to be vigilant. U.S. intelligence had of course been active against their Iranian adversaries, but U.S. operational objectives were to weaken Iran's covert action capabilities, rather than to destroy Iranian targets and kill people having their morning coffee.

The administration nonetheless saw Khatami's election and open-minded discourse as an opportunity. Indeed, it was, if limited in scope, given Khamenei's strong opposition to formal talks with the United States and, in Washington, the rejection of any accommodation to Tehran, regardless of who might be president. Although Khatami might not have been Khamenei's choice for the presidency, they shared a worldview that did not encompass diplomatic ties and direct contact with the U.S. government and maintained personal and official relations. Even if Khatami had wanted to move beyond people-to-people contact with Americans while pursuing his reform agenda at home, he would have been hemmed in by strong foes of rapprochement. On the U.S. side, it was not up to the president alone to offer suspension of sanctions against Iran. Congress held the whip and saw Khatami as just the human face of a bestial regime. All the White House could offer on the president's sole authority was permission for Iran to export rugs and pistachios to the United States. This was not the sort of windfall that would cause decision makers in Tehran to reassess their strategic priorities.

Nor was Khatami in a position, if he were even so inclined, to provide Clinton the one thing he needed to manage congressional animosity toward Iran, which was Tehran's acknowledgment of the IRGC's role in orchestrating the attack at Khobar Towers. In June 1999, the White House enlisted the Omani government to pass a secret message, since declassified, from Clinton to Khatami. The key passages were:

The United States government has received credible evidence that members of the Iranian Revolutionary Guard Corps (IRGC), along with members of Lebanese and Saudi Hizballah, were directly involved in the planning and execution of the terrorist bombing in Saudi Arabia of the Khobar Towers military residential complex on June 25, 1996. . . . Those responsible, however, have yet to face justice for this crime, and the IRGC may be involved in planning for further terrorist attacks against American citizens. . . . The United States has no hostile intentions towards the Islamic Republic of Iran and seeks good relations with your government, but we cannot allow the murder of U.S. citizens to pass unaddressed. . . . We need a clear commitment from you that you will ensure an end to Iranian involvement in terrorist activity, particularly threats to American citizens, and will bring those in Iran responsible for the bombing to justice either in Iran or by extraditing them to Saudi Arabia.[38]

Khatami replied as follows:

The allegations contained in the message attributed to President Clinton are inaccurate and unacceptable. The Islamic Republic of Iran views the recurrence of such unfounded allegations in the gravest terms. . . . The Islamic Republic of Iran bears no hostile intentions towards Americans and the Iranian people not only harbor no enmity, but indeed have respect for the great American people. At the same time, they shall vigilantly and resolutely defend their independence, sovereignty and legitimate rights against any threat.[39]

Well, it was worth a try. The best that can be said about this exchange is that both sides adopted a nonbelligerent stance and expressed respect for the other's civilization. These were useful signals, and on the Iranian side at least carried the hint of a stand-down and halt to terrorist attacks, at least against the United States. Clinton on the other hand made it clear that in the future, Iran should expect a U.S. military response. The result was nevertheless discouraging; the White House shut down the Oman channel and leadership communications appeared to come to an end.

The administration still sought a way forward before Khatami disappeared from the scene to be replaced by a hardliner. Diplomatic links were proposed, to no avail, and in March 2000, Secretary of State Madeleine Albright delivered a remarkably eloquent speech containing an apology for American interference in Iran's affairs: "In 1953 the United States played a significant role in orchestrating the overthrow of Iran's popular Prime Minister, Mohammed Mossadegh. . . . It is easy to see now why many Iranians continue to resent this intervention by America. . . . The United States and the West gave sustained backing to the Shah's regime . . . [which] brutally repressed political dissent. . . . The United States must bear its fair share of responsibility for the problems that have arisen in U.S.-Iranian relations."[40]

Even though Albright went on to catalogue Iranian acts that haunt the American imagination and would justify American enmity toward Tehran, her extraordinary acceptance of American complicity in events that short-circuited modern Iranian history was intended to elicit a response from Tehran that would initiate continued cordial contact. It was—in terms of diplomatic history—a bold departure. But Iran's leadership was unreceptive, and Albright's plea remained unanswered.

In the end, dual containment led to America's containment by Iran and Iraq. It forced the United States to maintain a large military infrastructure in the Persian Gulf, embrace sanctions policies that strained relations with NATO allies and Arab states, and distracted policymakers from more pressing concerns. Preparing for the Sunday morning talk shows, the NSC communications director would always be sure to remind Sandy

Berger, the national security adviser in Clinton's second term, of two things: first, that Sandy was the national security adviser, a point meant to rally him for media combat, and second, that Saddam "was in the box." This mantra was repeated as a signal to the public, the media, and the government itself: the U.S. grip on Saddam was so tight he had no room for maneuver and therefore was not a threat. The administration's policy toward Iraq was therefore on track.

What imparted a sense of "thou dost protest too much" in these claims was the fact that containerizing the dictator was not the declared aim of U.S. policy. The declared aim, as Indyk reminded Congress in mid-1999, was regime change.[41] But there was no question it wasn't working. And the longer it failed, the more entrenched Saddam, the more battered the Iraqi people, the more compromised America's reputation, and the harder the fight in the UN to keep sanctions going. The administration's one indisputable success was the systematic dismantling and destruction of Iraq's weapons of mass destruction and the infrastructure, research and development capability, and delivery systems that underpinned it. But the nagging belief that there was more—and enough of it to make a strategic difference—shackled the administration to a larger policy vis-à-vis Iraq that could only make things worse.

The administration, to be fair, appreciated these dilemmas. The way out, it calculated, was to revamp the sanctions regime to undercut international criticism. The United States, UK, and the Netherlands, which had a seat as a nonpermanent member on the UN Security Council, together proposed what they dubbed "smart sanctions," that is, less likely to hurt ordinary Iraqis yet still painful for Saddam and his inner circle. But by this time, the moment was lost. When I arrived in London in late 1999, I encountered the British chief of the general staff and asked him what he thought of the situation. He said that there were only three roads open. The French and Russian path, which was to reintegrate Iraq into the international community, a preference shaped as much by commercial interest as anything else; the U.S. and UK commitment to sanctions, whether or not these were "smart," which he intimated would not be sustainable; and third, a war that resulted in Saddam's death. This turned out to be prescient.

The Peace Process Grinds On

There was a third part to Clinton's Middle East policy, the peace process, which simmered in his first term and came to a rolling boil late in the second. It was something of a strange preoccupation. The possibility of a major war involving Israel, one that might draw in the United States, had been eliminated by the Egyptian-Israeli peace treaty of 1979, negotiated by President Carter. Strictly speaking, there was no compelling American strategic interest in a peace process after that. But like Ahab and his white whale, the Clinton administration was determined to forge peace agreements on parallel tracks between Israel and Syria and the Palestinians.

Architects of this peace process would deny that there was no strategic rationale for their secretive labors. In their view, the United States would never be able to pursue its strategic interests in the Arab world unless it was perceived as achieving a just solution to Israel's occupation of Palestine, and the team was therefore making a pivotal contribution.

As we have seen, previous administrations had also pursued the white whale with great determination. Jimmy Carter, as mentioned earlier, did so with great success, but at the cost of a loss of focus on the situation in Iran. In that case, diplomatic victory had been achievable because the issue in dispute—whether Egypt or Israel would control a desolate peninsula separating them—was negotiable, and both countries had already concluded for their own reasons that the cost of war exceeded the sacrifices demanded by peace. Reagan launched his own peace process, laid out the U.S. goal, and pushed the parties toward it. The Cold War was raging. An agreement would serve U.S. interest by reducing volatility in the region.

As Soviet influence in the Middle East waned and the risk of renewed large-scale conflict between Israel and its neighbors was gone, Washington nonetheless plowed onward with its peace process as though nothing had changed. The strategic argument still had traction, perhaps because the Clinton administration believed that an ongoing peace process would help keep Arab states on board U.S. policy toward Iraq. Administration officials might also have believed that it would encourage allies to be more supportive of Clinton's attempt to choke off Iran's economy. A powerful peace process lobby within the government was also important.

The lobby was motivated by a strong belief in a strategic imperative to peace between Israel on the one side and Syria and the Palestinians on the other. Peace would pave the way for closer U.S. ties to the Arab world, lower the risk of instability that might suck the United States into a war, and enable Israel, a democracy and friend of the United States, to flourish. These policy enthusiasts felt a deep responsibility for the security of Israel, which they believed would depend on a successful peace process that only the United States could bring to fruition.

They drove U.S. policy in this period on the back of major trends. The first was the administration's overall sense of leaving the debris of the Cold War behind and commitment to the great mission of enlargement. Skepticism about the prospect of an end to the Arab-Israeli conflict ran counter to the new mood of endless possibility. Second, there was the Madrid Conference that had brought Arabs and Israelis to the table together. Just as the magnificent military success of Desert Storm seemed both to open space for new initiatives while compelling the Clinton administration to deal with its unintended consequences, Madrid also appeared to part the waters while motivating those who had engineered it to surpass it.

In organizational terms, the peace process team had cultivated the reputation as bearers of a diplomatic secret sauce, fostering an impression of indispensability. Indeed, the process was tightly held. The rationales for secrecy were many and not entirely without merit. As any policymaker will tell you, it is far easier to develop diplomatic initiatives when no one—colleagues, the public, the media, or the relevant parties themselves—knows what is going on. Without secrecy, colleagues will rush to point out the weaknesses in your plan, advocacy groups and lobbyists will leap in to create political dangers for the administration, and foreign players will use their knowledge of internal U.S. deliberations to game outcomes, occasionally working through American pressure groups and members of Congress beholden to them, eager to vex the administration for partisan purposes.

This freedom of maneuver was linked to the location of the peace process team within the topography of the State Department, outside the Near East bureau and reporting directly to the secretary of state sans intermediaries.

The team was known as the office of the "Special Middle East Coordinator," or SMEC. As it happened, the key officials were all Jewish, which adds another factor to the determination with which a peace process was pursued. The members felt strongly about both U.S. and Israeli interests and believed that these interests were mutual and deeply intertwined. Thus, they were convinced as Americans and Jews that a peace process was vitally important to both the United States and Israel. They felt, accordingly, they had a historic opportunity to strengthen America's position in the Arab world while securing the future of a democratic Jewish state tightly aligned with the United States. This opportunity would be unlocked by a final status accord with the Palestinians and peace treaty between Israel and Syria.

It helped that in their idiosyncratic ways, they were all extraordinarily intelligent and capable of nuanced yet powerful self-expression, and that they believed in themselves as much as they believed in their shared purpose. In effect, they were the perfect senior staff. Having worked together on Madrid, all except Indyk, they were already a well-oiled machine.

However, they did not get much traction in Clinton's first term, in part because the president himself was leery of the commitment and not particularly confident in his command of the issues and because the Israelis and Palestinians were engaged in their own peace process outside the purview of the administration. Over time, conditions evolved toward deepened U.S. involvement and heightened tensions between Palestinians and Israelis. It was a roller coaster that was destined to jump the rails, claiming the life of an Israeli prime minister along the way and ending in a ferocious Palestinian uprising that killed thousands—mostly Palestinians—and destroyed much of Palestine's public infrastructure, setting its GDP back by decades.[42]

Oslo Usurps Madrid

At the outset of Clinton's first term, the talks that began in Madrid were shifted to Washington, where the Palestinian, Syrian, and U.S. participants met without making any significant progress. This paralysis suggested that as impressive a technical diplomatic achievement Madrid had been, that was all it had been. Taking advantage of an enormous display of American military power to press-gang Syrians, Israelis, and a few Palestinians-without-portfolio into a conference room made sense, since negotiations can start only by getting adversaries around a table. But proximity does not guarantee results.

With memories of Bush's military achievement receding, the evaporation of Russian influence on Syria, for good or ill, and the magic of Madrid fading, negotiators had little incentive to depart from their hardline positions. While these futile interactions played out, the Norwegian government invited a small number of Israeli and Palestinian academics to meet in Oslo to think out loud about ways to advance the peace process. The Palestinian leadership, still in Tunis, and the Israeli foreign ministry, headed by Shimon Peres, were kept informed by the participants, but avoided involvement. The fact that the Likud government under Yitzhak

Shamir had lost in a landslide to a Labor coalition led by a former army chief of staff, Yitzhak Rabin, in June 1992, opened the door to this experiment in informal diplomacy.

The State Department peace team was informed that these talks were going on but was not asked to join them. The Oslo group wisely aimed not to draft a treaty but rather the principles they believed should shape one, following the lead of the Camp David negotiations.

Oslo Triumphant

In the spring of 1993, Israeli diplomat Yossi Beilin judged that sufficient progress had been made to bring Peres into the picture. Satisfied that the Palestinian side could deliver Arafat, that the principles drafted by the team were both diplomatically negotiable and politically marketable within Israel, and that new prime minister Yitzhak Rabin could be persuaded to embrace them, he returned to Jerusalem intent on transforming these informal talks into formal negotiations.

Rabin reluctantly agreed to bless the process. He knew that some accommodation had to be made to Palestinian aspirations to stabilize a potentially volatile situation on the ground and keep the relationship with the United States, which had nearly capsized with Shamir at the helm, afloat. Rabin was also looking for ways to redirect the government's budget from supporting settlement expansion to education, since a shocking survey had recently shown that Israeli children were maleducated, unable to perform simple tasks. Rabin had been an early supporter of settlement activity, which the Labor Party had rationalized as essential to security. But the bloom was off the rose.

The negotiated declaration of principles Rabin decided to back would recognize the PLO as the legitimate representative of the Palestinian people, in part as an inducement to the perennially skittish Arafat to endorse the document, in exchange for Palestinian recognition of Israel's right to live in peace and security. Mutual recognition was widely regarded as an essential precursor to a meaningful agreement. In operational terms, it called for the phased withdrawal of Israeli forces from the West Bank and Gaza and the devolution of administrative functions there from Israel to an interim Palestinian authority. In conjunction with these steps, the Palestinians would elect a legislature called the Palestinian National Council and an executive to run the Palestinian Authority. It was presumed that this would be Arafat, who would be permitted to return to Palestinian territory from exile in Tunis along with his entourage. The interim agreement would sunset after five years, during which time Israel and the Palestinian Authority would negotiate the thorny core issues of Jerusalem's status as capital of a Palestinian entity—statehood was still not discussed—the return of Palestinian refugees, the question of borders, and the nature of Palestinian sovereignty.

When the news broke that the parties were close to an agreement and were operating with the approval of their respective governments, the U.S. team folded their own process, shifting to providing technical advice, helping to overcome sticking points in the draft, and encouraging the leadership on both sides to stay the course. It was the kind of thing the peace team did best.

Clinton decided that he would take ownership of the process at this stage. The White House invited Arafat and Rabin to a signing ceremony that took place on the South Lawn of the mansion, bathed in brilliant sunlight. The ceremony was capped by emotional remarks by Rabin and Arafat and Clinton's successful stagecraft in maneuvering Rabin into an awkward two-pump handshake with his Palestinian nemesis and counterpart.

Oslo Thwarted

Both Rabin and Arafat returned to publics that were less than enthusiastic about the deal they had signed. The response in the Knesset was vituperative. More ominous was the dawning realization of the settler movement and Israeli right wing that the Oslo agreement prefigured defeat for their plan to establish a so-called "greater Israel" from the Jordan River to the Mediterranean Sea. Progressive American Jews interpreted Oslo as the vindication of enlightenment and the Zionist project, their complacency matched only by the militancy of their counterparts on the other side of the political spectrum.

A little over two years later, on September 28, 1995, the parties inked the Israeli-Palestinian Interim Agreement on the West Bank and the Gaza Strip, usually referred to as Oslo II. This three-hundred-page agreement set forth the plan and timetable for turning the September 1993 Declaration of Principles into a road map leading to final status negotiations.[43] It contained detailed programs for the withdrawal or redeployment of the IDF, security cooperation with the newly formed Palestinian police, joint economic activities, and myriad other practical provisions.

While these arrangements were being made, the Clinton administration also facilitated a peace treaty between Jordan and Israel. This was not quite as challenging as contriving an agreement between a state and what amounted to an armed NGO, and both parties were highly motivated. The Hashemite king Hussein needed to surmount the obstacle to American aid created by Jordan's support for Saddam during Desert Storm, and Israel desired to reinforce Jordan's role as a security guarantor of Israel's right flank and buffer between Israel and a resurgent Iraq. The $200 million in military equipment and $700 million in debt forgiveness offered by the administration no doubt helped convince the king to take the plunge.

The Strategic Assassin

During the celebrations of these landmark agreements, two Jewish brothers in their midtwenties, Yigal and Hagai Amir, were thinking about how best to gut them. The brothers were Orthodox, not quite ultra-Orthodox but rigorous in their religious observance. They believed that the return of land controlled by Jews to non-Jews violated the will of God. As such, a person who transferred Jewish land to Muslims was guilty of a serious crime. Within this community, the question naturally arose whether Rabin, because of his complicity in the Oslo Accords, had committed a sin for which the appropriate penalty was death. In private, these speculative exercises were expressed as settled verdicts. Rabin was subject to *din moser*, the rule prohibiting the abandonment of Jewish lands to non-Jewish ownership, and *din rodef*, the rule authorizing lethal intervention to prevent such a betrayal from succeeding. The Amir brothers, like Muslim terrorists, preferred to carry out an attack blessed by one or more authoritative clerics. In this case, the death warrant was a *p'sak din*, essentially the equivalent of a fatwa.

Lest one think that the plot was completely on the fringe, in mid-November there was a rally against Oslo, attended by Likud Party leaders including Benjamin Netanyahu. Footage is widely available on YouTube. The demonstrators chanted "Death to Rabin," denounced him as a "traitor," and carried signs depicting Rabin in a keffiyeh and in a Nazi SS uniform. (The latter was hoisted by an undercover security officer seeking to blend in with the crowd.) The mood was ugly; the Likud eminences who were gathered in a building overlooking the packed plaza below decided, with one exception, not to address the mob. The exception was Netanyahu, who stepped onto a terrace and whipped his audience into a murderous frenzy. A few months earlier he had led a procession accompanying a coffin and brandishing a noose, both meant to signify the appropriate treatment for Israel's Oslo problem, namely the prime minister. The Amirs's precise plans might have been known only by their family and closest associates, but they reflected the beliefs of a much wider stratum of Israeli society, which was baying for Rabin's blood.

The October anti-Oslo demonstration spurred Rabin's approval for a pro-resolution, pro-peace rally in Tel Aviv on November 4. The atmosphere was all love and peace, Israeli-style. The Age of Aquarius feel of the video documentation of the event is still moving. As Rabin left the celebration and walked toward his car, Yigal Amir was waiting, armed with a 9mm Beretta pistol. Aiming at the center seam of the back of Rabin's suit jacket from a foot away, he fired three times, hitting him twice. Amir was immediately taken into custody and Rabin to a nearby hospital, where he died shortly after arrival. Shimon Peres took up the reins as prime minister, pledging to persevere in implementing Rabin's policies.

Spiraling Violence; Netanyahu's Return

The event ushered in a succession of horrors. Tucked away within the West Bank was a young, pious Palestinian, a Birzeit University graduate in electrical engineering named Yahya Ayyash, whose dream of working in Amman or the Persian Gulf had been denied by Israeli authorities. Ayyash placed his skills instead at the service of the Izz al-Din al-Qassam Brigades, an armed wing of Hamas. He devised powerful detonators using household chemicals and fabricated high-energy explosive devices that had been used as far back as April 1993 through August 1995, killing dozens of Israeli civilians. Most of the victims were on or queuing for public buses. He earned the sobriquet "the Engineer," or al-Muhandis in Arabic.

The Israeli domestic security agency, the Shabak, came up with a plan to kill the Engineer by slipping him a modified cell phone he could be counted on to borrow from an intermediary who was under the Shabak's thumb. Modified in this instance meant the insertion of an eavesdropping chip as well as 15 grams of RDX, a potent plastic explosive. On January 25, 1996, when an Israeli surveillance aircraft determined conclusively that the Engineer himself was on the line, the RDX in the phone was detonated.

This coup, which the outgoing head of the Shabak considered his legacy, plunged Israel into an even bloodier vortex as Hamas began a campaign of reprisals shortly after the forty-day mourning period for Ayyash had ended. In February and March 1996, Hamas staged four bombings, killing seventy-eight Israelis and wounding scores more. Had Peres scheduled a snap election immediately after Rabin's death, a traumatized Israeli electorate would have given him a substantial victory and pushed an electoral reckoning for the Hamas offensive far into the future. But he had delayed elections so that he could run as his own man, rather than as a stand-in for a martyred Rabin. As a result, Peres was left to face Netanyahu in an election that was going to be both a referendum on Oslo and on Peres's record of ensuring the safety of Israelis in the face of a Palestinian rampage. It was not an election Peres was destined to win. The match took place at the end of May 1996. Between then and May 17, 1999, Clinton was going to have to deal with Netanyahu.

The fact was that the administration managed it with some success. The peace team wrung out of Netanyahu's government further agreements relating to the implementation of Oslo II, especially the withdrawal of IDF units and transfer of administrative control of West Bank towns to the Palestinian Authority. But as both sides documented, there was large-scale noncompliance with their respective obligations. The Palestinians failed to stifle incitement, continuing to encourage violence against Israelis, reward terrorists, and teach schoolchildren to hate Jews. The Israelis pressed ahead with settlement construction and expansion, violated deadlines for withdrawal of military forces from Palestinian areas, and extracted U.S. concessions regarding the pace at which they would fulfill their commitments. The administration, fearful of disrupting fragile agreements and reluctant to get into arguments with Netanyahu, chose to give the two sides a pass instead of calling them to account for their failures to comply. Letting the parties get away with bad behavior encouraged further disregard for the agreements they had signed. The benefits accrued disproportionately to Israel, which was able to leverage Palestinian violations to justify their own. As a practical matter, the Palestinian violations could not impose strategic costs on Israel, while Israeli progress in settlement expansion and delayed redeployments would profoundly undermine Palestinian interests over the longer term. Whether or not the Clinton administration could have imposed discipline on both sides in equal measure, it was clear that under Netanyahu and Arafat, the promise of Oslo had withered.

Netanyahu Wobbles; Ehud Barak Takes Charge; Peace with Syria?

By the spring of 1999, Netanyahu was in serious political trouble. On his right, traditional allies blamed him for cooperating with the United States; on the left, there was dissatisfaction over the slow pace of talks. In May, Netanyahu lost by a landslide to Ehud Barak, then the most decorated soldier in the Israeli army, a former chief of staff with an IQ of 180.

Barak, from the Clinton administration's perspective, was God's gift. He was Labor and thus aligned nicely with the Democratic Party's ethos, possessed the credibility that only military command can confer, and was intent on getting signed peace agreements from the Palestinians and Syrians. Exploiting these virtues to the fullest, Barak was able to lure Clinton into successive diplomatic fiascos, before being rejected by voters himself in February 2001. Barak, as well as the administration's peace team, believed that the two ongoing tracks begun in the early 1990s—the Palestinian and Syrian—afforded a useful flexibility. If one track stalled, the other could be picked up. And since the Syrians and Palestinians would be wary of each other cutting a deal and leaving the other isolated, both would be motivated to keep the United States and Israel engaged.

When the Syrian track was prioritized, for example, it was said that Arafat felt like "the other woman." The administration had tried to energize the Syrian track in late 1995 and early 1996 at meetings held at the

Wye Plantation in rural Maryland, which established that there was, in fact, the possibility of an eventual peace agreement. Exchanges were not warm, but they were businesslike and addressed the issues in a pragmatic way. But under Netanyahu they languished. Barak was keen to restart them. The effort had a distinct advantage over the Palestinian track because the underlying issue was territorial control rather than irreconcilable national narratives.

During his leadership, Rabin had given U.S. peace process leaders what Daniel Kurtzer described as a "diplomatic gift. . . . Israel would be ready to meet Assad's requirements on territory, if Assad would be ready to meet Israel's requirements on security and peace."[44] This became known as the "Rabin deposit." It was clearly a probe, devoid of the details wherein the devil resides. But knowing that Israel was not anticipating an outcome in which it continued to hold any Syrian land was hugely important to Assad. Even still, Assad either rejected or demanded changes to Rabin's security requirements that, from Israel's perspective, were unworkable. With Oslo underway at the time and looking good, Rabin decided to switch focus to the Palestinian track, leaving Assad to stew in Damascus.

When Peres took office after Rabin's death, he told Washington that he would honor the Rabin deposit, but the ensuing talks never really coalesced. Assad, perhaps on the basis of American advice, thought, inaccurately, that Peres would be more flexible on security arrangements. Assad also understood the weakness of Peres's political position and apparently concluded that Syrian concessions would be wasted, rather than thinking that they might have the potential to strengthen Peres's prospects and thus Syria's outcome in the negotiation. Assad saw no difference between Labor and Likud on security matters and therefore perceived no risk in waiting for Peres's successor. This was a mistake.

Upon his victory over Netanyahu in 1999, Ehud Barak declared his eagerness for a deal with Syria. Clinton authorized and participated briefly in an unproductive U.S.-hosted round of talks in Shepherdstown, West Virginia. Barak kept pushing for a rematch, sure that he could find a formula that would win Assad's agreement. The obstacle, as it had been for years, was Assad's insistence on full Israeli withdrawal versus Israel's desire to retain a small strip of land on the northeastern shore of the Kinneret, or Lake Tiberias. For Syria, full withdrawal meant the line between the two countries as of June 4, 1967, when it had controlled that tiny section of lakefront. With Anwar Sadat, whom Assad had mocked for making peace with Israel, having gotten back every inch of Egyptian territory from Israel in 1979, the Sphinx of Damascus could accept no less.

Barak, the Clinton Whisperer; Lame Duck American President Meets Dying Syrian President to Press Israeli Case; Inglorious End to Syria Talks

In March 2000, Barak convinced Clinton to meet with Assad in Geneva to deliver an undefined concession to Assad that would break the deadlock. Clinton agreed. Time, after all, was running out both for his administration and for Assad, who was in ill health and would die within three months. Unfortunately, when the time came to meet with Assad, Barak turned out not to have anything new for Clinton to put on the table. The president was in the awkward situation of transmitting and defending an Israel offer that Assad had already rejected repeatedly. It was a hopeless and embarrassing job, especially given Assad's willingness to make the trip to Geneva from his deathbed. Explaining his, and by extension Syria's, emotional commitment to regaining the shoreline, Assad reminisced how, as a boy, he had swum in Lake Tiberius. When told this later, Barak mused that it was a good thing the young Assad had never swum in Lake Geneva. But the opportunity for a treaty had been lost, irrevocably, and that was not a joke.

Barak, the Clinton Whisperer 2.0; the Illusory Allure of Camp David; the End of the Clinton Presidency, the Peace Process, and Dual Containment

For reasons that are unclear, Clinton fell for the same ploy again during the summer of 2000, when Barak argued that the time was ripe for an Israeli-Palestinian summit meeting that Clinton would sponsor. Barak intimated that he had an offer in mind that Arafat could not refuse, especially in the pressure cooker of a meeting chaired by the president. At this stage, there was no evidence that Arafat was interested in considering any Israeli offers, which he anticipated would be unlikely to match the expectations of his constituents; with Oslo disintegrating and Palestinians' frustration riding high as Barak focused on the Syrian track, the mood was too brittle for Arafat to take any risks. The administration pressed ahead despite Arafat's hesitancy, seduced by Barak's siren song of a final peace agreement between Israel and the Palestinian people.

Clinton did his best to reassure Arafat in advance of the summit that there would be a preparatory process, a preliminary discussion of the issues so that he would have a sense of what the United States hoped to achieve, and Barak was ready to come to the table. He also promised that the troop withdrawals postponed by Barak would take place even if the summit failed and that failure would not be blamed on the Palestinian side alone. Clinton was going to break all these pledges shortly, but they were enough to get Arafat to Camp David, where the summit was to be held in an homage to Carter's 1979 diplomatic feat.

It did not work. Barak's approach was to hide his bottom line, if he had one, from both Arafat and Clinton, trying to get either or both to make interim concessions he could pocket on his way to the best deal possible. Arafat's approach was to wait for Barak to disclose his bottom line before making any concessions that would prove politically damaging should Barak's eventual offer be unacceptable to the Palestinian side.

As Robert Malley, a staffer at Camp David, has observed, the Palestinians' job in Oslo and at Camp David was to negotiate the terms of their own surrender. Through a combination of bad luck, military defeats over the years, and bad leadership, Palestinians were confined to an area about one-fifth the size of their land prior to 1947. They could not see a way to negotiate away even more. The popular perception of the time was that Arafat was passive and recalcitrant, unwilling to make a deal at all despite Barak's "generous" proposed package, which may or may not have actually been on offer.

Malley's sardonic take on the "generous offer" narrative remains the best assessment.

Had there been, in hindsight, a generous Israeli offer? Ask a member of the American team, and an honest answer might be that there was a moving target of ideas, fluctuating impressions of the deal the United States could sell to the two sides, a work in progress that reacted (and therefore was vulnerable) to the pressures and persuasion of both. Ask Barak, and he might volunteer that there was no Israeli offer and, besides, Arafat rejected it. Ask Arafat, and the response you might hear is that there was no offer; besides, it was unacceptable; that said, it had better remain on the table.[45]

The Clinton administration policy in the Middle East was hobbled by an attraction to faulty doctrines. It was also trapped by its predecessor's problematic legacy in Iraq. Dual containment, as we shall see, would ultimately lead to Iraq's destruction and an unbridled Iran. The administration missed or discounted conciliatory Iranian signals—the Conoco tender, the fax proposing a reset[46]—and, prodded by Congress, pushed on with a maximum pressure campaign against Tehran that led to a successful Iranian strike against the U.S. military in Saudi Arabia. Even when tensions eased, the administration was blocked by Congress from taking steps that might have yielded a less confrontational relationship in the years that followed.

The administration's peace process diplomacy did help Israel find a way to talk to the PLO and gave it the opportunity to achieve peace with Syria, but the doctrine of incrementalism, grounded in the view that with the parties far apart on pivotal issues, there was no alternative but step-by-step phased cooperation on small things, was pursued long after it was clearly ineffectual. And when Clinton, urged by Barak and spurred by his own quest for a legacy, finally lunged for a comprehensive deal, he failed. Fortunately for the administration's reputation, his successor's record was far worse.

CHAPTER FIVE

GEORGE W. BUSH

Wrong Man, Wrong Time

It was the "decision of one man to launch a wholly unjustified and brutal invasion of Iraq," former president George W. Bush said Wednesday before quickly correcting himself, saying he meant to describe Russian President Vladimir Putin's war on Ukraine.

"Iraq, too, anyway," he added under his breath to laughter from the audience during a speech at his presidential center in Dallas.

—WASHINGTON POST, 2022[1]

At some point in mid-1999, when I was still at the Clinton White House, Zalmay Khalilzad got in touch to suggest lunch. I was delighted. Zal was (and is) highly intelligent, imaginative, and something of a celebrity among national security policy wonks. He would go on to a succession of high-wire diplomatic posts under George W. Bush, Barack Obama, and Donald Trump, but back then he was still just a defense intellectual linked to powerful neocons. Lunch was bound to be stimulating. Zal had a pitch. Essentially, it was about the transformation of an area of southern Iraq already under U.S. military protection into something more than a no-fly and no-drive zone for Saddam's army. In his conception, the United States could take it over and use it as a base for training and equipping a Shiite force that, under the right conditions, would burst forth, march to Baghdad, and depose Saddam. I made the customary counterarguments. Suppose Saddam saw the threat and intervened quickly and brutally to nip this Shiite revolt in the bud? What if this rebel army emerged from its chrysalis only to fail to subdue Saddam's elite divisions around Baghdad? Outcomes like these would put U.S. prestige on the line. Washington would have no choice but to rescue its proxy army and finish the job by destroying Saddam's forces and the regime itself, which would defeat the purpose of a proxy army. If, on the other hand, one were looking for a policy that would force a hesitant, risk-averse Washington elite to change the regime in Baghdad through force of arms, Zal's idea could prove quite effective. I went back to the office thinking, *Well, I guess these guys are serious about starting another war with Iraq.* Fortunately, Vice President Al Gore seemed likely to defeat any Republican candidate the following November, so I did not give Zal's plan much more thought.

The election did not play out as anticipated. The vote was close and ultimately decided by the Supreme Court, which ruled that thousands of ballots cast in Florida for Al Gore were inadmissible owing to a technical flaw. Gore chose not to contest the outcome and left politics altogether. The result placed the country in the hands of a seemingly unserious person with no foreign policy experience, a limited interest in public policy— judging from his terms as governor of Texas—and a classic small government pro-business Republican mindset, but with one unique asset: he was a son of George H. W. Bush.

Characterizing George W. Bush is not as easy as it might appear to be. There is no question the spoiled frat boy who won the Electoral College vote in 2000 matured in office. He was derided as stupid by critics in part because he inherited his father's problem with English expression and in part because he was demonstrably narrow-minded, incurious, and impulsive. While there is no publicly available evidence of high intelligence, Bush's aggressive anti-intellectualism and crude approach to foreign policy dilemmas made him look less bright than he probably was. In the early days, his unsavory collaboration with cronies trying to steal land that was home to thousands of low-income Texans to build a football stadium created the appearance of moral ruthlessness in addition to obtuseness.[2] As his time in office lengthened, his thinking appeared to become somewhat more nuanced and his readiness to absorb unwelcome information grew. Steps he took toward the end of his second term showed an accommodation to reality and fewer reflexive responses to challenges overseas. They also demonstrated a more comprehensive view of U.S. interests, for example, by promoting programs to manage an HIV crisis in Africa and requesting congressional appropriations to counter the epidemic in countries that lacked the resources to do so on their own.

The Professionals Are Back

Bush's foreign policy team drew on the Vulcans who served in his father's administration. Dick Cheney, who had been Gerald Ford's chief of staff and George H. W. Bush's secretary of defense, was now the vice president but with license to focus on foreign policy and defense issues. Paul Wolfowitz, who'd been a senior State and Defense official, was the new deputy secretary of defense. Colin Powell, who had been the chairman of the Joint Chiefs of Staff, became secretary of state. His deputy was Richard Armitage, an assistant secretary of defense under Cheney. Donald Rumsfeld helmed the Defense Department; his résumé already included this post in the Ford administration, as well as being elected to Congress, running multinational firms, and qualifying as a fighter pilot. George W. Bush's national security adviser was Condoleezza Rice, who had been on the elder Bush's NSC staff. Richard Haass, who had served with Rice on the NSC staff, was made the director of the State Department policy planning staff.

The return of the Vulcans was greeted jubilantly by both neoconservative and garden-variety Republicans who had lacerated the Clinton administration for taking its eye off the ball. Michael Mandelbaum and Eliot Cohen, international relations scholars with solid reputations, had scourged Clinton's administration for practicing foreign policy as though it was "social work" and using military force haphazardly and without the essential will to win. The Clinton team had been mocked for an absence of serious purpose and reluctance to use American power to advance the national interest. According to Republican critics, Clinton's foreign and defense policy was the product of a cult of the amateur, exemplified in their view by Tony Lake, whom Kissinger had dismissed as a "good student of American foreign policy," conjuring up a boy wearing short pants and a beanie topped by a tiny propeller.

Rice, on the other hand, was thought to have not only a first-rate mind but an appropriately hard-nosed view of international relations. During the campaign, she authored an essay for *Foreign Affairs* in which she argued that the Clinton administration had failed to cultivate American allies, while letting rival powers, especially Russia and China, advance their interests at American expense. Although she referred to the Middle East as "a region of core interest to the United States and to our key ally Israel,"[3] she added little in terms of detail, perhaps because she had never worked on the region. But in a near verbatim (though uncredited) quote from Lake's earlier *Foreign Affairs* essay, she wrote, "As history marches toward markets and democracy, some states have been left by the side of the road. Iraq is the prototype. Saddam Hussein's regime is isolated, his conventional military power has been severely weakened, his people live in poverty and terror, and he has no useful place in international politics."

Clinton's role in weakening Saddam's military and the responsibility of both GHW Bush and Bill Clinton for impoverishing the Iraqi people was unworthy of notice; in the Rice worldview it was as though these things just happened. Rice concludes her essay with the non sequitur, "He

[Saddam] is therefore determined to develop WMD," which neither followed necessarily from her premise nor reflected the reality that Saddam had already abandoned his quest for WMD; and that "nothing will change until Saddam is gone, so the United States must mobilize whatever resources it can, including support from his opposition, to remove him." Though this had essentially been the Clinton administration's policy, which also relied on an ineffectual internal opposition to Saddam,[4] the incoming administration believed its own effort would fare better.

"Iran," she wrote, "presents special difficulties in the Middle East . . . Iranian weaponry increasingly threatens Israel directly. As important as Israel's efforts to reach peace with its Arab neighbors are to the future of the Middle East, they are not the whole story of stability in the region. Israel has a real security problem, so defense cooperation with the United States—particularly in the area of ballistic missile defense—is critical."

Thus, Iran was a problem for the United States because it was a problem for Israel. Israel's presumed vulnerability gave extra ballast to the Bush team's view that antiballistic missile defenses, of the kind then banned, should be funded. Rice's subtle pushback against a supposed Democratic view that all would be well in the region if only Israel made a peace agreement with the Palestinians—a case I never heard a Democratic policy official make—signaled that a Bush administration would not be so frivolous when threats could and should be countered militarily.

Yet the overall thrust of her essay on behalf of the Bush campaign was that the United States had more important business than maneuvering for advantage among less-than-great powers, which soon became her boss's view as well. The two figures, after all, meshed nicely. "I like to be around her," Mr. Bush told *The New York Times* in 2000. "She's fun to be with. I like lighthearted people, not people who take themselves so seriously that they are hard to be around. . . . Besides, she's really smart!" But not threatening. Bush went on to say that Rice "can explain to me foreign policy matters in a way I can understand."[5]

With the formation of Bush's team, the new mantra was "the professionals are back!" In the foreign policy realm, the focus was on China. The new administration had been critical of Clinton's stance, which they saw as too relaxed. By April, this change in approach to Beijing triggered a crisis involving a collision between a Chinese warplane and a U.S. spy plane. There were no casualties, but the crew of the American aircraft were detained on Hainan Island, where they had been forced down. The situation calmed down in part due to Bush's management of his own team, which was primed for confrontation, and his effort to line up allied governments to urge China to release the crew. This episode underscored the new emphasis on major allies and adversaries, including its perils.

Osama bin Laden Begs to Differ

While the Bush White House was concentrating on the major powers, Osama bin Laden, the head of the al Qaeda terrorist organization, was putting the finishing touches on what would be the 9/11 attacks. The administration had been briefed extensively on this evolving threat both by the outgoing national security adviser, Sandy Berger, who urged Rice to attend to it, and by George Tenet, director of Central Intelligence, a Clinton holdover, who said he was so worried about an impending attack that his "hair was fire." Rice, dwelling on big countries, considered the warnings about terrorists operating independently of states implausible; she later told the 9/11 Commission that investigated the attacks that Bush thought striking ragged terrorist groups would be "swatting at flies."[6] Bush himself told the Commission that he was more worried about a Saudi-Iranian alliance, a proposition so bizarre it raises serious doubts about whether he absorbed anything at all in his hundreds of briefings by CIA.[7]

As far back as January 2000, a former White House colleague, Dan Benjamin, and I had written in *The New York Times* that there would soon be a mass casualty attack against the United States by Sunni extremists.[8]

By then it was common knowledge among experts that a catastrophe was inevitable. It later seemed incredible that the Bush administration could be so heedless of the intelligence warning of an imminent attack, which had reached a crescendo in the summer of 2001. Still, Rice would not convene a meeting on al Qaeda until September 4, 2001, far too late to take the sort of action needed to thwart the terrible plot then nearing its climax.

The 9/11 attacks had a long tail. Depending on the time frame one applies, it could be said to have originated in the *Qital* verses of the Quran, which exhort Muslims to kill non-Muslims; the writings of Muhammad ibn al-Hasan al-Shaybani, the ninth-century Hanafi scholar who justified the killing of noncombatants; the edicts of a late-fourteenth-century cleric, Taqi al-din ibn Taymiyya, who endorsed the killing of impious Muslims; in the anti-Western fervor of Sayyid Qutb, a mid-twentieth-century Quranic commentator in Egypt; the founder of the Muslim Brotherhood, Hasan al-Banna, who opposed British rule in Egypt and favored an Islamic state; the works of Jamal al-din al-Afghani, an Indian Muslim theoretician of Islamic revivalism; the creed of Muhammad ibn abd al-Wahhab, the eighteenth-century expositor of a particularly rigid and exclusionist form of Islam that became the state religion of Saudi Arabia; the behavior of Arab authoritarians whose repression pushed political expression into mosques, where grievances were clothed in the language of religion, and who then failed to regulate effectively the infrastructure of religion, mosques, schools, and charities; the policy of Saudi royals who exported Muslim political and religious dissent to an array of countries, including the United States; to the strategy of Abdullah Azzam, a Palestinian-Jordanian paladin of the 1980s who preached the obligation of Muslims to free co-religionists from foreign rule; the example set by Che Guevara and other architects of anti-imperial insurgency; or the manifestos of Osama bin Laden, who formulated a strategy to liberate Muslims from their impious rulers, the "near enemy," by attacking the great power propping them up, the "far enemy," otherwise known as the United States. In truth, all these factors contributed to the evolution of holy war as it was applied in 2001 to targets in the United States.

The historian's dilemma is where to begin her or his story, recognizing that every effect has a cause, or many causes, some general and others specific, and that these can and do reach far back in time. Daniel Benjamin and I traced the historical context of 9/11 in our book *The Age of Sacred Terror*, which we wrote just after the attacks. The most relevant backstory begins in the mid-1970s, when Egypt's president, Anwar Sadat, was transforming the country's socialist economy into an extravaganza of crony capitalism. Younger Egyptians, who'd grown up under socialism, rallied against the new order. To help drown out the criticism, the government encouraged Islamists to compete against the Leftists for influence, especially on university campuses. After years of repression under Sadat's predecessor, Gamal abdel Nasser, the Islamists thrived.

The problem for Sadat was that the Islamists did not like his opening of the economy to the West, with its attendant corruption, adoption of un-Islamic behavior, and influx of foreigners. The name chosen by one Islamist group, al Takfir wal Hijra, "condemn and flee," summed up its program. Other dangerous organizations sprung up, like al Gamaat al Islamiyya, "The Islamic Group," which ultimately assassinated Sadat in 1981. To them, Sadat was nothing but a reincarnated Pharaoh, the archetypal tyrant of pre-Islamic Egypt, a relic of the age of ignorance.

During Nasser's suppression of Islamists in the 1960s, his targets had found refuge in Saudi Arabia. The Saudis were battling Egypt through proxy forces in Yemen, so it made sense to give aid and comfort to his domestic enemies. And the fugitive Islamists were inspired by the same spiritual sources as the Wahhabis, even if they weren't Wahhabi themselves and were distinctively committed to political change. So when a second wave of Egyptians washed up in Saudi Arabia as a result of the continuing Islamist war against Sadat and his successor, Hosni Mubarak, there were already Egyptians—and a great many young Saudis influenced by them—in the Wahhabi religious establishment.

During the 1980s, many of these pious young men traveled to Afghanistan to join the jihad against the Soviets. Bin Laden's al Qaeda—"The Base"—was set up to provide logistical support for the fighters within Afghanistan. The hub was in Peshawar, on the Pakistani side of the border facing the fabled Khyber Pass. Bin Laden called it simply Maktab al Khidamat, the "Services Office." The Soviets were defeated in Ronald Reagan's second term by a lengthy U.S. effort to hamstring Russian forces; as far as the Arab fighters were concerned, it was they who'd run the Soviets off Muslim land. Their victory left them eager for the next round.

The first Gulf War would have been the next opportunity. As we saw in the chapter on George H. W. Bush, bin Laden himself had urged the Al Saud to rely on these volunteers to defend Saudi Arabia from Saddam, rather than on a massive Christian army whose presence would defile the land of Muhammad and disgrace the Kingdom. But his proposal was understandably brushed aside by the Al Saud, who had been stampeded by Bush's prediction of an imminent Iraqi attack on Saudi Arabia. For bin Laden, who was already enormously popular among young Saudis, it was damning. In the view of restless would-be jihadis, the Kingdom then compounded its error by failing to intervene on behalf of beleaguered Bosnian Muslims during the Balkan wars of the 1990s.

The 1990s saw growing public criticism within the Kingdom of Al Saud rule. The "Awakening" movement spearheaded by two young Saudi clerics, Salman al-Awda and Safar al-Hawali, demanded reform. The clerics submitted petitions insisting upon greater political participation and on royal accountability. The response consisted of cosmetic institutional political changes and the usual mix of positive and negative incentives to welcome these changes as sufficient. But in 1992, the court also created a new ministry of Islamic affairs, which, among other things, poured money into the employment and overseas deployment of zealous young clerics who might otherwise cause trouble at home. These propagators of the faith were inspired, on the one hand, by Wahhabi disdain for infidels and deviant Muslims and, on the other, by a mission to counter oppression of Muslims everywhere. The Kingdom gave them diplomatic passports, salaries, travel expenses, and logistical support provided by the Saudi embassies in the countries to which they were posted. Aware that the governments of some of these countries would reject such missionaries, the Saudi government even instructed its diplomatic missions to conceal their actual purposes.

Bin Laden Goes Public

Apart from Saudi Arabia's penetration of foreign states by religious activists, Osama bin Laden had issued declarations in 1996 and 1998 declaring war against the United States and authorizing the killing of civilians in response to American aggression against Muslims worldwide. These statements jumbled together anti-colonial rhetoric, vitriolic condemnation of Arab regimes that betrayed their faith, anti-Semitic and anti-Israeli themes, judgments regarding the duty of Muslims to defend Islamic lands (including far-flung places like Spain, where Muslims once ruled), and finally, the assertion that all Americans, as citizens of a democratic state, bore responsibility for the actions of the administrations they had elected. Since those administrations had inflicted death and destruction on Muslim noncombatants, then American noncombatants were fair game.

Even before bin Laden jumped into the fray, jihadists of his sort had targeted the United States. In 1993, the World Trade Center was attacked by Ramzi Yousef, who was like a classic evil genius of pulp fiction brought to life in Pakistan. With the blessing of the Brooklyn-based "Blind Sheikh," Omar Abdel Rahman, Yousef planted a van jammed with explosives by what he thought was a key structural element in the underground parking lot under the towers. It detonated with tremendous force but failed to collapse the building. Yousef is now in a U.S. prison; the Blind Sheikh is dead.

Bin Laden's growing prominence was noted by CIA, which began to track him in the mid-1990s. The Saudis themselves were concerned enough by the mid-1990s to strip him of his citizenship and passport. But the government of Sudan was sympathetic to bin Laden's view of Islam and his anti-Western agenda and welcomed the cash he had to offer. Bin Laden settled there in Khartoum and transformed his organization into what the intelligence community called the Ford Foundation for terrorists, although at this point, he had not yet committed crimes against the United States and therefore could not be indicted. The United States turned to Egypt, which bordered Sudan and was not hung up on legal technicalities, to take bin Laden off the board. Cairo, however, declined to act. Bin Laden, in the meantime, was digging deeper into Sudan and plotting to strike the United States.

In 1995, jihadists struck the headquarters of the Vinnell Corporation's program office in Riyadh. Vinnell was responsible for providing logistical and other support for the Saudi National Guard. This arm of the Kingdom's military is unlike the U.S. national guard, which are reserve forces that report to state governors and generally assist civil authorities in emergencies, such as natural disasters. In contrast, the Saudi version is a praetorian guard, under the command of the crown prince, superbly equipped and trained to ward off internal threats to the royal family. Vinnell's office was both a symbolic and practical target. In the summer of 1998, bin Laden upped the ante by attacking the American embassies in Dar es Salaam, Tanzania, and Nairobi, Kenya. The strikes were carried out simultaneously and with great precision. The local organization was provided by the Al-Haramayn Foundation, a Saudi charity funded by the Kingdom, and an array of private donors. The Saudi link did not escape the FBI's notice. The CIA and State Department pressed the Saudis for help in stemming the flow of resources to groups that had the United States in their sights, and in investigating these deadly conspiracies. But as the CIA's White House liaison at the time has since written, the Saudis were fundamentally uncooperative.[9] The 1998 attacks—in combination with bin Laden's declaration of war that same year—should have impelled the Kingdom to crack down on the overseas operations of organizations it supported. Regrettably, they did not.

The Conspiracy Unfolds

And so it was that in January 2000, three Saudi officials, Walid Suweilam, Fahad al Thumairy, and Omar al Bayoumi, dispatched by the ministry of Islamic Affairs in Riyadh to the Saudi embassy in the United States, traveled to the King Fahd, Ibn Taymiyya, and Kurdish mosques in Los Angeles and San Diego to prepare for the arrival of Nawaf al Hazmi and Khalid al Midhar, the al Qaeda operatives in the vanguard of the 9/11 attacks.[10]

Nothing is inevitable, and the attacks of 9/11 were no exception. The Saudis, after the 1998 bombings, could have taken another look at the people they were deploying to the United States to ensure they were not secretly al Qaeda sympathizers. And U.S. government agencies could have worked together more effectively to nip the plot in the bud. The CIA, for example, knew that al Midhar and al Hazmi were members of al Qaeda, had identified them at an al Qaeda meeting in Kuala Lumpur, Malaysia, and noted that the pair had flown from Bangkok to LA. Unfortunately, the CIA did not provide essential information to the FBI about the entry of one of these al Qaeda operatives into the United States and the fact that another had gotten a U.S. visa. The deliberate withholding of this information essentially gave bin Laden's group a free pass to roam the country. And the Saudi government had inadvertently hired and deployed to the United States the support network for these operatives. Not that the FBI was blameless. In August 2001, its own field office in Minneapolis stumbled on a likely twentieth hijacker, Zacarias Moussaoui, and questioned him regarding his interest in flight lessons, but could not get permission from FBI headquarters to break into his computer. Had they been able to, it is probable that the plot would have been uncovered.

Disaster

Thus far, the record indicates that al Qaeda had been planning a major attack of some kind as early as 1998 without having settled on a particular plan. Moussaoui, for instance, who was interested in crop dusting, suggested the dispersal of poisons. Bin Laden's point man was Khalid Sheikh Mohammed, Ramzi Yousef's uncle, who apparently devised the outlines of what became the 9/11 attacks. The operational chief was a grim Egyptian engineer based in Hamburg, Germany. He assembled a crew of nineteen, including himself, or perhaps twenty if, as seems likely, Moussaoui was a participant in the plan. Money flowed from accounts in the United Arab Emirates, which was also home to two hijackers. The others were Saudi nationals and a lone Lebanese.

On September 11 they launched a coordinated suicide attack against three targets—the World Trade Center towers, the Pentagon, and either the White House or Capitol—reaching the towers and the Pentagon. Their weapons were hijacked civil aircraft loaded with fuel (and passengers). The attack against the White House or Capitol failed because the passengers on that aircraft overwhelmed the hijackers but tragically were unable to pilot the plane themselves. That flight, United Airlines 93 out of Newark, crashed near Shanksville, Pennsylvania. The aircraft driven into the north and south towers in New York burned so fiercely they melted the steel elements holding up the buildings. The two structures pancaked, killing all those above and on the floors penetrated by the planes and those below who could not get out before the structures collapsed. The plane that hit the Pentagon, American Airlines 77 out of Dulles, destroyed one of the building's five sides in an inferno of burning fuel and storm of flying glass and concrete. Altogether, the hijackers massacred 2,977 people, mostly Americans but also many foreigners unlucky enough to be in the World Trade Center that morning. Among the casualties was John P. O'Neill, who had recently retired from the FBI, where he had been a tireless enemy of al Qaeda, and had just started as the security director for the World Trade Center. He ran into the north tower after the impact of American Airlines Flight 11 from Logan Airport and never emerged. The south tower was destroyed nearly simultaneously by United Airlines 175, also out of Logan. Two decades after the attack, more than 1,000 victims remain to be found or identified.

The events of 9/11 were axial not just because they were the first successful attacks against the continental United States by a foreign adversary since the War of 1812, or the most profound intelligence failure since Pearl Harbor in 1941, but because they were a response to American activism in the Middle East. The attacks were a cruel, if only momentary, correction to the idea that the United States was the subject and the Arab world the object. Bin Laden's appalling raid against a civilian target demonstrated that the dynamic could be reversed. America could be acted upon, just as it had acted upon others. As a statement, it was both eloquent and repugnant. It also aroused the United States to a reply that was much deadlier than bin Laden's gruesome provocation.

The Administration Reels and Reacts; Iraq in the Frame

I was in the back seat of a London taxi when I heard a BBC presenter saying on the radio that a plane had crashed into the north tower of the World Trade Center. My first reaction was to shout, "He did it! He did it! He fucking did it!" The perplexed driver turned to ask who did it, and to tell me that the BBC was reporting the event as an accidental collision. My answer, of course, was Osama bin Laden. Back in Washington, it did not take the CIA much longer to convey the same judgment to the administration. By the time the administration had reassembled for an NSC meeting in the Situation Room four days after the attacks, Wolfowitz was quick to speculate on Iraqi complicity. Bush "testily" asked his counterterrorism adviser, Richard A. Clarke, whether Iraq was the perpetrator. Clarke said no, which should not have been a surprise to anyone. The deputy attorney general, Jamie Gorelick, who was later given access by the 9/11 Commission to Bush's daily intelligence briefings in the summer months preceding 9/11, confirmed that the spike in intelligence indicators of an impending attack was a regular feature. The information the CIA conveyed to the president clearly pointed the finger at al Qaeda, not Iraq.[11]

But for Wolfowitz and those persuaded by him, including the vice president and his chief of staff, Scooter Libby, Saddam was the monster under the bed. Wolfowitz and Libby had been seduced by Ahmed Chalabi, the exiled Iraqi fantasist who saw Saddam as the obstacle to his quest for the throne. Wolfowitz had also fallen under the spell of an academic Middle East specialist, Laurie Mylroie, who had cobbled together a mass of tenuously connected facts and guesswork to support the claim that Saddam was behind a range of evils, including the 1993 bombing of the World Trade Center and later the destruction of the Murrah Federal Building in Oklahoma City in 1995. Given her links to influential Washingtonians, the audacity of her claims, and collection of alleged evidence, she enjoyed access to senior policy officials, including me. As did others, I shipped her files to the CIA for an analysis and assessment. As far as the intelligence analysts were concerned, her evidence was questionable and her argument unconvincing. For proponents of Mylroie's case, however, rejection by the intelligence community merely confirmed its validity.

On the other hand, there was the undeniable matter of Saddam having plotted to kill George H. W. Bush on his victory tour of Kuwait after he'd left office and the fact that Saddam's regime had given shelter to anti-Israeli terrorist groups. There was a solid argument for Saddam's willingness to use terror to achieve his goals. There just wasn't any evidence that he had consorted with al Qaeda to attack the World Trade Center, the Pentagon, the White House, or the Capitol. Nevertheless, the notion that Iraq was involved took hold, fueling the preexisting commitment to regime change in Iraq that Condoleezza Rice had laid out in *Foreign Affairs*.

Subtly reinforcing the conviction that Iraq was the appropriate object of the U.S. response to 9/11 was a neocon belief that if only Iraq could be sorted out, it would make the perfect U.S. ally in the Middle East. Israel, of course, was a staunch partner and a democracy but, being a Jewish state, could not help the U.S. safeguard its interests in the Persian Gulf, since the Arab states could not then accept Israel's cooperation. Saudi Arabia was a valued partner, but its inability to muster a military force capable of operating effectively and obscurantist religious establishment reduced its strategic value. Iraq, in contrast, was a secular state, did not discriminate against female professionals as a matter of policy, educated and trained its own technocrats, fielded a large combat-hardened army, and even approached the threshold of nuclear capability back in the 1980s. The only barrier to this ideal alliance was Saddam Hussein.

While U.S. forces under General Tommy Franks were floundering in Afghanistan as bin Laden and his band escaped into the Tora Bora mountains and safe haven in Pakistan, preparations for war with Iraq were already beginning. Although the president stated repeatedly during the winter of 2001–02 that he had not decided whether to invade Iraq, the White House had already spun up the Pentagon war-planning process and begun to divert surveillance and reconnaissance platforms from Afghanistan to the Middle East. Senior military officers, their hands full with an ongoing war in Afghanistan, were incredulous. Meeting informally, they reviewed the bidding, concluding that Iraq was too weak to be a threat to the United States and that it could be taken down at any time, so there was no good reason to hamstring military operations in Afghanistan in order to move against Saddam in the near term. These views got an unofficial hearing, but the impending decision seemed inevitable, and military commanders elected not to resist.

War Planning

The ensuing planning was hampered by disagreements within the Pentagon about the size of the invasion force needed to topple Saddam. Donald Rumsfeld, the secretary of defense, had been impressed with the "Revolution in Military Affairs" ushered in by Desert Storm. The term referred to the application of advanced computing techniques to military operations.[12] Amazing progress in data processing and sensing technologies had made truly precise weapons a real possibility. Precision meant that wars could be fought by fewer troops. Decisive results could be achieved by smart munitions delivered with stunning accuracy against targets that underpinned the enemy's efforts: headquarters elements, air defenses, communications nodes, heavy vehicles and artillery, missile launchers, you name it. Rumsfeld saw his moment to reshape U.S. military power from its legacy Cold War structure and doctrine to one that would incorporate the revolution in military affairs. He would future-proof the country's defense capabilities.

An invasion of Iraq would therefore be both a blessing and a curse. A blessing because it would enable Rumsfeld to experiment with his concept for a redesigned military, a curse because the necessities of the war itself would inevitably get in the way of the transformation he had in mind. It's hard to change horses in midstream. Rumsfeld's solution to this challenge was to try to ensure that the war would be fought as quickly as possible and not tie down his forces any longer than necessary. His thinking was reinforced by *Shock and Awe*, a monograph written by a Beltway defense consultant, that reads like a cross between a Tom Clancy novel and an Avengers comic book. It was clearly intended for men in the policy establishment who saw themselves as death-from-the-sky warriors, prepared to do what needed to be done. Essentially, it argued that a strong blow against selected targets using the new military tools would shatter the morale of the enemy and precipitate his rapid collapse. A French officer in 1914 imbued with the "cult of the offensive" would have recognized this idea immediately;[13] as would an American officer studying doctrine in the years after Vietnam.[14] In Rumsfeld's mind, "shock and awe" tactics would meet his requirement for a war that would be won decisively by a swift, overwhelming assault.

This infatuation with a caricature of Germany's blitzkrieg strategy aligned nicely with the president's attraction to preemptive war. In June 2002, Bush elaborated on this concept in a speech to West Point cadets.

"We cannot defend America and our friends by hoping for the best. . . . If we wait for threats to fully materialize, we will have waited too long. . . . And our security will require all Americans to be forward-looking and resolute, to be ready for preemptive action when necessary to defend our liberty and to defend our lives."[15]

The appeal of preemption is intuitive. If you are sure the other guy is going to shoot you, that he can't be deterred from immediately taking the shot or dissuaded from doing so, it makes sense to shoot first. You live to fight another day, your adversary doesn't. Thus, the reward for preemption is large and the penalty for restraint is proportionately harsh. Actual examples of this situation in international relations are few and far between, however, and seemed not to apply to the actual threat posed by Iraq. For instance, the CIA's view was that Iraq was five to seven years away from a nuclear weapon.[16]

Rather than preemption, Bush was describing a strategy of preventive attack, whereby you see a potential adversary walking in the general direction of the Walmart gun counter, and preferring to be safe than sorry, gun him down then and there. The official version of the prevention option, labeled as "preemption" to suggest that the situation was critical and use of force inescapable, appeared in the summer of 2002 in the

Bush administration's *National Security Strategy of the United States*: "There are few greater threats than a terrorist attack with WMD. To forestall or prevent such hostile acts by our adversaries, the United States will, if necessary, act preemptively in exercising our inherent right of self-defense."[17] As Condoleezza Rice framed the problem, "We don't want the smoking gun to be a mushroom cloud."

Dick Cheney's view, according to interviewer Ron Suskind, was that "if there was even a one percent chance of terrorists getting a weapon of mass destruction—and there has been a small probability of such an occurrence for some time—the United States must now act as if it were a certainty." Suskind then quotes him saying that "our analysis" matters much less than "our response."[18] Cheney's suggestion was that lashing out violently, even or especially in the absence of proof, would be a more potent deterrent to challenges from other quarters. Leading news outlets facilitated the marketing of such claims by reporting them uncritically, enabling senior officials to point to, say, *The New York Times* as the source when they repeated them in public.[19]

In fairness to the administration, anxiety about the prospect of nuclear terrorism had gripped Washington policy analysts and some members of Congress from the mid-1990s onward. This mood fused with a long-standing concern about nuclear proliferation and the damage even a small nuclear weapon could cause. (Now that the United States seems to have accommodated to around one million dead as the result of a mishandled pandemic, worries about a radioactive device contaminating Central Park seem quaint.) But in the wake of the 9/11 attacks, which clearly aimed to cause mass casualties, cognitive bias—the kind of mistake that is hardwired into human thinking—also led many to assume the proximity and violence of the event was the beginning of a trend, rather than the singular event it was, and to overestimate the damage inflicted by the attack. The "blood lust" Bush confessed to feeling at the time infused these perceptions with the potential for spiraling violence.[20] The economic markets, interestingly, were not prey to these misconceptions or passions.

An elite committee—"White House Iraq Group"—set up under Republican political strategist Karl Rove concluded that the best approach to co-opting American public opinion would be to say that Iraq was on the verge of a nuclear weapons capability and was prepared to use it against the United States in league with al Qaeda. Not for nothing is Rove considered a gifted propagandist. These fabrications engendered a 71 percent approval rating for war in March 2003.[21]

Did the president really believe this? Apparently so, judging by his enthusiastic endorsement of ambiguous and contested evidence, or when he referred incorrectly to an IAEA report that he thought had said Iraq was six months from a nuclear bomb, saying, "What more do you need?" A month later, in October 2002, he stated that Saddam was "a man that we know has had connections with al Qaeda. This is a man who, in my judgment, would like to use al Qaeda as a forward army."[22] Given his reflexive thinking, inattention to detail, confidence in his own "judgment," self-righteousness, and impulsive bellicosity, there's little reason to doubt that Bush believed his own assertions about Saddam. He might have been self-deceptive but was not necessarily deceitful.

The Uniformed Services Beg to Differ

Those who would fight the war had a different view from the civilians selling shock and awe and fantasies of grateful Iraqis. They had little doubt that they would prevail over the enemy within months at the most, but they anticipated a post-conflict phase marked by guerilla warfare and taking responsibility for basic societal needs once Saddam was knocked from his perch. The then-new army counterinsurgency handbook stipulated that to maintain order, the United States would have to deploy 20 soldiers for every 1,000 Iraqis, which presupposed an occupying force of at least several hundred thousand personnel. Given this demand, it made little sense to move forward until the hunt for al Qaeda in Afghanistan was wrapped up, freeing additional troops for a complex operation in Iraq.

A shoving match between Rumsfeld and Wolfowitz on one side and the uniformed military on the other was bound to be won by the civilian leadership. The army chief of staff, General Eric Shinseki, was forced out, a signal to the ground forces commanders and Central Command that it was time to get with the program. Agreement remained elusive, however, as each cut that military planners made to the size of the invasion force elicited requests from Rumsfeld to cut more deeply. Wolfowitz wanted to know why the job couldn't be done with a brigade, a relatively small maneuver unit of about 5,000 soldiers.

Because military campaign plans are intrinsically complicated, every adjustment of the force size created a ripple effect, necessitating hundreds of other revisions. With enough staff working hard enough, these interlocking accommodations could be made. But the effort crowded out the planning for Phase IV of the operation, which concerned the post-conflict stabilization of a country that would be awash with weapons and freshly knocked back on its heels. The State Department had produced reams of paper laying out the issues that would confront the United States after defeating the Iraqi army, but reports that describe problems, even where they suggest possible solutions, do not amount to plans. And without a plan, the military cannot act.

Cheney, as early as February 2002, was sure the United States was going to take out Saddam. He had already established what amounted to a parallel government to push the war planning process forward, while the formal machinery of government ground onward in the absence of a presidential decision to go to war. In a speech before a veteran's convention, Cheney declared that Saddam was linked to 9/11, that he was preparing weapons of mass destruction for imminent use against the United States, that Iraq was one year away from possessing nuclear weapons, and the Iraqi people would welcome the U.S. force that was going to liberate them from Saddam's tyrannical rule. Colin Powell, who had embraced the role of Hamlet in this period, complained to Rice at the NSC that Cheney's speech was out of line. There had been no decision to go to war. Cheney offered to revise the speech for a subsequent appearance before another veteran's group. He followed through by shortening his remarks, but not by deleting anything he had said about Iraq.

The *Greatest* Greatest Generation

The notion that the United States would be welcomed as liberators is curious in the present context but seems to have been widely shared within the administration. It was reflected in the code name chosen for the expected invasion, "Cobra II." The original "Cobra" was the Allied rollback of Nazi power from western Europe, begun with the Normandy landings of June 1944. One would have thought that the implied comparison between the Third Reich, an immensely capable military power that for a time had occupied nearly all of western and eastern Europe as well as much of North Africa, and Saddam's Iraq, a country of 25.64 million people already humiliated in battle with the United States and crushed by sanctions, would have provoked laughter. Similarly, the comparison of Saddam and Hitler should have been risible to anyone who knew anything about either villain. The only trait uniting them was a tendency to strategic misjudgment.

Any doubt about the administration's delusions of grandeur should have been resolved by the Pentagon's code name for the occupation of Iraq, "Eclipse II," inspired by the official name for the U.S. occupation of West Germany following the surrender of Nazi forces on May 8, 1945. Although the occupation of Germany is generally remembered as more skillful and efficient than it was, the Eclipse of that era had been given a lot of thought, unlike its successor. In contrast to the detailed occupation plan Dwight D. Eisenhower had requested two and a half years before

Germany was defeated, neither Central Command nor the Joint Staff gave any thought to how Iraq would be managed in the wake of combat.

But given the administration's view of itself as embarking on a world-historic campaign to destroy a malignant entity on the scale of Nazi Germany and liberate its captive population, it is perhaps unsurprising that decision makers foresaw a jubilant Iraqi population showering U.S. troops with bouquets. Yet even this expectation was odd, given that defeat and occupation triggered a massive wave of German suicides.[23]

Saddam Does Have WMD, Right?

Cheney's belief that Saddam was close to a nuclear weapons capability and was preparing to unleash other weapons of mass destruction on the world seems to have had no basis in U.S. intelligence analysis. In fact, the administration had never asked for such an assessment. The only large-scale coordinated intelligence assessment of Iraq's weapons of mass destruction program was completed in 2002 at the request of Congress, not the White House or any other executive branch department.[24] Bush himself never read it. According to the staffer who managed access to classified materials in the Capitol vault and kept a log of users, less than a half dozen members of Congress read beyond the executive summary of that report, and only a small number even looked at it.

Intelligence analysts wrote in the report that Iraq had continued its WMD programs and "if left unchecked, it will probably have a nuclear weapon during this decade," but they had faced obstacles in completing the assessment. The most important was that Saddam had expelled UN inspectors from Iraq in November 1997, so five years had elapsed during which Saddam could in theory have launched a personal Manhattan Project without anyone outside Iraq noticing. Given UNSCOM's skepticism of its own success, one might have expected that analysts in a Bush II administration would take seriously the possibility of a secret Iraqi program.

And because intelligence analysis is often inferential, especially in the absence of corroborative data, the fact that Saddam acted as though he had WMD fueled the belief that he really did have something to hide. There was also a natural preference to avoid risk—if you were an intelligence analyst and you judged, for example, that Saddam could strike Israel with nuclear weapons, but turned out to be incorrect, then no harm, no foul. If, on the other hand, you argued that Saddam had no nuclear weapons capability, and Iraq suddenly destroyed a U.S. ally with an atomic bomb, the consequences of getting it wrong would be quite severe. The success of al Qaeda's surprise attack—combined with the administration's conviction that Iraq was behind it—made a worst-case assessment the analysts' best bet.

In London, the compilation of what came to be known as the "dodgy dossier" documenting Saddam's active pursuit of WMD was underway. The security service tasked with compiling the dossier was instructed that "10 Downing Street wanted the dossier to be worded to make as strong a case as possible in relation to the threat posed by Saddam Hussein's WMD," virtually mirroring Bush's instruction to George Tenet and Colin Powell. The intelligence community on both sides of the Atlantic was being marshaled not for independent evidence-based assessments, but rather to market a preordained decision to go to war. As in the United States, a cluster of conjectures was proffered as proof. Blair insisted that "the assessed intelligence has established beyond doubt . . . that Saddam has continued to produce chemical and biological weapons, that he continues in his efforts to develop nuclear weapons."[25]

What Were They Thinking?

In November 2002, I was summoned along with several distinguished scholars of Iraq, and strategy more generally, to meet with Prime Minister Tony Blair at 10 Downing Street. On the other side of the table were Blair, Foreign Secretary Jack Straw, and Blair's right-hand man, Jonathan

Powell. Neither Straw nor Powell spoke during the hour and a half we were interrogated by Blair, who raised two primary questions: First, was regime change in Iraq a good idea? And second, would Iraqis be better off with Saddam or without him?

The answer to the first query was that Iraq was fundamentally unstable and that the sudden elimination of Saddam from the scene would unleash possibly severe intercommunal violence. Pursuing regime change in Iraq would therefore not be a good idea, at least in the short term. The answer to the second was, it depends on which Iraqis. Certainly, some would be better off, or at least see themselves that way, while others would be left worse off, some in the worst possible way. Suffering under tyranny is not distributed evenly. Blair responded with perhaps feigned incredulity, asking again if we thought that Iraqis would be better with Saddam than without him. Although the discussion dragged on, it never advanced beyond this pseudoanalytical nonquestion. Walking back to our offices from the prime minister's residence, we concluded that war was inevitable and not far off.

Nettled by the reluctance of the intelligence community to corroborate Iraqi complicity in 9/11, the White House set up an independent intelligence unit within the Pentagon under Douglas Feith, the undersecretary for defense policy, whom CENTCOM commander General Tommy Franks had labeled "the fucking stupidest guy on the face of the earth," to get to the bottom of the matter.[26] Feith's team tirelessly plowed through thousands of intelligence files but ultimately failed to make their case. Although at some point soon thereafter, Bush himself stopped pointing to Saddam as the mastermind of 9/11, Dick Cheney waited to do the same until 2006.[27]

The Quest for International Legitimacy

Intelligence on Iraq's supposed weapons of mass destruction was crucial because the administration was seeking the United Nations' blessing for invasion. Whether such a blessing was necessary, or even useful, was debated within the administration. The State Department, not surprisingly, assessed that the international—and to some degree domestic—legitimacy of regime change in Iraq would be buttressed by UN authorization. The Office of the Vice President and the Defense Department downplayed the value of legitimacy, a nebulous concept to begin with, insofar as perceptions of illegitimacy could not impede a U.S. assault, and because the exuberance of the liberated Iraqis would eclipse any prewar Security Council authorization for the use of force.

Nonetheless, Bush, perhaps recalling his father's administration's campaign for international approval for Desert Storm, concluded that the benefit of a UN Security Council authorization for war outweighed the risk that authorization might be refused, or accompanied by conditions that hampered U.S. freedom of action.

This was all good and well, but the Security Council would not recognize far-fetched claims about Iraqi complicity in the 9/11 attacks as relevant or valid. The case had to be made in terms of Iraqi noncompliance with UN demands, as expressed in UNSC resolutions. UNSCR 687, which the first Bush administration had elicited from the Security Council, demanded among other things that Iraq surrender its weapons of mass destruction and agree to the dismantling of infrastructure linked to WMD as well as intrusive inspections. Any successful appeal to the UN would have to be grounded in evidence of Iraqi disobedience.

On November 8, the Security Council approved Resolution 1441, which accused Iraq of being in material breach of UNSCR 687 and demanded Iraq's cooperation within thirty days in a renewed UN inspection effort, but without specifying penalties for noncompliance.[28] This was not quite good enough for the administration's purposes, which required a clear UN go-ahead for an attack if Iraq failed to comply within forty-eight hours. To wring this second resolution from the Security Council, a U.S. National Intelligence Estimate concluding that Iraq was working on WMD would be a good start, but it couldn't just be handed out in the UN in New York. It would require a strong performance, in the flesh, by an administration official with a reputation for integrity, experience, and caution. Looking at Bush's team, there was just one person who fit the bill: Secretary of State Colin Powell.

Powell Carries the Ball but Not Quite into the End Zone

Most of what is known about Powell's role in the inexorable march to war we know from Powell himself. The political skills that brought him to the nation's top military command a decade earlier had kept him in the public eye and made him a natural choice for secretary of state. He cultivated an image as the adult in the room: steady, deeply experienced, the architect of a miraculous feat of arms against Saddam in Desert Storm, but also the voice of restraint in counseling a swift end to hostilities and stanching the temptation to lay siege to Baghdad.

A year and half later, when the war was underway and the coalition effort was foundering, Powell used Bob Woodward to let the public know that, in fact, he'd always thought an invasion of Iraq would fail. Exploiting Woodward's technique of using unattributed quotations to give readers a "you are there" feeling, Powell was able to gut his adversaries within the administration and burnish his credentials as the mature one, without leaving any fingerprints.

According to Woodward, Powell had presented Bush with his Pottery Barn rule, warning Bush that if he broke Iraq, he would own it.[29] His message was that an invasion of Iraq might prove harder to manage than others in Bush's entourage believed, and simply walking away would not be a feasible option if things went wrong. Lawrence Wilkerson, an army colonel serving as Powell's aide, added that Powell had been unimpressed by the administration's WMD case against Iraq.

More recently, Powell unburdened himself to *The New York Times*

Magazine about his role.[30] It turns out that in the summer of 2002, Powell met with Jack Straw in Long Island to compare notes, agreeing that Bush had already decided on going to war and that Blair could not be trusted to steer Bush in a different direction. But the meeting produced no plan of action, apart from a mutual assurance that having lost the fight in their respective capitals, it was now their duty to stay at their posts to prevent further problems. "I'm sort of not the resigning type," Straw said. "Nor is Powell. And that's the problem."

It certainly was. Indeed, according to Straw, if Powell had resigned, he would have too. In the summer of 2002, had prominent members of the UK and U.S. cabinets left their posts in protest, the momentum driving war preparations likely would have slowed considerably as Congress and Parliament, as well as the media and public in both countries, grappled with the earthquake. This might well be only a surmise, but the moment was, nonetheless, a plausible point at which war might have been averted.

Powell had raised the Pottery Barn rule with the president shortly before the forlorn seaside chat with Straw, at a meeting of the war cabinet on August 5, which included Bush's first briefing on the war plan by Tommy Franks. Powell took the opportunity to share the gist of the State Department's view of the extreme complexity of the postwar challenges. "I told [Bush], 'Removing Saddam is the easy part,'" Powell said. "'You'll be the proud owner of 25 million Iraqis in 18 fractious provinces.'" Bush asked Powell, "What should I do?" This, in retrospect, was Powell's moment to recommend against going to war. He still had credibility with the president, who might still have been open to persuasion. But instead, he offered Bush technical advice about going to the UN before going to Baghdad, and left it at that.

Bush had a deep anxiety that the administration's UN case was inadequately linked to terrorism, which in Bush's view was what Americans cared about. Meanwhile, others debated the reliability of an Iraqi intelligence source, code-named Curveball, being run by the German intelligence service. Curveball had long been assessed by U.S. operatives as a fabricator, the CIA term for "liar," but the war hawks insisted on the credibility of Curveball's claims about an Iraqi biological weapons program that he had apparently just made up to impress his handlers. Iraqi water trucks were said to be chemical weapons decontamination vehicles. Vans were assessed to be mobile biological weapons production vehicles. Industrial tubes described as being manufactured to tolerances suspiciously higher than such tubes in the United States turned out to actually be machined to the same specifications as the American versions.[31] The CIA assessed that Iraq had 500 tons of chemical agent, but when asked to source the estimate, explained that the figure dated from 1991 and assumed that none of the contraband had been found and destroyed by UN inspectors.

Powell had his own intelligence chief, Carl Ford, mobilize his analysts to separate the wheat from the chaff. They did so in a crash project, concluding that there was essentially no wheat to be found amid the chaff. Declassified documents show that Ford's experts judged thirty-eight of the claims that the CIA presented to Powell as well supported were at best "weak."[32] Thus, when Powell told Barbara Walters in 2005, "There was some people in the intelligence community who knew at that time that some of these sources were not good and shouldn't be relied upon, and they didn't speak up. That devastated me," one would be entitled to judge two of his three claims as false and self-serving. People in the intelligence community did speak up, including Powell's day-to-day intelligence advisers, and there is no evidence that he was "devastated," a term generally understood to signify severe and overwhelming shock or grief.[33] Powell understood that the case for Iraqi WMD was nothing more than a haphazard jumble of uncorroborated reports, unfounded assumptions, complete falsehoods, and bad leads. Disinclined to blow the whistle or clash with the White House in private, he worked with Tenet to transform it into something that could survive scrutiny.

In the event, Powell's presentation impressed his American audience but failed to win over the Security Council to a second resolution giving Saddam forty-eight hours to turn over the weapons of mass destruction that were no longer in his possession. Although his argument, that a tight, firm deadline was necessary because Saddam was trying to run out the clock, appealed to some UN delegations, the Security Council as a whole was unpersuaded. The French reaction to Powell's speech was withering.[34] The German prime minister was no less forgiving.[35] And the secretary-general of the United Nations, the pro-American Kofi Annan, declared that the war violated international law.[36] Which party actually had the law on its side remains open to debate.[37] The main argument for illegality was the U.S. failure to exhaust nonviolent alternatives before launching the war[38]; the opposing argument was that the doctrine of self-defense permits "anticipatory" military action.[39] This was the weaker argument because it depended on the nature of the threat Iraq posed to the United States, and whether it was sufficiently imminent and serious to justify recourse to self-defense. And as was understood at the time by Powell's own intelligence analysts, this was not the case. Powell had pointlessly embarrassed himself. But the penalty was paid by others who had no say in the matter, as is usually the case when Washington's elite missteps. In this case, Powell retained his celebrity status, wealth, and influence. Democrats and Republicans in the years since remained eager for his endorsement and mourned his death in 2021.[40]

Bush Pulls the Trigger

By March 2003, with disputes over the war plan resolved, the State Department sidelined, forces deployed, war fever at home whipped up, British support assured, and Saddam apparently dithering, Bush was ready to begin the war he'd never explicitly decided upon.[41] Even the start time was impromptu. Tenet, believing he knew where Saddam was holed up, informed Bush that "we got the son of a bitch" at a rural location known as Dora Farms. Tenet's bluster was only half true. Saddam was a son of a bitch, but the CIA had no idea where he was. Bush ordered the start of hostilities moved up in order to launch an air strike on Dora Farms, which absorbed two 2,000-pound bombs and dozens of cruise missiles. There can be little doubt that the neighbors were shocked and awed. Saddam, however, was in Baghdad. That night, Wednesday, March 20, 2003, Bush spoke briefly to the nation from the Oval Office, saying, "On my orders, coalition forces have begun striking selected targets of military importance to undermine Saddam Hussein's ability to wage war."[42]

The war was over in three weeks. The speed of victory underlined the fact that Iraq had not been a threat to the United States. The administration nonetheless packaged the conquest of Iraq as a colossal achievement. On May 1, Bush landed on the deck of the USS *Abraham Lincoln*, an aircraft carrier. The bridge was draped in an enormous banner emblazoned with the words "Mission Accomplished," although these two words had been cut from Bush's subsequent speech by Rumsfeld, who was in Baghdad and already conscious of the difficulties U.S. forces had yet to face. Rather than chopper onto the ship, which was only thirty miles off the coast of California, Bush arrived on a jet in a dramatic arrested landing, which is when the incoming aircraft lands at a high speed and is snagged by a cable attached to the deck before it plunges off the other end of the carrier. Bush climbed out wearing a flight suit, as though he had piloted the plane, making quite an impression. A *Wall Street Journal* columnist and former Republican speechwriter wrote dreamily, "And there was the president, landing on the deck of the USS *Abraham Lincoln*, stepping out of a fighter jet in that amazing uniform, looking—how to put it?—really hot. Also presidential, of course. Not to mention credible as commander in chief. But mostly 'hot,' as in virile, sexy and powerful." The author, Lisa Schiffren, further noted, "You don't see a lot of that in my neighborhood, the Upper West Side of Manhattan."[43]

Bush Declares Victory

Bush's speech was an amalgam of disparate themes. Roughly half was about terrorism and al Qaeda, rather than the country he had just attacked. He stated:

> The liberation of Iraq is a crucial advance in the campaign against terror. We've removed an ally of al Qaeda, and cut off a source of terrorist funding. And this much is certain: No terrorist network will gain weapons of mass destruction from the Iraqi regime, because the regime is no more.
>
> . . . We have not forgotten the victims of September the 11th. . . . With those attacks, the terrorists and their supporters declared war on the United States. And war is what they got.
>
> . . . Any outlaw regime that has ties to terrorist groups and seeks or possesses weapons of mass destruction is a grave danger to the civilized world—and will be confronted.[44]

In another part, focused on America's love of freedom, Bush linked his administration to Roosevelt's and Reagan's, declaring that this generation had shown mettle comparable to the generation that destroyed Germany and Japan by advancing "across 350 miles of hostile ground, in one of the swiftest advances of heavy arms in history. You have shown the world the skill and the might of the American Armed Forces." As we will see, the invasion of Iraq was against virtually no opposition, with total air superiority and over flat terrain. For perspective, it might be useful to recall General George S. Patton's Order 70 issued to the Third Army in 1945:

> In the period from January 29 to March 22, 1945, you have wrested 6,484 square miles of territory from the enemy. You have taken 3,072 cities, towns, and villages, including among the former:

Trier, Coblenz, Bingen, Worms, Mainz, Kaiserslautern, and Lud-wigshafen. You have captured 140,112 enemy soldiers and have killed or wounded an additional 99,000, thereby eliminating prac-tically all of the German 7th and 1st Armies. History records no greater achievement in so limited a time.[45]

Bush allocated the rest of his speech to applause for shock and awe and the revolution in military affairs. In context, it was a discordant note. One explanation might be that the drafters wanted to highlight these tech-nical factors for U.S. adversaries listening to the speech, signaling that resistance would be futile. Separate but related was Bush's pride in the precision of U.S. weapons as a brake on noncombatant casualties. This is always worth pursuing, but Bush did not account for the damage already done to Iraqi civilians or the civilian casualties that the invasion was bound to cause in the coming years.

Perspective

In contrast to this stew of boastful swagger and crude threat—and in light of the Bush administration's insistent evocation of the Second World War—it is instructive that victory over Nazi Germany was telegraphed to Washington by General Eisenhower in just a single sentence: "The mis-sion of this Allied Force was fulfilled at 0241, local time, May 7th, 1945. [signed] Eisenhower."[46]

Without diminishing the courage, discipline, and competence of U.S. military personnel, which remain second to none, their defeat of Iraqi forces took little effort. My former colleague at the RAND Corporation, Stephen Hosmer, was commissioned by the air force to analyze the rea-sons for the virtually instantaneous collapse of Iraqi military forces. His book, which drew heavily on interviews with prisoners of war as well as Iraqi regime officials, is still the definitive treatment of the topic.

First, there was Saddam's "congenital optimism, excessive self-confidence, and poor understanding of international and military affairs." These traits combined to undermine Saddam's readiness to take steps that might avert a U.S. attack, such as agreeing to the inspections that had been demanded. Saddam didn't believe there would be a war, until it was too late. Even then, he assumed that a war would be waged from the air without a ground component and that, however terrifying the bombardment, it would be survivable. If the United States were to invade, Iraqi forces would still be able to bleed the intruders enough to force the United States back to the conference table, leaving the regime intact. Delusions abounded. Tariq Aziz, the Iraqi foreign minister who was fluent in English and knew something about the outside world, believed that the war would not happen because the Archbishop of Canterbury had preached against it.[47]

Saddam was also worried, as always, about internal security. Fears of a coup or subversion kept most Iraqi regular military divisions strung out along the border with Iran. Not even the penetration of coalition forces prompted Saddam to reconsider this positioning of his army. To prevent any single element of his military and security apparatus from rebelling successfully, he placed family and clan members in command of major formations and ensured that they reported to him through separate chains of command. Saddam kept his lightly armed palace guard within the capital, and distributed his elite Republican Guard armored and mechanized divisions in a circle around the city instead of combining them into a powerful maneuver force, thus leaving them vulnerable to defeat—one by one—by coalition units. Saddam himself moved constantly to avoid assassination, which made him hard to kill, as the failed strike against Dora Farms had shown. The downside was that it made coherent command and control of Iraqi forces, let alone the development of a cogent defense plan, impossible.

Further weakening Iraq's defensive capability, Saddam apparently never went through with scorched-earth tactics that might have been expected, such as laying mines, blowing up bridges, or flooding terrain essential to the coalition advance. Saddam's groundless conviction that the coalition attack from the south toward Baghdad was a mere feint and that the real thrust would come from the north via Jordan led him to order key units away from the fight, clearing the way for the invaders.

The invaders, moreover, utterly outgunned the Iraqi army. The defenders had plenty of heavy weapons and other gear, but it was obsolete and no match for U.S. forces, which fielded state-of-the-art armor and tank crews with finely honed gunnery skills. The defenders also had no protection against the onslaught from the skies above. Making the confrontation even more lopsided was the mutually reinforcing effects of inadequate training and incompetent leadership. Per Hosmer:

The central reason for the lack of Iraqi resistance in [Operation Iraqi Freedom] was the Iraqi military's extremely poor motivation and morale. Events showed that the vast majority of the officers and troops . . . mostly deserted their units before being engaged by Coalition ground forces. *In the course of the march up to Baghdad, U.S. ground forces rarely confronted cohesive enemy units of even battalion size.* When major combat ended, not a single organized Iraqi military unit remained intact, because all the Iraqi troops that had survived the war had "self-demobilized" by going home.[48] (Italics added.)

In a nutshell, the best armed forces in the world took on those among the worst in the world, whose troops had mostly gone home before the fighting started, and won.

The War after the War

U.S. control of the situation quickly unraveled as locals began looting government ministries. Over the course of three weeks, Iraqis stripped over half the state ministry offices down to the studs. The equipment was the first to go, then the furniture, and finally the wiring and pipes behind the walls. The employees, if they were not among the looters, were elsewhere waiting for the storm to blow over. This burst of mayhem was a sign of things to come.

For those who might later have wondered what Donald Trump's adviser, Steve Bannon, meant when he urged the end of the "administrative state," a close look at Iraq following the U.S. invasion would be clarifying. Even after a decade of sanctions, Iraq was still an administrative state, in the sense of having a budget, a government to execute it, and a bureaucracy to deliver services. On the day before the U.S. assault, this apparatus was working, if only in a fitful, creaky, and ineffective way. The steadily rising prevalence of corruption was a reliable indicator of the decline of government services, which in part was a by-product of economic sanctions. Nonetheless, the structure existed. The instantaneous decapitation of the Iraqi government by the United States simply blew away the government's administrative capacity to carry out basic functions, while the occupying army had no ability or resources to replace what it had destroyed. The result was anarchy.

When a population is precipitously deprived of a central government authority, it will begin to look elsewhere for the security and support it needs to survive. This search for security will begin with family and extend to wider circles of trust. The resulting market for suppliers of these goods is the ultimate free trading arena, attracting entrepreneurs, often with guns, who are happy to replace the local order that had disappeared along with the state. The market naturally breaks into segments along ethnic or sectarian lines, in part because the security entrepreneurs bill themselves in these terms to secure a share of the overall market for order amid chaos. It's a question of branding. As this process evolves, society as a whole begins to split along sectarian or ethnic grounds as well. The occupiers, who knew very little about politics and society in Iraq, observed this restructuring of Iraqi society and concluded wrongly, though understandably, that Iraq had always been a hopelessly divided country. A more accurate assessment would be that Iraqi society had been largely integrated, particularly in Baghdad and its environs, and it was the U.S. invasion and decapitation of the regime that set sectarianization in motion. The entry of the United States was the equivalent of an asteroid colliding with the earth.

Clueless in Baghdad

In 2002, when I was assigned by the State Department to a London-based think tank, a colleague and I convened a meeting of top Iraqi scholars living in Europe, by choice or necessity, to explore the likely impact of an American invasion. For funding, I approached an old friend working in Rumsfeld's office, offering to share the findings of our project in return for support. The response was negative. My contact explained that an expression of interest by the Office of the Secretary of Defense would be tantamount to an admission that the secretary did not know what he was doing. Support was eventually provided by another agency via the U.S. embassy in London, but that agency was pushed aside in the rush to war and had no influence on the management of post-conflict policy.

Willful ignorance proved persistent. As the *Washington Post* Baghdad bureau chief Rajiv Chandrasekaran described in his fine book on the occupation, the government set up by the United States, known as the Coalition Provisional Authority (CPA), was jammed with Republican Party loyalists whose only qualification was a political connection to the Bush campaign. For the most part, they knew next to nothing about the Middle East, Iraq, or military operations. Their presence squeezed out career U.S. officials with deep experience, if not in Iraq, then elsewhere in the region.[49]

The United States did not have diplomats in Iraq from 1991 until 2003, so direct knowledge of Iraqi politics and governance in the intervening years was largely unavailable, apart from information gleaned by UN inspectors, aid workers, Iraqi expatriates in the Gulf and Jordan, or foreign diplomats. Even the most well-meaning appointees seemed to be disconnected from reality. When I was asked in the winter of 2004 to serve as an aide to the new Iraqi national security adviser, Dr. Mowaffak Baqr al-Ruba'i, I politely declined, pointing out that I was Jewish and that my ethnicity could prove controversial just as the first post-Saddam Iraqi administration was trying to get its sea legs. Though there were Jewish American diplomats in Iraq at that point doing useful things involving intensive day-to-day interaction with Iraqis, such as managing one of the U.S. provincial reconstruction teams, none had the visibility that would accompany a U.S. aide to al-Ruba'i. The reply to my refusal illustrated the depth of the challenge facing the United States. I was told that I did not understand that we were dealing with a new Iraq, where such religious distinctions no longer mattered. Upon reading this message, my unspoken thought was that we were in for serious disappointment.

The CPA was headed by Jerry Bremer, who had served as an aide to Kissinger while he was in the foreign service and then briefly helmed a new counterterrorism office at the State Department, before retiring from government and landing at Kissinger Associates as an international business consultant. Bremer was undoubtedly chosen because, in addition to being camera ready, even a bit Kennedy-esque, he had a reputation as a good manager and ultra-smooth diplomat. Regardless, the job unfortunately required both more managerial savvy and diplomatic finesse than he possessed.

It was also true that when Bremer was asked to replace Jay Garner, the down-to-earth, plainspoken, and unphotogenic retired major general who'd been handling reconstruction, Iraq still looked like it might be a success story. Bremer's expectations might therefore have been unrealistic. His lack of adult supervision compounded the problem. His position was made answerable to the Secretary of Defense, rather than to State or the White House, and Rumsfeld lacked the interest and patience to oversee the myriad technical, organizational, logistical, and political problems that inundated the CPA. The military did its job and got rid of Saddam. It was time, in his view, to move on to other things. Thus, there was no check on Bremer's impulsive management style.

Bad Decisions

In his single year as head of the CPA, Bremer made three serious mistakes that, taken together, destroyed whatever chance the United States might have had to stabilize Iraq. The first was his decision to divvy up Iraqi ministerial portfolios along ethnic and sectarian criteria, a system known as muhasasa tai'ifiya, or sectarian apportionment system,[50] on the advice of Iraqi expatriates who had cultivated U.S. sponsorship between the Gulf wars. It had the effect of enshrining sectarian division as an ordering principle for Iraqi politics. By validating a sectarian order—and in doing so, compelling Iraq citizens to interact with a government structured along these lines—Bremer's decision reinforced the sectarian dynamic in the street, where security entrepreneurs, or, more bluntly, warlords, were brutally taking control. Ethnic and sectarian political leaders took advantage, starting with Shiites, whose chief cleric, Ayatollah Sistani, set up an electoral list, followed by Kurds with their list, both trailed by the Sunni-flavored nonsectarian "national" list. There were, therefore, no political parties, as in Western democracies, but ethnic and sectarian blocs pursuing their own particularistic agendas.

During this period, the interagency process in Washington appears to have concurred in a proposal to de-Baathify Iraq. This was yet another peculiar reflection of the administration's view of the war as being on the scale and significance of the defeat of the Third Reich. In that earlier era, the United States and other Allied powers occupying Germany determined that German society would have to be de-Nazified before a successor German state could be trusted with the responsibilities of governance. Since the Nazi Party explicitly embodied the perverse ideals of annihilationist anti-Semitism, operated the Gestapo and the SS, oversaw the concentration camps, and had a prominent role in furthering Hitler's goals, the occupiers rightly concluded that party members should be excluded from the administration of a new Germany.

The phenomenon of states ruled by both a party and a "real" government was not all that rare in the twentieth century. In the Soviet Union and the People's Republic of China, for example, the communist parties shared in the rule over their respective societies. In Germany and Italy, fascist parties operated similarly. This mode of control had an impact on thinkers and activists in the Middle East, where two Syrians, a Christian and a Muslim, founded the Baath, or "Renaissance," Party, which evolved as a tool for popular mobilization and implementation of government policies. Its main branches were in Iraq and Syria. In both countries the dictatorial regimes that ultimately seized power, the Assads in Syria and Saddam Hussein in Iraq, had used the Baath Party as their ticket to ride to power. In the process, these rulers drained the Iraqi and Syrian Baath parties of influence and power, as they did to the rest of civil society in their countries, but retained the parties as a kind of Potemkin organization to which all loyal Iraqis or Syrians were expected to affiliate.

U.S. occupiers disregarded these facts about Iraqi politics and the role of the Baath in the Iraqi state. Bremer and his colleagues' identification with the Greatest Generation, battling the worst evildoers ever to stalk the earth, led them to confuse the vacuous and forlorn Iraqi Baath Party with the Nazi Party's coercive apparatus. It was only logical therefore that Iraq be de-Baathified. Bremer, moreover, wanted to arrive in Iraq with a bang. As he put it in his instructions to the CPA, "It is desirable that my arrival in Iraq be marked by clear, public and decisive steps. . . . These should reinforce our overall policy messages and reassure Iraqis that we are determined to extirpate Saddamism."[51] But there was no such thing as Saddamism, nor did the Baath have much to do with Saddam's ungentle approach to rule.

De-Baathification, in practice, deprived tens of thousands of ordinary Iraqis who had no influence whatsoever on the government in Baghdad, no role in the suppression of dissent, and no command responsibilities in the armed forces, of their livelihoods. It was as though the United States, through its senior-most official in Baghdad, had decided to follow through on decapitating the regime by dismantling whatever administrative capacity still existed and creating, by the stroke of a pen, an enormous class of destitute workers in an unstable, poverty-stricken country whose infrastructure had been destroyed by bombing and mass looting. This was the second of Bremer's blunders.[52]

The trifecta was completed by Bremer's unilateral decision, uncoordinated with the U.S. government as a whole, to disband the Iraqi army.[53] Military planners had been worried for months before the invasion that the number of U.S. troops deployed for the war would be too small to control events on the ground once the Iraqi army had been defeated.[54] It was understood, at least by the command staffs, that the sudden evaporation of government authority would release unruly behavior, much of it lethal. The Pentagon therefore baked a role for the Iraqi army into the plan for securing civil order upon the elimination of Saddam's government by coalition forces. The idea was that U.S. authorities would tell Iraqi soldiers to return to the barracks, or simply go home, and await their recall to active duty. In the meantime, they were to be paid and assured of their prewar status.[55]

These troops would then be mustered by the CPA to carry out civil affairs duties, including enforcement of law and order and reconstruction. This approach had been briefed to the president on March 12 by Doug Feith, who was in charge of postwar planning,[56] and blessed by the president, Rumsfeld, Powell, Rice, and the commanders on the ground.

It made a lot of sense. As the briefing framed the issue: "Cannot immediately demobilize 250K-300K personnel and put on the street."

On May 22, Bremer wrote to Bush outlining his plan to dismantle Saddam's "military and intelligence" structures. Bush apparently approved without inquiring too closely. At the NSC meeting the next day, Bremer announced that he was immediately going to disband the Iraqi army. No one around the table had evidently heard anything about this, apart from the president, who had already agreed. This fact in itself would be a conversation killer at an NSC meeting. Bremer's later weaselly claim that no one at the meeting complained should therefore be dismissed. Powell was not even in Washington; the ground commander in Iraq, the chairman of the Joint Chiefs of Staff, and the CENTCOM commander, as well as the army chief operations officer, had been completely in the dark. General Abizaid, the CENTCOM commander, later pointed out that Arab regimes maintain large armies in part to purposely keep potentially rebellious unemployed young men off the street. The notion of letting them loose in Iraq was crazy. But Bremer played his hand well, in terms of narrow bureaucratic gamesmanship, by going offline to the president, otherwise keeping his intentions secret, and disclosing the plan at an NSC meeting as a fait accompli to clueless colleagues. The situation was just a small sample of how the Pentagon and the Office of the Vice President ran the entire war effort.

This foolish maneuver also failed to account for Saddam having distributed weapons caches throughout the country (perhaps to arm an insurgency, though there is no evidence that Saddam had planned for one). So, not only did many soldiers return home with their service weapons, but there were also large stockpiles of guns and ammunition within easy reach of most towns. And even if the Iraqi army was not the most competent, its members at least knew how to operate a weapon, how to aim it, and, after May 23, at whom to point it.

Where's the Exit?

As street violence escalated and the awkward mix of CPA political hacks and career specialists tried to get Iraq up and running again, a debate began among senior officials that would pulsate over the next four years. At root was the question, How soon can we get out of here? It was not just competence that was in short supply. There was a scarcity of the sustained interest and commitment the situation demanded. On the ground commander's part, this was comprehensible. The military was assigned to the task of destroying the Iraqi army and toppling Saddam. It had succeeded admirably. The administration from which the military took its orders had made the decision to keep the invasion force lean and mean, and to withdraw it once its mission was accomplished. Yet here they were, suffering from whiplash as the command was told to redeploy from Iraq and then back into Iraq. The military was once again stuck with a stabilization mission, which it had not expected, was not trained for, and was too few in number to carry out effectively.

Over the first five years of the occupation, violent civilian deaths, not including deaths due to the shattered health-care sector, climbed steadily from 13,887 in the first year, cresting in the fourth year at 30,571, and totaling to 92,614 in year five. These deaths should be thought of as adding to the large numbers killed in the first Gulf War and by the sanctions imposed in the interwar period. The numbers would grow considerably when civil war returned to Iraq in 2014.[57] The number of U.S. troops killed in action during this period rose as well, starting from 315 in the actual invasion and immediately afterward, to 713 in 2004, 673 in 2005, 704 in 2006, 764 in 2007, and 221 in 2008. Nearly 32,000 were wounded in battle, many grievously so.[58]

In that first year, the U.S. military commander, Lieutenant General Ricardo Sanchez, was by all accounts in over his head; an appropriate if unfortunate match for Bremer, who he hated. This was the moment that U.S. military strategy in Iraq took shape. Army and Marine Corps units were congregated in large bases from which they would sortie out to conduct sweeps of MAMs—"military age males"—and, where the armed resistance dared to fight, to pulverize it. There was, at that stage of the war, little conception of it as a counterinsurgency. As the insistent analogies with the Second World War and emphasis on shock and awe would suggest, the war was seen not as a hearts-and-minds-winning endeavor carried out using selective force and a lot of economic assistance, but rather as a no-holds-barred fight against a brutal state, its die-hard defenders, foreign fighters there to challenge the new Shiite-dominated dispensation and its American enablers, and the Shiite militias eager to consolidate their position in the new order.

Exemplary Errors

There were landmarks amid the carnage. In March 2004, rebels in the city of Fallujah in Anbar province captured four contractors who were guarding food convoys to U.S. bases. They tortured them, set them on fire, and dragged them through the streets before hanging the charred corpses from a bridge trestle. This atrocity capped an escalating series of confrontations between protestors and the American troops that had been inserted into Fallujah in 2003 despite the calm that prevailed there after the invasion. The display of mutilated corpses left the command in Baghdad with little choice but to respond vigorously, which it did in two successive sieges that eventually leveled about 60 percent of the city.

As Fallujah was being subdued, *60 Minutes* broadcast an April 2004 segment covering the abuse of Iraqi prisoners at Abu Ghraib, a Saddam-era prison about thirty kilometers west of Baghdad.[59] Television coverage was supplemented by work by the investigative journalist Seymour Hersh in *The New Yorker* magazine.[60] The excesses were documented by the perpetrators themselves, who photographed one another mistreating the prisoners. Some, though not all, of the torment could be classified as torture. The very idea of the United States invading Iraq, inflicting a great deal of damage to liberate the country from Saddam's rule, and then packing his most notorious prison with young men caught up in indiscriminate sweeps only to be abused by American soldiers was hard to fathom.

Even the Bush administration understood that these incidents undermined U.S. credibility. Rumsfeld allegedly offered to resign, since the prison system was a military responsibility, but he was nonetheless retained. As one might expect, the commander of Abu Ghraib, Brigadier General Janis Karpinski, who had repeatedly warned her superiors of problems at the prison, was demoted and vilified, while her immediate superiors went on to desirable commands back home. The administration's objective was to establish that the scandal was an isolated event, triggered by the irresponsible local commander of an out-of-control military police battalion and unrelated to the underlying gap between policy and the resources provided to carry it out.

The Mailed Fist

A year and a half later, in November 2005, U.S. troops operating in Haditha, a farming town in northwestern Iraq, killed twenty-four civilians, including women and children. The provocation was the loss of a fellow marine the previous day.[61] At this point, Lieutenant General George Casey had been in command of U.S. forces in Iraq for six months. His objectives, which were set by the White House, were twofold. First, his forces were to kill terrorists; second, he was responsible for the creation of an Iraqi army capable of providing security for Iraq against threats from within and without, so that U.S. forces could withdraw. The first task was straightforward and, with a few exceptions, executed with gusto by Casey's division commanders, especially Ray Odierno of the 4th Infantry

Division. The approach, by and large, was that of the mailed fist. Rules of engagement, that is, guidance regarding who can be shot and under what conditions, reflected this tough approach to the objective. They were also quite confusing. The rules of engagement were continually revised in a piecemeal fashion to reflect new and unanticipated ambiguous situations. These revisions came too often and too quickly for army lawyers to pause and issue an up-to-date, comprehensive set of rules. As a result, few units ever really knew precisely what the latest legal determinations were, or whether their unit's information was current.

The prevailing uncertainty about legitimate targets in tactical situations that could be hair-raising for both Americans and Iraqis led many units to embrace a "shoot first and ask questions later" approach to their patrolling. Commanders, taking their cue from the top, prized aggressiveness while avoiding casualties of their own. The result was a high civilian death toll, which tended to undercut whatever tolerance U.S. forces could elicit from the population. One commander quoted by Thomas E. Ricks, the chronicler of the war, trotted out an old axiom to the effect that he wanted ordinary Iraqis to fear his troops more than they feared the insurgents.

Despite some temporary local exceptions to this approach, Casey, with Washington's backing, stuck to it, while internecine violence and attacks against U.S. troops increased. The exceptions proved important. In Tel Afar, a small city in northwestern Iraq, the brigade commander, Colonel H. R. McMaster, applied a more selective, balanced strategy in 2005 to win trust and isolate jihadists from the population. David Petraeus followed a similar plan in the larger northern city of Mosul. McMaster and Petraeus subsequently emerged as advocates of a new strategy that would abandon Casey's treatment of Iraq as "Injun country" controlled by a network of Fort Apaches.

However, by mid to late 2006, it was becoming clear to some in Washington that the U.S. occupation of Iraq was destined for catastrophic failure.

The Iraq Study Group, a blue-ribbon commission headed by James Baker, George H. W. Bush's secretary of state and Reagan's treasury; Lee Hamilton, a Democratic representative with foreign policy credentials; and assorted other luminaries of both parties, summarized it as follows:

> Attacks against U.S., Coalition, and Iraqi security forces are persistent and growing. October 2006 was the deadliest month for U.S. forces since January 2005, with 102 Americans killed. Total attacks in October 2006 averaged 180 per day, up from 70 per day in January 2006. Daily attacks against Iraqi security forces in October were more than double the level in January. Attacks against civilians in October were four times higher than in January. Some 3,000 Iraqi civilians are killed every month.[62]

The demolition in February of the tenth-century Shiite al-Askari shrine in the city of Samarra, just ninety miles north of Baghdad, was correctly seen by most observers as the starting gun of a civil war. But the realization of impending doom among Washington decision makers was slow in coming. Policymakers are all too human, hardwired to discount facts that conflict with their preconceived ideas and quick to assign outsize significance to information that supports their fantasies. In 2006, the administration accentuated the positive. There had been two elections, one with strong turnout; Bush had, at least in his own mind, bonded with his Iraqi counterpart, Nouri al-Maliki, an old-fashioned Shiite chauvinist; Saddam Hussein had been captured and subsequently executed—Bush kept Saddam's pistol as a trophy in his private study—and U.S. forces were killing a good many terrorists, including the al Qaeda kingpin Abu Musab al-Zarqawi, who died following an air strike on his safe house northeast of Baghdad in June 2006. At the same time, however, the country had slid from rioting, rampant crime, and a wave of assassinations into civil war, with the United States caught in the middle.

The Search for Solutions

The trend might have been obscure to policymakers, especially Bush and Cheney, but it was perfectly clear to outsiders. On the one hand, there was the Iraq Study Group, which concluded that the situation was simply irretrievable, a powerful statement by the tattered remnants of a once-dominant foreign policy establishment. The group's conclusion resonated with the public mood and the administration's own instincts.

On the other side, there was a small, tightly knit group of neoconservatives at the American Enterprise Institute (AEI), a right-wing think tank, to whom the Iraq Study Group were defeatists whose prescription was simply to cut and run. To some extent, the underlying dispute was about the nature of American reputation and credibility, which both sides agreed were central to the deterrence of U.S. enemies. For the old guard, the risk to reputation would increase, perhaps dangerously so, if the U.S. remained committed to an unwinnable war. The shadow of Vietnam haunted them, even though the U.S. loss there had little effect on its credibility in the final years of the Cold War. The best course was to declare victory and pull out.

On the right, it was thought that reputation would best be preserved by leading the new Iraqi government to victory in the civil war, or at a minimum stanching it, in order to give Iraqi politicians the breathing space they needed to govern fairly and effectively. Even those who favored quickly extricating the U.S. from Iraq asked whether it was possible to cut and run with your pants around your ankles. The neocon group believed, not unreasonably, that the kind of recovery they hoped for would be impossible without more troops on the ground.

Under ordinary circumstances, think tankers have only limited influence on the party in power. But these were not ordinary circumstances. The analysts at AEI found a partner in Jack Keane, a recently retired four-star general, former vice chief of staff of the army, and decorated combat veteran. Forceful, articulate, and well-connected, Keane united these advocates of an increase in the U.S. force presence with counterinsurgency experts to formulate a new strategy for the Iraq war. The issue for the group was not solely a troop increase, but what the additional troops would actually do.

Their answer was to kill terrorists without detaining or killing others, protect the population against predatory groups, deal with Iraqis as though they were human beings with inherent dignity, and channel resources to the population to improve quality of life. This was classic counterinsurgency doctrine as conceived by the French and British in their colonial wars and subsequently learned the hard way by U.S. forces in Vietnam. But for the U.S. Army, Vietnam was like a first marriage you can't bear to think about. The field grade officers from that era had spent the next fifteen years restoring the Army and Marine Corps to their stature before the Fall. U.S. ground forces still consisted of the heavy formations that had combined firepower and mobility to grind its adversaries to powder from the Civil War under Ulysses S. Grant to World War II under George S. Patton. This was the army that had ejected Iraq from Kuwait in 1991, during which H. R. McMaster, then an obscure young officer, staged what then seemed like the last tank battle likely to be fought. But the vast tank armada that swept across the Iraqi desert in 1991 was a coda, rather than prelude. And it certainly was not the ideal force to cope with an Iraqi civil war fought largely by lightly armed insurgents in cities and towns.

The army as an institution was reluctant to revert to a counterinsurgency mission. To be sure, this disdain was driven by an officer corps committed to the way of war they had trained for, the tools they had mastered, the doctrine they had absorbed. But it also derived from a belief that the U.S. military should be optimized to fight powerful enemies possessing the industrial and technological prowess of the United States and capable of supplanting its hegemonic position. To that end, ground forces perfected for counterinsurgency operations would be the wrong ones when push came to shove. "Big Army" was therefore unlikely to favor Keane's campaign for change, at least in the Iraq war zone. Casey, who had little choice but to continue plowing the same furrow, refused to talk to Keane.

Keane, as it turned out, didn't need the ranking army bulls. He had made inroads at the White House while making effective use of officers he had mentored during his long career who were now generals themselves. It was a classic squeeze play. One of the officers he had promoted was David Petraeus, who after two tours in Iraq had been assigned to Fort Leavenworth, where he oversaw the production of the army's new counterinsurgency manual. Petraeus's biography is well known, but it's worth underscoring his uncommon intelligence, ambition, discipline, and sheer physical endurance. To some degree these qualities are shared by all soldiers who achieve four-star rank, as Petraeus ultimately did. Yet most are not promoted for their imagination. Indeed, researchers at West Point have concluded that promotion boards "penalize officers for conceptual ability."[63] Petraeus was an exception to the rule.

Keane and his allies in the West Wing, especially the national security adviser, a straightforward lawyer named Stephen Hadley, prodded Bush to acknowledge that the U.S. effort in Iraq was sinking fast. Public support for the war, especially in the wake of the November 2006 midterm elections that put the Democrats in charge of Capitol Hill, could no longer be propped up by talking points about light at the end of the tunnel. The situation called for actions, not words. The result was the "surge."

The Surge

In December, Bush approved the deployment of more troops to Iraq. Demonstrating his tendency to blame others for his mistakes, he surprised Casey in a videoconference by coldly denouncing what he implied was

Casey's strategy rather than the strategy set forth by the White House years earlier. Shortly thereafter, he fired Casey, who was given a soft landing by the army as chief of staff, cut Rumsfeld loose, nominated the ubiquitous Robert M. Gates as secretary of defense, and named Petraeus as the new commander in Iraq; Ray Odierno, who underwent a miraculous conversion to the counterinsurgency faith, was made his deputy. Under new management, the Pentagon found an additional five brigades for duty in Iraq. On January 10, 2007, the surge was announced by Bush in a speech delivered at the White House.

This bold maneuver is widely thought to have been a turning point in the war. Five years later, Petraeus, then a civilian who'd resigned from the CIA in momentary disgrace for supplying his mistress with classified information, explained to readers of *Foreign Policy* "How We Won in Iraq."[64] The claim that "we won" is problematic, considering the distance between the outcomes and the objectives of the U.S. effort.[65] But the objectives were unclear once Baghdad fell to U.S. troops and evolved during the course of the war. What is true is that after a sharp two-year spike in U.S. and Iraqi casualties—as was inevitable once 30,000 additional troops entered the fray and were deployed throughout neighborhoods in cities and towns across Iraq—the overall level of violence did decrease.

What might have happened without the surge is unknowable. What is knowable is that the space the surge was supposed to provide for the emergence of effective and democratic Iraqi government was not used for this purpose. As Iraq scholar Toby Dodge recounts in his book *From War to Authoritarianism*, the surge, against the backdrop of invasion and occupation, made Iraq safe for a corrupt, undemocratic ruling elite in Baghdad.[66]

Surge enthusiasts point to the alleged mobilization of the Sunnis of Anbar province, a resistance stronghold, against al Qaeda. There is some truth to this claim, inasmuch as Petraeus was shrewd enough to offer financial and tactical assistance to a movement that had been underway prior to the surge, and to label it "Sons of Iraq," a snappy phrase suffused with the scent of patriotism. The Anbar Awakening, as it was also called, was actually an attempt by local tribes to expel Sunni extremists they had previously welcomed; in effect, the surge commanders inadvertently armed the tribes against the state. The surge also coincided with the final stages of the ethnic cleansing and forced migration of Sunnis by Shiite militias from much of Baghdad, the completion of which would likely have lowered levels of violence regardless.

The end of surge operations signified the end of the war. A depleted Bush administration signed a Strategic Framework Agreement with the Iraqi government in 2008, which mandated the departure of U.S. troops from Iraq in 2011. Iraqi governments would continue to flounder through the next two U.S. administrations, torn between Washington and Tehran, unable to control national territory, shot through with corruption, and incapable of providing basic services to the Iraqi people.

The Freedom Agenda

Two other elements of the Bush administration's Middle East program remain to be addressed: The Freedom Agenda, or "Forward Strategy of Freedom," and the Middle East peace process. Neither of these initiatives was consequential, but they were both promoted by the administration as if they were, and both reflected a baseless conception of the United States as exceptionally influential, at least during Bush's two terms.

In 2003, even as his team was trying to decide what to do with the 68,000 troops then based in Iraq, Bush gave a speech in which he sounded startlingly like a Middle Eastern conspiracy theorist. "Sixty years of Western nations excusing and accommodating the lack of freedom in the Middle East," he admitted, "did nothing to make us safe. . . . As long as the Middle East remains a place where freedom does not flourish, it will remain a place of stagnation, resentment, and violence ready for export."[67]

Of course, for the past several decades, the United States' closest significant other in the region had been Saudi Arabia. During this long stretch of time, no one would have mistaken the Kingdom for a place where freedom flourished, either in terms of democracy or the liberty of women, gay people, or religious minorities. On the other hand, the political opposition was largely to the right of the Al Saud. They objected to elite corruption but believed the cure lay in stricter enforcement of Islamic law by the state and a larger role for clerics in policymaking. The United States could have urged the Al Saud to open up the political system to accommodate critics, but it is at best unclear that this would have yielded a Kingdom more in tune with American values.

In Egypt, a repressive government was tolerated because it kept the peace with Israel, was essential to the rapid movement of U.S. fleets from the Mediterranean to the Pacific Ocean during the Cold War, and, in the following years, was an avid hunter of jihadists. Yet, throughout the Arab world, the United States tried for years to leverage its military and economic relationships to improve the human rights situation in problem countries while spending money to spread the practical knowledge local democratic activists needed to push for reform. Nonetheless, the opposite became the stump speech for the administration. In 2005, Condoleezza Rice, as secretary of state, told an audience in Cairo, "For 60 years, my country, the United States, pursued stability at the expense of democracy in this region here in the Middle East—and we achieved neither. Now, we are taking a different course. We are supporting the democratic aspirations of all people."[68] One thing was clear. The administration identified stability as the problem and labored mightily to fix it.

In defense of the administration, democratic peace theory, a set of ideas put forward by Immanuel Kant, an eighteenth-century German moral philosopher, and taken up by twentieth-century American political theorists, was then at the height of its influence. According to this theory and a great deal of statistical evidence, it seemed that democracies did not go to war, at least against other democracies, meaning that more democracy would lead to less war. It was also thought that democracy favored development: rule of law was essential to impartial enforcement of contracts, which was good for business; a free press ensured transparency of government policymaking and limited corruption; and universal suffrage gave everyone a stake in the system. Inevitably, there would be exceptions to these general rules, but on the whole, democracy, in Winston Churchill's words, might well be "the worst form of government, except for all the others."

Yet there were serious objections to democratization as a policy objective.[69] The most obvious was that since the occupation of Germany and Japan, democracy had not been successfully imposed by force of arms. And in the cases of Germany and Japan, there was no long history of foreign domination; instead, both countries had experienced periods of democratic government, even if those experiences were short-lived and unlike the American version of democracy. Iraq, in contrast, had historically been ruled by foreign empires, including the Mongols and, for five hundred years, Ottoman Turks. Between World War I and 1958, it was ruled by Great Britain through royalty imposed on Iraq by politicians in London. At no time was Iraq able to develop a robust constitutional order or experiment with democracy as a political way of life. And since 1980, Iraq had been at war with either Iran or the United States—not the conditions that favor the emergence of popular rule and embrace of civil liberties. Even if the U.S. efforts to implant democracy had been competent, the ground was too stony for the flower to take root.

Is Democracy in the Middle East a Good Thing for the United States?

Then there was the more fundamental problem of the compatibility of democracy and U.S. interests. There was abundant, relatively reliable polling that showed democracy and Islam being compatible as far as Muslims were concerned. Their eager participation in elections bears this out—voter turnout in free elections in the Middle East often surpasses turnout in Western countries, especially the United States. And when Arab opinion of the United States is surveyed, majorities or pluralities say they admire American democratic political institutions. On the other hand, majorities everywhere in the Arab world at that time were quite clear about their extremely unfavorable views of American policies, particularly those that affected Arab interests.[70] To critics of democratization as an American goal, it seemed clear that while the result might be good for Arabs, it would be less so for Washington's regional strategic interests. Skeptics, especially among Middle East scholars and old diplomatic hands, also believed that authoritarian resilience and strength would inevitably triumph over the zeal of reformers, who could be coopted, jailed, or killed if they crossed the line.[71]

Bush was generally careful to link democratization to U.S. security. In his view, terrorism of the sort that led to the nightmare of 9/11 was the product of autocratic rule and poverty. Thus, terrorism could be eliminated by democratization, which would solve the problem of autocracy and the thwarted desire of Arabs for a political voice, while improving economic development. Bush's beliefs were, as usual, strongly held, hazy, and disconnected from reality.[72] The U.S. government's own data from this period showed clearly that most terrorist attacks took place within democratic countries. This is still true—the vast majority of terrorist attacks in the United States are carried out by domestic opponents of the prevailing order, mostly on behalf of white supremacy.[73] For the most part, terrorists were irredentists, separatists, or social revolutionaries for whom Western-style democracy was not radical enough. There was little direct evidence to suggest that the 9/11 attackers, let alone their terrorist counterparts in Europe or South Asia, were launched on the warpath by poverty.[74]

Like many of the ideas that shaped Bush's policy choices, his notions about the roots of Muslim radicalism were both strange and easily checked, if he had had the necessary curiosity and intellectual energy. For instance, the nature of suicide terrorism was clearly established among terrorism experts. A now classic 2003 study had shown that a key driver of terrorist self-sacrifice was foreign occupation, rather than economic hardship or even religion.[75] If the White House had been paying attention, there might at least have been some preparation for the terrorist bloodbath that the invasion and occupation would unleash.

Underpinning Bush's pitiable quest to be the avatar of freedom were the twin convictions that power automatically conveyed influence and that everyone's view of freedom was identical. Both views were mistaken, or mostly so. Force can coerce or even compel, but influence hinges on the power to persuade.[76] This power, in turn, depends on conceptions of shared interest, the presence of affinity groups in the country the United States is trying to influence—that is, groups that are legitimate in the eyes of their compatriots and which have favorable views of the United States—and a degree of mutual trust. Not one of these conditions applied to the U.S.-Iraqi relationship. Power therefore could reasonably be expected to intimidate a ramshackle and demoralized Iraqi army, but was not going to influence Iraqi perceptions of the United States or views on how best to run their own country. As far as Arabs were concerned, the invasion of Iraq could be satisfactorily explained by Washington's desire to rid the world of Israel's enemies and to seize control of Middle Eastern oil. From this perspective, American justification of the war as an altruistic exercise, a gift of freedom, was not going to buy much influence.

The majority of Middle Easterners do, like most people, want freedom, the ability to organize themselves without foreign interference and in a way that meets their needs and desires. These do not necessarily correspond to American formulas, especially since Americans themselves hold

vastly different, even antithetical, conceptions of democracy and freedom.[77] During the COVID pandemic, many Americans defined freedom
as the right not to wear a mask; at other times, freedom meant the ability
to refuse to provide goods and services to same-sex couples. Other Americans believed that these were not rights at all and that they negated the
very meaning of the term. These differences were not trivial. The dispute over masks is assessed to have killed hundreds of thousands of
Americans.[78] These deep societal divisions have shaped the history of
the American republic virtually since its inception; they were, in fact,
deliberately exploited by Republican strategists to engineer Bush's own
narrow electoral victories. The glib assumption that there was anything
like a singular American conception of freedom, and that it must somehow be the object of Arab yearning, reflected the Bush administration's
intellectual incapacity and moral vacuity. There was simply no reason to
expect everyone in the Middle East to agree on fundamental things that
we could not agree on at home.[79]

Democracy for Egyptians?

Apart from Iraq, the forward strategy of freedom focused on two developments. One was in Egypt, where then president Hosni Mubarak had
locked up Ayman Nour, an appealing political rival of the sort one could
imagine getting elected to Congress by a progressive district in the United
States. From Washington's perspective, he personified the kind of non-
threatening, youthful, secular-leaning, and pro-Western instincts that
would favor incremental reform and, not incidentally, preserve U.S. influence in a post-Mubarak era. Condoleezza Rice had endorsed his pursuit of office as a gentle prod to Mubarak to undermine revolutionary
sentiment by opening the political sphere to a new generation of moderate politicians. Mubarak was rather less impressed and pointedly arrested

Nour despite Rice's protests, forcing her to cancel a planned trip to Cairo.[80] (Nour was eventually released, after the charges against him were discredited, but was defeated by a member of Mubarak's security service in a race to keep his seat in the National Assembly.)[81] Bush, however, nonetheless deserves credit for the relatively free parliamentary elections in 2005, in which the Muslim Brothers got 20 percent of the seats.

The other battleground for freedom was Palestine. In June 2002, as plans to invade Iraq began to solidify, Bush made a peculiar speech about the Israel-Palestine conflict, advancing a groundbreaking claim of U.S. support for Palestinian statehood, while stipulating conditions that no one thought the Palestinians could meet in the foreseeable future, if ever.[82] Bush's paradoxical remarks revealed his clashing instincts. On one hand, there was a genuine, if shallow, sympathy toward Palestinians under occupation. On the other, there was the belief that democracy and good governance, as he viewed them, were the indispensable prerequisites to independence. His preoccupation with democracy was linked to his analysis of 9/11, which had rendered terrorism as the ultimate sin and hatred of freedom and dearth of democracy as its main causes.

There could be no doubt that the Palestinian Authority established during the Clinton administration under the Oslo Accords was not a democracy. The head of the authority was still Yasir Arafat, who ran the government as a private fiefdom; even if he was not the initiator of terrorist attacks against Israel, he certainly did little or nothing to stop them. The al Aqsa intifada that had begun toward the end of the Clinton administration was snowballing. Ariel Sharon, who was elected prime minister of Israel in February 2001, was intent on crushing the revolt. On May 18, he authorized the use of F-16 fighter bombers against the densely packed Gaza Strip; the following year was marked by escalating reciprocal violence between Israel and Palestine.

When Hamas attacked a Passover seder and massacred twenty-eight celebrants, for Sharon and an enraged Israeli public, enough was enough.

The IDF entered the West Bank, besieged Arafat in a bunker and his fighters in a church in Bethlehem, and fanned out, moving into cities assessed as safe havens for Palestinian gunmen. On May 7, Palestinian militants struck again, this time in Rishon LeZion, a sizable coastal city just south of Tel Aviv, killing sixteen and wounding fifty. Three weeks later, Israel began building a security barrier intended to seal off the West Bank. Two days afterward, a Palestinian suicide bomber attacked a bus in Jerusalem, killing sixteen passengers.

Such was the backdrop to Bush's speech. The coda came shortly afterward in the shape of a 2,000-pound bomb dropped by an American-made F-16 onto the Gaza apartment building occupied by Salah Shehada, the Hamas military commander. Shehada was killed, but so were his wife, daughter, and thirteen others, who were judged later by an Israeli investigative commission to have been uninvolved in military activities.[83]

The speech was part of a pattern—of enthusiasm for initiatives that the administration subsequently failed to tangibly support—in Bush's first term. In 2003, the administration promoted a peace plan with a "Road Map" beginning with "ending terror and violence, normalizing Palestinian life, and building Palestinian institutions," to be completed in May 2003; followed by a six-month transition period "focused on the option of creating an independent Palestinian state with provisional borders and attributes of sovereignty"; then a final phase scheduled for 2005, when the parties would reach a "permanent status agreement and end of the Israeli-Palestinian conflict."[84]

Implementation of the plan would be supervised by the Quartet, consisting of the United States, EU, UN, and Russia. The Quartet was headed by a series of heavy hitters, including James Wolfensohn, former head of the World Bank and world-class fundraiser for the Palestinians, followed by Tony Blair, the former British prime minister, also exceptionally well-connected to the deep-pocketed Davos elite. Although the Quartet made some technical progress during this period, the ongoing uprising and the administration's distraction by escalating strife in Iraq combined to stymie progress on the Road Map.

Divisions within the administration also hampered any advances. Although Rice thought the issue was important, as did Powell, they were outweighed and outfought by Elliott Abrams of the NSC, who was influential on Capitol Hill and among neoconservatives more generally. I met with Abrams during this period to discuss how the RAND Corporation was compiling practical things the Palestinians would need to accomplish to maximize prospects for a successful state. Abrams was cordial but told me that the planning effort was pointless because, as he put it, there would not be a Palestinian state. He knew what he was talking about.

The Sharon government, in the meantime, was working on a plan to rid itself of responsibility for Gaza and freeze the peace process by unilaterally withdrawing from territories, rather than negotiating departure, which would sidestep demographic worries and render irrelevant negotiations about things that Israel did not wish to negotiate, such as the status of Jerusalem, the refugee problem, and borders. But for Hamas, the withdrawal created new room for maneuver. This would turn out to be a lingering, bloody problem.

The transition from Bush's first term to his second had seemed to promise a more effectual approach to the peace process. Rice was now the secretary of state, Abrams was sidelined, though not out of the picture entirely, and Cheney was less able to push Rice around now that she was a cabinet member. Moreover, her former deputy Steve Hadley was now national security adviser, giving Rice a direct line to the adjoining square and oval offices in the West Wing.

Bush, however, was still president, hence the mismanagement of the two Arab-Israeli crises and single initiative of his second term. In December 2005, Sharon, obese and in poor health, had the first of two back-to-back strokes, which took him out of action. (Sharon died in 2014, having been in a coma for eight years.) In April 2006, the cabinet officially removed the comatose prime minister from power and replaced him with Ehud Olmert, a career Likud politician who was adaptable, pragmatic, and intelligent but lacked Sharon's charisma and authority. Bush was facing cyclonic violence in Iraq, the failure of CENTCOM's strategy and, at home, the aftermath of Hurricane Katrina, which destroyed much of New Orleans in August 2005. This disaster was compounded by the administration's botched response and Bush's apparent cluelessness regarding the extent of the damage and the operations of his own government. Olmert and Bush were not the ideal duo to deal with Arab-Israeli troubles.

Israel and the United States Accidentally Place Hamas in Charge of Gaza

For Bush, the Freedom Agenda pointed to a way forward in Palestine. The United States would fund the second-ever Palestinian elections; the plan was that Palestinian moderates would trounce Hamas, push it aside in Gaza, and ultimately unify Palestinian parties under a banner of nonviolence and accommodation with Israel. Democracy experts had discouraged the push for elections because balloting benefits the better organized rather than the more moderate parties, but the fact that successful elections had been held in Iraq under challenging conditions and polling had indicated Palestinians' preference for Fatah, the moderate party, imparted unwarranted confidence in both Washington and Jerusalem.

When the elections were held on January 25, 2006, and hailed by expert observers as free and fair, Hamas won by a landslide, winning 74 of 132 seats in the Palestinian legislature. Over the course of the next year, a discredited Fatah lost control of Gaza to Hamas, dividing Palestine into two opposing parts, politically and geographically.[85] The elections had strengthened the violent faction Washington sought to subdue and made Washington's trusted Palestinian ally into a joke. When I asked the NSC official responsible for the policy that led to elections what he had been thinking and whether he was happy with his enemy's victory, he doubled down, insisting that despite appearances to the contrary, the result was desirable because it would eventually expose Hamas for the evil that it was.

Another Lebanon War

Having inadvertently humiliated Mahmoud Abbas, the Fatah Party leader, and made a negotiated solution to the Israel-Palestine conflict exponentially harder to achieve, the administration confronted its second crisis. On July 12, 2006, Hizballah foolishly skirmished with an Israeli patrol, killing some soldiers and capturing others. Their objective was to trade prisoners for four detainees in Israeli custody.

Olmert, as the untested successor to a war hero and esteemed strategist, was motivated to prove himself by hitting hard and chose to attempt to clear Hizballah from southern Lebanon. The air force and navy destroyed thousands of Hizballah missiles and launchers in the first twenty-four hours of the war before turning to infrastructure, first to impede the movement of reinforcements to the south and to trap Hizballah fighters already there, then on to critical facilities, such as power plants, to put pressure on the Lebanese government. When Hizballah persisted in launching rockets at Israel, Olmert ordered a ground invasion.

It was clear that Israel could not win, in the sense of destroying Hizballah's infrastructure, weapons stocks, and strong political influence from Beirut down to the Israeli border. And there was no hope for a successful blockade of Lebanon that would prevent Iran from replacing Hizballah's losses as long as Syria, which controlled Lebanon's longest border, was at odds with the United States and Israel.

Given these inescapable realities, prolonging the war would be strategically pointless as well as a humanitarian disaster. Bush's conception of diplomacy as a tool of the weak and use of force as the universal solvent led him to egg Olmert on rather than restrain him, and to undermine UN efforts to mediate a cease-fire until Olmert himself had had enough. The course of the conflict severely damaged Olmert politically. At one point, he was Google bombed: if the phrase *kishalon harutz*—"utter failure"— was typed into the search field, it would lead to the prime minister's office website.[86] Israel had brought its full might to bear on Hizballah but failed to achieve its objectives. By surviving the onslaught, a reckless Hizballah, responsible for many civilian casualties given its deliberate deployment among noncombatants, was able to declare victory.

Yet Another Last-Minute Harpoon
Launched at the White Whale

As Bush entered the last phase of his presidency, the Quartet was still at work and Palestinians and Israelis were trying to hammer out bits of the road map without the United States in the room. The administration came up with an idea for a conference, which they referred to as a "meeting" to differentiate the gathering from the failed conferences staged by previous administrations, notably at Madrid under George H. W. Bush and Camp David under Clinton.

The striking thing about the meeting, which ultimately took place at the U.S. Naval Academy in Annapolis, Maryland, was that it succeeded in attracting the participation of nearly every significant Arab state on a take-it-or-leave-it basis. Relatedly, it foreshadowed the approach that Bush's Republican successor would adopt in terms of its underlying notion that an Israeli-Palestinian peace agreement would have to be underwritten by regional Arab states. As the idea evolved, it was as though such an agreement would not be with the Palestinians but with those Arab states, who would be responsible for upgrading Palestinian living standards until its politics matured enough to make a peace agreement viable. Despite the mostly vacuous rhetoric that enveloped the meeting, it did kick off a process, but one that was left to drift by a listless, hands-off administration.

There is little doubt that Olmert and Abbas were committed to reaching an agreement. Olmert had already publicly endorsed the establishment of a Palestinian state and declared that Israel would be prepared to make "painful" concessions toward that end. As his thirty-six meetings with Abbas unfolded—and as his deputy Tzipi Livni's talks with Ahmed Qurei, Abbas's negotiator, progressed—he made a number of meaningful commitments, including giving the international community authority over the Holy Basin, the awkward term for the physical area encompassing Christian, Muslim, and Jewish holy sites.[87]

However, Olmert had been an unpopular leader. The inconclusive Lebanon war and subsequent blue-ribbon commission damning his leadership was one factor in his failure to consolidate power. He also slipped up in a response to the Iranian president's apparent call for Israel's destruction by inadvertently referring to Israel as a nuclear weapons state, a status that Israel has never officially acknowledged, prompting calls for his resignation.[88] It was allegations of corruption, for which he was convicted and sentenced to prison, that ultimately brought him down.[89]

In this version of history, the peace process collapsed because of avoidable contingencies, just when Israelis and Palestinians were finally willing to strike a deal. With Olmert announcing his departure from his party's leadership in anticipation of indictment, Abbas was understandably reluctant to agree to a pact negotiated with an Israeli prime minister on his way out, especially since not everything had been nailed down. Olmert's reluctance to record his territorial offer on a map for Palestinian (and American) scrutiny, for fear of a leak in Israeli media, did not help matters. Ultimately, the only map was one sketched by Abbas on a dinner napkin in mid-2008, based on one Olmert showed him but would not hand over.

The role of the United States would normally have been to provide bridging proposals. Apart from pointing the way toward compromises that the parties might have missed, such proposals offered the parties the opportunity to claim that concessions were forced on them by Washington, leaving leaders on both sides fireproofed against accusations that they had willingly abandoned cherished positions.

But the administration offered no such clever expedients to either party, apparently on account of Bush's belief that it was not his role to provide them and, in any case, that the United States could not want peace more than the parties. Peace process orthodoxy gives pride of place to diplomacy. Most of the participants are professional diplomats, and others function as such even if they are not foreign service officers. Diplomacy itself is a process. Sometimes the process is understood to be the purpose, as when the parties are too far apart to reach agreement, but incremental gains made in apparently futile talks are seen to constitute a basis for progress should the objectives or context change, or simply as a way to keep from coming to blows. At other times, the parties share a perception that agreement is possible but blocked by differences over relatively minor matters. In that situation, there is a premium on diplomats' tactical skills to finesse sticking points, paper over problems, get to yes. If the Olmert-Abbas talks were of this species, Bush's and Rice's resistance to getting their hands dirty by intervening with the bridging proposals devised by their peace team was inexplicable and tragic in its implications.

Was this the case? With the history written by the diplomats and the archives not yet open, it's hard to say. The primary sources are the participants themselves, and they seem determined to protect their reputations, or to defend the positions they embraced at the time. In January 2011, there was a large-scale leak of Palestinian documents dating back to Oslo, including minutes recorded by Palestinian notetakers.[90] Although their release was initially thought to have incinerated the reputations of Abbas and his chief negotiator, Saeb Erekat, a careful reading reveals a

Palestinian negotiator generally trying to be creative within the broad outlines of Palestinian policy and confronting a somewhat inflexible Israeli counterpart.

On balance, outsiders cannot judge whether the parties were close to a final deal that would have been reached had Washington only pitched in. My own sense, given the rightward drift of Israeli politics in this period, the lingering impact of the al-Aqsa uprising on Israeli opinion, and the broad popularity of Benjamin Netanyahu's later rejection of Obama's attempt to revive the peace process, is that Olmert could not have made his concessions to Abbas stick. They were too good to be true. And in the case of borders, too good to be shared for the record. Whether Abbas came to this conclusion or, as a political matter, could not strike a bargain while Israeli forces were operating Gaza, or thought he would get a better deal from succeeding Israeli and American leaders, remains unclear.

Daniel Kurtzer, the diplomat who headed the U.S. embassy in Israel during this period, concluded:

> The story of the Bush administration's approach to the peace process in the Middle East is fundamentally a saga of missed opportunities and inadequate preconceptions that left the prospects for peace far weaker when Bush left office. . . . For their inability to mesh power with diplomacy effectively, the president and his administration bear significant responsibility.[91]

Why the Poor Results?

The attacks of September 11 might not explain Bush's failures in the Middle East, but they do partly account for why the administration found itself in over its head. The situation called for a cool head under fire, a capacity to perceive shades of gray, a good listener who, unlike Bush, would not keep Saddam's Glock 18 in his White House study because "he really liked showing it off" and "was really proud of it."[92]

The al Qaeda 9/11 attacks must be seen in the context of the U.S. entanglement with Iraq, which originated with George H. W. Bush. If the United States had either opted for diplomacy and sanctions back then or gone all the way to Baghdad, Saddam Hussein would not have come up on the radar before the dust had settled in lower Manhattan. And if the elder Bush had dealt with Iraq in 1991 as he did, but the younger Bush had not become president, surrounded by his father's defense and foreign policy team, Iraq would not have come into Washington's gunsight.

Some would go further and argue, as in this book, that had the United States not deployed 500,000 soldiers to the Kingdom of Saudi Arabia in 1990–91, Osama bin Laden would not have decided upon attacking the United States. The role of accident is truly striking. Had, for example, Al Gore's legal team been more adept or aggressive, he might have won Florida and become president; there is no one who believes that Gore would have responded to 9/11 by invading Iraq.

The Beginning of the End

In 1956, Great Britain under Prime Minister Anthony Eden invaded Egypt, with the objective of forcing the ouster of Gamal Nasser, the country's popular leader. The mission failed. Britain was humiliated. Upon Eden's death, his 1977 obituary in *The Times* (London) acidly observed, "He was the last Prime Minister to believe Britain was a great power and the first to confront a crisis which proved she was not." Although U.S. power in the early 2000s far exceeded Britain's might a half century earlier, one could easily substitute a few words and have a crisp summary of George W. Bush's role in the Middle East and beyond. When the crisis of 9/11 erupted, Bush believed the United States was the greatest power on earth and would sweep all before it. Acting on this belief, he lost wars in Iraq and Afghanistan and killed, or caused to die, hundreds of thousands of people. Karl Marx, paraphrasing Engels, wrote that world events repeat themselves, the first time as tragedy, the second time as farce.[93] Comparing Britain's effort under Eden in 1956 to exert control over the Middle East with Bush's in 2003, the first was the farce, while the second was the tragedy.

CHAPTER SIX

BARACK H. OBAMA

Live and Learn

Don't do stupid shit.[1]

—PRESIDENT BARACK OBAMA,
COMMENTING ON MILITARY INTERVENTION

You know, the strategy that was crafted in Washington didn't always match up with the actual threats that were out there. . . . You make things a little bit better . . . and that's in no way a concession to this idea that America is withdrawing or there's not much we can do. It's just a realistic assessment of how the world works."[2]

—BARACK OBAMA

Barack Obama was unlike George W. Bush in nearly every respect, beyond background and worldview. Obama was the self-made man that Bush was not, even if Bush promoted himself as the archetype of the rugged independent wildcatter and oil millionaire. One will always wonder, although probably not deeply or for very long, whether things would have worked out quite so well for Bush if he had not sprung from a dynasty of millionaires embedded in a network of powerful politicians.

Obama's parents were itinerant academics. His father was Kenyan by birth, his mother American. Despite persistent Republican claims, championed initially by Donald Trump, that Obama was not a citizen, he had in fact been born in Hawaii and was a citizen by birth. Just as Bush had been endowed with ancestral wealth and powerful connections, Obama had been bequeathed exceptional intelligence, capacity for hard work, and notable self-confidence. He parlayed these qualities into an academic career in Chicago and then, via grassroots organizing, into Illinois politics and then the U.S. Senate and the presidency in 2008.

Obama entered office just as the Great Recession of 2008 was erupting, thanks to the cynical business practices of banks that had been progressively deregulated in the years since Reagan took office in 1981. Bush, on the other hand, had entered office with a tailwind of record growth and a distinctly favorable strategic environment. Whatever initial ambitions Obama might have had in the realm of foreign policy were instantly compromised by the need to stanch the recession before it became a full-blown depression. *The Onion* headline reporting Obama's election victory—BLACK MAN GIVEN NATION'S WORST JOB—seemed particularly apt.[3]

The economy was at the precipice. By the end of 2009, 20 million jobs in construction, real estate, financial services, and the auto sector disappeared. Between December 2007 and October 2009, the U.S. unemployment rate rose from 4.9 percent to 10.1 percent; including marginally attached workers, part-time employees, and discouraged workers who simply dropped out of the labor market, total unemployment was estimated to be 16.3 percent. Real GDP fell 4.3 percent between the last quarter of 2007 and the summer of 2009, the steepest drop since the end of World War II. Home prices fell approximately 30 percent and the S&P 500 index fell 57 percent in just six months, from October 2007 to March 2008. The net worth of U.S. households and nonprofit organizations shrank by 8 percent from $69 trillion in 2007 to $55 trillion in 2009. This was a shattering blow, and it was Obama's job to soften it and pave the way toward recovery in the face of Republican deficit hawks and inflation fear-mongering. He succeeded.[4]

But he had to fight every inch of the way against a political opposition for whom "the single most important thing we want to achieve is for President Obama to be a one-term president," as majority leader Mitch McConnell clarified for those who hadn't gotten the message by 2010.[5] Apart from the prospect of an economic apocalypse, the new president was intent on devising a program to widen access to health care and then getting it through a Republican gauntlet backed by the medical and insurance industries. According to Hillary Clinton, secretary of state in Obama's first term, "Obama basically said, 'You know, we've got this major economic crisis that may push U.S. into a depression. I'm not going to be able to do a lot to satisfy the built-up expectations for our role around the world. So, you're going to have to get out there and, you know, really represent U.S. while I deal with, you know, the economic catastrophe I inherited.'"[6]

Nevertheless, Obama did have several foreign policy objectives that he hoped to achieve in his first term. The first was to pull U.S. troops out of Iraq on the timetable negotiated by George W. Bush. The second was to put the U.S. approach to the region on a different footing, emphasizing his administration's departure from regime change as America's modus operandi. Setting the stage for a return to Israeli-Palestinian negotiations was a third. Blocking Iran's path to a nuclear weapon was the fourth and most ambitious goal. Overall, it was not an unreasonable agenda, but in December 2010 the Arab Spring was ignited by the self-immolation of a Tunisian vegetable seller. The ensuing convulsions across the region led to a U.S.-backed invasion of Libya, regime change and an Islamist government in Egypt, civil war in Yemen, and an ill-fated U.S. intervention in Syria that triggered Russian involvement. The Iranian role in Syria in turn made the pursuit of a nuclear deal with Tehran more difficult by spurring opposition in Congress to any agreement with the Islamic Republic.

Meanwhile, the U.S.-Israel relationship was transformed by the open alliance of the Republican Party and the Israeli government. These developments were capped by the murderous emergence of the Islamic State first in Iraq, then Syria. The chaotic intensity of Obama's first term led to a narrow focus in the second on finalizing a nuclear agreement with Iran and beating back the Islamic State.

Settling the Settlements Problem

Obama was determined to put a tougher U.S. stance against Israeli settlements at the center of the peace process. He may have been freer to do so in part because there were no peace process professionals in the West Wing to tell him it would probably not work. This was not necessarily a bad thing; the triumph of hope over experience can lead to bad outcomes, but so can the triumph of experience over hope. In this instance, the White House chief of staff, Rahm Emanuel—judged by *The New York Times* in 2009 as "perhaps the most influential chief of staff in a generation"— believed that it could and would work.[7] Emanuel's father had been a member of the Irgun, the right-wing Jewish militia that flourished in British-ruled Palestine. His uncle had been killed by Arabs in 1933. Emanuel himself had spent two weeks on an Israeli military base in 1991 as a kind of volunteer cum tourist. He and others seemed to feel that this pedigree would fireproof him against charges of anti-Zionism or pro-Palestinian bias. In one meeting shortly after Obama took office, Emanuel told officials responsible for Middle East policy that the United States would compel Israel to concede to the administration's demands regarding the settlements question. As he told *New York* magazine, "We were enunciating twenty-plus years of U.S. policy. The difference was we weren't just lip-synching it."[8]

Israeli settlements in the West Bank had been established shortly after the IDF ejected Jordan from west of the Jordan River during the Six-Day War of 1967. A combination of messianic zeal and practical military thinking led to a fairly rapid expansion of the settlement enterprise. When Obama took office in January 2009, the settler population was over 478,000, about 40 percent of whom were living in East Jerusalem, the sector of the city that had been in Jordanian territory until the 1967 war, or in suburban enclaves clustered along the old cease-fire line. The rest lived in settlements scattered throughout the West Bank.[9]

Settlements have complicated the task of negotiating an agreement by populating parts of the West Bank so densely with Israelis, especially ultra-Orthodox Israelis, over such a long period of time that the return of these conurbations to Arab sovereignty has become hard to imagine. They are also problematic because they disrupt the contiguity of Palestinian land; the various bits of Palestinian territory are separated from each other by areas that are settled by Israeli Jews.

Contiguity is vital to Palestinian economic growth: the need to go through multiple checkpoints introduces delays that cause produce to spoil while necessitating the duplication of assets and infrastructure in areas that are cut off from one another. If Palestinian refugees were to return to a new Palestinian state, demographic pressures and the need for consolidated territory would naturally be greater.

Every American administration has opposed settlement activity, usually relying on a rhetorical formula combining the concepts of illegitimacy—the fourth Geneva Convention forbids occupying powers to transfer their own population to conquered territories—and unfairness, since settlement activity prejudged negotiations by simply taking land that was meant to be bargained over.

Despite the failure of Bush's Road Map to foster progress, it did make clear that settlements were a problem that had to be tackled if the process were ever to advance.[10] Although Israeli public opinion was increasingly divided about the settler movement, many Israelis saw it as the embodiment of a pioneering spirit that was central to Israel's national myth as their country became more urban, wealthy, and consumerist. By this time, the settler population was large enough to influence national elections.

Worlds Collide

Attention now turned to Benjamin Netanyahu's first trip to the United States in his second stint as prime minister. In the May 18, 2009, meeting, Obama proposed that Netanyahu order a halt to all settlement activity to pave the way for renewed negotiations with the Palestinians. Obama's request took Netanyahu completely by surprise. After leaving the Oval Office, the prime minister walked down the hall to Vice President Biden's office, where, according to one of the staffers there, he had turned "completely white." He paced around as though caged in Biden's smallish office, repeating rhetorically, "How am I supposed to do this!? I can't do this!" The avuncular Biden did his best to calm the agitated Netanyahu, but there was little the vice president could say. A settlement halt was what the president expected.[11]

Netanyahu's next stop on the trail of tears was Congress. With the Senate in Democratic hands, the White House had been able to coordinate in advance with the informal Israel caucus on the settlements issue, as well as with American Jewish community leaders in an ongoing process. Domestically, there was little if any pushback. Settlements were just hard to defend.

Obama followed through in his Cairo speech on June 4, 2009. "Israelis," he said, "must acknowledge that just as Israel's right to exist cannot be denied, neither can Palestine's. The United States does not accept the legitimacy of continued Israeli settlements. This construction violates previous agreements and undermines efforts to achieve peace. It is time for these settlements to stop."[12]

Netanyahu's Countermoves

Pointing to opposition within his cabinet on the right, Netanyahu said that he might be able to compromise, if Obama were to get an important Arab state, such as Saudi Arabia, to take a public step toward recognizing Israel and give him the political cover to do Obama's bidding on settlements. Involving the Saudis looked like a delaying tactic meant to put the onus on Obama, but it was framed as a good-faith effort to cooperate, so Obama told his aides that he would go directly from Cairo to Riyadh to convey the Israeli request.

The trip was a fiasco. The Saudi monarch was unreconciled to a Jewish state in the Middle East and skeptical about Netanyahu's ambitions. Obama was an unknown quantity who had opted to use their first encounter to flack for Netanyahu. Saudi diplomats had warned off their American counterparts, but to no avail. Obama's requests were modest—a Saudi trade office in Israel, or overflight rights for commercial aviation headed toward Israeli airports from Asia—but in "the context of the king's perception of Israeli treatment of Palestinians, these minor concessions looked like a cosmic betrayal of Palestinians and a stain on the honor of the al Saud."[13]

This episode got relations between the new administration and the Saudi leadership off to a bad start, and the sourness never really seemed to dissipate. The results of the meeting had strengthened Netanyahu's hand since Obama had failed to deliver, while alienating a potential ally in Saudi Arabia. Obama had been played.

When Obama took office, the old verities with Saudi Arabia applied. There was a brief convergence of interests as the administration imposed tougher sanctions on Iran, but the Saudis saw Iranian support for Bashar al Assad as a threat about which the United States was doing nothing. Tensions began to seep into the relationship. Obama was personally disdained by the Saudis, and he was unconvinced of the Kingdom's strategic importance to the United States. When the United States—and then other countries—began to negotiate a nuclear agreement with Iran instead of further intensifying sanctions or attacking Iran militarily, the Al Saud concluded that there was no point to working with Obama. Better, in their view, to wait for a Republican.

Biden Tries to Reassure Netanyahu

In May 2010, Obama threw a Hail Mary pass, sending then vice president Joe Biden along with former senator George Mitchell to reassure Israel of the U.S. commitment to its security and to start a round of proximity talks, in which Mitchell would shuttle between Jerusalem and Ramallah, the capital of the Palestinian Authority on the West Bank, in the hope of prodding the two sides to meet directly before the ten-month partial freeze on settlements, which had been grudgingly negotiated, expired. While Biden was pledging the administration's "absolute, total, unvarnished commitment to Israel's security," the Israeli interior ministry announced that 1,600 new housing units would be constructed in Ramat Shlomo, an ultra-Orthodox settlement that abuts the Palestinian towns of Shuafat and Beit Hanina north of East Jerusalem.[14]

Given Biden's status and his diplomatic mission, the insult was remarkable. Netanyahu assured Biden that construction, if it did happen, would not begin immediately. Biden had little alternative but to accept this, but as one prominent Israeli columnist wrote, "To wipe the spit off his face, Biden had to say it was only rain."[15]

Back to Basics

In Netanyahu's Oval Office meeting, his condescending posture toward Obama was widely noted by the media and commentators. In part, this was aimed at a domestic audience that relished the spectacle of an Israeli leader humiliating an American president, but it was also a reflection of Netanyahu's deep personal disdain for Obama.

For Netanyahu, it was not just Obama's approach to technical policy questions that was bad for Israel. There was something deeper. As a Black American, Obama had his own narrative of oppression and dispossession. Even as an elected president, Obama was derided as a charlatan who was merely pretending he was an American citizen, and was condemned as failing to love the country he falsely claimed as his own. Israelis grasp that their claim to American support rests largely on our sympathy for the suffering of diaspora Jewry and the sacrifices Israelis made to create and defend a state in a hostile region. Many seem to believe, wrongly in my view, that a president with his own people's history of enslavement and discrimination—based on its color—will be less than impressed by the tribulations of Jewish history and thus less inclined to wholehearted support for Israel. This is one reason why Trump was universally popular in Israel, while Obama was viewed with suspicion.

Ross's End Run

Dennis Ross, in the role of mature overseer for the NSC Middle East office, was pursuing a separate effort he believed would produce a breakthrough.[16] He began to meet in London with his Israeli counterpart, Isaac Molho, and with Hussein Agha, a Palestinian academic based in Britain, to draft a set of principles that would serve as the basis of an Israeli-Palestinian final status accord.[17] The idea was to generate the document outside of the three governments, but with the knowledge of the leaders of all three parties. If the negotiators came up with an agreed text that was quietly blessed by the leaders, it could be introduced into whatever lumbering, official peace process maneuvers were taking place at the time and lead to a relatively rapid resolution of the conflict.

But it quickly became clear that the Israeli and Palestinian negotiators were mismatched and neither of them had any reasonable expectation of their work ever being recognized by their respective leaders. Ross's welcome in the Oval Office seemed to wane as time went by. One of Ross's carefully cut and polished rhetorical gemstones was about "the Two Bibi's." There was the Bibi who understood that a two-state solution was essential to a prosperous, secure, and democratic future for Israel, but there was also the Bibi who was still in thrall to dreams of a territorially "greater Israel" and disinclined to take risks for peace. In Ross's analysis, the United States had to strengthen the first Bibi while working overtime to help overcome his more cautious instincts. By the early fall of 2011, Obama seems to have concluded that there was in fact only one Bibi and that it was the second.[18]

Gluttons for Punishment

Despite the lack of progress, in Obama's second term thoughts returned to whether to resume the peace process. In early December 2012, there was a small, informal meeting in the Situation Room, in which White House and senior State Department officials discussed whether it was time for yet another whale hunt. For a negotiation to produce results, the power of the presidency had to be brought to bear. Given the uncertainties involved and the president's other priorities, was another round of peace talks a sensible investment of the president's scarce time and perishable credibility? Despite the skepticism voiced by participants in the meeting, the decision was to try again.[19]

Obama gave the job to John Kerry, who deputized Martin Indyk, the author of dual containment, to carry out day-to-day talks with Israel and the Palestinians. It was a dismal phase in a fading process. Kerry's style of personal diplomacy, which meant that there was no U.S. notetaker at pivotal meetings with Netanyahu, led to confusion and accusations of bad faith. Deadlines for a Palestinian return to the table came and went while Kerry and Indyk were stuck in a frustrating loop, trying to keep Israel committed to a temporary and ambiguous settlement freeze while the Palestinian side dithered. Proposals to keep Netanyahu on board ranged from releasing Jonathan Pollard, the Israeli spy, from prison to providing the Israeli air force with a squadron of the newest U.S. fighter aircraft off the assembly line. Kerry dragged out these negotiations, which neither of the parties wanted, until nearly the end of Obama's term in office. Failure led to recrimination. At the end of 2016, Obama instructed the U.S. UN delegation to abstain from voting on a resolution condemning Israeli settlements (as well as Palestinian transgressions), rather than voting against it. For the Israelis, this was a perfidious act, which reinforced the appeal of the incoming Trump administration.

The Arab Uprisings

Beginning in December 2010 with a popular revolt in Tunisia and the flight of its longtime kleptocratic ruler, a succession of uprisings tore through the region. A generation of scholars and diplomats imbued with a belief in the "robustness of authoritarian rule" were taken by surprise. Their broad thesis—apparently shattered by the turbulence in Tunisia, Libya, Egypt, Yemen, Syria, Iraq, Bahrain, Jordan, and Lebanon—had been that state and society in these countries had struck a so-called authoritarian bargain. Under this informal arrangement, governments would guarantee a modicum of employment, basic services, and security, and in exchange the population would forgo the kind of political participation that might undermine the control enjoyed by ruling elites. When states failed to live up to their side of the deal, they had security services to quell disorder resulting from popular resentment. Often, these states also forged strong ties to outside powers, especially the United States and, before 1989, the Soviet Union, that could be relied on to provide the resources necessary to ensure domestic security.

With the fall of the USSR, counterterrorism cooperation slowly replaced the Cold War structure of alliances. After 9/11 and Bush's insistence that countries were either with the United States or against it, Middle Eastern authoritarians were happy to define their domestic opposition as terrorists and lay claim to American funds, intelligence, equipment, and political support.

The late 1980s and 1990s had been tough on Middle East economies that had no significant oil revenues to fall back on. Incessant international pressure to liberalize their economies widened the gap between rich and poor in these countries, reduced subsidies on staples, increased unemployment, and cut investment in basic infrastructure. Authoritarian rulers therefore leaned more heavily on coercion and depended on the United States to finance it. Because these rulers had the arms and the apparent willingness to use them, most observers believed that nothing could change.

For reasons that are still debated, in the early 2010s, mass demonstrations broke out across the region despite the risk of state violence. In two cases early on, Tunisia and Egypt, the hated leaders were quickly toppled. Angry people elsewhere must have assumed that the same could happen in their own countries. Moreover, the security forces in Tunisia and Egypt, at least up that point, had not turned their guns on unarmed protestors. Satellite television broadcasts and social media distribution of images and videos captured by ubiquitous cell phones had a big impact on public opinion everywhere Arabic was spoken.

The West was strongly supportive. The uprisings were instantaneously romanticized. Here at last was proof of the victory of liberty. Dictatorships were collapsing because they lacked the will to defend their rotten systems. In some of these countries, activists had been getting help from Western governments for years, raising Western expectations of support for their revolutionary activity and the stability of the postrevolutionary order in successor states. Applause from the Obama administration and, in the case of Libya, supportive military intervention, reinforced perceptions that the imbalance between state power and oppressed peoples would be remedied once the United States put its thumb on the scales. The experience of Libyans and Egyptians seemed to bear this out.

For the Obama administration the Arab Spring was no less a surprise than it was to everyone else. There had long been a suspicion in official Washington that at some point prolonged repression would trigger revolution; it was a leitmotif in U.S. diplomatic discourse with friendly autocratic regimes. The generic talking point was that political reform now could head off a revolution later, with the underlying image being the steam valve, which if not loosened every once in a while, would create pressures that would blow up the boiler.

If you were on the Arab side of this conversation, you would be thinking about the King's Dilemma: The more I loosen up, the more will be demanded, and the greater the likelihood that I'll have to use force. Thus, incremental reform leads inexorably to increased repression.[20] You would therefore politely allow the American diplomat to make his or her case and then change the subject.

Yet now the revolution was here and, contrary to Gil Scott-Heron's expectations, it *was* being televised.[21] The White House and NSC staff were thrilled. *The New Yorker* had already profiled Samantha Power and Dennis Ross as Obama protégés seeking to change the pattern of American support for autocratic regimes. Others on the staff, such as Michael McFaul, an academic student of democratization in eastern Europe and the ill-starred future ambassador to Moscow; Gayle Smith, a migration expert;

and Ben Rhodes, an aspiring novelist and speechwriter who would be named a deputy national security adviser, argued that the Obama administration should no longer practice "business as usual." This phrase was meant to capture the transactional and realpolitik values they believed, largely correctly, had historically regulated U.S. foreign policy.[22] They saw the protests against Hosni Mubarak in Egypt as an opportunity to rewrite the rules.[23]

Obama and Mubarak

Obama's pro-democracy aides started by advocating a break between Washington and Mubarak as the Egyptian president came under increasing pressure toward the end of January 2011.[24] Clinton suggested that Frank Wisner, who had been ambassador to Egypt and was as plugged in as anyone to regional elites, be sent to Cairo to reason with Mubarak. As ambassador to Egypt in the late 1980s, Wisner had hunted the quail he served to guests at the residence and kept a supply of white port on hand. He was inclined to see Egypt as a country needing a firm hand at the tiller. Obama authorized the trip.

As those who knew Wisner, Clinton especially, could have predicted, Wisner advised Mubarak to avoid a sudden departure, which was precisely the opposite of Obama's intention. When Wisner made his message public at a gathering of the international A-list in Munich, the president was furious. A few days later, Obama, after speaking to Mubarak on the telephone, stated publicly that it was "not the role of any other country to determine Egypt's leaders." But "what is clear, and what I indicated tonight to President Mubarak, is my belief that an orderly transition must be meaningful, it must be peaceful, and it must begin now."[25] In his memoir, Obama explained that if he had been a young Egyptian, "I'd probably be out there" protesting. Responding to allegations of hypocrisy, he wrote:

I might not be able to stop a China or a Russia from crushing its own dissidents, but the Mubarak regime had received billions of U.S. taxpayer dollars; we supplied them with weapons, shared information and helped train their military officers; and for me to allow the recipient of that aid, someone we called an ally, to perpetrate wanton violence on peaceful demonstrators, with all the world watching, that was a line I was unwilling to cross.[26]

There was certainly a strong logic at work. Regardless, with huge crowds of demonstrators surging through public spaces in Cairo and Alexandria, police stations throughout the country under attack, and the risk of a breakdown in public order, the generals who were the power behind the throne had concluded Mubarak was endangering their own interests and had to go. Their interests were primarily in the smooth management of the vast business enterprises owned by the Egyptian military. If, in the view of these power brokers, the key to restoring order in Egyptian megacities was Mubarak's imprisonment, then it was a small price to pay.

Questions about Obama's wisdom in nudging Mubarak from power have therefore never made much sense, given that Mubarak was ejected not just by the street but by the very power structure with which the United States was allied. Even if Obama had concluded that U.S. interests were best served by a Mubarak regime and signaled that Washington would support the use of force against protestors, Mubarak's own team would still have removed him.

Tremors in the Gulf and Israel

Although this was abundantly clear at the time, foreign governments reliant on U.S. support concluded that Obama had forced out a friendly ruler who would have survived the uprising against him if the United States had only stood fast. At the top of this list was Israel.[27] They seemed to believe that if the United States would abandon Mubarak, it would readily throw other allies to the wolves if the relationship became a burden. The UAE and Saudi Arabia expressed similar fears. The administration's efforts to clarify that the U.S.-Egypt relationship was not being abandoned were to no avail, largely because its interlocutors could not readily tell the difference between themselves and the states they ruled. They, in effect, were their states. So, to repudiate a country's ruler, as Obama had done with Mubarak, was to repudiate the state.

The worldviews that the parties brought to the crisis were mutually unintelligible. Antagonism and its underlying anxieties were deepened by irreconcilable understandings of democracy. For the United States, it was all about institutions: free and fair elections, universal franchise, freedom of speech and assembly, and peaceful and orderly transfers of power. There would be winners and losers, of course, but there was always the next election.

For the Israelis, democracy was not an ideal form of government for societies where free elections could bring to power the wrong party—one, for example, that might refuse to transfer power if it lost the next election. The U.S. reply was that a thoroughgoing embrace of these institutions by the government and continuous reinforcement of their legitimacy would reduce the risk that any party could get away with a seizure of power. The UAE and Saudi Arabia are monarchies, so they were naturally wary of democracy.

While the United States and regional allies wrangled bitterly over the issue, the White House was divided between business as usual and the new democratic order. One of the deputy national security advisers staged debates between those who were seen as, or professed to be, advocates of one or the other of the two positions. The issue that crystallized these discussions was the proper approach for the United States to take toward the military junta then functioning as the caretaker government in Cairo.

Obama, Egypt's Generals, and Elections

Shortly after Mubarak was removed from power, I hitched a ride to Cairo with General James Mattis, then head of U.S. Central Command, and came back to report that if elections were held, there would be an Islamist government in Cairo. I speculated that this outcome would presage the beginning of the end for the tight U.S.-Egyptian relationship forged at Camp David in 1979. I did not take a position on whether that would be a good or bad thing. My sense was that Tom Donilon, Obama's second national security adviser, was skeptical, if only because a change would inject new uncertainties that would have to be managed. Yet there was a sense in the West Wing and at the State Department among the political appointees that the revolution in Egypt created the opportunity, for the first time, of a durable, genuinely people-to-people relationship between the United States and Egypt; one which did not entail U.S. military and intelligence support for a repressive and unpopular regime.

These competing perceptions of the revolution influenced U.S. decision making about parliamentary elections. Those who thought the generals were doing a reasonably good job of holding things together, and that rushing into elections might not be a great idea, took the view that more time would enable opposition groups with a secular agenda to form parties capable of winning elections.

The other side, which won out, regarded the generals as plotting to reassert the old regime's control over a praetorian state that would thwart the revolution and close off the path to democracy. These officials acknowledged the disadvantage that fledgling secular contestants would face in an election against extremely well-organized and disciplined Islamists. But they judged that the sooner elections were held, the closer to the exit the generals would be. The key was to help moderates win elections, which would require the presence of NGOs and official Americans on the ground to tutor democratic activists and newly formed political parties. The generals ruling Egypt took this about as well as Americans would take an influx of foreign NGOs and officials aiming to fix American politics. From the standpoint of pro-democracy U.S. officials back in Washington, the persistence of military rule was a greater threat to democratization than a decisive victory for Islamists in an unfettered election.

The irony was that the generals themselves favored early elections. Given the serious difficulties Egypt was bound to face in reconstituting a political order of any sort and in reviving its economy, the generals were anxious to return to a behind-the-scenes role while their reputation was still intact and allow an elected civilian leadership to take the blame for hard times.

As expected, the Islamist parties trounced their secular opponents in parliamentary elections. The elections were carried out efficiently and without any evidence of abuse, which was a real achievement. But this phase was punctuated by serious disturbances. A mob of protestors stormed the Israeli embassy in Cairo and were moments away from precipitating a massacre when Egyptian commandos finally intervened.

Then the generals, irritated by badgering from Washington regarding their performance and strident calls for them to transfer power, arrested an American democracy activist in Cairo, who, incidentally, was the son of the U.S. secretary of transportation. This cabinet member's call to Obama inquiring into his son's status was the first inkling the president had that U.S. handling of the transition in Egypt was not going well. There was some thought given to freeing the young man through a subterfuge, but the teapot tempest was resolved through negotiations before the situation escalated.

To settle the debate about business as usual versus democratization, the White House convened an interagency tabletop exercise intended to encourage senior officials to think through their policy priorities when faced with a plausible but hypothetical scenario. The outcome revealed a decided consensus on the importance of preserving the Egypt-Israel peace treaty, ensuring continued privileged access to the Suez Canal in wartime, and a cooperative framework for U.S. and Egyptian counterterrorism operations. Notable for its absence was any interest in or reference to political reform. The White House had apparently been presiding over a government that did not define democratization as a strategic interest worth mentioning. The old ways die hard.

Islamists Triumphant

Egypt held presidential elections in the summer of 2012. It was a crowded field, which required a runoff election. The Islamists, in the form of the Muslim Brotherhood, won by a narrow margin against Ahmed Shafik, a legatee of the old political order. The results revealed just how deeply and evenly Egyptian society was split. The winner, Mohamed Morsi, was a ponderous U.S.-trained engineer, substituted by Muslim Brotherhood leaders for a preferred candidate disqualified for having an American grandparent in his lineage. He was in over his head from the outset of his presidency. His inexperience, management style, and inability to transcend his image as a minor functionary in a secretive organization all hurt his ability to deal with the crises sweeping through the country. However, his handling of two regional flare-ups, ensuring Egypt's compliance with its treaty with Israel after an inadvertent Egyptian military error violated the treaty terms, and participating constructively in a diplomatic arrangement for a cease-fire between Israel and Hamas, suggested that at least in the realm of international politics, the Muslim Brotherhood would act in much the same way that previous governments had acted.

Morsi was also a paranoiac with real enemies. The security agencies—the archetypal deep state—were probably responsible for shortages of fuel and other commodities that enraged a divided society exhausted by nearly two years of postrevolutionary turmoil. It is quite likely that the security services stoked popular resentment and played a role in organizing large demonstrations against Morsi. His response was to issue an edict that criminalized opposition to his government, or to him personally. This move merely fed the frenzy and forced the United States to distance itself from Morsi, which, in turn, made him more vulnerable to domestic opposition.

Counterrevolution

Obama tried unsuccessfully to counsel Morsi, encouraging him to give ground in order to avoid confrontation with his opposition. But by the summer of 2013, the smell of blood in the water brought out huge crowds—on the scale of the protests that led to Mubarak's ouster—demanding Morsi's resignation. His refusal was met by an ultimatum from the chief of the general staff, Egypt's most senior military commander, Abdul Fattah al-Sisi, to step down. Morsi's rejection of the ultimatum swiftly led to his imprisonment and subsequent death. It also led to the wholesale slaughter of peaceful Muslim Brotherhood demonstrators in a majoritarian counterrevolution.

The Libyan "Shit Show"

As democracy rose and fell in Egypt, the opposition to Muammar Qaddafi's rule in Libya was inspired to challenge his regime militarily. The name "Libya" was first applied to the territory in the 1930s and not used officially until its independence as a monarchy in 1950. The northern part of Libya had been split between two tribal confederations as far back as Roman times, and the wedge between the western half, centered on Tripoli, and the east, under Benghazi, remained wide under Qaddafi, who hailed from the west. Benghazi was therefore the natural place for a revolt to begin.

Qaddafi was, to say the least, an eccentric ruler. Over the years, his behavior became more baroque; when the demonstrators in Benghazi declared their independence, he responded in bizarre and vitriolic terms, pledging to hunt the rebels, or "greasy rats," by "cleansing the city by going from house-to-house." He defended his tough response by noting that he was doing nothing more than what U.S. authorities had done to quell the revolt in Waco, Texas, referring by name to the Branch Davidians, sectarians largely killed off in a raid by federal law enforcement.[28]

This defense did not exactly win Obama's approval. The White House was bombarded by calls from David Cameron and Nicolas Sarkozy urging the president to demand that Qaddafi step down. Qaddafi's bloody-minded remarks on February 24 motivated the UN Security Council to impose sanctions on the Qaddafi government on the twenty-sixth.[29] As Qaddafi's forces engaged the rebels, the casualty toll rose, prompting the Security Council to pass a resolution that authorized the use of "all necessary measures" to protect the Libyan people from Qaddafi, established a no-fly zone over Libyan territory, and "designated" an assortment of Libyans to become subject to sanctions, including freezing of their assets.[30]

The resolution scratched more than just one itch. Western European states were increasingly eager to demonstrate that they could take military action, and this was as good an opportunity as ever. The enemy was puny, the battlefield nearby, and the cause was verified as just by the United Nations. Washington, fearful that NATO would lose its reason for being with the collapse of the Soviet Union, had long pressed Brussels to participate in "Out of Area" operations, meaning interventions outside the European theater of operations. NATO had assumed responsibility for some activities in Afghanistan, but here was a contingency in which European NATO members could take the lead. And by taking the lead, the United States was spared the need to allocate forces to Libya amid the withdrawal from Iraq and the surge in Afghanistan. Those in the administration, like Samantha Power, who lobbied for the adoption of the "responsibility to protect"—"R2P"—as a legal justification for use of force, were elated. Intervention in Libya would put Washington on the slippery slope to further applications of this doctrine, which, over time, would make it the right sort of business as usual. In this instance of the long-running tussle between values and interests as the appropriate driver of foreign policy, values were defined as an interest and endowed with strategic import.

The resolution was also emblematic of the humbling of post–Cold War Russia and the apparent triumph of a Western liberal order. In an earlier era, Moscow would have vetoed such a resolution, both to protect an ally and to deprive its adversaries of UN cover for interfering in the affairs of other countries. This time, the Russian president, Dmitry Medvedev, a Vladimir Putin protégé keeping the presidential throne warm for Putin's return in a rotation scheme, instructed the Russian UN delegation to abstain from rather than veto the resolution, thereby allowing it to move forward. Moscow's rationale was likely that abstention would preserve its influence over events without sacrificing its opposition to Western intervention. When the strikes against Qaddafi's forces began, Putin was furious, and a disgraced Medvedev claimed that he had been misled regarding the use of force. Clinton dismissed Russia's reaction, asserting that the phrase "all necessary means" could not have been construed as anything other than an authorization for the use of force. The Russians, she implied, had known exactly what they were doing. The problem, however, was that Putin was soon going to swap jobs with the ineffectual Medvedev, and for him, it was never too late for buyer's remorse, or retribution.

Obama's recollection suggests an impatience born of ambivalence and heightened by the cloudy thinking among his aides on the prosecution of the war. In his 2020 memoir, he writes about an initial meeting with his staff as events in Libya were thought to be spinning out of control.

"All right," I said. "I'm not ready to make a decision yet. But based on what I'm hearing, here's the one thing we're not going to do—we're not going to participate in some half-assed no-fly zone that won't achieve our objective."

I told the team we'd reconvene in a couple of hours, by which time I expected to hear real options for what an effective intervention would look like, including an analysis of the costs, human resources, and risks involved. "Either we do this right," I said, "or we stop pretending that we're serious about saving Benghazi just to make ourselves feel better."[31]

He opted in favor of air strikes, believing that a regime siege of Benghazi would mean that "at best, a protracted conflict would ensue, perhaps even a full-blown civil war. At worst, tens of thousands or more would be starved, tortured, or shot in the head. And at the moment at least," he reflected, "I was perhaps the one person in the world who could keep that from happening." Qaddafi, however, had neither the track record nor the capacity to wage this kind of all-out war. It remains unclear how Obama had formed this baseless, but consequential, notion.

Libyan Liberation

Once the shooting started, the tussle over how to achieve a quick win began. An attempt to convince Qaddafi's associates to abandon their leader and agree to a transition went nowhere.[32] Efforts to assemble an African coalition against Qaddafi ran aground. The establishment of a government in exile proved to be technically challenging.

The English-speaking professors selected as prospective executives of a post-Qaddafi government were precisely the sort of well-meaning activists who get shot by warlords as they step off the airplane upon their triumphant return to the capital. The question of who would help a shattered

Libya pull itself together once the fighting was over went unanswered. When a delegation of British general officers and diplomats showed up at the White House to discuss a division of responsibilities, I walked into the meeting with a chest bruised by Deputy National Security Advisor Denis McDonough's prodding index finger as he repeated his instruction: "No ownership." This was fine with me, but I did wonder who would take ownership of Libya's stabilization in the absence of the United States, or what the point was of decapitating the leadership of a state that had struck a useful deal with the United States—to fight jihadists, abandon its nuclear aspirations, accept responsibility for Pan Am 103 and compensate the victims' families—and which would assuredly devolve to anarchy once the deed was done. As it turned out, no one took responsibility, although there was some gloating. Not for nothing did Obama label the war against Qaddafi "the worst mistake" of his presidency.[33]

As the fighting intensified, my NSC counterpart for counterterrorism and I met with colleagues from other departments on a weekly basis to track the reverse flow of Libyan jihadists returning from the locations to which Qaddafi had forced them to flee. Libya and Tunisia had contributed sizable contingents to the jihad in Iraq and South Asia, young men with no prospects at home, or violent opponents of Qaddafi's who had gone into exile to avoid capture by his security services.

U.S. experts had been tracking these fighters and were disconcerted to see them coming home to roost. Qaddafi's government, under fire, rapidly lost the ability to keep them out. In a previous administration, I had been the senior director on the NSC for counterterrorism and subsequently wrote two books on the jihad with Daniel Benjamin, who was now Secretary Clinton's counterterrorism adviser. I was sensitized to the terrorism dimension in a way that many of my colleagues in the Obama administration were not. Libya seemed to be turning into a game preserve for battle-hardened militants.

On the ground and in the air, the anti-Qaddafi coalition trudged along, unable to force a decisive end to the ragtag conflict. Commitment began to wane among the combatant countries, whose parliaments and publics had been promised swift victory. The Norwegians, who were carrying out a disproportionately large number of strike missions, cut back on their air component. NATO militaries, never truly battle ready, were running out of bombs, and parliaments were wary of appropriating funds for renewing stockpiles.

Of course, it is also true that they were running out of targets. This was not Saddam's vast mechanized force and elaborate infrastructure, but rather the pathetic husk of a state. On the U.S. part, the military commitment was so half-hearted that when a third Predator drone was required to keep an eye on the regime's abandoned chemical weapons depot at Al Waddan in southern Libya, it was only after much agonizing that one was redeployed from a training facility at Fort Huachuca in Arizona.

The coalition finally caught a break on October 20, 2011, when Qaddafi was discovered hiding in a drainage pipe near Sirte, his old stomping ground, where he was sodomized with a bayonet and shot by his ebullient captors. Only at that point could NATO stand down so that Libya's rebel factions could turn on one another, while predatory outsiders including the UAE, Turkey, Russia, Qatar, and Egypt could feast on the carrion of the state. International post-conflict responsibility was transferred to the United Nations.

A Tragic Coda

Over the summer of 2012, the State Department authorized the removal of the military site security team in Tripoli that had been guarding the reopened American embassy.[34] This was disconcerting news. Militants were swirling around Libya's big cities, organizing themselves into an array of militias under the command of warlords with jihadist connections. This was not the time to be lowering our guard. I asked my Libyan affairs officer to check in with his counterpart at the State Department, but the bureaucracy there was resentful of NSC micromanagement; he therefore got no insight into the reasoning behind the drawdown. An appeal to the West Wing to intervene was declined because the issue for decision was in the purview of the counterterrorism directorate, not the Middle East and North Africa office. And at the State Department, the decision was made by the long-term undersecretary for management, Pat Kennedy, and the diplomatic security service, a department backwater, rather than the counterterrorism bureau. A disaster was not foreordained, but was a growing probability.

On the night of September 11, 2012, probability became certainty when jihadis attacked a U.S. diplomatic outpost in Benghazi and a nearby CIA facility. The attacks began with shooting and the liberal use of diesel fuel to set fire to the compound. This phase killed two people, Christopher Stevens, the U.S. ambassador to the transitional Libyan government, who had disregarded the advice of his security chief not to visit Benghazi, and Sean Smith, an information officer.

The survivors were rescued by a team from the CIA facility. Relief, however, was short-lived. The CIA team and rescued State Department personnel came under murderous and highly accurate mortar fire, which took two more American lives, Glen Doherty and Tyrone Woods, both former Navy SEALs, before the battle subsided. The CIA team drew jihadist blood as well. Unlike the melee at the diplomatic outpost, where the defenders were out in the open, engulfed in oily smoke and unable to return fire, the CIA personnel were able to use their firepower to keep intruders at bay.

From the moment the first reports of an assault arrived in Washington and regional military commands, the White House began to coordinate an all-out effort to stage a rescue operation. But the laws of physics are unfortunately immutable. The necessary troops were stationed too far away and the transportation assets to get them to Benghazi could move only so fast. Perhaps the incident would have been less costly, or not even have happened, had the State Department requested the continuing deployment of security forces to diplomatic installations in Libya. We will never know. But if troops had been on the ground in Libya, they would likely have reached the beleaguered personnel sooner than they did from Italy.

This tragedy was the result of incompetence, a perennial challenge for large organizations, and certainly not malign intent. Led by then Representative Mike Pompeo, congressional Republicans, including Devin Nunes and Trey Gowdy, seized on the disaster as proof of the administration's evil designs, rather than inexcusably poor planning. They claimed that the White House deliberately withheld assistance to the stricken installations, for reasons that accusers found difficult to explain.

But with Hillary Clinton in the frame, Republican allegations of homicidal conspiracy came only too naturally. Logic was not the issue. The only official who paid a price was Susan Rice, then the permanent U.S. representative to the UN. She had had nothing whatsoever to do with the awful fate of the Americans in Benghazi, but as a senior member of the administration, she was assigned along with others to face the Sunday morning news anchors. Using talking points prepared by the intelligence community, she indicated that the assault of the U.S. outposts was a spontaneous reaction to a movie depicting Muhammad as a fool and that jihadists joined the protest only once it was underway.

New information soon disproved this preliminary assessment. Republicans accused Rice of deliberately lying to create the impression that the jihadist threat had diminished on Obama's watch. She instantly became unconfirmable as secretary of state, which had been the next stop on her swift ascent, and was ultimately named national security adviser to Obama in his second term. It goes without saying that for Libyans, there was no soft landing.

Civil War in Syria

Syria would fare far worse. Beginning on March 6, 2011, pro-reform demonstrators joyously swarmed the streets of Syrian cities, demanding the departure of Bashar al-Assad, the hereditary ruler. In broad terms, the events that had played out in Tunisia, Egypt, and Libya had electrified young Syrians. If Ben Ali, Qaddafi, and Mubarak could all be stripped of Western recognition and overthrown by popular revolutions, why not Syria? Bashar Assad's attempt to liberalize Syria's economy had widened the gap between rich and poor; there were not enough jobs for a burgeoning youth population; and a drought some linked to climate change had ravaged the agricultural sector. These grievances blended with Islamists' violent rejection of Assad rule going back to the 1970s, which had simmered since the elder Assad crushed a Muslim Brotherhood revolt in 1982.

The spur to revolution was similar to the catalysts elsewhere. Instead of a poor street vendor abused by police or the fatal beating of an activist in Cairo, in the Syrian city of Daraa, it was the killing of juveniles who'd spray-painted a utility building with anti-regime slogans. Having insisted on Mubarak's departure before any serious violence had been done and bombed Libya in anticipation of large-scale killings that had not yet occurred, the administration could do no less than condemn Assad's resistance to reform.

Donilon, formerly a lawyer for the mortgage giant Fannie Mae, immediately proposed that economic sanctions be imposed on Syria and chaired numerous Principals Committee meetings on how best to squeeze the Assad regime financially. Government analysts accustomed to telling policymakers what they want to hear, under the guise of supporting the administration's policy instincts with data to back them up, seized on the so-called Sunni business class as a pillar of regime support that could be shattered by sanctions.

Donilon's approach seemed to assume that these Sunni merchants would hold a board meeting and vote Assad out because he was bad for business. Syria experts then and since would have conceded the existence of a Sunni business class, while ridiculing the assumption that it was in any way politically influential. Day-to-day, low-level Syria specialists in the government who had worked on these issues for years were unanimous in their accurate assessment that Assad would never give up. These views never made it to the situation room because policymakers generally do not like to be told that their policy goals are detached from reality.

Misconceptions were reinforced by the U.S. ambassador to Syria, Robert Ford, who insisted that Assad was going to be toppled in the near term. As he told senior officials, he had looked out his office window, seen a roadblock, and concluded that Damascus was about to fall to the rebels. His defense attaché appeared at the White House to brief me on the military dimension of the growing conflict and assured me that the Syrian army was incapable of keeping its vehicles operating in the field. The army, he said, would quickly grind to a halt.

Fred Hof, a former army colonel serving as the State Department Syria envoy, believed that Assad was a coward who would crumple and run under pressure from the rebels. Obama had authorized outreach to Syria early in his presidency through two channels, a small conventional NSC and State Department delegation[35] and another below-the-radar approach involving Hof and Dennis Ross to explore a far-reaching three-way deal between the United States, Syria, and Israel.[36] Given this level of contact, it is unclear how these fantasies about Assad evolved, but they were catnip to policymakers now enmeshed in a complex war in Libya, who were hoping the Syrian problem would go away.

While the State Department was pulling together a diplomatic strategy, other parts of the government were mobilizing to deal with the risks posed by Syria's gigantic stockpiles of deadly chemical weapons. The fear was that if one or more of the military bases where these munitions were stored fell to rebel forces, then there would be no hope of locating, recovering, or neutralizing these poisons. They could be sold to the highest bidder, used by terrorists, or simply disappear.

An intense effort was made to map the storage depots, figure out how to contact the responsible commanders, and come up with a plan to destroy the stockpiles before they could be liberated. The Israelis were a crucial partner in this urgent task. Given the nature of the challenge and the lack of weapons that could reliably destroy stockpiles without risking a catastrophic public health crisis through an accidental release, it was a relief when the Assad regime itself became aware of the problem and centralized its munitions at bases less vulnerable to capture.

As the fighting spread, it seemed stuck in low gear until June 6, 2011, when rebels in the mountain town of Jisr al-Shughur in northwest Syria ambushed a company-sized Syrian unit on its way to reinforce a local base, which was also attacked. About 120 regime troops were killed in these engagements.[37] The cat was now out of the bag. Regime violence, which up to that point had more to do with incompetence, poor command and control, and opportunistic sadism, would now be more systematic.

The Obama administration was boxed in. On August 18, the president spoke: "For the sake of the Syrian people, the time has come for President Assad to step aside. The United States cannot and will not impose this transition upon Syria. It is up to the Syrian people to choose their own leaders, and we have heard their strong desire that there not be foreign intervention in their movement."[38]

This was the voice of a president determined not to be dragged into somebody else's civil war. In the process of withdrawing from Iraq and watching Libya disintegrate, Obama was hammering home the theme of "no ownership." Still, his remarks did mention pressuring Assad, who had already inflicted more casualties on his own people than had Qaddafi before being selected for forced retirement by the United States. For many observers, especially the Syrian opposition, Obama's commitment to "pressuring Assad to get out of the way of this transition" negated his strong assertion that the "United States cannot and will not impose this transition upon Syria." A combination of clumsy speechwriting and wishful thinking created expectations of U.S. intervention in the months that followed.

Pressure amounted to increasing sanctions in the hope that the regime, which was thought to be spending $1 billion per month, might be bankrupted within a year. But no one knew exactly how much cash the regime could lay its hands on, so the year could easily stretch out to two or even three. Diplomatic isolation was another approach. The United States formed an international group called the Friends of Syria, which would meet to excoriate the regime and elicit financial pledges to fund the opposition and provide humanitarian aid. It is unlikely that these measures kept Assad awake at night.

The United States also funded an external opposition political leadership, which proved largely ineffective since it was disconnected from the action on the ground within Syria. Before long, it was subsumed under a larger governing structure stuffed by Qatar with Muslim Brotherhood figures, whose religious orientation ran counter to Washington's notion of a secular post-Assad Syria. The UN was also involved, trying to forge cease-fire agreements and a negotiating agenda for reforms that would be acceptable to both sides. For the opposition, no outcome that left Assad in power, even on an interim basis, was acceptable; for the government, any outcome without Assad in power was unthinkable. These efforts therefore went nowhere.

Back-to-back speeches by Assad in January 2012, declaring the regime's intention to fight to the bitter end, made it somewhat harder to maintain the image of an adversary about to crack.[39] In February, the

West Wing asked for a paper outlining the full range of options available to deal with the disaster. They ran the gamut from doing nothing to introducing ground troops. Intermediate measures—blockade, arming and training opposition forces, enforcing a safe zone within Syria for the opposition forces of the Free Syrian Army—were spelled out as well. Robert Ford, on behalf of the State Department, dismissed the paper on the grounds that the regime would soon collapse and that no such measures would be necessary. None of the other relevant agencies was any more eager to leap into a quagmire.

The Russian Angle

With policy formation more or less paralyzed, the focus turned to enlisting Russian cooperation. There was still a lingering faith in the power of Hillary Clinton's "reset" of U.S.-Russian relations. Donilon seemed to think that he could make headway with his Russian counterpart, Nikolai Patrushev, a taciturn former general. But the Libya resolution had poisoned the well. Clinton's applause for Russian reformers and legislation sanctioning Russians involved in the death of a crusading journalist also narrowed the space for cooperation on Syria. Nonetheless, Russian diplomats managed to seduce their U.S. counterparts by insisting that "Russia was not wedded to Assad."

The subtext was that Moscow would settle for anyone so long as they looked, talked, and acted just like Assad. My talks in Moscow with Putin's Middle East adviser made this perfectly clear. In his view, the United States was no different from the imperialist governments that carved up the Ottoman Empire after World War I, and I was an American reincarnation of Lawrence of Arabia. By standing with Assad, Moscow was blocking yet another Western ploy to rob the Arabs of their destiny. Beneath this self-dramatizing presentation of Russian motives was a steely self-interest and clarity of purpose that was manifestly absent in Washington.

The State Department, convinced that the Russians were pliable, developed a transition plan for Syria, whereby the government and the opposition would share power. Each side could reject players on the other side who they deemed unacceptable, a bit like jury selection. In theory, the opposition would consent to the participation of second-tier regime members, but oppose Assad and his immediate circle. The second-tier apparatchiks would naturally agree to this arrangement since it would guarantee their survival, or at least give it better odds than a civil war that culminated in the destruction of the entire regime. In reality, of course, Assad *was* the regime and no one below him believed that it would survive his departure. The Russians and the United States signed a communiqué in Geneva. It remained in force for about a half hour, until Sergei Lavrov, the Russian foreign minister, and Clinton gave dueling press conferences, each jubilant over the decisive victory of their respective clients. It seemed that the Russians were wed to Assad after all.

Shifting Strategies

With diplomacy running out of gas, the administration began to consider arming and training the opposition. An incredible attack on seemingly indispensable regime figures in Damascus on July 18, 2012, stirred imaginations in Washington.[40] Somehow, the opposition had succeeded in tunneling under the streets of Damascus to the basement of a government building where the organizers of Assad's counterinsurgency met to plot strategy. The saboteurs detonated a bomb that killed most of the key planners, including Assef Shawkat, Assad's brother-in-law and confidant. Certain things were beyond doubt. The opposition had first-rate insider information on secret regime deliberations and schedules. It also had excellent operational security, which allowed it to carry out a daring, complex operation without detection. Moreover, the regime was suddenly shorn of its leadership in the war against the rebels. Yet, the regime proved to be astoundingly resilient. Assad kept his nerve and the regime held it together, regrouped, and went on fighting.

Arming and training the opposition was a knotty proposition. Skeptics in the West Wing asked government analysts to assess the effectiveness of previous U.S. arm-and-train programs for foreign insurgents.[41] The ensuing report cited academic studies showing that outside aid of this kind, especially in the absence of boots on the ground, had little or no effect on the outcome of the conflict. There were also careful scholarly assessments of the negative effects of such arms transfers on the structure of insurgencies, especially where there was more than one external source of arms. The result was fragmentation as each group or warlord sought to attract and control the largest share of weapons. Ultimately, in Syria, this process led to a consolidation of the insurgency under jihadist groups that outfought and absorbed their moderate rivals.

Accordingly, the first time a proposal to arm the Syrian opposition was brought to Obama, it was shot down. From his perspective, taking the armed opposition under America's wing would open a bidding war with Iran, which the United States could not win, simply because Syria was so much more important to Tehran than to Washington. His doubts were fueled by the sterility of the discussion. None of the cabinet members could define a U.S. interest in Syria that would justify intervention; and none could explain how intervention would produce a political outcome in Syria that aligned with U.S. values and objectives.

Clinton and defense secretary Leon Panetta said that "we had to have skin in the game," apparently so that when the opposition won, the United States would exercise influence in Damascus by virtue of its prior support. This is not what Wall Streeters meant when they dreamt up the phrase "skin in the game," which originally referred to the small sum tricky investors would put into dubious deals so other potential investors would think risky bets were safer than they really were. In any case, the slogan was no substitute for argument. Both Susan Rice and Denis McDonough spoke at length against arming the opposition. Donilon, who sided with Clinton, maintained a frustrated silence.

Proponents of arming and training opposition forces chipped away at Obama's resolve in the months that followed, capitalizing on a growing despair over Assad's brutal response to the insurrection and desire to do something—anything—that might put him on the defensive. Iran was becoming more involved in supporting the regime and Lebanese Hizbal-lah, whose access to Iranian weapons ran through Syria, deployed nearly five thousand fighters to beat back territorial gains made by opposition forces. Persian Gulf states wanted to get involved as well to thwart an Iranian attempt to establish a permanent presence within an Arab state. David Cameron, the British prime minister, tried to enlist Obama in harebrained schemes that called to mind Peter Sellers playing James Bond. David Petraeus, who had joined the administration in 2012, pressed incessantly for intervention, until his resignation amid scandal. By the spring of 2013, Obama had relented and American and Gulf Arab weapons were pouring into the armories of rebel forces.

The Red Line

Interventionists appeared to have caught their break the following sum-mer, when regime forces unleashed a horrific chemical attack on Ghouta, an opposition-held suburb of Damascus.[42] Almost exactly a year before, in an informal Q&A, Obama had said,

> We cannot have a situation in which chemical or biological weap-
> ons are falling into the hands of the wrong people. . . . We have
> been very clear to the Assad regime but also to other players on the

ground that a red line for U.S. is, we start seeing a whole bunch of chemical weapons moving around or being utilized. That would change my calculus. That would change my equation.[43]

In the aftermath of the Ghouta atrocity and quick confirmation of the regime's guilt, advocates of intervention deployed the juxtaposition of "red line" with "chemical or biological weapons" in Obama's remarks of the previous year to assert that the administration had vowed to respond militarily to a regime gas attack. In a curious echo of the widely propagated misreading of Obama's 2011 speech urging Assad to "get out of the way," an off-the-cuff remark regarding the transfer of chemical weapons from Syrian stockpiles to either Lebanese Hizballah or the armed opposition and vague references to a "red line" and a changed "calculus" was transformed into a binding commitment to war against the Assad regime.

Yet perceptions matter, and the impetus to teach Assad a lesson took over. Obama and Cameron quickly agreed to launch a joint air campaign aimed at bases associated with Syria's chemical weapons. On Tuesday, August 27, they spoke at length about the battle plan, which went swiftly awry. On Thursday, August 29, a confident David Cameron, the prime minister who would later foolishly pledge a referendum on Brexit to kill the initiative, went to Parliament for support for air strikes. He was slapped down 285–272 by members who recalled Blair's partnership with Bush in a war based on false claims about weapons of mass destruction.[44] The next day, Cameron told Obama that Britain would not participate.

Obama was not interested in acting unilaterally. He thought the United States had dropped enough bombs on Arab countries during the previous decades; if it was going to drop more, he wanted an ally to share the dismal experience. The question now was how to back out of an awkward situation. Working with McDonough, he devised a stratagem to engineer a congressional roadblock so he could portray the White House as stymied by an irresponsible Congress afraid to use force.

Although *The New York Times* described this maneuver as one of the riskiest of Obama's presidency, he could have been fairly confident that war-weary Democrats would oppose him, as would tough guys, like John McCain, who wanted more decisive use of force, and Republicans who claimed not to trust Obama with a military operation. However, few members would want to be on record as voting against hitting Assad, so the measure would most likely never go to the floor. Obama would therefore not bear the stigma of losing a major vote, but he could still accurately assert that he'd gotten a red light on the Hill.

In his Rose Garden remarks, he teed up his request for congressional approval, saying, "I'm prepared to give that order, but having made my decision as commander in chief based on what I am convinced is our national security interests, I'm also mindful that I'm the president of the world's oldest constitutional democracy." Thus, he would be reluctant, perhaps even remiss, to use force without the approval of the people's elected representatives. Twisting the knife, he continued, "What message will we send if a dictator can gas hundreds of children to death in plain sight and pay no price?"[45] As anticipated, this was a message Congress could live with perfectly well in order to avoid the political consequences of holding a vote.

The Question of Credibility; Russian Rescue

Credibility obsessives still levied heavy criticism. By declaring the intention to strike Syria but failing to follow through, Obama had damaged America's reputation for resolve, inviting further challenges to American interests. The weakness of this claim lay in the fact that the United States did not have an overriding interest in Syria, even if it did have an interest in enforcing norms regarding the use of chemical weapons. Rational would-be challengers to the United States therefore would not take Obama's decision as a signal that it was now open season on vital U.S. interests.

Fortunately, the Russians came to the rescue by proposing that in lieu of air strikes, the UN might remove and destroy Syria's chemical weapons stockpiles, with Moscow guaranteeing Assad's cooperation. This did not directly confront the interventionists' kvetching about America's reputation, but it did enable the administration to change the subject, arguing, in the words of Jon Finer, then Kerry's chief of staff, that "we strongly believed it was better to get 1,300 tons of chemical weapons out of the hands of the Syrian regime, or let them fall into the hands of ISIL."[46]

There are several versions of this story, told by participants with different perspectives and perhaps motives. Ben Rhodes, the White House foreign policy messaging expert and one of the deputy national security advisers, credits John Kerry with the initiative.[47] An alternative account emerging from the NSC staff was that Kerry did float the idea, but in the form of a facetious remark about Assad, which the Russians took literally and ran with.

The precise lineage of what was a brilliant concept might never be fully clarified. But the results were impressive. By the time the UN's Organization for the Prohibition of Chemical Weapons finished in 2014, 96 percent of Assad's declared stocks had been destroyed. Though Assad did continue to use chlorine for years after he surrendered his astronomically more potent nerve agents, chlorine gas is so easy to make that its use would have been much more difficult to prevent.

Assad on the Ropes

The influx of weapons, money, and foreign jihadists into Syria at this stage of the war was beginning to put the regime under serious strain. By the Spring of 2015, Assad's forces had been pushed out of Idlib, losing the city of Jisr al-Shughur, out of Palmyra, and was in control of only a shrinking section of northwestern Aleppo, the most important Syrian city apart from the capital. The Islamic state was carving out a large chunk of Syrian territory in the eastern part of the country, establishing a capital for its "Caliphate" in Raqqa on the northeast bank of the Euphrates about 100 miles from Aleppo. Regime forces were losing a great many soldiers and paramilitary fighters. Many were Alawite, the sectarian minority that constituted much of the regime. It looked as though the ruling sect might suffer a demographic collapse. At this time, I was out of government and on a business trip to Beirut when I received a call from a journalist based in Syria, passing along a Syrian government request for me to meet with Assad in Damascus. I was not opposed to this in principle, but the United States and Israel had just assassinated the external operations chief of Hizballah in Damascus, and I was not eager to drive across the Bekaa, a Hizballah stronghold, when the wrong people might be contemplating revenge.[48]

On returning home, I notified the White House and State Department of this development. There was interest at the White House in exploring the opportunity. Rob Malley, the new coordinator for Middle Eastern affairs at the NSC, was open to ideas that might de-escalate the conflict, especially since the armed opposition was dominated by Islamists not very different from al Qaeda, and it was scarcely obvious why the United States would destroy the Assad regime just to provide a state for jihadists. And, as he told a reporter in 2018, the administration efforts to weaken the regime was "part of what fueled the conflict rather than stopped it."[49] We spoke about the concessions the United States would want from Assad and what the administration might be willing to do in return.

I was consulting in this period to the Middle East Institute, a small think tank that had just avoided bankruptcy through a miraculous gift from the UAE and Saudi Arabia, arranged by one of the American advisers to the UAE crown prince. The Gulf states were just learning what the Israelis had long understood, that think tanks could be valuable tools for disseminating the views of their sponsors and influencing Washington opinion. The Middle East Institute was the UAE's first acquisition. When

I met with an institute manager about the call, I was told that visiting Syria would cause the UAE and Saudis to withdraw their funding. Moreover, given UAE and Saudi mistrust of Obama, the institute could not possibly appear to cooperate in any quasi-diplomatic initiative blessed by or linked in any way to the White House. As a precaution against the possibility that its Gulf donors might get wind of our discussion, the institute quickly moved to end our contract.

Unencumbered, I returned to Beirut and then traveled onward to Damascus by road. The armored SUV that picked me up at the border hurtled toward the capital at nearly 100 miles per hour; ISIS positions were only ten miles from the road and jihadists were harrying traffic with rocket propelled grenades. Assad was alone when we met the next day. In the course of a two-hour conversation, I offered my assessment that the Obama administration could not easily see a possibility of reconciliation over the mountain of corpses he had created. By taking concrete actions, including a halt to the use of indiscriminate weapons—barrel bombs and chlorine gas—facilitating the delivery of food and aid to rebel-held areas, and releasing prisoners, however, Syria might create the conditions for renewed contact and possibly de-escalation. I emphasized that I was not carrying a message from Washington, I was out of government, and was in Damascus only as an expert observer in search of ideas about how to reduce the level of violence where political compromise was not in the cards. The gist of Assad's reply was that he could see taking these steps if, in return, Washington would press Ankara to stop infiltrating jihadists into Syrian territory. This condition did not seem unreasonable, especially since Turkey's flirtation with ISIS had been a concern for Washington. He asked how he should proceed. I suggested he put these commitments in writing and communicate them to the White House. I told him I had no idea if there would be a response. It would be a shot in the dark.

On the way home, I briefed the UN envoy Stefan de Mistura in Geneva on the conversation. Boarding a plane in Lausanne, I bumped into Rob Malley, who was traveling with the U.S. team negotiating the Iran nuclear deal. I reviewed the meeting with Assad, and we talked through what a letter from Assad might look like. I continued the discussion in New York with the UN undersecretary for political affairs, Jeffrey Feltman, a colleague who had served as an assistant secretary of state for Near Eastern affairs. Back in Washington, I had dinner with Malley, who said that he had raised my meeting in Damascus with Susan Rice, who was against entertaining an overture from Assad. Malley explained her position in a way any Middle Easterner would understand. Assad, he said, was in a desperate situation; why throw him a lifeline? From my perspective, this is the very moment when a lifeline can extract important concessions; this is just when one enters bargaining mode. As a tactical approach, this was unconvincing to the West Wing, and the fact was that the optics were terrible. As a political matter, there could be no contact with the Syrian regime regardless of the potential benefits. With some regret, I signaled contacts in the region that there was no prospect for a deal along the lines I'd discussed in Damascus, and there the matter ended. Malley, in retrospect, mused that turning off the channel to Assad had been a mistake, but of course there was no going back.

Moscow Makes Its Move

In a coda to this story, I traveled to Moscow in early spring and met with Putin's Middle East adviser in a private capacity. We talked about the situation in Syria, Assad's difficulties, and Russia's perception of the diplomatic situation. In a jarring remark, he told me that "Russia would not permit the capital of Syria to move from Damascus to Raqqa." He seemed to be signaling the possibility of Russian intervention to prevent what he feared could be the defeat of the Assad regime by an Islamist insurgency. Back in Washington, I shared with Malley my perception that Russia seemed to be on the brink of a military commitment. As the summer wore on, my Twitter feed conveyed a growing number of references to Russian aircraft arriving in Syria. I revisited the issue with Malley, who reassured me Washington and Moscow were on the same page.

It emerged at the end of September that the two capitals were actually on different planets. The Russians intervened with about sixty aircraft, a small number by American standards, but enough to make a large difference in the military balance. Obama denied that the Russian move had taken the White House by surprise. He told *60 Minutes*, "We knew that [Putin] was planning to provide the military assistance that Assad was needing because they were nervous about a potential imminent collapse of the regime."[50] At this point, whether on the basis of flawed intelligence analysis or wishful staff thinking, Obama's talking points mocked Russia for having entered a "quagmire." (This line persisted through the Trump administration as well.) Syria did indeed pose risks for those who meddled in the civil war, but Russia had intervened with the minimal force necessary to achieve the narrow but crucial objective of keeping its client in power. Putin was not there for nation building, peacekeeping, stabilization, or reconstruction, objectives that had sunk the United States in genuine quagmires in Vietnam and Iraq.

The fact was that Syria and Russia shared a history from the late 1950s through the fall of the Berlin Wall. Tens of thousands of Russians had served in Syria over the years, sometimes intermarrying, and many Syrians during the Cold War had studied in the Soviet Union. The Russians had had intelligence and naval facilities in Syria and had rearmed Syrian forces in the wake of each defeat they suffered in Arab-Israeli wars. The two countries were on the same side throughout the prolonged slog of the Cold War.

The United States, of course, was on the other side. Washington had been as loyal to its ally, Israel, as Moscow had been to theirs. Few Americans had traveled to Syria or had close ties to the country. It was enemy territory. And the feeling was mutual. One night in 2012, I was in the bar at the Metropolitan Club in Washington with the scion of a legendary Damascene literary family, one of many opposition representatives pushing for intervention. As he ran up my tab, I asked him how Syrians' views of the United States would be changed by a U.S. effort to unseat the Assad regime. He replied that there wouldn't be any change . . . we'll still hate you. This struck me as both eminently fair and admirably frank. It was also an eloquent explanation for the difficulty members of the National Security Council had had in articulating the American interest in who ruled Syria.

One of the threads running through media commentaries following Russia's intervention was that Obama's Syria policy had invited Russian aggression. David Ignatius, the celebrated channel for Washington leakers with an agenda, typified the trend.[51] In a way, this view was accurate for the wrong reasons. It was not Obama's allegedly hands-off approach, but rather his aggressive intervention by arming and training opposition forces. The avalanche of weaponry for the opposition enabled them to make the territorial gains that had pushed Assad's back to the wall. Obama had been right at the outset: U.S. involvement would trigger a bidding war it could not win. Russian intervention proved him right.

The question is why Obama abandoned his initial instinct. A survey of colleagues who were involved in the decision-making process in the second term, suggested, first of all, there was a feeling, or perhaps a conviction, that the United States had to act to stop the violence, but that the lessons of regime change were too daunting. Indeed, talk about a Russian quagmire merely echoed in a subconscious mode the thoughts of policymakers regarding U.S. intervention.

Second, and related, was the "no ownership" mantra favored by Denis McDonough. An overt thrust toward regime change would surely confer ownership, and of a sharply divided and traumatized society. And misperceptions about Syria, which continued to burden administration planning, fed the view that rather than regime change, all that was needed was enough military pressure to compel Assad to enter negotiations in order to avoid defeat on the battlefield.

Third, the U.S. ability to arm and train the opposition without admitting publicly that it was doing so meant that the United States could engage militarily without taking "ownership." This looked like a policy that would check all the boxes, but Washington was easily outbid because its competitor, Russia, was entering at the invitation of a regime that was still functioning, could use air power with impunity, and was battling a rebel movement dominated by jihadists. The Obama administration nevertheless continued to arm and train the opposition through its second term, even as the Russians attacked the recipients. And nowhere in the Arab world did Moscow pay a diplomatic price for doing so.

The Rise of the Islamic State

At the same time, a small U.S. military contingent had deployed to northeastern Syria to mobilize a largely Kurdish counteroffensive against the Islamic State. The overall force also included a sizable Arab tribal contingent, a fact that often gets lost in reporting on the anti-ISIS campaign. This was the beginning of the end of the Syrian civil war. Aleppo was retaken by Assad in the summer of 2016; the following year, a pulverized, ISIS-controlled Raqqa fell to a Kurdish-Arab force supported by U.S. troops and aircraft. Between the Russians and, ironically, the Americans, the challenge to Assad's rule that emerged in 2011 had been defeated. Victory had a Pyrrhic tinge; the country's infrastructure had been largely destroyed, its population impoverished and dispersed, and its resources squandered.

The anti-ISIS campaign was enmeshed in the difficult departure of U.S. forces from Iraq. In a joint 2008 press conference in Baghdad with Iraqi prime minister Nouri al-Maliki, George W. Bush had explained to an Iraqi and international audience that the agreement the United States and Iraq had signed "lays out a framework for the withdrawal of American forces in Iraq—a withdrawal that is possible because of the success of the surge." The withdrawal would begin in 2009 with the drawdown of U.S. troops from Iraqi cities and then, in 2011, from the entire country.[52] Al-Maliki, putting a different, pugnacious spin on the agreement, stated that "incomplete sovereignty and the presence of foreign troops are the most dangerous, most complicated and most burdensome legacy we have faced since the time of dictatorship. Iraq should get rid of them to protect its young democratic experiment."[53]

The United States and Iraq subsequently tried to negotiate a follow-on agreement that would have permitted the continued deployment of troops for training and other purposes, but it fell apart over a U.S. requirement that military personnel who committed crimes while stationed in Iraq would be prosecuted by U.S. authorities and, if convicted, serve their sentence in the United States. Although this was a genuine obstacle to a negotiated agreement, it was also a convenient rationale for the two sides to walk away from a deal. Despite the fact that al-Maliki and many Iraqi parliamentarians considered U.S. forces useful and would concede privately that a residual force should remain in Iraq, the national assembly, with the exception of Kurdish members, refused even to vote on the agreement the United States had approved. The idea was political poison. Too many ordinary Iraqis saw the United States as occupiers rather than liberators. And Obama had campaigned on a promise to withdraw from Iraq and was determined to follow through on it.

This where the matter stood until the summer of 2014 when a successor to al Qaeda calling itself al-Dawla al-Islamiya fil Iraq wa al-Sham, or "The Islamic State of Iraq and the Levant" (ISIL), or ". . . Iraq and Syria" (ISIS), which had been fermenting in Syria, burst into Iraq. Its fighters quickly took control of Fallujah and Ramadi, Sunni cities in Anbar province, and then attacked Mosul, Iraq's second-largest city. The Iraqi troops shed their uniforms and fled, abandoning an army's worth of tanks and other vehicles as well as firearms, ammunition, and other vital supplies. Upon taking Mosul, ISIS fighters advanced southward with the apparent intention of invading Baghdad and also rampaged through parts of Iraqi Kurdistan, devastating its Yazidi population, enslaving the women and killing the males. The Iraqi state, reeling from a humanitarian and strategic disaster, appeared on the brink of defeat. Iraqi Sunnis, the losers in the civil war ignited by the U.S. invasion, were alienated by the backhanded treatment they got from the fiercely partisan Shia government and welcomed—or simply submitted to—the invaders, facilitating their conquest. Those who did not were killed or imprisoned.

Now for the Finger Pointing

Observers across the political spectrum blamed Obama. Writing as an "honest liberal," Peter Beinart branded Obama's Iraq policy as "disastrous."[54] John McCain slammed Obama for conforming to Iraqi realities rather than shaping them, an accusation no one could ever level at the Bush family.[55] Senate Majority Leader John Boehner blamed Obama for trashing Bush's victory.[56] James Traub, a centrist who has cultivated a reputation for responsible journalism, wrote that Obama "left a mess behind" in Iraq. While acknowledging that shaping reality in Iraq was not in Obama's power, he stipulated that "the fact that you can't do everything doesn't mean you can't do anything."[57] Leon Panetta, a former congressman who reappears in Democratic cabinets or as White House chief of staff as a kind of default choice, told NBC News, "I think when we stepped out of Iraq, in many ways, we created this vacuum in which not a lot of attention was paid to what was happening in Iraq or what was happening in Syria with the extremists who were developing a base of operations there."[58] Ironically, Jim Jeffrey, the U.S. ambassador to Iraq for much of this time, and no fan of Obama's—Jeffrey was later a Trump appointee—was the one commentator who really captured the situation in a *Wall Street Journal* op-ed.

> Could a residual force have prevented ISIS's victories? With troops we would have had better intelligence on al Qaeda in Iraq and later ISIS, a more attentive Washington, and no doubt a better-trained Iraqi army. But the common argument that U.S. troops could have produced different Iraqi political outcomes is hogwash. The Iraqi sectarian divides, which ISIS exploited, run deep and were not susceptible to permanent remedy by our troops at their height, let alone by 5,000 trainers under Iraqi restraints.[59]

The controversy over the withdrawal in the wake of the eruption of ISIS was inflamed by accusations of intelligence failure and, on the other side, politicized intelligence.[60] Obama himself fueled the fire. On *60 Minutes*, when asked to comment on Director of National Intelligence James Clapper's assessment that the intelligence community had underestimated ISIS while overestimating the capacity of Iraqi forces to fight, Obama replied, "That's true. That's absolutely true. Jim Clapper has acknowledged that I think they underestimated what had been taking place in Syria."[61] The intelligence community did not take this lying down, insisting that there was a "paper trail" showing that it had its eye on the ball and could not be justly blamed for the White House failing to act on the available information.[62] According to Major General Paul E. Funk II, a commander of the U.S. training mission in Iraq, the Iraqi army "really did become relatively complacent, and then flat out just didn't train—just didn't spend the money to do it, didn't maintain the systems, and therein lies the problem."[63]

Dozens of intelligence analysts at CENTCOM complained to the Defense Department inspector general that their gloomy assessments of the bitter mood among Iraqi Sunnis and the foothold that a burgeoning ISIS was gaining in the Jazeera, the great swath of land straddling the Syria-Iraq border, had been reduced to a mellower pitch as they percolated to the top of the command chain.[64] There was some merit to these claims. And, of course, intelligence analysts are rewarded for predicting calamities but generally unpunished for false alarms.

The interest of the military leadership, in contrast, is in depicting conditions as favorable, owing to the effectiveness of combat operations. So the shift in tone would have come naturally. At the end of the day, Obama was attentive to the polished and relatively optimistic reports he received from the Defense Department. He probably was genuinely surprised by the sudden show of ISIS power. The then head of the Defense Intelligence Agency, Lieutenant General Michael Flynn, later Trump's indicted national security adviser, was particularly deranged by Obama's remarks because he heard them as an excuse for Obama's own failure.[65]

Grinding Down the Islamic State

Amid the controversy, the administration managed to assemble an international anti-ISIS coalition, deploy U.S. forces to the theater, and provide military and intelligence support for the Syrian Democratic Forces (SDF) battling ISIS on their side of the border, and elite Iraqi units on their side. U.S. forces on the ground concentrated on training, tactical support, and special operations. Shi'a militias, called to arms by Ayatollah Sistani, the influential cleric based in the Iraqi city of Najaf, bought crucial time for the anti-ISIS coalition to enter the fray. Effective use of American airpower gradually wore down ISIS forces. Targeted killing and air strikes, however, do not take and hold ground. This task was left to Iraqi and SDF troops, which did what was asked of them. ISIS had no safe haven, even if the Turks were friendly, and apart from a pocket in Idlib in northwest Syria, nowhere to run. Internationally, they had no friends. The governments of Iraq, Iran, the United States, Russia, Jordan, and Israel, in addition to the myriad other members of the coalition, wanted to see ISIS crushed. The Islamic State, as a Middle Eastern geopolitical entity, was living on borrowed time from the moment of its inception. Its defeat entailed horrific destruction in what amounted to siege warfare and urban combat resembling the battle of Stalingrad. Believing in the nobility of sacrifice and lacking any refuge, ISIS adherents fought to the death.

What to Do about Iraq?

The larger issue was how a new administration should grapple with the effects of the previous administration's policies. Sometimes the answer is simple. For example, your predecessor signs an executive order prohibiting the entry of Muslims to the United States; you revoke it and sign your own executive order permitting entry. But Iraq posed a more profound problem, logistically and otherwise. By 2009, there were still between 136,000 and 150,000 troops in Iraq, an elaborate base structure, and immense equipment stockpiles. The departure of such a large force would inevitably rock the boat. But both George W. Bush and Barack Obama converged on withdrawal.

Their positions at the start of their administrations, however, differed. Bush saw himself as responsible for his father's legacy: the disarmament of Iraq and its transition to democracy, otherwise known as regime change. But by the end of his second term, Bush had evidently concluded that the United States had reached the limit of what it could do in Iraq and committed the United States to withdraw its forces from Iraq by 2011, come what may.

Should Obama have reversed Bush's policy? Or should he have attempted to "shape Iraqi realities," as commentators like to say, differently? These questions invoke ethical, political, and strategic concerns.[66] What did the United States owe Iraq, having invaded and unleashed a storm of violence after years of debilitating economic sanctions? One reparations-focused argument for retaining U.S. military forces to keep the peace was that it was the least that could be done for an unsteady Iraq.

Other advocates of remaining voiced an obligation to Americans who died to create a new Iraq. To withdraw before the job was done, however one defined the job, was to betray their sacrifice. Politically, by 2011, about 75 percent of Americans supported the withdrawal, although Republicans were more inclined to stay.[67] As one prominent historian recently summarized the implication of shifting popular views of ongoing wars, "When the public, or enough of them, withdraw their support for wars, as they did in Russia in 1917, in Germany in 1918 and in the 1960s and 1970s in the United States during the Vietnam War, it is difficult if not impossible for governments to fight on."[68] Iraq was not exempt from this broad truth.

Breakthrough with Iran

The capstone of Obama's Middle East policy was the negotiation of the 2015 agreement with Iran that made it impossible for Tehran to build a nuclear weapon without having to create a separate, completely secret nuclear infrastructure. (The discovery of any such effort would quickly invalidate the agreement and expose Iran to severe sanctions.)

Recent administrations of both parties have been concerned about Iran's nuclear ambitions. There is a broad consensus in Washington that nuclear weapons were too powerful to spread beyond the small nuclear club that obtained them in the first decade or so after their invention, for many reasons: there could never be absolute confidence in the restraint of leaders in a serious crisis, the ever-present possibility of an accident, and the fact that any use of nuclear weapons would engender an environmental and humanitarian catastrophe with global impact. And then there is the question of human judgment. Soviet misinterpretation of a 1983 NATO exercise brought the world to the brink of war. Moscow's launch of a first strike was only narrowly averted by an officer who wasn't convinced that the exercise was actually cover for an impending American attack.[69]

The main diplomatic tool for preventing the spread of nuclear weapons is the multilateral Non-Proliferation Treaty (NPT), which entered into force in 1970 and has since been renewed. The nuclear powers are obligated by the treaty to assist other countries in the peaceful use of nuclear energy, in return for a verifiable pledge never to develop nuclear weapons. In addition, the nuclear powers pledge to reduce and ultimately eliminate their own stockpiles. Iran signed the NPT the day it was opened for signature.

The Eisenhower administration first offered Iran, then ruled by the shah, help in building a civil nuclear energy program. Suspicions about Iran's nuclear intentions grew over time. A 1974 Special National Intelligence Estimate, commissioned by Henry Kissinger, did not pull any punches.

> There is no doubt however of the Shah's ambition to make Iran a power to be reckoned with. If he is alive in the mid-1980s, if Iran has a full-fledged nuclear power industry and all the facilities necessary for nuclear weapons, and if other countries have proceeded with weapons development, we have no doubt that Iran will follow suit. Iran's course will be strongly influenced by Indian nuclear programs.[70]

India pursued a covert weapons capability under the cloak of a civil nuclear program, detonating its first small bomb in 1974 and a much larger fusion device designed as a warhead in 1998. It is now an acknowledged nuclear weapons state.

In 2007, the intelligence community produced a new National Intelligence Estimate specifically on Iran's program. Its key point was that Iran had had a nuclear weapons program from some point in the 1980s until 2003, when cost-benefit calculations led to its suspension, but that it continued to pursue uranium enrichment. Some policymakers felt a combination of sanctions and isolation would force Iran to decide whether it wanted nuclear weapons capability or economic growth. Yet diplomatic efforts to reach an agreement that would get sanctions suspended proved fruitless.

In 2005 talks with European negotiators, Iran offered to limit enrichment to low levels—that is, too low to make a bomb—and to ratify and carry out the additional protocol to the NPT safeguards agreement, which would mean much more intensive scrutiny of Iran's activities and facilities. The Bush administration, according to then British foreign secretary Jack Straw, pressured the EU countries involved in the talks to reject Iran's proposal.[71] By the time talks resumed in 2009, an interval studded with UNSC resolutions condemning Iran's continuing enrichment, the number of centrifuges spinning in Iran had more than doubled, from 3,000 to 7,000.

The 2007 National Intelligence Estimate warned that "convincing the Iranian leadership to forgo the eventual development of nuclear weapons will be difficult given the linkage many within the leadership probably see between nuclear weapons development and Iran's key national security and foreign policy objectives, and given Iran's considerable effort from at least the late 1980s to 2003 to develop such weapons."[72]

Although the NIE earned the mockery of Henry Kissinger, who wrote that "the Key Judgments blur the line between estimates and conjecture," and Representative Pete Hoekstra, ranking member of the House Permanent Select Committee on Intelligence, who dismissed it as "a political document in 2007 to embarrass President Bush which everyone uniformly agrees was a piece of trash," its main conclusion, the view that anything Iran agrees to is "inherently reversible," came to be adopted by the opponents of Obama's 2015 deal with Iran.[73]

The next National Intelligence Estimate, in 2010, was also beset by controversy. According to *The New York Times*, U.S. analysts had received information in the late 2000s suggesting, but not proving, that Iran had restarted its nuclear weapons program.[74] Though the report was worrying, it was hard to interpret with any certainty; the analytical community relies on methodologies intended to reduce the risk of false alarms, and the Iraqi WMD fiasco loomed. Any scuttlebutt picked up by analysts about the Iranian program restarting would have to be complemented by other kinds of information acquired in different ways, in a belt-and-suspenders approach. Politicians and policymakers privy to intelligence are free to cherry pick to support their preconceptions. The analysts march to the beat of a different drum.

In this case, the debate about the status of Iran's program burst into the open. Amid the storm, analysts stuck to their prior assessment that Iran's program was on hold. One official told *The New York Times*, "I'd say that I have about 75 percent confidence in the assessment that they haven't restarted the program," while another stressed that "Iran is the hardest intelligence target there is. It is harder by far than North Korea. . . . In large part, that's because their system is so confusing," which "has the effect of making it difficult to determine who speaks authoritatively on what." What's more, he said, "we're not on the ground, and not having our people on the ground to catch nuance is a problem."[75]

Just as Obama was looking to chart a course regarding Iran's program, there was a bureaucratic knife fight over exactly what Iran was doing and with what intention. Several assumptions about Iranian thinking could be made. The first is that, like North Korea, Iran had considerable incentives to develop nuclear weapons, or be able to do so quickly. The United States had branded Iran as an axis of evil in need of regime change, and recently, it had easily pushed Iraq out of Kuwait, destroyed Saddam Hussein's regime, and occupied Iraq. But the United States, it seemed obvious, would not have been in the regime change business if the targeted regimes had nuclear weapons—North Korea was the evidence for the view that nuclear weapons capability kept the Americans at bay. America's shredding of Qaddafi's regime after Libya had halted its own nuclear program reinforced the conviction that a military nuclear program was a good thing to have.

The Israelis were armed with hundreds of missiles and nuclear warheads, while Iran had no nuclear weapons capability at all.[76] If Iran were ever to decide the time had come to challenge Israel militarily, a few nuclear weapons in Tehran's cupboard could block Israel's resorting to its own. And would the United States think seriously about challenging the regime if Iran could retaliate with nuclear weapons against the UAE, Saudi Arabia, or the U.S. Fifth Fleet in the Persian Gulf?

The temptation to develop a weapon, or to be able to produce one on short notice, must therefore have been strong, but opposition to it by Israel, the United States, and in NATO capitals was equally determined, not least because it might lead other countries in the neighborhood, particularly Saudi Arabia, to acquire nuclear weapons.

Saudi crown prince Mohammed bin Salman has already threatened as much.[77] And Israel, considered by Iran to be an illegitimate presence in the Middle East and unworthy of existence, was especially invested in blocking Iran's nuclear progression, considering that Iranian president Mahmoud Ahmadinejad said that it should be "wiped off the map." The precise meaning of the Farsi phrase translated as "wipe Israel off the map" has been vigorously debated. It is possible that it was meant to be metaphorical. But for the intended target, these distinctions could scarcely be reassuring when heard against the background noise of Iranian centrifuges busily spinning enriched uranium.

Obama calculated that there was room for maneuver. The administration's approach combined several complementary initiatives. The first was to reinvigorate sanctions by making them fully multilateral with UNSC authorization and widening their impact on Iran's economy. The second was a sequence of public and private diplomatic overtures, offering a hand in friendship to Iran, if Tehran would unclench its fist, in his 2009 State of the Union address.[78] He followed up with a conciliatory letter to Iran's ruler, Ayatollah Khamenei, urging cooperation on regional issues,[79] then a video message to the Iranian public and leadership, in which he referred to Iran as the "Islamic Republic," its official name.[80] He said, "In this season of new beginnings, I would like to speak clearly to Iran's leaders. My administration is now committed to diplomacy that addresses the full range of issues before us, and to pursuing constructive ties among the United States, Iran, and the international community. This process will not be advanced by threats."[81] Khamenei responded, via remarks to a crowd of worshipers in Mashhad, in skeptical, if not quite dismissive terms, saying, "They chant the slogan of change, but no change is seen in practice. . . . [But] should you change, our behavior will change, too."[82]

The process was rocky—another letter from Obama went unanswered[83]—but these steps were essential because sanctions in the absence of diplomacy offered no clear endpoint, while doing nothing to stem Iran's enrichment of uranium or construction of thousands of centrifuges. European and UN support for intensified sanctions was also crucial. Allies had faulted the Bush administration for its reliance on punishment to elicit cooperation, or perhaps more accurately, obedience. In their view, sanctions were a tool to force Iran to negotiate—a lever, not a sledgehammer. Obama's approach was a relief for other states involved in the process and impelled their help in enforcing sanctions.

In addition, Salem ben Nasser Al-Ismaily, a fixture in the small Omani business elite who would later be named chairman of Ithraa, Oman's investment promotion and export development agency, showed up in Washington on Memorial Day weekend in 2009 and got a meeting with Dennis Ross, who was then working for Clinton at the State Department. Presenting himself as an Omani emissary on behalf of Iran, Al-Ismaily handed Ross a paper proposing U.S.-Iran talks on sensitive issues such as the nuclear program and even Iranian support to Hizballah. Though he read the document with a "ton of salt," as he put it, Ross got the go-ahead from Clinton to continue meeting with the Omani envoy.

This channel was quashed temporarily after Iran's brutal response to public anger over irregularities in the government's conduct of the elections, which prompted Clinton to seek tougher UN sanctions against Iran. The Iranians had also arrested three American hikers on what U.S. authorities believed were bogus charges. This provocation, presumably staged by Iranian opponents of talks between Washington and Tehran, turned out to be a blessing in disguise for the administration's diplomatic objectives, if not for the unfortunate hikers. Al-Ismaily reappeared to negotiate the protracted release of the hikers and arrange for the government of Oman to pay the sizable fines—really, ransom—demanded by Iran.

This transaction removed an obstacle to resuming communication between the United States and Iran while affirming Oman's bona fides as an intermediary. The pace picked up in the winter of 2009–10, with the release of the first of the hikers. Ross and Puneet Talwar, the NSC senior director for Persian Gulf affairs, traveled to Muscat, capital of Oman, for consultations. In January, Clinton stopped in Muscat to meet with Sultan Qaboos, the then ruling monarch. During the course of the year, Obama called Qaboos twice, evidently concluding that Qaboos could be relied upon. Qaboos had met with Khamenei, he told Obama, and he was open to talks. There seemed little risk in following up.

Entering stage left was then Senator John Kerry. He saw his opportunity in the detention of the hikers, injecting himself into the equation. In the process, he developed a working relationship with Al-Ismaily, the ubiquitous Omani envoy, meeting him in Washington, Rome, and London. Kerry was not exactly freelancing; he had told Obama in the Oval Office that the moment was ripe to open a back channel and coordinated his talking points with Donilon.

However, Clinton and her staff at the State Department suspected Kerry was floating an unauthorized concession to Iran's insistence on its right to enrich uranium for its civil energy program. This was guaranteed by the NPT, but from Washington's perspective, Tehran had forfeited the right to enrichment by lying about its secret efforts to develop a nuclear weapon. These efforts might be on hold, but there was damning evidence that they had been made in the past. By mid-2012, both Obama and Clinton decided that this issue could not be left to an energetic member of Congress and believer in the power of personal diplomacy. Kerry himself insisted that "we made it crystal clear to them" that there would be no right to enrichment, but he was known to believe that this claim was unsustainable. The White House and perhaps even Clinton probably shared this view, but whether and how to concede Iran's right to enrich in the context of nuclear negotiations was a delicate question politically, strategically, and tactically.

Unacknowledged talks proceeded in Oman under the cover provided by Sultan Qaboos. The tension within the administration over the timing of the talks was not easily overcome while Clinton was still secretary of state. She believed that there was still more economic pain to be imposed on Iran. Until the United States had put Iran all the way through the wringer, there would be no way to know what Tehran's bottom line really was. By releasing the pressure prematurely, the United States might end up making more concessions than necessary. On the other hand, Obama had to consider the possibility that Iran's insistence on the right to enrichment and sunset clause for certain restrictions were irreducible and that pulverizing Iran economically would only heighten its determination to develop nuclear weapons. With the relatively moderate Hassan Rouhani, who was known to be interested in a deal, running for Iran's presidency, it might not be the ideal time to discredit reformers.

While the Oman process was inching forward, the Israelis were getting impatient. Washington took a three-part approach to keeping Israel from attacking Iran on its own. Donilon set up periodic consultations with his Israeli counterpart, Yaakov Amidror, a taciturn retired general who seemed to be a reliable transmitter of messages to and from the prime minister's office.[84] These meetings, which alternated between Israel and the United States, were generally unpublicized. In fact, participation was sharply limited, and the subject matter categorized as super-confidential, as a way to drive up the demand for entry on the Israeli side. From the U.S. perspective, the more Israeli professional military and intelligence personnel vying for space in the room, the less risk that politically motivated Israeli participants might be able to mischaracterize or withhold U.S. information.

Amusingly, there were limits to the Israelis' own tolerance for partisan mischief; for example, they excluded their ambassador to the United States, Michael Oren, a Likud political hack originally from the New Jersey suburbs, from key gatherings. Even his own government regarded Oren as untrustworthy and a loose cannon. During sensitive meetings at the White House, he was usually left pacing the pavement outside the building at the insistence of the Israeli delegation, an unwitting demonstration that perhaps the prime minister's office considered the issue too important to be left to the foreign ministry.

In these sessions on Iran, the U.S. goal was to impress upon the Israeli participants the extent of U.S. preparations to destroy Iran's nuclear facilities, should Iran ever be on the verge of producing a weapon. The message was that the administration was willing to use force against Iran and, moreover, had offensive capabilities the Israelis lacked.[85] In operational terms, the Israelis could hit Iran, but only at substantial risk. A comprehensive strike against the key nodes of Iran's nuclear infrastructure would require nearly the entire Israeli air force, much of which would be occupied in patrolling the air space traversed by the attackers, protecting the refueling tankers flying in foreign airspace, and suppressing Iranian or perhaps other air defenses that could knock out Israeli bombers.

The Iranian centrifuge hall beneath the mountain at Fordow, near the clerical city of Qom, was impervious to Israeli bombs, so commandos would have had to blow off the doors, descend to the lower chambers, and destroy the equipment, but the Israeli air force had no aircraft that could have gotten the operators there. The U.S. presentations at these meetings showed that, compared with Israel's air force, the U.S. Air Force could demolish Iran's installations without breathing hard. The United States had aircraft carriers that could be parked close to Iran, allowing fighters and bombers to carry out more sorties, with bigger payloads and more time on target. The administration had accelerated the procurement of the BLU 57, or "massive ordnance penetrator" (MOP), a 30,000-pound GPS-guided bomb with a casing so hard it could bury itself 200 feet below the surface of a mountain before exploding with seismic force.[86]

Just as important, the United States had airplanes that could actually carry such a device over intercontinental distances, namely the batwing B-2 stealth bombers based at Whiteman Air Force Base in Missouri. By the end of 2011, there was a stockpile of 16 MOPs at the base, more than enough to grind Iran's underground facilities to powder. Israel lacked a MOP, however, as well as an aircraft that could lift one off the runway.[87] And in the case of war, Iran would almost certainly have been able to reconstruct its nuclear production facilities as soon as the smoke cleared, so the Israelis would have to mount these incredibly challenging air and ground campaigns every couple of years. For the United States, this was feasible, for Israel, probably not.

How effective these show-and-tell sessions were in dissuading Israel from going it alone, perhaps with the aim of starting a conflict the United States would be forced to finish, is hard to say. I think most of the Israelis involved simply concluded that it was a pity that the United States had such great weapons but no president willing to use them, though I believed Obama was quite ready to use force against Iran if it developed a nuclear weapon, particularly since he staked out this position repeatedly in public. Yet even within the administration, and outside it, there were those who had their doubts. Nevertheless, one official who was consistently closely aligned with Israeli perceptions and policy preferences, and was skeptical of Obama—Dennis Ross—also believed that Obama was ready to pull the trigger.

The Israelis pressed for access to the MOP/BLU-57 and V-22 Osprey aircraft. The Osprey is an airplane with engines that can point horizontally forward for normal flight, or pivot upward to transform the airplane into a helicopter for vertical takeoff and landing. The Osprey, in short, was the perfect aircraft to transport Israeli special forces to targets in Iran and get them out again without requiring an airstrip. Jerusalem had asked the George W. Bush administration to buy the BLU-57, but Bush refused. He was already dealing with two wars and was not eager to get dragged into a third because the Israelis bit off more than they could chew, or because their air offensive against Iran led to attacks against U.S. friends on the Arab side of the Gulf who would need to be defended.[88] Obama adopted Bush's position on the transfer of weapons that might tempt Israel to act rashly or without adequate regard for U.S. interests.

On a separate track, according to *The Washington Post*, the United States and Israel were collaborating in the development of computer malware intended to disrupt Iran's nuclear enrichment efforts. The *Post* wrote that the bug was tested by the Israelis at their nuclear facility at Dimona in the Negev desert. Called Stuxnet, the special code was inserted into software that Iran, as well as many other countries, used to control machine operations.[89] Once embedded in Iran's computer system, the malicious code instructed centrifuges to run at extremely high speeds, destroying delicate components. At the same time, the attackers fed faked data to Iranian technicians monitoring the centrifuges so that the machinery looked as though everything was just fine.

Media reports suggest that Stuxnet was destructive but that its impact on Iran's enrichment activity was uneven.[90] The cyberattack was exposed when the malware escaped from Iran's system via the internet and began interfering with computer-controlled industrial processes in Europe. The director of the CIA and then of the U.S. National Security Agency at the time, Michael Hayden, looked back on the attack as relatively successful.[91] It is thought to have been the first known instance of cyberwarfare and has been studied carefully by the U.S. military and probably others as well.[92] Israeli intelligence also augmented the use of cyberweapons by systematically killing off Iranian scientists linked to the nuclear program.[93] One assassination took place in 2007, but the pace picked up during the period of U.S.-Israeli cooperation on Stuxnet, when another five scientists were allegedly shot, poisoned, or blown up—four fatally—between 2010 and 2012.[94] Iran attempted unsuccessfully to reciprocate, trying to kill Israelis in India and the Georgian Republic.[95]

As the Oman process appeared to show some promise, Obama's interest in collaborating with Israeli undercover operations faded. According to the *Wall Street Journal*'s account of interviews with knowledgeable Israeli officials, "Mossad leaders compared the covert campaign to a 10-floor building: The higher the floor, they said, the more invasive the operation. CIA and Mossad worked together on operations on the lower floors. But the Americans made clear they had no interest in moving higher—Israeli proposals to bring down Iran's financial system, for example, or even its regime."[96] As far as the White House was concerned, cyber sabotage, sanctions, and Israel's liquidation of Iranian scientists seemed to have gotten Iran to the table. These tactics had therefore outlived their usefulness and, if continued or ratcheted up, might well be counterproductive.

The White House was also not interested in sharing information about ongoing talks with Iran in the Oman channel with Israel, although it was a tough call. If excluded, Israel might act precipitously; if included, Netanyahu could be relied upon to leak details of the negotiation to the media and friends in Congress in the hope of derailing the talks. His track record of public appeals to Congress to reject Obama's Iran policy was irrefutable. The Israelis, however, knew what was going on behind their backs. Amidror, their national security adviser, taunted U.S. officials, saying that Israeli intelligence had tracked the tail numbers of aircraft going in and out of Oman and put two and two together.

The Israelis then spied on the Iran talks in order to glean details of the negotiation that Israel could share with members of Congress in order to incite opposition to the deal and provide Republicans with ammunition to discredit the administration by portraying it as soft on Iran and dangerous to Israel.[97] As one administration official explained to *The New York Times*, the Israelis "tell part of the story, like how many centrifuges we might consider letting the Iranians hold. . . . What they don't tell you is that we only let them have that many centrifuges if they ship most of their fuel out of the country."[98]

Some senior Israeli officials, including the legendary head of the Mossad from 1998 to 2002, Efraim Halevy, and Netanyahu's own Mossad chief, Meir Dagan, were astonished by this. "I've never seen such an effort, almost in broad daylight, to involve ourselves in internal American politics, to work on the ground to try to effect a political outcome," Halevy told *The Wall Street Journal*. Dagan added, "Friendly countries are not supposed to do this to each other."[99] The Israelis responsible justified their activities with public complaints about the United States withholding information. Extraordinarily, they faulted the administration for not disclosing to them Obama's bottom line, that is, the one thing a negotiator, let alone the president, would never divulge in a strategic negotiation.

Two former negotiators, Gary Samore and Robert Einhorn, both look back on the skirmishing as the result of the administration's decision not to inform Israel of the secret Oman talks. But Israel's use of intelligence information gathered by eavesdropping on negotiators to interfere in American politics suggests that regardless, Netanyahu was fully committed to obstruction and prepared to go to extremes to prevent a deal.

The irony is that both the United States and Israel thought of their respective tactics in identical terms. Obama and Netanyahu were each looking to buy time: the Israelis through assassination, sabotage, cyber-attacks, support for increasingly punitive sanctions, and physical destruction of Iran's nuclear infrastructure; the United States through a negotiated agreement that would make it hard for Iran to build weapons for ten or fifteen years. The Americans, pointing to the large number of centrifuges that had been built by Iran while under severe economic sanctions and the short time it would take Iran to rebuild bombed installations, argued that a negotiated agreement made more sense.

The Israeli response was, yes, it would make more sense, but only if the agreement forced Iran to permanently relinquish its right to enrich uranium and the duration of the agreement was until the end of recorded history. The Israelis appeared to believe that Iran would ultimately accept these terms if the United States kept up the pressure, returning to negotiations only when Iran was on the edge of collapse. The U.S. team, which was dealing with actual Iranians, thought this assessment was unrealistic.

As U.S.-Iranian talks dragged on, Israel began to think more seriously about striking Iran. By early 2012, worrying signals were picked up in Washington, where officials swiftly shared their anxieties with *Washington Post* readers via David Ignatius.[100] He wrote portentously that Netanyahu had not made up his mind, "But senior Americans doubt that the Israelis are bluffing. They're worrying about the guns of spring—and the unintended consequences."

Leon Panetta, then secretary of defense, was described as expecting an attack in late spring. Ignatius also referred to Ehud Barak as telling the White House that Israel was backing out of an annual Mediterranean naval exercise because of funding problems. He made this point while munching on hot dogs and beer in Donilon's office. Barak then met with Obama backstage at a meeting with Jewish groups to make the case for striking Iran. It was later revealed that Barak and Netanyahu tried three times to get Israeli cabinet approval for a strike in 2010 and 2011 but were thwarted by the army chief of staff and two right-wing ministers, who were said to be incredulous at the idea that Israel would take on such a task while risking its relationship with the United States.[101]

By November 2012, there was evidence, none of which was definitive, that Netanyahu was edging toward military action. As a precaution, the Pentagon ordered the positioning of U.S. ships and aircraft near Iran in case Tehran lashed out at U.S. allies in the Gulf or Israel in the wake of an Israeli strike. Netanyahu, in the meantime, had been led to believe by Barak that Obama had agreed to transfer the BLU 57 and Osprey aircraft to Israel. Calling Obama to thank him, he was told that the transfer had never even been considered. Conversations with Panetta and others suggested that the Israeli defense minister had gotten ahead of his skis, or perhaps thought that having Netanyahu put Obama on the spot would spring the desired equipment. It was a surreal moment.

Faced with a possible crisis, Donilon pulled together a small group to swap views on whether or not Netanyahu would attack Iran.[102] One participant said no, explaining that Netanyahu was too "chickenshit." Whether this was the right answer for the wrong reason will never be known, but as *The Atlantic* magazine later reported, "chickenshit" became the in-house code name for the Israeli prime minister.[103] John Kerry had to call Netanyahu and apologize.[104]

Diplomatic Probes Become Serious Negotiations

In June, national elections in Iran put Hassan Rouhani in the presidency. He was closely tied to Khomeini's regime and had good revolutionary credentials—without them, he would not have gotten prior approval to run for office. Although his campaign points were somewhat coded, it was clear that his approach to dealing with Iran's economic woes would be to shed Western sanctions, which would entail a nuclear deal. As the chief negotiator in earlier rounds of nuclear talks, Rouhani had a grasp of the issues and a sense for the other side's objectives. He also had the benefit of the groundwork done by U.S. and Iranian officials during their meetings in Oman. He was, therefore, the right person at the right time, a fact that Obama quickly grasped.

Despite rapid agreement on the interim deal, including cooperation "with respect to verification activities to be undertaken by the IAEA to resolve all present and past issues"[105] (bureaucratese for resolving suspicions Iran had created through earlier deception), the final agreement was not signed until July 14, 2015. The April 2020 leak of an interview with Iranian foreign minister Javad Zarif shed some light on what might have caused the delay. It was widely assumed that there was internal Iranian resistance to an agreement, if only because such a groundbreaking deal must have been as controversial in Tehran as it was in Washington. But according to Zarif, the Islamic Revolutionary Guard Corps and its charismatic leader Qassim Soleimani had been working against the proposed deal from the outset of negotiations. Soleimani had even traveled to Moscow to urge that Russian support for the deal as a member of the P5+1 be dropped. Zarif had had the unenviable task of tabling IRGC objections intended to kill the process, managing the negative P5+1 reaction, then neutralizing his adversaries in Tehran until their next attempt to hobble negotiations. But the more significant implication of the leak was that Zarif had won the battle despite IRGC resistance.[106]

The Joint Comprehensive Plan of Action (JCPOA), from a U.S. perspective in 2015, was a good deal. It reduced the number of centrifuges at the Natanz facility from 19,000 to 5,060 until 2025. The enrichment facility inside the mountain at Fordow would be limited to research and development until 2030, with its centrifuge number capped at 1,044. To make it hard for Iran to fuel a secret installation, monitoring was expanded from the mining stage through waste disposal, while procurement of nuclear-related material would be conducted through a joint commission. To block the pathway to a plutonium bomb, there would no longer be heavy water production at the Arak plant, which would be redesigned to make weapons-grade plutonium there impossible. Iran's uranium stockpile would be limited to 300 kilograms and enriched to a maximum of 3.67 percent, compared with the 90 percent required to fuel a warhead. This limit would be in force through 2030. Iran also signed and ratified the Additional Protocol to the Nuclear Non-Proliferation Treaty, which rendered permanent the most important verification measures.[107]

Congress Mobilizes against the Deal

Even as these terms were being negotiated, Congress was working to stymie whatever agreement might emerge. Arkansas Republican senator Tom Cotton, for example, took the extraordinary step of writing, along with forty-six other Republicans, to a foreign head of state, Ayatollah Khamenei, telling him that whatever agreement Iran signed with the Obama administration would be revoked by the next administration.[108] Senator Bob Corker, a Tennessee Republican, joined Ben Cardin, a Maryland Democrat, to draft a bill that would, among other things, make a deal subject to congressional approval. Their hope was that Obama would veto it, which would signal two things: that the White House was not confident Congress would green-light a nuclear deal, and that the president was short-circuiting Congress's role in foreign policy to implement a deal that would serve the interests of Iran. Obama's approach to this stratagem was to persist in negotiating for a bill he could live with. Corker and Cardin had little choice but to go along.[109]

The bill Obama finally accepted granted Congress the authority to vote to disapprove the deal, rather than to vote to approve.[110] It would be easier for Democrats to vote against disapproval than to vote for a nuclear deal, no matter how good it was. As a matter of grave consequence, a vote to disapprove would require 61 votes, or a two-thirds majority in the Senate, rather than a simple majority of 51. While the White House could not be completely secure in the likely count, the assessment was that Democratic defectors would be few enough that the threshold would not be passed.

Both sides took no chances. AIPAC reportedly spent $40 million to defeat the JCPOA. Working with Senator Corey Booker of New Jersey, a protégé of right-wing rabbi and media personality Shmuley Boteach, AIPAC told Democrats that a vote against disapproval would not hurt them if they also voted for a military assistance package that would give Israel the ability to attack Iran. Senator Mitch McConnell organized an effort to portray the Democrats as filibustering a vote on the JCPOA. There was no filibuster, but his aim was to assert that there was one, garner 61 votes for cloture—that is, an end to the filibuster—and then bring the JCPOA to the floor for a separate vote requiring only a simple majority. The Democrats, including those who opposed the JCPOA or were fence-sitting, rejected McConnell's ploy, which seemed to be more about wrong-footing Obama than preventing Iran from obtaining a nuclear weapon.[111] The White House facilitated a P5+1 delegation to brief Senate Democrats. Their argument was essentially that neither they nor the Iranians were going to return to the table to renegotiate the agreement, regardless of a congressional vote to disapprove. Nor would they enforce sanctions against Iran if it was in compliance with the agreement.

Ultimately, opponents of the deal were undercut by the absence of any plausible alternative. This was not a remediable problem because there was, in fact, no alternative, except no deal at all. And the one Democrats were looking at promised to keep Iran out of the nuclear weapons business for at least fifteen years. Iran could cheat, but verification procedures would make that difficult. If cheating was detected, the reimposition of sanctions could be triggered by the United States alone. P5+1 consensus would not be required. And as a last resort, there was a military option at hand. Thus, on September 10, the Democrats were able to block a Republican resolution for disapproval, and the JCPOA became a done deal.

In an otherwise dreary, if eventful, two terms of Middle East engagement, the completion of the JCPOA was a remarkable strategic achievement. By blocking Iran's path to either a uranium- or plutonium-fueled nuclear weapon for at least fifteen years, the administration secured time and space for the United States and its allies to advance their interests without the threat of regional nuclear proliferation. This diplomatic feat had little to do with hopes for renewed relations with Iran, let alone reconciliation. It was about solving an urgent proliferation threat without going to war. That was the real breakthrough.

By the end of Obama's second term, the lingering illusions that had led to interventions in Iraq, Syria, and Libya had dissipated. In April 2016, Obama said in an interview with *The Atlantic* that the Middle East was simply not a productive arena for strategic investment.[112] One suspects that he already held this view by the middle of his first term, by which time the Arab Spring was imploding, Israeli prime minister Benjamin Netanyahu had collaborated with the Republicans to humiliate him before a joint session of Congress, and the Arab Gulf states had made it known that they considered him unreliable, even feckless. Their attitude toward Obama, who they privately referred to as "the slave" or "the black dog," was fiercely antagonistic. From their perspective, Obama had collaborated with their worst enemies—the Muslim Brotherhood in Egypt and the Islamic Republic of Iran—and therefore merited contempt. Yet there was evidence of cooperation as well. Hedging their bets, for example, the Saudis heeded Obama's plea for lower oil prices in advance of his 2012 reelection bid.[113]

Obama had earned Netanyahu's battering by saying things out loud that everyone knows but are not supposed to be said: that Israeli settlements in the West Bank are an obstacle to peace with the Palestinians; that the border between Israel and a Palestinian state should be based on the June 1967 armistice line and adjusted through land swaps; that the Persian Gulf has to be shared with Iran; that negotiations are preferable to war for resolution of disputes; and that U.S. interests were shifting toward the Pacific and it would have to "rebalance" its diplomatic and military commitments accordingly.

In the 2012 election, Mitt Romney, his Republican opponent, claimed that Obama had thrown "Israel under the bus" and "disrespected" it, though military assistance to Israel had reached record levels during Obama's first term.[114] (Those levels would be exceeded in his second term.) As it turned out, this image of Israel flattened by the Democratic bus was not a major factor for Jewish voters, who cast their ballots more or less in the same ratio for Democrats as they had in previous elections.

The lesson was that the Jewish vote, to the extent that it mattered at the national level, was not going to be swayed by policy toward Israel. The sensible approach for the White House was to go along with Israeli requests that Congress would grant anyway, as long as Israel did not undermine U.S. strategic interests, such as bombing Iran while the United States, the permanent members of the UN Security Council, and the EU were negotiating limits on its nuclear program. On strategic matters, the White House gets to decide what is in America's interest.

CHAPTER SEVEN

DONALD J. TRUMP

The Deal of the Century

They're chopping off heads of people because they happen to be a Christian in the Middle East.[1]

Jews in the United States must "get their act together" and show more appreciation for the state of Israel "before it is too late."[2]

We protect Saudi Arabia. . . . And I love the king, King Salman. But I said, "King—we're protecting you—you might not be there for two weeks without us." . . . We defend many of these nations for nothing, and then they take advantage of us by giving us high oil prices. Not good.[3]

—DONALD J. TRUMP

Donald J. Trump might be the man who needs no introduction, but his foreign policy posed interpretative challenges that demand one. Submerged beneath the chaos of Trump's administration were fixed ideas about the world that found expression in his presidency's foreign policy. He rejected altruism, but most scholars and practitioners would agree that altruism is but a small and ambiguous factor in international relations anyway. More unconventionally, he conceived of the world as populated by winners and losers, conmen and suckers, and interactions as zero-sum games. This perspective naturally made him suspicious of negotiated agreements. Why would one party consent to a binding arrangement with another unless he believed he had successfully snookered the other guy? This was more than just a perspective. It was a business philosophy and a hardwired understanding of human interaction. That a negotiated agreement might represent gains for both sides struck him as inconsistent with self-evident realities.

Apart from this basic instinct, there is not very much to go on. Trump seems to have been nearly unique in his indifference to the mechanics of foreign policy, strategic doctrine, or anything resembling coherent thought about day-to-day events and their links to larger, longer-term national concerns. His comprehensive ignorance of the conduct of foreign policy clouded even his occasionally sensible, if crudely formulated, impulses. Where this ignorance intersected with deeply unwise initiatives, such as the wall along the southern border, the resulting fiascos obscured whatever systematic thinking might have gone into the policy. Trump's scattered and impulsive management style further impedes understanding, since it inevitably left unclear whether a dormant issue he had previously raised was important to his strategic outlook, but simply forgotten, or had never held any significance at all. Until the archives of the administration are declassified and released to the public, these will remain open questions.

How the Sausage Was Made

The very structure of the policy process in Trump's administration was baffling. The first presidential decision of most postwar administrations has been to set up the national security policy process. The gist of this drill is to determine who sits on the National Security Council. Trump's included, for example, Steve Bannon, an administration political propagandist, but excluded the chairman of the Joint Chiefs of Staff, who by law is the president's military adviser. This may seem minor, if dangerous, but it reveals not just the president's ignorance of the policy process but that of his key advisers as well. Policy direction is generally provided by the president, but it is shaped and transformed into actionable programs by the machinery of government. In Trump's case, there was no fully assembled machinery, just a pile of gears, circuit boards, nuts, and bolts tossed haphazardly onto the Situation Room conference table.

The National Security Council is the apex of a vast set of interlocking mechanisms meant to produce policy options for presidential decision. Its composition owes not just to tradition but to a practical necessity that transcends party. Mike Flynn, a retired general who had been cashiered by Obama, was Trump's first national security adviser. He was a person of exceptionally poor judgment, subsequently convicted for lying to the FBI about his illegal involvement with Russia and Turkey. As chair of the Principals Committee, the name for the National Security Council when the president is not at the head of the table, Flynn should have insisted that the right cabinet-level officials be included. That he appears not to have done so was an early signal that Trump's administration was not likely to develop policy through a careful process.

A pattern emerged whereby Trump would declare policies that were either ignored by the agencies supposed to carry them out, or not backed up by analysis or any sort of game plan. Frequent changes in the upper ranks of the administration and on the National Security Council staff reflected and perpetuated the disconnect between the West Wing and the rest of the government. The intensely politicized atmosphere in key agencies isolated appointed officials from career professionals, which further disrupted the creation and implementation of workable policies. Trump's reliance on immediate family members, as though the government was *la cosa nostra*, was yet another irregularity shrouding the administration's policy process. Given the bizarre workings of this system, it will take historians years to disentangle the quality and purpose of foreign and defense policy decisions made in the Trump years from the zany actions taken to carry them out, where any organized action was taken at all.

Another complication was Trump's murky personal interest in policy outcomes. The records introduced in his two impeachments, the report of an investigative counsel appointed by the Justice Department, several intelligence community assessments, and media reporting document Trump's deep ties to the Kremlin. These led him repeatedly to give Russia a pass to pursue its objectives regardless of American interests and led Moscow to do what it could to get and keep him in the White House. A former head of Israel's Mossad told me, quite seriously, that the election of Donald Trump was the result of the most successful covert operation he had ever witnessed. It's fair to say that his experience in this domain would make him a rather good judge.

Trump also seems to have relied on Arab funding to sustain losing real estate investments. Time and again, Trump seemed not to differentiate between his private business interests and his responsibility for foreign and defense policy. Aside from his business interests, there were also his political calculations. Politics does not always stop at the water's edge, despite the civic spirit behind the cliché, but in most administrations, politics at least slows down. In Trump's administration, it gushed forth.

Unexpected Continuities

Like Bill Clinton, George W. Bush, and Barack Obama, Trump came into office seemingly determined to humble Iran. However, Trump was convinced that Iran had been enriched and emboldened by his predecessor. By the time both Clinton and Obama left office, they were attempting to fashion a working relationship with the Iranian regime. Bush, by contrast, at first cooperated with Tehran in Afghanistan but was then bled by it in Iraq, while hawks in Washington sloganeered about how "real men go to Tehran" and "the road to Tehran runs through Baghdad."

With at least one crucial exception, Trump continued Obama's second-term Middle East policy. Obama had delegated the Israel-Palestine peace process to John Kerry on the assumption that it would be fruitless. Trump's approach was predicated on the same insight, and he proceeded to develop the idea of an economic peace between Israel and Palestinians on the West Bank that would not require political concessions neither side was prepared to make.

Despite some over-the-top admiration for the dictatorial instincts of Egypt's president Abdul Fattah al-Sisi and Saudi Arabia's crown prince Mohammed bin Salman, Trump's position toward these governments was not markedly different from Obama's. The same could be said about Syria, which the gullible Trump was fooled by his mendacious advisers into thinking the United States had left,[4] or Iraq, from which the United States had largely withdrawn in 2011 on a timetable dictated by the Bush administration. Under Trump, U.S. bases in Iraq were being closed down and consolidated,[5] while military intervention devolved to the one-off killing of Iran's Quds Force commander, Qassim Soleimani, in January 2020.[6]

Both presidents rejected the "endless war" paradigm. Both saw the Arab-Israeli peace process as at a dead end. Neither wished to be entangled in the Syrian civil war, although Obama hedged by approving a huge program to arm and train so-called moderate opposition groups. Both wanted to flee Afghanistan. Here again, Obama hedged, apparently against his better judgment. Trump did not. He started a stampede that would lead U.S. forces out of Afghanistan during Biden's first year in office. And despite the Obama administration's sincere support for the Arab Spring revolutions, there was not much it could do to advance them once they had occurred in the absence of congressional approval of a large increase in foreign aid. But Trump went further by deriding the spirit that animated the revolts.

Although Obama and Trump were obviously dissimilar in temperament, values, and intellectual capacity, they shared a declining sense of the utility, purpose, and effectiveness of American engagement, and es-pecially of military intervention, in the Middle East. Neither was moti-vated to compete with Iran, Russia, or Turkey for control of territory that he assessed to be of little relevance to critical U.S. interests; in the case of Saudi Arabia and the UAE, both concluded the United States is likely to continue to enjoy preponderant influence without having to go to war for it. As Obama completed his second term, it was unclear whether his administration's approach was a fluke or the harbinger of a trend. Until late in his term in office, Trump's rhetoric and actions seemed to confirm a trend.

Like Obama, Trump could play the activist in the Middle East, de-spite his instincts. Unlike the interventions of his predecessors, his activ-ism was, with the important exception of Iran, small-scale and relatively cost free. You get what you pay for, however, and the United States got very little return in strategic terms. Trump's single consequential act was to pull the United States out of the Iran nuclear deal. In that instance, the returns were negative. And his Middle East policy did not help him get reelected, despite the applause it received from evangelical voters.

Trump Tramples Nuke Pact

The administration's policy toward Iran—as compared with its rhetoric—was initially unclear. Even as the White House deplored Iranian foreign policy, derided the JCPOA, vowed to crush the IRGC, and castigated Iran's government for its illiberal practices, it continued to confirm Iran's com-pliance with its obligations under the JCPOA for Congress every ninety days. For Trump, this was frustrating. It was as though Iran's compliance with the agreement was, to him, an underhanded ploy to violate it. In April 2017, therefore, he declared that Iran was not living up to the "spirit" of the nuclear deal, because Tehran continued to expand its regional influ-ence.[7] As Steve Miller, Harvard's expert on non-proliferation, said at the

time, the very notion of a 150-page document of mind-numbing technical detail having a "spirit" made no sense. Iran's regional activities and
ballistic program were not covered by the agreement, which focused on
the nuclear issue alone.

After a year of begrudging certifications of Iranian compliance with
the agreement, Trump felt that the only way to escape the trap, in his mind,
of rewarding Iran for bad behavior was to get out from under U.S. obligations to certify Iranian compliance and continue to suspend nuclear-
related sanctions by ripping up the deal. In May 2018, he declared that it
"was a horrible one-sided deal that should have never, ever been made. It
didn't bring calm, it didn't bring peace, and it never will. . . . We cannot
prevent an Iranian nuclear bomb under the decaying and rotten structure
of the current agreement. The Iran deal is defective at its core." Moreover,
he said that withdrawal from the deal showed that "the United States no
longer makes empty threats."[8] He formally withdrew the United States
from the deal and reimposed sanctions on Iranian oil sales and other
transactions that had been suspended in exchange for Iran's compliance
with limits on its nuclear program. His declared objective was to compel
Iran to submit to a renegotiation of the agreement so that its defects, from
the administration's perspective, would be eliminated. The administration apparently believed, in these words, that the United States "could
have its cake and eat it too," meaning that Iran would continue to comply
with the terms of the deal indefinitely despite the U.S. violation of the
agreement.[9] The administration defended the reimposition of sanctions
and addition of new ones, saying that they had deprived Iran of the funds
to press its aggressive regional agenda, while also contending that Iran's
meddlesome behavior was worse than ever. The impression was of an
administration flying by the seat of its pants.

The administration's tools were primarily economic sanctions. As we
have seen, sanctions can be an alternative to war, or a prelude to it. In the
latter sense, sanctions serve as a prod to get one's adversary to lash out,

providing the pretext for a war that one expects to resolve the underlying dispute once and for all. Sanctions in this context have the added virtue of weakening the opponent in the period leading up to the anticipated clash. In this case, severe economic sanctions would starve Iran of resources for its armed forces, making victory for the United States in a potential military contest swifter and easier. This was the Roosevelt administration's implicit strategy vis-à-vis Japan in 1940–41. American economic sanctions designed to deprive Japan of essential imports were understood as incentivizing Japan's military government to move against the United States while simultaneously weakening Tokyo's ability to wage a long war. Not that the White House wished for a Japanese attack, but policy makers understood that sanctions would leave Tokyo with little choice. So this was a policy with a pedigree.

Early in the administration's single term, it was unclear whether Trump's objective was forcing Iran back to the table or maneuvering Tehran into a war. When Trump withdrew from the JCPOA and intensified sanctions, Tehran could have responded in ways that would have heightened tensions and led to a fight. But it played it cool, remaining in compliance with its JCPOA obligations and offering Washington no pretext for escalation. Iran waited a full year following Trump's 2018 departure from the JCPOA before beginning a phased withdrawal of its own.

War with the Islamic Republic, however, was not the only possible implication of U.S. withdrawal from the JCPOA, although the others' likelihood and weight were harder to gauge. These included the difficulty of negotiating future arms control or non-proliferation agreements, owing to Trump's dismissal of the JCPOA as a "political agreement" binding only on the administration that signed it; the weakening of the transatlantic alliance against the backdrop of a resurgent Russia; the risk of regional nuclear proliferation should Iran, unconstrained by the JCPOA, sprint for a bomb; an empowered China and Russia; and the erosion of the dollar as a reserve currency as a result of secondary sanctions imposed by the Trump administration on firms that violated U.S. sanctions on Iran.

Teasing out the incremental effect of the U.S. withdrawal from the JCPOA on conditions that were already corroded is tough. For example, walking away from the JCPOA was a serious affront to the European governments that had worked hard to conclude it. For the British, French, and Germans, the agreement transcended a mere technical arrangement with Iran regulating its nuclear program. It was, rather, a symbol of a new European effectuality, of an ability and determination to alter the course of international developments in a way that served a serious, shared interest.

The effect of U.S. withdrawal from the JCPOA on future arms control and non-proliferation agreements is also tricky to predict, in part because the longer-term reputational effect of Trump's defection is unclear—will it undercut other countries' trust in the United States to keep its word, or will it be looked back on as an aberration?—and in part because we might already be in a post–arms control era, in which case the question is moot.

The debate over reputation, how it forms in the eye of the beholder, and how it influences their behavior, has preoccupied observers since Thucydides's *Peloponnesian War*.* It would be fair to assume, at a minimum, that reneging on the JCPOA is unlikely to enhance a U.S. reputation for scrupulous integrity.

Hence, what was one of the few success stories in multilateral arms control and non-proliferation diplomacy—as opposed to non-proliferation

---

* In the mid-1990s, a combination of archival research and social psychology experimentation cast doubt on the real-world significance of reputation, especially in crises. For the moment, this revisionist wave has generated a useful reaction, and the debate seems to have devolved to a kind of middle ground. Reputation is important, but generally in serial encounters over similar issues in a specific geographic area. In crises, where adversaries have historically focused on the other's sense of the stakes involved and his capacity to defend them, reputation seems to be less a factor.

by force—has now been jettisoned, along with the rules-based Non-Proliferation Treaty regime, the bedrock of international non-proliferation policy. Rather than strengthen the rules-based NPT architecture, withdrawal from the JCPOA subverts it. In its place, we may be back to an unconstrained Iranian civil nuclear program, one that is much less transparent, with only the threat of force to contain it.

If Iran Goes for a Bomb, What Will Its Neighbors Do?

A nuclear-armed Iran was long thought to be the catalyst for proliferation on the Arab side of the Gulf, though proliferation experts have questioned this conventional wisdom for several reasons.[10] A nuclear fuel cycle is extremely difficult to engineer, build, and maintain. Fabricating a weapon with the enriched uranium or plutonium produced by the fuel cycle is yet another immense challenge. And having weaponized the fuel, there remains the task of reducing the size of the "physics package" to fit on a missile and harden it enough to survive reentry into the atmosphere.

For the handful of states that have succeeded in creating a stockpile of deliverable nuclear weapons, the effort has been sustained, intensive, immensely expensive, and generally reliant on outside help. In the Arabian Peninsula, the money is ample, but the expertise and technological infrastructure is not. Ironically, the decision to go for a bomb would be complicated by the multilateral measures put in place over the last decade to hamper Iran's nuclear program.

Although the Saudis have contended that nuclear power is economically essential and have negotiated with a range of suppliers, they have moved slowly until now. Under a new leader, this could change. Crown Prince and now prime minister Mohammed bin Salman has smashed many of the unspoken rules of the game in an attempt to transform the Kingdom. His iconoclasm is especially evident in the security realm. Under his command, Saudi forces are engaged in Yemen against the Houthis, a political faction backed by Iran, and the Kingdom has put itself forward as a bulwark against Iran. In March 2019, he stated that "Saudi Arabia does not want to acquire any nuclear bomb, but without a doubt if Iran developed a nuclear bomb, we will follow suit as soon as possible."[11] There is little reason to doubt his intent. That Saudis have wanted to preserve the nuclear weapons option can reasonably be inferred from their unwillingness to agree to a U.S. prohibition on enrichment as a condition for the transfer of U.S. nuclear technology. The crown prince's declaration did not magically erase the obstacles to a nuclear weapons capability. But his resources, determination, and pattern of risk-taking behavior could combine to surprise Washington.

There is also the question of the economic boomerang effect of unilateral sanctions. Successive U.S. administrations have relied on economic sanctions in the absence of coercive alternatives to the use of force. In most cases, sanctions are counterproductive. They strengthen authoritarian regimes and punish ordinary people. But they satisfy the need to be seen to be doing something to defend U.S. interests where the will to fight for them is tenuous, or the stakes are not that high. Under some conditions, however, they can be effective, as they were against Iran in weakening Iran's economy during the years preceding Tehran's agreement to negotiate stringent limits on its nuclear program. While this had no effect on the pace of Iran's nuclear efforts, it did make sanctions relief politically essential. The election of Hassan Rouhani in 2013 provided an opening, and the Obama administration was prepared to deal. And the sanctions were especially punitive because they were multilateral. There was no way for Iran to evade them.

To replicate the wall-to-wall impact of pre-deal multilateral sanctions, without the cover of a UN Security Council resolution, Trump intended to levy sanctions against other countries that violated U.S. unilateral sanctions. These extraterritorialized measures can be extremely effective when the United States has the whip hand; in this instance, by virtue of the fact that international transactions are largely denominated in dollars. Trump made it clear that the United States would enforce sanctions on any country that, for example, bought Iranian oil. And the United States would essentially block any foreign firm doing business with Iran from the U.S. banking system. Among other things, the United States is in a position to seize or block U.S.-based assets of offending firms.

Whether or not these measures are effective in the short term, states could develop countermeasures over the long run. Most obviously, they could shift incrementally and slowly toward other currencies for trading purposes. The Chinese are already establishing companies whose only trading partner is Iran. Dollars are not a factor in this equation, and there are no U.S.-based assets for Washington to hold hostage. Other countries will likely follow suit. As China debuted as the champion of free trade, and the United States under Trump bowed out of multilateral trade pacts while weaponizing U.S. financial institutions, the lure of the dollar as a reserve currency was liable to shrink. The Obama administration was alive to this danger; presumably, Biden's is too. It's worth recalling that the British pound was a reserve currency for a century and then, suddenly, it was not.

The Other Guy Gets a Vote Too

In September 2019, Trump, perhaps sensing that he had maneuvered the United States into a cul-de-sac, pivoted, beseeching Iranian president Rouhani to meet him in New York to discuss renewed nuclear talks. Not long after, the administration looked the other way as Iran attacked or seized tankers in the Persian Gulf, shot down a $220 million U.S. military drone, and, pounded oil installations in Saudi Arabia with an avalanche of rockets.[12] The absence of any U.S. rejoinder left open the question of whether Trump was rethinking his policy toward Iran, perhaps sensing that maximum pressure was not going to win maximum cooperation.

Iran then rejected another round of negotiations in favor of increasing its enrichment of nuclear fuel, but without taking the step of removing IAEA inspectors. The United States abruptly switched gears once again and targeted a leading Iranian official, Qassim Soleimani, commander of the Islamic Revolutionary Guard Corp's expeditionary unit, the Quds Force.[13]

The killing took place on January 3, 2020. The provocation for the strike was supplied on December 27, 2019, when rocket fire at an Iraqi base near Kirkuk, in northern Iraq, killed a U.S. contractor, in one of a rash of such attacks at bases across the country. Shortly afterward, the administration announced that Kata'eb Hizballah (KH), one of the largely Shia militias that form part of Iraq's hybrid military infrastructure, was responsible for the attack. No evidence for this assessment was publicly disclosed, which does not mean it was lacking. Kata'eb Hizballah was founded by Abu Mahdi al-Muhandis, a prominent Iraqi Shia politician who sought shelter in Iran from Saddam between 1979 and 2003, and then from the United States between the mid-2000s and 2011. U.S. aircraft subsequently raided five KH installations, killing nineteen fighters in what then Defense secretary Mark Esper called "defensive precision strikes." Predictably, Iraqis objected to U.S. air strikes against a militia that had fought ISIS, and they demonstrated rowdily around the American embassy in Baghdad. Shortly afterward, U.S. strikes killed Soleimani, along with al-Muhandis and several others, as they were leaving the Baghdad airport.[14]

Targeting Soleimani would seem to have been prohibited under Executive Order 12333, which forbids U.S. employees to assassinate or conspire to assassinate foreign officials. Although it is up to the president whether to comply with it, in one form or another this order, which originated in the congressional reaction to CIA assassination plots uncovered in the 1970s by the Senate's Church Committee, has been adopted by every administration from Gerald Ford's to Barack Obama's. It has persisted until now mainly because no one has thought it would be a good idea to legitimize assassination, given how hard it is to protect our own public figures.

Iran declared that it would confine its response to military targets, and on January 8 it struck two U.S. bases in Iraq with twelve missiles. Though there were no casualties, scores of U.S. and Iraqi military personnel as well as civilian workers could have been killed. The weapons used were not accurate enough for Iranian decision makers to have been certain that only unoccupied facilities would be struck. They must have assumed, therefore, that the attacks might well draw blood and, if they did, that Trump might escalate the conflict. It appears that the poor quality of Iranian missile guidance systems, precautions taken on the bases to shelter personnel after advance warning of the attacks, and sheer luck prevented the situation from worsening.

If, on the other hand, the administration wanted a war with Iran because it believed a war would be short and end in a victory parade down Constitution Avenue, then it must have assumed that killing Soleimani could provoke one, leaving the United States the undisputed master of the Persian Gulf region. This is not as outlandish as it sounds. The United States has the capacity to carry out a coordinated, sustained air campaign that would be highly destructive and capable of locating and killing Iranian political, military, and intelligence leaders and dismantling their ministries. The assumption that a comprehensive aerial assault could bring about a revolution against the Iranian regime was not necessarily deluded, though the likelihood that it would go disastrously wrong was high.

The Decision to Risk a War

The manner in which the options to respond to the contractor's death were presented to Trump raises additional questions about his decision. According to participants, the president was shown PowerPoint slides in the canonical Beltway form of three alternatives, which we encountered in an earlier chapter, ritually characterized as (a) nuke 'em, (b) surrender, and (c) my option, so that the decision maker is herded toward "my option" by two others that are patently infeasible or absurd. In this case, the options were "kill Soleimani," "refrain from responding to the rocket attack that killed the contractor," and "work with the Iraqi government to fix the problem." No one, at least in the pre-Trump world, would have expected a president to choose the most extreme option. As criticism of the assassination mounted, White House aides were quick to point a finger at Secretary of State Mike Pompeo for persuading the reluctant Trump to give the order. There can be little doubt, based on his long-standing views of Iran's Islamic government, that Pompeo endorsed the move, even though it is known that he later opposed a full-scale war against Iran.[15]

Although Iran's leader, Ayatollah Khamenei, would later state that Iran would retaliate decisively at some point in the future,[16] there was nonetheless a spasmodic response four days after Soleimani's death, when twenty-one rockets landed in the huge American diplomatic compound in Baghdad, killing an Iraqi worker. According to a Trump tweet, the missiles came from Iran, but U.S. Central Command attributed the launch to a "rogue" Iranian-backed militia.[17] The national security cabinet met at the White House on December 23 and finalized "deterrence" options that were to be presented to Trump.[18] Dire warnings from the White House to Iran soon followed,[19] yet cooler heads prevailed.

One could posit a number of explanations for Trump's decision to kill Soleimani, but the one that leaps to mind is impeachment. Although Soleimani's death did not appear to leave the United States better off strategically, it did appear to leave Trump better off politically by pushing impeachment out of the headlines, dominating the news cycle with images of himself as a decisive wartime leader, dividing the Democratic Party on a foreign policy issue, and mobilizing a Republican base that tends to admire toughness. The assassination was plotted in an uncommonly narrow circle to minimize dissent. Nonetheless, there were participants who have since said that they saw no evidence of Soleimani's alleged plans to attack the United States in Iraq, despite the administration's public assertions about a "sinister" scheme. According to a senior administration official, "The DoD was not all in agreement that killing the second most popular person in Iran at an international airport in Iraq was a good idea."[20] Soleimani was too prominent a figure and too closely aligned with the Supreme Leader for Iran to forgo some kind of retaliation.

The Trump administration must have felt that it had protected the president's political flank by displaying a willingness to fight. Conflict would have enabled the United States, in the administration's collective imagination, to press for renewed talks, provided that Iran did not foreclose that option by killing Americans. Trump spoke to the nation from the White House on January 8 to announce a cessation of military action, unspecified new economic sanctions, demands to negotiate a new nuclear deal, and, bizarrely, his best wishes for Iran's leaders. According to senior Arab Gulf officials, Brian Hook, Trump's point man on Iran, told them the president was "desperate" for a deal. Trump thought he could replicate his stunt involving the North American Free Trade Agreement (NAFTA), which was unpopular with his base. In that case, he tore up the existing agreement, insisting that it was a terrible deal, and then proceeded to sign essentially the same agreement, claiming he had extracted a better deal. In response to Trump's speech to the nation, Iran's foreign minister, Javad Zarif, tweeted that Iran was not going to carry out additional attacks. It was also clear that Iran was not going to participate in a replay of Trump's NAFTA charade.

Would the United States have been willing to carry out the scorched earth policy threatened by Trump? It seems unlikely. There would have been pushback from within the Pentagon, as there was in the virtually immediate reaction to Trump's onetime threats to destroy culturally significant sites in Iran. The spectacle of the United States systematically battering what is actually a weak country would have spurred international outrage that would force an early cease-fire. Under an attack of such intensity, Iran would have targeted U.S. interests and its allies in the region. Israel would likely have found itself under a missile barrage from Lebanon, many Iraqis would have lashed out, and the Iranian regime would have been sure to take the fight to capitals on the Arab side of the Gulf. The United States would indeed be the undisputed master, but of a smoking, shattered landscape.[21]

Own Goal

The U.S. withdrawal from the nuclear agreement failed to compel Iran to enter into negotiations over a broader and more restrictive one. As the Trump administration drew to a close, the United States and Iran remained at a standoff. In late December the U.S. Navy sent a nuclear submarine armed with 154 cruise missiles into the Gulf and staged two deployments of B-52 bombers[22] to the region, amid talk of impending Iranian retaliation for the anniversary of the death of Soleimani and the death of Mohsen Fakhrizadeh, a scientist who oversaw the country's nuclear efforts, who was presumably killed by Israel.[23] Fakhrizadeh's death on November 27 was widely interpreted as a spoke in the wheels of renewed talks between the incoming Biden administration and Tehran.[24]

Iran's reaction to the assassination of the scientist was expressed in a law passed by its parliament requiring the government to begin enriching nuclear fuel in earnest. Now at the 60 percent level, Iran has made it clear that it is now capable of going all the way to weapons-grade uranium very quickly. Iran also took the opportunity provided by Trump's attempt to destroy the JCPOA by installing centrifuges of increasing sophistication and efficacy. U.S. government experts assess that Iran could now build a bomb within six months from the day it started production. At the time the JCPOA was signed, the "breakout period" was a full year.

As the odor of high explosives dissipated, then, the United States faced the prospects of a nuclear-armed Iran; an Iraq that was less stable than at any time since ISIS erupted in 2014 and where Iran's influence will grow while that of the United States recedes; the eventual loss of U.S. access to bases in Iraq; the suspension of anti-ISIS operations; a growing divide between the United States and its European allies; and new opportunities for Russian and Chinese aggrandizement. As tensions began to subside, it appeared that their only clear benefit had accrued to Trump's ill-fated reelection campaign, which underscores Trump's instinct for exploiting the public good for personal gain.

Israeli Strategy

The evolution of American policy in the region has been unsettling for Israel. Unlike with the Arab Gulf states to which it has low-key or clandestine ties and that no longer pose a conventional military threat, Israel does not have the option of détente with Iran. Between the disconcertingly radical way Iran speaks about Israel—replete with threats to obliterate it—and actual Iranian intentions, there is no mistaking a persistent Iranian effort to position itself to attack the Jewish state. Iran's posture recalls the earlier campaign of Arab states bordering Israel and of the pre-Oslo Palestinian strategy toward it, which was to maintain pressure, accept defeat in war without conceding defeat, and prepare for the next round. Each cycle was presumed to chip away at Israel's resolve, self-confidence, and, ultimately, capacity for self-defense. However, Israel's costly victory in the 1973 war and the peace with Egypt in 1979 and Jordan in 1994—coupled with the collapse in 1989 of Syria's Soviet arms supplier and bankroller—buried this Arab strategy. The so-called first-tier states eventually absorbed the enduring fact of their military inferiority and accepted Israel's presence in the Middle East.

Just as the old Arab strategy was fading, the 1979 Islamic Revolution in Iran gave it a new lease on life. The Iranians have pursued it through their support for Hizballah in Lebanon, where, in effect, Iran now shares a border with Israel, as well as for terrorist groups and Hamas in Gaza. In recent years Soleimani had advanced these goals through his command of the Quds Force, entrepreneurial diplomacy, and force of personality. Ideology drives Iran's opposition to Israel: its existence is an affront to the divinely ordained moral order that in the regime's view should govern the universe, or at least the regional structure of interstate relations. This has placed Israel in an awkward position: adjustments to its foreign policy, or plausible concessions of any kind, cannot address the underlying motivations of Iranian animosity.

These new circumstances have produced a revised Israeli security strategy known as "the campaign between the wars," or by its Hebrew acronym, Mabam.[25] This strategy, which might best be described as a permanent offensive, has resulted in at least 158 strikes against targets in Syria since 2013, in which about 2,000 missiles or bombs were delivered by Israeli warplanes.[26] The number could well be much higher.[27] It is a campaign of growing reach and audacity that has encompassed targets Israel assessed as related to Iran as far away as Beirut and the Bekaa Valley in Lebanon to the northwest[28]; al-Tanf on the Iraqi-Jordanian border; and Anbar province in Iraq in attacks apparently staged from northeastern Syria.[29] Given that the U.S. controls Iraqi airspace, the Trump administration evidently decided that acceding to Israel's strikes there outweighed its interest in Iraq's stability or the pretense of regard for its sovereignty.

Mabam carries considerable risk for Israel of provoking the very attack it seeks to deter.[30] There is the risk of escalation should Tehran decide to respond more effectively than it has in the past, perhaps killing Israeli civilians in the process, thereby necessitating an Israeli response that may escalate in unforeseen ways. For the Israelis, there is also the danger of alienating a future U.S. administration by collaborating with Trump's in the destabilization of Iraq or dragging the United States into a regional war with Iran that would not serve American interests.

The Abraham Accords

This brings us to the other major Middle Eastern initiative of the Trump administration: the Abraham Accords.[31] These encompass peace treaties between Israel on the one side and the United Arab Emirates, Bahrain, Morocco, and Sudan on the other.

Like U.S.-Soviet arms control agreements of a bygone era, the accords reflect and codify existing realities rather than create new ones. Although both Israel and the UAE have guarded their security ties carefully over the years, Americans doing business in the UAE have often bumped into Israelis thought to have defense or intelligence connections. There have been hiccups in the relationship, but on the whole, it has been something of an open secret.

Both countries perceive Iran as an enemy but also feel threatened by the Muslim Brotherhood. Hamas is an offshoot of that organization, which makes the Brotherhood suspect in Israeli eyes. And as a transnational group advocating both democracy of a limited sort and Islamic law, the Brotherhood is anathema to the UAE, which is attempting to secularize while maintaining an authoritarian system. When the Muslim Brotherhood won the presidency in Egypt in 2012, Israel and the UAE both saw it as a dangerous development.

But the UAE is not looking for a war with Iran and will not be eager to host Israeli forces determined to fight one. Given that Israeli and Emirati interests were largely met through existing tacit arrangements, the immediate spur to the Emirates' initiative probably lay in the prospect of

Israeli annexation of parts or all of the West Bank.[32] The UAE understood that Israel would defer this in return for diplomatic recognition. There was also the question of money: an experienced investor explained to me that the trade relations made possible by the Abraham Accords will make many Israelis rich and many Emiratis richer. According to Israel's finance ministry, formal trade will grow from virtually nothing to $500 million in a few years.[33] Thus far, trade volume is lopsided with Israeli imports from the UAE exceeding exports by a considerable margin. If the UAE is able to acquire major Israeli tactical systems, such as the Iron Dome antimissile launcher, the number could be much higher.[34]

To close the deal for the Abraham Accords, the Trump administration offered incentives to Arab signatories. To the UAE, it was acquisition of the F-35 stealth aircraft. Typically, this would not have been possible because it would have undercut Israel's qualitative military edge, which is guaranteed by U.S. domestic law.[35] Trump also appears to have offered the prospect of sophisticated Growler electronic warfare aircraft and long-range Reaper drones. Prime Minister Netanyahu privately assured Trump that the sale of F-35s would not be an issue,[36] although Benny Gantz, the deputy prime minister, and Israeli military and intelligence officials challenged him on this.[37]

Morocco was persuaded to sign the accords by a shocking reversal of the U.S. position on Western Sahara, which Morocco has claimed for years in defiance of the wishes of the tribes living there.[38] After long insisting that the status of the territory had to be negotiated,[39] the United States endorsed Moroccan control. Washington won over Sudan by dropping it from the U.S. list of state sponsors of terrorism.[40] Bahrain, nominally independent of Saudi Arabia, signed the accords in lieu of Riyadh, where King Salman bin Abdulaziz al-Saud's opposition to a treaty with Israel in the absence of progress on Palestinian rights has blocked the crown prince's freedom of action.

Trump and Iraq

One wonders, in retrospect, how the Trump administration viewed Iraq. It had always suspected that Iraq was an enemy in league with Iran, a view that was linked to resentment about Iraqis'—and particularly Shias'— ingratitude for America's "generous" sacrifices on their behalf. This ahistorical petulance was exhibited by National Security Advisor Robert O'Brien,[41] who in his justification for Soleimani's assassination recalled how "the American people have been extraordinarily generous with their lives and with their treasure to the people of Iraq, to help them move forward. So, you know, we'd certainly be very disappointed if there was some sort of adverse decision by the Iraqi parliament, the Council of Representatives, with respect to our continued ability to assist the people of Iraq." Ryan Crocker, a former U.S. ambassador to Iraq, bemoaned Shias' disloyalty to their U.S. saviors. "No one [in Iraq]," he told *The New York Times*, "is going to speak up for us, despite all we've done and in spite of the mistakes. . . . All we've given Iraq, and the Shia in particular, were things they could never have dreamed of before 2003."[42]

That the president had been stewing in these grievances is clear from his reaction to Iraqi demands that U.S. forces withdraw from Iraq after Soleimani's death: "We have a very extraordinarily expensive air base that's there. It cost billions of dollars to build. We're not leaving unless they pay us back for it." Unless the United States exits Iraq on a "very friendly basis," Trump said, the United States "will charge them sanctions like they've never seen before ever."[43] Given that approximately 200,000 Iraqis died as a consequence of Operation Iraqi Freedom, the recipients of all that largesse might have taken a skeptical view of Trump's crass collection notice.[44]

These resentments help explain the willingness of the administration first to acquiesce in Israeli air strikes against Iranian targets in Iraq and then to carry out its own, regardless of the continuing presence there of several thousand U.S. troops mostly engaged in training activities and force protection. Strikes in Iraq, whatever the justification, were likely to further hamstring its weak government and erode whatever goodwill the United States had cultivated. The vote on January 5, 2020, in the Iraqi parliament to expel U.S. forces from the country, although it is not binding, was a foregone conclusion from the moment the U.S. missile killed a prominent Iraqi politician and militia leader and an Iranian guest of the state.[45] The rare public denunciations by revered clerics of the Sistani family reflect Iraq's deep alienation from the United States: in his letter of condolence to Iran's Supreme Leader, Grand Ayatollah Ali al-Sistani extolled "the unique role [Soleimani] played in many years battling ISIS in Iraq and all his efforts and sacrifices related to this are unforgettable."

To the extent the United States cared about its legacy in Iraq and its enormous investment—hundreds of billions of dollars and thousands of Americans killed or wounded—in Iraq's future, the assassination of Soleimani and Muhandis was a mistake. If, however, the administration had written off Iraq as good for nothing more than a staging ground for Iran's regional aggression, then there was no legacy to protect.

Trump and Syria

It is hard to pinpoint Trump's aims in Syria. He was beholden to Moscow and therefore loath to criticize Russia's support for the Assad government, the object of Washington's ire. Iranian support for Assad was easier to condemn, but there was not very much the United States could do about it. The Kurds had been vital to the U.S. anti-ISIS campaign, but Trump was enamored of Turkey's president Recep Tayyip Erdogan, an authoritarian as Trump envisioned himself. And Erdogan was seeking to destroy the Syrian Kurdish military and political community that the United States had cultivated. In contrast to Obama, Trump ordered air strikes against targets related to Syrian chemical weapons in April 2017 and then a year later in April 2018. The latter attack, a more violent raid, was carried out with French and UK forces. Neither attack had any effect on the viability of the government of Damascus or the weapons it used against the opposition. But leaders in all three capitals judged that the use of chemical weapons warranted a response, even if it was destined to be ineffectual. For Trump, these were opportunities to differentiate himself from Obama and showcase his role as commander in chief.[46]

Overall, though, Trump was increasingly unhappy with the U.S. presence in Syria once ISIS had been suppressed in 2017. The White House seemed to have no interest in overthrowing the Assad regime and had not deployed enough troops in the right locations to engage Iranian movements, or those of its proxy forces. The only mission for U.S. troops appeared to be to protect the Syrian Kurds who had borne the brunt of the fighting against jihadists in Syria, and who needed protection from Turkish ground and air forces that had entered Syria to push back, or just kill, the Syrian Kurds occupying territory along the border with Turkey. As far as the U.S. military and State Department were concerned, this was a moral and strategic obligation. U.S. Central Command, along with then Defense secretary James R. Mattis, had assured the Kurds that the United States would never abandon them, despite Trump's clearly expressed desire to get out of Syria—he initially ordered U.S. troops to withdraw in December 2018.[47]

The pushback in Washington against that decision reflected decades of Kurdish lobbying, the Kurds' favorable reputation as combatants in the war against ISIS, and lingering American guilt over the betrayal of the Iraqi Kurds decades before. Trump retreated, but only temporarily, until October 2019. As of this writing, there are still 900 U.S. troops in Syria who are working with their Kurdish co-combatants and Arab tribal elements to block an ISIS resurgence, but these forces have been pushed away from the border by the Turkish army and its undisciplined Sunni

Arab protégés. The events surrounding the Turkish campaign reflected Trump's grifter instincts, the absence of a policy-making system, and the furious opposition of his own party to Trump's careless attitude toward Syrian Kurds. The fuse was lit by the White House summary of a call between Trump and Tayyip Erdogan, the Turkish president, which said, "Turkey will soon be moving forward with its long-planned operation into Northern Syria. The United States Armed Forces will not support or be involved in the operation, and United States forces, having defeated the ISIS territorial 'Caliphate,' will no longer be in the immediate area."[48] In other words, Trump, seemingly on a whim, was leaving the Kurds to Erdogan's tender mercies.

The House of Representatives rejected the withdrawal 354–60; in the Senate, Mitt Romney called it "a bloodstain on the annals of American history." Still, Trump was initially unfazed, only acknowledging that his order "was unconventional . . . [but] sometimes you have to let them fight like two kids. Then you pull them apart." As outrage grew and Erdogan marshaled his forces to take on the Kurds, Trump had second thoughts, which prompted an idiotic letter—there is simply no other word for it—to Erdogan, warning him not to go overboard.[49] Trump gushed,

Let's work out a good deal! You don't want to be responsible for slaughtering thousands of people, and I don't want to be responsible for destroying the Turkish economy—and I will. . . .

I have worked hard to solve some of your problems. Don't let the world down. You can make a great deal. [Syrian Kurdish commander] General Mazloum is willing to negotiate with you. . . .

History will look upon you favorably if you get this done the right and humane way. It will look upon you forever as the devil if good things don't happen. Don't be a tough guy. Don't be a fool! I will call you later.

Erdogan reportedly threw the letter into a wastebasket and gave the order for Turkish forces to embark on Operation Peace Spring, as the invasion was called.

It was a bloody mess. Within weeks, the administration had reinserted troops, but only after the Turks and their jihadist allies had rampaged through Kurdish towns and villages along the Syrian border. This time, the president had a compelling reason to reassert control: revenue from Syrian oil fields. When Erdogan visited the White House shortly afterward, Trump explained, "We're keeping the oil. We have the oil. The oil is secure. We left troops behind only for the oil."[50] Separately, he elaborated on this point, saying, "What I intend to do, perhaps, is make a deal with an ExxonMobil or one of our great companies to go in there and do it properly . . . and spread out the wealth."[51] He then handed a small Delaware-based company run by Republican donors, Delta Crescent Energy, the contract to manage Syrian oil fields occupied by the United States and its Kurdish allies.[52] Defense Secretary Mark Esper, who replaced Mattis after he had resigned in protest of Trump's order to withdraw troops from Syria, publicly contradicted Trump's assertions. According to Esper, U.S. troops had gone back in to fight ISIS, rather than secure profits for American companies. It was also widely observed that expropriation of Syria's natural resources was a violation of international law.

Jared Kushner, Viceroy

Jared Kushner, the president's son-in-law and heir to a real estate fortune, was named assistant to the president and special adviser shortly after Trump took office. He had had a rocky start, thanks to his failure to disclose contacts with Russian officials, prompting the denial of his top secret security clearance. The situation was further complicated by the disclosure of Kushner's attempt to get a dedicated encrypted line installed in his office, linking him directly to the Kremlin, so that his conversations would be inaccessible to others, including U.S. government agencies.[53] The yearlong tug-of-war between the White House and the arbiters of security within the intelligence community and FBI was only resolved by Trump's direct intervention. Kushner had already been involved in day-to-day policy deliberations. He became Trump's go-to guy for managing serious domestic problems, such as prison reform or, later on, COVID response.

In the Middle East, Kushner had two portfolios. The first was the peace process. Trump's closest advisers on this issue, Jason Greenblatt, his first Middle East envoy, and David Friedman, his ambassador to Israel, were orthodox Jews with links to the settler movement on the West Bank. Both were senior executives within the Trump Organization in New York. Trump's public statements early in his administration signaled an open-mindedness to whatever ideas Israel and the Palestinians might agree on. Despite his rejection of the institutionalized peace process geared to Palestinian independence and sovereignty, he was certain that a deal could be struck. The underlying dispute was over real estate, so he was the one to make it happen, where diplomats were bound to fail.

Kushner was entrusted with devising the deal. He started by shrugging off conventional peace process wisdom as well as the usual pieties about a two-state solution, which was not an unreasonable premise for a new plan. The gap between Israelis and Palestinians looked unbridgeable. Palestinian politics were broken. Hamas and Fatah continued to contest the leadership of the national movement, producing endless deadlock. Palestinian politicians were corrupt, security forces were loyal to individuals rather than institutions, there had not been legislative elections for well over a decade, and the economy barely limped along. The Palestinian leader, Abu Mazen, was in his mid-eighties, uninspiring and a symbol of a necrotic system.

Israeli occupation caused some of these problems and made others worse. The burgeoning Israeli population in settlements clustered along the old border and dotting the landscape of the West Bank reinforced Palestinian perceptions that Israel was uninterested in a deal and intent on imposing a fait accompli. Given these unpromising conditions and the collapse of Kerry's recent effort to secure an Israeli-Palestinian agreement, the new proposal was limited to an economic peace. The premise was that the Palestinians were never going to obtain their political goals. There would be no fully contiguous Palestinian territory on the West Bank; no borders that aligned with pre–June 1967 lines; no capital in Jerusalem; no concession to the right of Palestinian refugees to return to their homeland; and no sovereignty, except of a kind that bore only a slight resemblance to the real thing. Since Israel held all the cards, it was well past time for Palestinians to rethink their vision for the future.

The idea was that, in exchange for accepting political realities, Palestinians could secure a glowing economic future. From Kushner's perspective, this did not mean that statehood was off the table for all time. Rather, having accepted the terms of an economic peace, Palestine would be able to cultivate its political garden as well and ultimately grow into the kind of society ready and able to commit to a true, lasting peace with its Israeli neighbors.

The essential elements of this approach were, first, to demonstrate to the Palestinians that they were isolated. As the administrations saw the situation, there was no country, other than the United States, that cared about them or their political aspirations. Arab neighbors were fed up with their recurring demands for financial support, disorderly politics, and inability to strike a deal with Israel. Within Israel, they had alienated all but a tiny minority of leftist cranks. The Palestinians, in short, would have to be put in the penalty box, as Kushner phrased it, where these unwelcome truths could be impressed upon them. The United States, for example, would cut off aid to Palestinians, close down its diplomatic installations in Jerusalem that linked Washington to the Palestinian leadership, and move the U.S. embassy from Tel Aviv to Jerusalem, signifying American rejection of the long-standing doctrine that the status of Jerusalem was to be negotiated between Israelis and Palestinians. The Palestinians would soon see that they had no defenders within the international community. Because they had no defenders, there would be no pushback against Israel or the United States.

Second, because even this kind of plan would require Israeli cooperation, Washington would have to hold Israel in an especially close embrace to prepare it for the proverbial "painful compromises" Kushner's initiative would allegedly entail in the future.

Last, the process would have to be internationalized. An economic peace relied on capital, which neither Israel nor the United States would supply. The fuel had to come from the wealthy Arab states in the Persian Gulf, which, in deference to Trump and Kushner, would overcome their reluctance to invest in the Palestinian economy and subsidize the budget of the Palestinian Authority until the gains from the economic peace were realized.

There was an undeniable internal logic to this plan, but it did not appear connected to the observable reality of Palestinians' desire to be rid of Israeli occupation and run their own show, even into the ground. The RAND Corporation had proposed something along the lines of the Kushner plan in the early 2000s, which most Palestinians rejected precisely because it was not linked to a political goal. A decade later, fewer Palestinians believed that a state was in the cards, but they nonetheless interpreted an economic peace as both the justification and scaffolding for continued occupation.

Kushner did consult former peace negotiators, in particular Aaron Miller, who recounted their conversation in a blog posting. Miller's message for Kushner was that his plan would be dead on arrival, but the fact that previous peace plans crafted by officials who were steeped in the issues had died either on the operating table or in the recovery ward did not help experts like Miller establish their credibility with Kushner.

Not that Kushner's own credibility was impressive, at least outside of Jerusalem. His plan was described in the media as "the Monty Python sketch of Israeli-Palestinian peace initiatives." In his self-defense, Kushner revealed that he had read twenty-five books on the Middle East process, although which books they were remains unknown.[54]

However, failure could not be averted despite Kushner's special brand of advocacy:

> You have 5 million Palestinians who are really trapped because of bad leadership. So what we've done is we've created an opportunity for their leadership to either seize or not. If they screw up this opportunity—which, again, they have a perfect track record of missing opportunities—if they screw this up, I think that they will have a very hard time looking the international community in the face, saying they are victims, saying they have rights. . . .
>
> The Palestinian leadership have to ask themselves a question: Do they want to have a state? Do they want to have a better life? If they do, we have created a framework for them to have it, and we're going to treat them in a very respectful manner. If they don't, then they're going to screw up another opportunity like they've screwed up every other opportunity that they've ever had in their existence.[55]

The real problem, he told reporters, was that Palestinian leaders were "hysterical and stupid." He insisted that "if they stop saying crazy things and engage, they will see there is an opportunity here." It turned out that one of the crazy things Palestinian leadership was saying was that it had not been allowed a glimpse of the plan and therefore an opportunity for an informed response.[56]

In a conversation with Christiane Amanpour, Kushner offered viewers his advice on how best to approach his plan: "What I would encourage people to do is try to divorce yourself from all of the history that's happened over the years." History, unfortunately, is one of those things that must be taken into account in any such negotiation. Referring to dismissive assessments of his plan, he pointed out, "I've been getting criticized for the last couple of years by all the people who have tried and failed for not doing this the same way they have, okay?" He was irritated by the obliviousness of critics to the sheer amount of work he had put into his plan, insisting, "Past proposals have been 2 to 3 pages—this is an over 80-page proposal with a map. Never been done before."[57] Although this claim was absurd, he probably believed it to be true.

The move of the embassy from Tel Aviv to Jerusalem had long been required by legislation, but over time, successive administrations had invoked a clause in the law that waived the requirement to relocate the embassy if the move threatened to provoke a violent Arab or Muslim response. Right-wing American Jewish voters and evangelicals opposed the use of the waiver because they supported Israeli control of Jerusalem and its determination that Jerusalem was the country's capital. It was not until these constituencies became indispensable to the electoral viability of a particular administration—Trump's—that official Washington seriously considered relocating the embassy.

The move was condemned for an array of reasons, some valid and some less so. It was true that according to the UN Security Council, the political status of Jerusalem and sovereignty over it were questions reserved for negotiation. Hence the fact that until the transfer of the U.S. embassy to Jerusalem under Trump, the only diplomatic missions headquartered in Jerusalem belonged to a couple of small countries that had been compensated generously by the Israeli government for their loyalty. On the other hand, Jerusalem was unarguably Israel's capital. Except the Defense Ministry and Mossad, the entire apparatus of Israel's government, including the parliament, the prime minister's office and residence, Hebrew University, and the national cemetery were all situated in Jerusalem. This was not a scenario that would ever be reversed. Nor was it likely that the unification of Jerusalem under Israeli law would change, regardless of negotiations that might or might not be revived. Moving the embassy to Jerusalem, therefore, could be justified as a sensible concession to reality.

Critics contended that however much the move might align with common sense, it put the United States on the wrong side of an important legal dispute and was a clear sign that Washington had abandoned its admittedly uneven interest in Palestinian rights entirely, and would cause the Muslim world to explode in indignant rage. Thus, the embassy move would be worse than a sin; it would be a mistake. But the Trump White House, to the extent they gave this any thought, bet correctly that Israel would move swiftly to stanch Palestinian protests on the West Bank and that demonstrations in response to the move in regional capitals, especially Cairo and Amman, would be dispersed immediately by security forces.

The ceremony in Jerusalem marking the administration's decision was revealing, insofar as there were no non-Orthodox Jewish clergy present and that most of the VIPs were American evangelical leaders. Also absent were diplomats representing other countries. It had the appearance, and reality, of a campaign event to reinforce evangelical support for the president by demonstrating that once again, he had delivered to the evangelical community in a way that no other president had done. Through evangelical eyes, the juxtaposition of Trump, the Holy City, and Temple Mount was powerful, visible evidence of Trump's election by God to further Christian goals.

The Unity of Elites

Kushner's other job was to court the Saudi elite. Mohammed bin Salman's missteps had by now imperiled the U.S. embrace that had constituted one of the pillars of Saudi rule. Americans have never particularly liked Saudi Arabia. Its use of oil as a weapon in 1973, spectacles of public executions and reports of other human rights violations, suspicions that Saudi leaders were complicit in the September 11 attacks, and a widespread distaste for Islam have combined to form a popular image of a corrupt, cruel, anti-Semitic absolute monarchy. Gallup polls of Americans over many years have shown that the majority of respondents have held unfavorable views of the Kingdom. It was only during Desert Storm, when Washington went out of its way to portray Saudi Arabia as a valiant ally in the campaign to liberate Kuwait, that expressions of a "very favorable" view broke into the double digits—11 percent. For the most part, it has hovered around 5 percent.

Yet the relationship between Jared Kushner and MBS was evidence of the Kingdom's enduring influence in Washington, despite public revulsion. The Kushner-MBS dynamic resembled the chummy relationship between the George W. Bush White House and Bandar bin Sultan, son of Saudi Arabia's former defense minister and the ambassador to the United States from 1983 to 2005. Endowed with essentially unlimited resources owing to his father's matter-of-fact corruption, Bandar courted the rich and famous. The photo of Bandar, Bush, Dick Cheney, and Condoleezza Rice lounging on the White House balcony shortly after the September 11 attacks illustrates the cozy intimacy that then prevailed.

Kushner's bond with MBS similarly reflected class affinity, shared financial interests, and self-conceptions as men who matter. In policy, it reflected a disregard for human rights, a desire to curtail Iranian influence and to see the clerical regime in Tehran crippled or replaced, and an impulse to recast Middle Eastern politics, not just by humbling Iran but by cutting the Gordian knot of Israeli-Palestinian animosity. Their relationship also embodied the self-dealing crony capitalism that keeps Middle Eastern regimes—and increasingly the United States—afloat. One result of this trend is the subversion of American strategic interests through bilateral deals that favor the financial interests of their ruling elites.

A case in point, according to an investigation by the House Committee on Oversight and Reform, was a secret Trump administration effort to supply Saudi Arabia with nuclear power plants, despite the opposition of its own lawyers and strategic planners. The Saudi plan to develop nuclear power had been circulating for several years and on its face is uncontroversial. Saudi oil is best sold on the hard currency markets, while domestic power needs, especially for electricity and desalinization, could be better met by nuclear energy (but even better met by solar power). Russia, China, and South Korea were competing for lucrative nuclear power–related construction contracts in the Kingdom. American company Westinghouse Electric—which declared bankruptcy in 2017, owing to the high cost of its reactor design, but has since emerged from it—had been seeking a contract to build nuclear plants in Saudi Arabia, but U.S. firms are subject to stringent export restrictions designed to prevent foreign countries from using U.S.-built reactors to produce nuclear fuel, which could be used for weapons. The Saudis, however, insisted on producing their own nuclear fuel; they turned to lobbyists in Washington to make their case and pressed it more strongly after Trump became president.

Saudi interests meshed with Trump family financial dealings. In 2007, Kushner's company bought 666 Fifth Avenue in New York City, a poorly timed and disastrously negotiated deal that eventually placed him in serious financial jeopardy. In 2018, Brookfield Asset Management Inc., an investment company with around $330 billion of assets under management, including real estate, renewable power, infrastructure, and private equity, took a $1.1 billion lease on the property, bailing Kushner out. Brookfield also now owns Westinghouse Electric. To make matters murkier, the disgraced former national security adviser Michael Flynn, while an adviser to the Trump campaign—and apparently during his brief tenure at the White House and after his departure—was deeply involved in the lobbying effort to approve the sale of reactors to the Saudis, and he presumably stood to make a great deal of money if the deal went through.

This would be a dangerous move. As previously noted, MBS pledged to secure a nuclear weapons capability if Iran were to do so. A Saudi capacity would almost certainly reinforce Iran's desire to acquire its own. Two new and adversarial nuclear powers separated by one hundred miles of Persian Gulf waters is an alarming prospect. The construction of a facility for producing ballistic missiles in the Kingdom has also provoked suspicion of Saudi nuclear aims. The Trump administration said that it would enforce the restrictions governing the transfer of nuclear technology, while cautioning that the Russians or Chinese may construct Saudi reactors instead.

All in all, Kushner was rewarded lavishly by the Saudi crown prince for his support. Within six months of leaving the White House, an investment firm Kushner set up to capitalize on the Abraham Accords was given $2 billion by Saudi Arabia over the objections of its own investment officers. From the crown prince's perspective, however, one can see why this would be a prudent investment in the return of the Trump family to the White House in 2024.[58]

In the United States, outrage at the murder of the Saudi dissident journalist Jamal Khashoggi by a hit team dispatched by the thin-skinned Crown Prince Mohammed bin Salman persisted. In Senate testimony in November 2018, Secretary of State Mike Pompeo derided senators for "caterwauling" about human rights when the Iranian wolf was at the door. Secretary of Defense James Mattis denied that there was a "smoking gun" that indisputably proved the crown prince had ordered Khashoggi's death, but the circumstantial evidence was convincing enough for Congress to dismiss his assessment as a cover-up and for the Senate to pass a resolution holding MBS personally responsible. In January 2021, the intelligence community declassified its own assessment, which concluded that the crown prince had ordered Khashoggi's murder. As we will see in the next chapter, the Kingdom's key role in the global oil market and the sheer amount of cash the U.S.-Saudi relationship throws off within the United States would force anger over Khashoggi's murder to coexist with old ways of doing business.

On the whole, Trump's Middle East looked worse than Obama's four years earlier. Iran was enriching uranium to 60 percent and installing centrifuges to begin stockpiling nuclear fuel. Trump had driven Iran out of compliance but not back to the negotiating table, or to the battlefield.

Trump, and Kushner, left no advances in the peace process for Biden to exploit, but, in fairness, there was probably no interest in either Israel or among Palestinians in yet another round of talks. Whether the Abraham Accords turn out to be anything more than a conduit for capital flows between the Gulf and Israel remains to be seen. If the accords have strategic implications, they might not necessarily help Biden's administration. Instead, they could embolden Israel and Emirati actions toward Iran that escalate uncontrollably. Trump left Biden messy situations in Libya and Yemen, but to be fair, it was scarcely likely that Washington could accomplish much on its own in either country. In Syria, Trump left Biden a volatile situation. At the time of writing, an empowered Erdogan, no friend of the United States, presides over a jihadist protectorate in the northwest corner of Syria, nominally ruled by Abu Mohammed al Jolani, head of Hayat Tahrir al Sham, the successor to Syrian al Qaeda. Turkey is threatening Syria's Kurdish population, Israel is bombing targets across the length and breadth of the country, and U.S. sanctions have locked the Syrian people into a dungeon of sheer misery while leaving the regime itself undamaged. In Iraq, Biden is faced with an unresolved conflict with both the government in Baghdad and factions aligned with an influential Iran, while autocrats in important capitals like Cairo have become more openly oppressive. But the America that Trump has bequeathed to Biden is not in much better shape. It is, however, a much higher priority.

CHAPTER EIGHT

JOSEPH BIDEN

Back to the Future?

If we ever needed a visual reminder of the continuing grip oil-rich autocrats have on U.S. foreign policy in the Middle East, we got it today. One fist bump is worth a thousand words.[1]

—REP. ADAM SCHIFF, ON BIDEN'S FIST BUMP WITH
SAUDI CROWN PRINCE MOHAMMED BIN SALMAN

We will not walk away and leave a vacuum to be filled by China, Russia, or Iran.[2]

—PRESIDENT BIDEN DEFENDING THE FIST BUMP

My background and the background of my family is Irish American, and we have a long history of—not fundamentally unlike the Palestinian people with Great Britain and their attitude toward Irish Catholics over the years, for four hundred years.[3]

— PRESIDENT BIDEN ON THE PLIGHT OF THE PALESTINIANS

Given the wreckage Trump left behind at home and in areas of strategic salience abroad, the Biden administration has not had much time to spare for Middle East issues. Its foreign policy agenda has been shaped by the looming question of how best to come to grips with Xi

Jinping's China. Taiwan has reemerged as a flashpoint, creating the conditions for confrontation. Russia's invasion of Ukraine and the reverses it has suffered, owing in part to U.S. weapons transfers, has raised the specter of nuclear weapons use by a cornered Putin. In contrast, the Middle East, with the significant exception of Iran, poses no plausible serious challenge to U.S. interests or opportunities to advance them. Although oil and gas supply has been caught up in the economic warfare that shrouds the fighting on the ground between Ukraine and Russia, leading to Biden's fleeting appeal to Saudi Arabia to boost production, changes in the oil market have contributed to Washington's pivot from the Middle East. The United States alternates with Russia and Saudi Arabia as the world's largest producer of fossil fuels, the cost of renewable energy is dropping, electronic vehicles are poised to dominate the automotive sector, and the effects of global warming are lending a bit of urgency to a shift away from oil.[4] Demand, on the other hand, will remain high in the near to medium term. According to McKinsey & Company, by 2040, supply will have to increase by 38 million barrels per day to meet demand; even if the energy transition proceeds rapidly, an unlikely scenario, demand will exceed current supply by 23 million barrels per day.[5] According to investigative reporting by the *New York Times*, "The Kingdom is working to keep fossil fuels at the center of the world economy for decades to come by lobbying, funding research, and using its diplomatic muscle to obstruct climate change action." Indeed, the Saudi oil minister vowed to pump every" last molecule" of oil underneath his country.[6] Uncertainties about Russian and Iranian participation in the market suggest that the gap might be even wider. Thus, even if the United States doesn't need foreign oil, it will be facing higher prices over the long run.

Biden was Obama's point man on Iraq during his vice presidency, and Tony Blinken, the new secretary of state, was Biden's point man. They understand Iraq and its problems well and know many Iraqi politicians. Unlike Trump, who regarded Iraq as enemy territory and its people as in thrall to Iranian clerics, Biden sees it in more nuanced terms and has avoided taking steps that weaken the Baghdad government's credibility by infringing on its sovereignty, or demonstrate callous disregard for Iraqi lives, as Trump did by pardoning the American contractors convicted of murdering fourteen civilians in 2007.[7] Iraqi politics blew up in 2022 as one faction tried to overturn the spoils system that was imposed by the United States and has regulated Iraqi politics ever since. The tragic irony was that even the United States realized that the spoils system had to go if the Iraqi government was ever going to deliver a better life for its citizens. But Moqtada al-Sadr, the politician who was pressing violently for the change, was himself one of the worst actors on Iraq's political stage and an implacable enemy of the United States. Washington's ability to intervene was limited—long gone were the days when the White House could choose the Iraqi leader—but Trump's killing of prominent and popular figures in Iraq had alienated the moderate Shia, thereby cutting off an avenue of influence. Under the circumstances, the United States has wisely kept a low profile. Iran's response to the intra-Shi'a split that marked the political standoff was likewise subdued. Biden's advisers were also directly involved in the Iran nuclear talks, so unlike Trump's, they have intensive experience negotiating with Iranians. But Trump clearly shifted the center of gravity of American punditry on Iran to the right.

The new administration therefore has been focused on how best to restore the pre-Trump status quo with Iran; what if any benefits it can extract from the Abraham Accords; whether to adjust its military and diplomatic posture in the Persian Gulf; and what to do about Syria, which Turkey, Iran, Israel, Russia, the United States, and an assortment of jihadists are picking apart while its population slowly starves.

Iran Nuclear Deal

Biden has declared his intention to reenter the JCPOA (Joint Comprehensive Plan of Action). Rather than reverse Trump's withdrawal from the agreement immediately upon entering office, Biden took his time. He was overwhelmed with domestic issues and had just faced down a Republican move to delegitimize his election. The Iranians, in the absence of sanctions relief authorized by the JCPOA and U.S. participation, were enriching uranium to relatively high levels. The mood in Washington seemed to be that Iran had to be put back in its cage before the United States reentered the JCPOA. Iran has already rejected direct talks with the United States to revive the current agreement but, the thinking went, was so eager for sanctions relief that it would go along with talks about future talks.

These negotiations, after all, would entitle Iran to raise issues of its own. When the United States brings up its ballistic missile capability, Tehran will no doubt point to the UAE's F-35s and offer to consider limitations on Iranian missiles in return for corresponding limits on the UAE air force. U.S. accusations of malign activities in Syria will be met with the observation that Iran is helping Syria at the government's request: Who, the Iranians will ask, invited the United States? And what right does the United States have to seize Syrian oil fields and hand them to an obscure American firm?[8] Who backed a brutal Saudi air campaign in Yemen? Who violated Iraqi sovereignty by killing a senior Iranian official visiting Iraq?

The lyrics of this opera had already been written, but since many of the JCPOA provisions do not expire until the end of 2030 and others sunset in 2025, beyond Biden's first term, both sides have time to temporize. The Iranians will be especially cautious, since they will not be certain that whatever they agree to with Biden will survive past his term in office.

The worry for Washington is what Israel will do if Iran continues to enrich nuclear fuel to high levels. A May 2022 report by the International Atomic Energy Agency (IAEA) stoked this fear. Unshackled from its JCPOA commitments by Trump's policy of "maximum pressure," Iran has stockpiled enough 60 percent enriched uranium-235 that when enriched to 90 percent—well within Iran's capability—Tehran could fuel a bomb within ten days. This specific breakout time frame is important because it is short enough to take place between IAEA inspections and therefore not detectable in a timely fashion. Weaponization would still take up to two years, but once Iran had stockpiled enough highly enriched uranium, the fabrication of a deliverable munition would be harder to uncover. Moreover, Iran's current stockpile of 20 percent enriched uranium gas—now at 238 kilograms—and its higher-capacity centrifuges indicate that it could produce enough weapons-grade material for a second weapon in a matter of weeks.[9]

"Maximum pressure" was also supposed to deter Iranian attacks against the United States in Iraq. According to the U.S. intelligence community, however, attacks against U.S. forces in Iraq by Iran-aligned militias quadrupled following the Trump administration's withdrawal from the JCPOA.[10] While the JCPOA talks have been back in play, there has been a tacit truce.

An Israeli attack against Iran is not out of the question. Depending on how Iran reacts to an Israeli assault, the United States could be sucked into a war with the Islamic Republic. With Chinese aircraft regularly buzzing around the boundaries of Taiwanese air space, Russia's invasion of Ukraine, inflation and interest rates still rising in late 2024, a Republican controlled House of Representatives, and the COVID pandemic lingering, an Israel-Iran war involving the United States would be one crisis too many.

As long as talks last, and hopefully longer, the Biden administration will have succeeded in preventing Iran from developing nuclear weapons, thereby reducing the risk of a regional war and nuclear proliferation on the Arab side of the Persian Gulf. Iranian malign regional activities are not a direct threat to the United States, but they trouble its friends, particularly Israel, the UAE, and Saudi Arabia. These activities include the aforementioned attack on Saudi oil facilities; the occasional launch of Iranian missiles by Houthi rebels at Saudi Arabia and the UAE in response to Saudi air strikes, or simply to provoke them; indications of Houthi interest in using Iranian missiles against Israel; the independence of Iraqi militias aligned with Iran; Iranian-backed militias in Syria used mainly as cannon fodder by Assad in a fading civil war; and Iran's ongoing attempts to transfer advanced missiles and other weapons to Lebanese Hizballah.

Nearly all these provocations were made possible by U.S. blunders or those of its allies, and all have proved difficult to reverse militarily. Iran's grip on Lebanon originated in the failed U.S. and Israeli intervention there in the early 1980s, although there is evidence that Iran had begun to nurture the Shiite "resistance" shortly after the revolution in Iran. Its presence in Iraq was made possible by the war against Saddam Hussein from 1991 to 2003 and the ensuing civil war. Iran's involvement in Yemen was made possible by a Saudi and Emirati effort to roll back Houthi gains in a civil war that ravaged the country. Its engagement in Syria was a function of Iran's dependence on Damascus for diplomatic support, resupply of Lebanese Hizballah, and of course the threat posed by Sunni jihadists.

The Biden administration lacks the strategic incentive and domestic political support to dislodge Iran from its various regional footholds, which continue to galvanize opposition to the nuclear agreement. Given constraints on the administration and the needs of the countries where Iranian influence has become entrenched, it would seem logical to mobilize Arab capital and simply outspend Iran, which is economically weak, facing large-scale nationwide protests, and organizationally challenged. In Syria, Tehran can organize soup kitchens and militias and build small schools, but it cannot rebuild the country's energy grid, replace its healthcare delivery system, and resuscitate its transport sector.

The Gulf states have the resources and incentive to do this, but not necessarily the motivation. Investment aimed at crowding Iran out of Syria and alleviating a humanitarian crisis is currently deterred by U.S.

sanctions against non-American entities engaged in financial transactions in Syria.[11] In the unlikely event that the Biden administrations drops or relaxes these sanctions, Arab clout in Syria might grow, and Iran increasingly squeezed out.

Iraq could absorb investment in its agribusiness, industrial, and hydrocarbon sectors; Yemen desperately needs investment in infrastructure and desalination capacity—it is out of water—and while Iran can supply the Houthis with missiles and rockets, it cannot meaningfully improve the quality of life for Yemenis. Lebanon is in a state of profound crisis triggered by the collapse of a banking sector structured as a pyramid scheme. Its reconstitution will be a serious challenge, and Iran has no capacity to prevent Lebanon from going over the precipice.

This sort of initiative is one of the few that can take U.S.-Saudi relations in a productive direction. Despite disgust at the crown prince, mainly among Democrats, since the murder of his critic Khashoggi in 2018, the Saudi connection is too sturdy to derail.[12] The Kingdom has spent over $37 million lobbying in Washington, has funded, along with the UAE, a multimillion-dollar think tank, and has invested more than $1 billion in the U.S. tech sector, while endowing universities and hospitals.[13]

Jake Sullivan, Biden's national security adviser, has rightly repudiated the "blank check" Trump handed to Muhammad bin Salman, which implicitly condoned murder, kidnapping, domestic repression, the siege of Qatar, and indiscriminate bombing of Yemeni civilians, but the inertia of the U.S.-Saudi relationship will impede meaningful change.[14] Early in his presidency, Biden initially restricted his communication with Saudi Arabia to King Salman and refused to talk to the crown prince. He also initiated a review of arms sales, cut off U.S. support for Saudi operations in Yemen, and took the Houthis off the U.S. list of terrorist organizations. Arms sales, however, continue, while a January 2022 Houthi missile attack against the UAE has prompted calls to put the Houthis back on the terrorism list and renew sanctions. The administration, as noted earlier, has also released a redacted version of the intelligence assessment that the crown prince was deeply involved in Khashoggi's murder.[15] Yet according to administration sources, "the Biden administration stopped short of directly penalizing Crown Prince Mohammed bin Salman, calculating that the risk of damaging American interests was too great."[16] Biden explained to an international audience of national security grandees in Munich on February 4, "We're going to continue to support and help Saudi Arabia defend its sovereignty and its territorial integrity and its people."[17]

This was a timely statement. On February 24, 2022, Russia invaded Ukraine. Western states quickly agreed on a set of punitive economic sanctions on Russia intended to drive up the cost to the Kremlin of its aggression, in the hope of bringing the fighting to a halt. These sanctions were punishing as well to the states imposing them. Russia supplied a vast amount of oil and gas to the global energy market. The market, however, was tightening severely as demand spiked following the height of the pandemic, during which energy use had plummeted. The result was a swift and brutal wave of inflation that broke over Western economies. For Biden, whose party was fighting for its life, this was a dangerous development. Even though his administration had not caused the rise in prices and could do little to counter them, voters blamed Biden for the pain at the pump.

In similar situations in the past, U.S. presidents had reached out to Saudi Arabia to use its swing capacity to boost supply, thereby moderating price. Two factors made the Saudis initially unreceptive to such a plea. One was Biden's disdain for the crown prince and Saudi Arabia, which he vowed to make an outcast for the murder of Jamal Khashoggi.[18] Referring to the Kingdom, he declared, "I would make it very clear we were not going to in fact sell more weapons to them. . . . We were going to in fact make them pay the price, and make them in fact the pariah that they are," adding that there is "very little social redeeming value in the present government in Saudi Arabia" and that he would "end the sale of material to the Saudis where they're going in and murdering [Yemeni] children." This last promise related to the ongoing Saudi air campaign against Iran-backed Houthi rebels in Yemen. Saudi air strikes had been notably indiscriminate, killing many Yemeni noncombatants, especially children.

The second obstacle was Saudi Arabia's OPEC+ agreement on production quotas, which included Russia. By agreeing to increase production above established OPEC+ limits, Saudi Arabia would appear to be doing Biden a favor, while disregarding Russia's interest in maintaining high oil prices. Conversely, by sticking with the existing OPEC+ agreement, the Kingdom would appear to be complicit in Russia's war on Ukraine and favoring Moscow over the United States, Riyadh's long-term friend and protector. Saudi Arabia chose to stand with Russia for the first three months of the war in Ukraine, despite pleas from Washington to side with Ukraine and the West. In late May 2022, however, the Kingdom reversed this stance for several reasons: as a result of Western sanctions, Russia could not meet its own production targets under the OPEC+ agreement, so Moscow was really no longer a party to it; Riyadh's fear of a Western recession that would reduce demand for Saudi oil over the longer term; and because Russia's actions in Ukraine were so egregious, the Saudis could no longer afford to be seen as propping up the Kremlin's finances.

As these circumstances evolved, the Biden administration was moving to repair the damage to its relationship with Saudi Arabia. Bill Burns, the CIA director, made an undisclosed trip to the Kingdom and met with the crown prince in April 2022.[19] Burns's trip triggered speculation about what the United States was prepared to offer the Kingdom in return for abandoning Russia and limits on oil production. Secretary of State Blinken and Jake Sullivan, the national security adviser, met with a "senior Saudi defense official" around the same time, fueling speculation that a major change in U.S.-Saudi relations was in the offing.[20] Conflicting statements from the White House about a possible presidential visit to the Kingdom on the tail end of meetings in Israel solidified expectations of dramatic moves. Accusing Biden of betraying the memory of Jamal Khashoggi by cozying up to his executioner, moderate Democrats opposed the visit.[21] The trip was postponed, probably to prepare the ground more thoroughly for "deliverables," things that Biden could display to justify an encounter with the crown prince.[22] The announcement that two small islands long claimed by Egypt would revert to Saudi sovereignty, and rumors of Saudi permission for Israeli commercial aircraft to cross Saudi airspace and schedule flights to the Kingdom for Israeli Arabs and Palestinians to visit Mecca, were interpreted as straws in the wind. These small steps, observers thought, would lead to U.S. security guarantees for the Kingdom and a Saudi-Israeli peace treaty under the rubric of the Abraham Accords. This proposition seemed all the more plausible in light of a simultaneous UAE push for security guarantees. The UAE had fought in Afghanistan against the Taliban and hosted U.S. air and naval forces at its airfields and ports, but considered that the United States was taking its cooperation for granted. When Houthi missiles launched from Yemen struck the UAE in January 2022, the initial U.S. response was muted. The Emiratis, however, declared that the attack was their 9/11 and insisted on a commensurate response from Washington, which hadn't dispatched so much as a Hallmark card. The UAE wanted the Houthis to be put back on the U.S. terrorism list, from which they had been removed to facilitate cease-fire negotiations underway in Yemen and security guarantees befitting a close, if informal, U.S. ally.

While the United States refused to redesignate the Houthis as terrorists, it did agree to explore security guarantees of some sort. The United States and UAE already have a defense cooperation agreement that obliges the United States to consult with the UAE if it is attacked. It is hard to see what more the United States can offer. The fact is, the United States does not make security guarantees. A close look at the Treaty of Washington, which established NATO and declares that an attack against the territory of one NATO member is an attack against all, goes on to say that member states would be required only to consult with the defending member state and "to take such action as it deems necessary." There is no automatic commitment to go to war on that country's behalf.[23] It seems unlikely that whatever the State Department's lawyers devise, it won't meet Emirati expectations. Nevertheless, the symbolism of a rebranding of the current defense cooperation agreement might reassure the UAE and deter its adversaries, especially given the tempo of U.S. activity at Emirati bases.

The Saudis do not have a defense cooperation agreement like the one that regulates the U.S.-UAE relationship, so even an agreement promising consultations in a crisis would signify a material strengthening of the bilateral security relationship. And as an executive agreement, it would sidestep the need for Senate approval. This would be a hard sell. Khashoggi, after all, was an American resident and a columnist for *The Washington Post*.

Biden did make the trip in mid-July, timing the visit to coincide with a Gulf Cooperation Council meeting in Jeddah. This had the virtue of submerging his own presence in a gathering of a gaggle of regional leaders. His meeting with the crown prince was led with a fist bump, an awkward alternative to a handshake. Biden raised human rights with him, but these points were waved off; the fact was that Biden was there, in the Kingdom he had excoriated, meeting with the man he had accused of murder. The White House subsequently issued a long list of deliverables, including the return of Tiran Island to Saudi control; opening Saudi airspace to flights going to and from Israel; a Saudi pledge to sustain a truce in Yemen; a global infrastructure program to stabilize supply chains; and cooperation on cybersecurity, clean energy, telecommunications, public health, space exploration, maritime security, and air defense. As for "the egregious murder of Jamal Khashoggi," Saudi "commitments with respect to reforms and institutional safeguards . . . to guard against such conduct in the future." Oil production, the real point of the visit, was billed as cooperation on energy security. This consisted of an expression of gratitude for a 50 percent increase in production levels above the Kingdom's OPEC+ targets for July and August. This didn't have much impact at the pump, since traders had already factored that into their pricing, but it was better than nothing. The White House added that "further steps" were anticipated that would stabilize the market. This vague expectation was not accompanied by a reference to Saudi concurrence.[24] It was just as well since within a few months, Saudis were cutting production by 100,000 barrels per day, and by October was slashing output much more radically.[25]

The question raised by all this frenetic activity is whether it signals an intensified commitment to Gulf security and a return to the era before Obama and Biden began to rebalance toward Asia. This seems unlikely. If it were not for the war in Ukraine, spiraling inflation, and the expected loss of the House and possibly the Senate to the Republicans, the administration would probably not have been talking about new security-related commitments in the Persian Gulf. It seems unlikely that Biden's successor will break with the focus on Asia and restore the old U.S. posture in the Persian Gulf. China will, if anything, be a more formidable competitor, and tensions over Taiwan as U.S. strategic ambiguity becomes less ambiguous are not going to fade. Jared Kushner, moreover, has repeatedly advised the Saudi crown prince to make no agreements with Biden, but rather to wait for Trump's return, when the benefits to Saudi Arabia (and profits for Kushner's investment fund) will be much greater. Under Biden, the U.S. relationship with the UAE, on the other hand, will likely stabilize, but the Emiratis, like the Saudis, will continue to see Biden as a speed bump on the road to a more accommodating Republican administration.[26]

Biden and Israel

The U.S.-Israeli relationship has shed the excesses it acquired under Trump, who appointed as ambassador a Trump organization lawyer strongly supportive of settlers and annexation.[27] Biden has already reversed policies that stripped Palestinians of aid and diplomatic access in Washington.[28] Security assistance is locked in throughout Biden's first term by the ten-year Memorandum of Understanding signed by Obama in 2016. Some of the systems Israel wants to buy with U.S. assistance are necessary to attack Iran, such as refueling tankers, vertical landing and takeoff aircraft, and a bunker-busting bomb that is too heavy for any Israeli plane to carry.[29] This presages a future request for strategic bombers, the sale of which is currently prohibited by a U.S.-Russian arms control treaty.[30]

In the six months following Biden's inauguration, Netanyahu came out swinging, warning the president-elect that "there can be no going back to the previous nuclear agreement."[31] Netanyahu also warned that "with or without an agreement we will do everything so [Iran is not] armed with nuclear weapons."[32] There are countervailing voices, primarily retired intelligence officials, but Israeli opponents of the JCPOA still dominate the discussion, as when Israel's chief military officer noted that anything resembling it "is bad and must not be permitted." They will enjoy the warm welcome of congressional Republicans.

Biden caught one of the few breaks in his administration thus far when Benjamin Netanyahu lost the Israeli elections in June 2021 to a broad coalition united by the desire to end his long reign.[33] Netanyahu's departure, coupled with the new government's interest in restoring a semblance of cordiality in Israel's relations with the United States, will afford Biden a bit of political breathing room as he deals with more urgent issues. Netanyahu's successors, Naftali Bennett of the far Right and the centrist Yair Lapid, took up Netanyahu's fervid opposition to the JCPOA. Lapid, who will face Netanyahu in November 2022 elections, declared that Israel will not be bound by the JCPOA.[34] Since Israel is not a party to the agreement, this was not exactly breaking news, but as a campaign talking point, it sounded tough enough to secure his political flank against Netanyahu. Lapid, as did his predecessor Bennett, dispatched senior delegations to Washington to whip up congressional resistance to a deal with Iran and persuade the administration that reentering the JCPOA would be foolish. Their slogan, a retread of the pitch that permeated the 2015 campaign against the deal, was that Israel did not oppose any deal with Iran, just the JCPOA.[35]

There is little that Biden can do to counter the aggressive anti-JCPOA campaign, though it is clear that he will try. The U.S. air strike against Iran-backed militia camps in Syria on February 25, 2021, was a gesture to those who claim that the deal does nothing to interdict or punish Iran's "malign activities."[36] Official U.S. statements explained the strike as a signal of the administration's intention to protect American lives and deter Iranian aggression.[37] Sources in Syria indicated that the U.S. aircraft buzzed the targeted location repeatedly before releasing their bombs, to give residents the opportunity to get out of the way.

It seems scarcely likely that this stratagem will pay off. Oklahoma Republican senator Jim Inhofe, author of *The Greatest Hoax: How the Global Warming Conspiracy Threatens Your Future*, declared on February 1, 2021, that a return to the JCPOA is a nonstarter. Saying that "the original Iran deal, after all, was a gift to the Iranian regime," he laid out the principles for a new deal that would be acceptable to Republicans. It would have no sunset clauses, include no provision for enrichment, and end Iranian development of ballistic missiles and regional meddling.[38] In other words, congressional Republicans will not support any deal that would be negotiable with Iran. Some Democrats may well embrace this position too.

In early 2022, the U.S. and Iran were dancing around a return to the table; most observers judge the incentives for the parties to finesse the tangle over terms as strong enough for a way to be found. This has proved illusory. A deal brokered by the EU over the summer collapsed as Iran withdrew its commitment to clarify anomalies identified by the IAEA in its enrichment record. Tehran further fouled the nest by targeting current and former U.S. officials and an Iranian dissident in the United States for assassination and then gloating over the attempted murder of the famed author Salman Rushdie at a literary festival in upstate New York.[39] These maneuvers appeared designed to sabotage the talks, but it was equally possible that the new Iranian government under Ebrahim Raisi believed that Iran could get away with its abrogation of its IAEA commitment because Biden needed a nuclear deal to ensure the success of Democrats in the November elections. This was a virtually perfect misunderstanding of the state of play, but unlike the previous leadership, Raisi has no experience of the United States or its politics. The attempted assassinations might well have seemed to decision makers in Tehran to be business as usual and no reason for the United States to link them to the deal. If so, they were wrong.[40] Opinions in Washington are divided over what the effects would be of a failure to reach an agreement. Some think cratered talks will lead Iran to accumulate fuel for nuclear weapons and that Israel will respond militarily, while others concede that Israel might step up sabotage operations and assassinations of Iranian scientists but would not take actions that could spiral into full-scale war. From this perspective, it matters rather less whether or not the JCPOA is revived.

As for the Israeli-Palestinian conflict, Biden's advisers perceive no benefit to restarting the peace process, despite pleas from Palestinian leaders, because the parties are too far apart and the distance is widening. Although there are many on both sides who would welcome an agreement, the deals they envision ask too much of the other's political system, society, and leadership. U.S. reengagement would be ineffectual, producing the worst of all worlds for the administration, where it would look powerless in the face of Israeli opposition while paying a high domestic political price for its ineffectual efforts. As an indication of Israel's friends' readiness to punish Biden for taking steps they view as counter to Israel's interests, AIPAC's political action committee funded thirty-six members of Congress who voted to deny Biden's electoral victory and prevent him from taking office on January 6.[41] When pressed on its financial support for Americans backing an insurrection and subverting democracy, AIPAC stated that this was "no moment for the pro-Israel movement to become selective about its friends."[42]

Biden and Syria

As for Syria, Blinken has expressed his regret at Obama's having done "too little" to stanch the civil war that has consumed hundreds of thousands of lives and forced the migration of half its population. The question is how Blinken's regret will shape U.S. policy. Reflections over George H. W. Bush's incitement and abandonment of Iraqi Shias in 1991 filled Paul Wolfowitz and others with regret that later drove them toward a second war with Saddam Hussein. Thus far, Blinken has spoken of more energetic U.S. diplomacy aimed at a political transition in Syria. This is all to the good but leaves unanswered how U.S. policy will address the welfare of the Syrian people during this interregnum. Does the United States pulverize Syrian society with sanctions, as it did in Iraq between Desert Storm and Operation Iraqi Freedom? Or does it roll back current sanctions to allow reconstruction and stabilization operations to be conducted by non-Americans even though they will in effect benefit a murderous regime? This is a profound ethical challenge that Biden has had to navigate.[43]

In October 2022, a fifth round of elections in Israel brought Netanyahu back to power in conjunction with leaders of a once-banned racist party. Netanyahu awarded the party control of the interior ministry and is considering handing over the defense portfolio as well. This would give a faction committed to expulsion of Arabs from Israeli-controlled territory authority over the West Bank. The reaction of the U.S. ambassador to Israel was indicative of the Biden administration's posture toward Netanyahu's triumphant return: "Congratulations and Mazal Tov to PM Netanyahu, [. . .] the State of Israel and the People of Israel on the formation of a new government. The United States looks forward to working with you to enhance our already incredibly strong relationship & unbreakable bond." In other words, the administration was not going to spend scarce political capital in Washington to tangle with the new government. Yet it might have no choice. Netanyahu's coalition encompasses ultra-right wing parties, Otzmah Yehudit ("Jewish Power"), Tzionut HaDati ("Religious Zionism"), and Noam ("Pleasantness"), which together endorse expulsion of Palestinians, annexation of the West Bank, reducing civil liberties of Israeli Arabs, and undermining the rights enjoyed by Israel's LGBTQ+ population. The leader of the Jewish Power party has been given the post of national security minister with authority of the national police, border police, and a military force on the West Bank. He will be in a position to cause mischief that would draw the United States into disputes with Israel regardless of Biden's reluctance to get involved.[44]

In terms of the overall approach to the region, those insisting upon American leadership are in opposition to the campaign against the "endless wars" that now appear to have ended, at least in the Middle East. Even the chairman of the Joint Chiefs of Staff has mused publicly about closing or shrinking the headquarters of the Fifth Fleet in Bahrain.[45] And as troops are drawn down from Iraq and Afghanistan, the numbers of support personnel in the Persian Gulf could diminish.

The Biden administration has had more urgent priorities than regional developments that do not threaten core U.S. interests. To prevent the Republicans from gaining control of both houses of Congress in the 2022 midterms and sinking its policy initiatives, it had to deliver economic improvements for the lower half of American wage earners unprecedented in the postwar period. In addition to overseeing nearly $2 trillion in stimulus funding, the administration has managed to pass a $1.9 trillion COVID-19 relief plan, $1 trillion bipartisan infrastructure program, $280 billion industrial policy bill, sharp expansion of veterans' benefits, and a $485 billion Inflation Reduction Act that tackles both climate change and health care. The administration had little choice but to subordinate most potential congressional flashpoints over foreign policy to these crucial goals.[46]

The Balance Sheet

Since the end of the Second World War, America's overriding purpose in the Middle East has been to secure two states, Israel and Saudi Arabia. Like the warp and weft of a tapestry, they weave in and out of the wider story, sometimes invisible, but always indispensable. They hold the story together. And so have these two states appeared throughout this book. Major episodes—the wars in Iraq, clashes with Iran—might appear to be unrelated to this core purpose, but they are ultimately linked to it. Saddam's pursuit of nuclear weapons and the means to deliver them was a problem for the United States because he might have used them against Israel, or to deter Washington from intervening on behalf of Saudi Arabia. Iran during the shah's rule already had aggressive intentions toward the Gulf Arabs, and that threat intensified with the revolutionary regime that replaced him, which also declared Israel to be its mortal enemy.

In the last phase of the Cold War, the main threat to these quasi-allies, directly or indirectly, was the Soviet Union. As Soviet power declined and then collapsed, so did this threat. A decade later, the 9/11 attacks rescrambled it. The Bush administration's response to 9/11 was justified in multiple ways, which were ultimately narrowed down to enforced democratization in the service of regional stability. Israel benefited from the elimination of Iraqi military power and especially the end of Saddam's nuclear program. On the other hand, the defeat of Iraq strengthened its other, more dangerous, regional adversary, Iran. On balance, therefore, U.S. post-9/11 policy did not really improve Israel's strategic position, despite Israel's lobbying for a war against Iraq. The effect of the war on Saudi security was similar. The Saudis had feared Iraq and participated in Desert Storm. But, again, Iraq's defeat empowered Iran, which also threatened Riyadh. In the Saudi case, the irony lies in the Kingdom's refusal to cooperate in the U.S. effort to rein in al Qaeda before 9/11 and, worse, its deployment to the United States of Saudi officials who helped the 9/11 hijackers carry out their attacks.[47] As for Iraq itself, perhaps in the fullness of time, observers of a thriving, democratic Iraq will look back on the Iraq war and conclude that it was both just and successful. But who, from that hypothetical vantage, will be able to say that a war that killed hundreds of thousands of ordinary Iraqis sped its road to democracy? And who can say now that many years hence, Iraq will even matter to U.S. strategic calculations, despite the blood and treasure that America invested there?

At the inception of America's post-WWII immersion in the Middle East, the vulnerability of Saudi Arabia and Israel appeared striking. Israel was surrounded by hostile Arab states, some backed by Moscow, and its survival looked far from certain to the ordinary observer. Still, though American diplomats harbored an ambivalence toward Israel until the late 1960s, the United States simply could not have allowed another Holocaust. And Saudi Arabia, for much of this time, appeared to be within easy reach of Soviet military power.

In the intervening decades, these two states have come a long way. No one should now seriously question the survival of either. Indeed, the surest sign of their security is their willingness to challenge the United States when their interests diverge from Washington's. The Abraham Accords, which link the United Arab Emirates and Israel and, in the not-too-distant future, Saudi Arabia, are a vivid emblem of this new dispensation. So was Netanyahu's readiness to intervene in U.S. politics and align the Israeli state with one American political party. The unavoidable conclusion is that, despite the scorn heaped on U.S. policy for its serial blunders, and notwithstanding the more modulated critique offered in this book, Washington succeeded in accomplishing the two goals it had set for itself in the post-war era. The question is, at what cost? And would these states have survived, even prospered, had these costs not been incurred?

Success, of course, has many sources. Israelis and Saudis are in large measure responsible for their own survival. Many Israelis have died to give their country life and to sustain it. Its government has adroitly maintained the backing of a succession of foreign powers—the Eastern Bloc, France, Germany, and, most crucially, a resolute United States. The Saudis faced different perils, but the tacit guarantee of U.S. protection would not have meant much if the Al Saud had not managed the affairs of the Kingdom and its resources with some skill. Over time, both countries changed. They became more self-confident as immediate threats to their security diminished, their wealth grew, and their diplomatic reach expanded. Israel, in part as a result of protracted conflict, has shifted to the right and, owing to a burgeoning Orthodox population, is gradually taking on a different political and cultural hue. As these developments have unfolded, prospects for an Israeli-Palestinian peace agreement have withered.[48]

Saudi Arabia has undergone an equivalent shift in a much shorter time. The MBS ascendance signifies the emergence of a very different kingdom from the one with which the United States forged deep ties following the Second World War. He is trying to engineer a new Saudi society and recast the state as a regional power. He has also established a reputation for heedless cruelty. Whether he will succeed or be undermined by a backlash emanating from conservative elements in Saudi society or the elites he has suppressed is impossible to foresee. But for now, he holds the reins.

The Good, the Bad, and the Ugly

I am often asked if the United States deserves credit for anything during the period covered by this book. Three things come to mind.

The first is the amount—well over $100 billion—in U.S. economic and humanitarian aid to the Middle East between 1946 and 2018.[49] The United States could have extended a great deal more, especially by converting the even greater sum of military aid into economic assistance. But Congress reflects the will of its constituents, many of whom do not wish to allocate tax dollars to the care and feeding of American children, let alone foreigners. Assistance also was largely confined to countries whose governments were aligned with the United States, or, as in the case of Iraq, was owed American largesse to repair the damage it had inflicted. Nevertheless, U.S. aid left many people better off, mostly through project assistance that improved access to clean water, sanitation, or other public goods. There is little to no evidence, however, that U.S. presence fostered the only sustainable force for improving public welfare, namely sustained, equitably shared economic growth. Second, the United States made a good-faith, if ultimately futile, effort to carve out space for Palestinian sovereignty while preserving Israel's security. Although this phase of the peace process was—and still is—rationalized as important to U.S. strategic interests, the fact was that after the Cold War, the peace process was no longer a strategic necessity; activists within the U.S. government who continued to pursue a peace agreement were animated by sentiment and moral concern. They can point to memos they wrote during those years that underlined strategic considerations, but the truth was that long after the strategic rationale waned, American diplomats pursued an Israeli-Palestinian peace because they believed it was the right thing to do.*

---

* U.S. diplomats and other public servants, including my former colleagues and current friends, point with justified pride to some related successes, including the diplomatic achievement of maintaining close ties to Israel and Saudi Arabia during the long period preceding their de facto mutual recognition. This was a neat trick, but it must be conceded that Saudi ties to the United States were driven primarily by their threat perceptions. As long as the United States was regarded as a reliable guarantor, the Saudis would have found a way to overlook the close U.S.-Israel relationship. Relatedly, my colleagues who specialized in the peace process argue that Carter's conclusion of a peace treaty between Israel and Egypt was a singularly important contribution. By eliminating the risk of another Egyptian-Israeli

Then there was Obama's achievement of the nuclear deal with Iran, a diplomatic masterstroke. Its demise has been used by opponents of the deal to claim that it was so flawed as to be politically unsustainable. Yet there is no question that its destruction by Donald Trump had everything to do with Trump and little to do with the deal itself. So, yes, the United States can point to accomplishments the past four decades, even if it has abandoned the one of greatest current strategic import.

As of early 2022, there are relatively few U.S. combat personnel in the Middle East, though thousands of Americans sustain U.S. bases in the region. Actual "boots on the ground," however, have mostly been brought home. The course of the Russia-Ukraine war, North Korean saber-rattling, or escalating Chinese threats to Taiwan will likely draw in forces that in a previous era would have been in the Middle East. Expert commentators still tend to emphasize the continuing strategic significance of the Middle East, recommend that the U.S. military presence there should be beefed up, and talk of a regional vacuum that Russia and China will fill to America's detriment. Yet we are now in the third successive presidency that seems unimpressed by this assessment, perhaps because it reflects the outlook of those who empowered Iran by crushing Iraq and repudiating an agreement that limited its nuclear ambitions. Russia, meanwhile, has

---

conflict, it made future large-scale land wars impossible. The underlying idea is that such wars would have required at least two Arab parties. With Egypt off the table, so was war. But with Egypt's expulsion of its Soviet backers in 1972 and embrace of the United States in the aftermath of the 1973 Yom Kippur War, renewed conflict with Israel was already improbable. No doubt a treaty created a more stable reality, particularly for war planners in Cairo and Tel Aviv. But the new era had been introduced by Sadat's war and turn to the West, not by Jimmy Carter. Colleagues also make the case for George H. W. Bush's Madrid Conference, which brought Arabs, including Palestinians, together with Israelis to work out a pathway to peace. But their case rests on what Bush would have accomplished in the second term he did not have. The counterfactual is that the technical achievement of Madrid would have been parlayed into a final status accord. Well, maybe. But what we do know is that rather than submit to a multinational process orchestrated by Washington, the Israelis and Palestinians chose to negotiate an agreement on their own, resulting in the Oslo Process. What we also know is that this process failed.

little clout in the Persian Gulf, and has a foothold in just one Middle Eastern state, Syria, which one would not normally consider a jewel in the crown. China needs oil from both Iran and the Arab Gulf states and therefore has a vital interest in ensuring that the two sides of the conflict do not threaten each other. This is a stabilizing dynamic. The threat China and Russia pose to U.S. interests in the Persian Gulf is often ill-defined, but appears to devolve to loss of access to Persian Gulf oil. Donald Trump pointed out in 2019—perhaps not quite accurately—that the United States does not need Saudi oil.[50] The United States does import Saudi oil, although not in large amounts, and the price of that oil remains tethered to developments in the world energy market. But the United States could get along well enough if Saudi oil were cut off. If the United States and China were at war, it would be the Chinese who would be cut off from Persian Gulf by U.S. Navy submarines prowling the straits that link the Indian Ocean to the Pacific.

Finally, there is the home front: 9/11 was the result, and cause, of deep U.S. involvement in the Middle East. From what can be divined from bin Laden's utterances, the U.S. deployment of 500,000 troops to Saudi Arabia in 1990–91 impelled him to kill Americans; he was offended by the damage done by U.S.-led sanctions against Iraq; and he was angry about U.S. support for Israel. What could the United States have done differently? This book has tried to answer this question, but counterfactuals, while suggestive, are inevitably unsatisfying because, after all, they never actually happened. In this coda, perhaps it suffices to say that outcomes are not inevitable. They may be shaped by deep, impersonal forces underpinning everyday realities, but they result from choices that governments make from among available options at a given moment. This recounting points to roads not taken.

A prominent national political player told me several years ago that 9/11, on balance, had represented a good deal: forty years of cheap oil for 3,000 killed on one day in 2001. That is certainly one, albeit chilling and repulsive, perspective. It begs a number of questions, however, from whether cheap oil was in fact a good thing and how the savings from cheap oil compared with the enormous financial costs—$5 to 7 trillion—incurred by the United States in response to the attacks (however mistakenly) and to the 7,000 killed in action, 32,000 wounded in action, 8,000 dead contractors, 30,000 suicides committed by active duty personnel and veterans, all in addition to the 3,000 killed on 9/11; to the related financial and economic crises that have jeopardized American political cohesion and democracy; to the immense domestic surveillance system and militarized policing that have aggravated that democratic crisis.[51] And had cheap oil not been so easily available, the climate crisis we are now facing might not be quite as severe. As the planet bakes in the coming years, the United States will suffer, but not as much as the population of the Middle East and North Africa. No doubt the rivalries that drive conflict in the region will persist, but amid climatic changes that will cause food and water shortages, render territories uninhabitable, and force millions into perpetual migration. These waves of climate refugees will crash against Europe, while the United States will have to cope with the desperation of migrants from the overheated lands to its own south.

A net assessment suggests that the United States would have been better off today had it not been so eager to intervene in the Middle East. Fortunately, America's era there is drawing to a close, and probably not a moment too soon.

Will it ever resume? It is certainly possible, and there is broad precedent. But a return to anything like the scale of America's post-9/11 wars of counterterrorism is unlikely. The scale of military engagement will be much smaller than the engagement in the Asia-Pacific and Europe, and perhaps more like Washington's diffident post–Cold War presence in Latin America.

Between the early 1960s and mid-1970s, Southeast Asia was the target of U.S. intervention. First Vietnam, then Laos and Cambodia became fierce arenas for U.S. military action. Roughly 47,000 American battle deaths were recorded in those places, while U.S. bombing of North Vietnam is thought to have killed one million Vietnamese. Forty-five years later, this intensely violent phase has not recurred and few observers see reengagement on this scale as likely. Nonetheless, the United States maintains about 93,000 soldiers and 86,000 marines in the region. Pacific waters are patrolled by the navy's Seventh Fleet—the largest of its forward-deployed forces, which includes some 50 to 70 ships and submarines and 150 aircraft—as part of a standing strategic effort to contain China. In the coming decade, these forces could plausibly find themselves at war with China over the future of Taiwan.

Europe was a major theater of operations in two World Wars. Most Americans who were not indigenous were immigrants from Europe or descended from them. These included many millions of German immigrants, a bloc that contributed to President Wilson's reluctance to join the Great War until Germany's missteps forced his hand. Intervention, when it came, was costly—117,000 killed in action in just a year—and U.S. disillusion with the results fed isolationism during the roaring twenties and depression years until Nazi Germany arose as a clear strategic threat. The ensuing war left the United States responsible for western Europe and faced with another rival, the Soviet Union, which, like Hitler's Germany, appeared bent on control of the continent. The Marshall Plan and the creation of NATO bound the United States and Europe together. The Cold War and construction of the now much debated "rules-based, liberal international order" was mostly a U.S.-European project. With German unification and the collapse of the Soviet Union, NATO's borders grew to include new members eager to be linked to western Europe and the United States. The United States now maintains 100,000 troops in Europe; the Russia-Ukraine conflict, in which the United States is deeply involved, will probably drive that number higher. Thus, U.S. security and prosperity have become tightly intertwined with both Europe and Asia over more than a century of dramatic interaction.

In Asia, U.S. trade with China alone was worth $555 billion in 2020; in Japan, it was over half that amount. Hundreds of billions of dollars of trade also continue to flow with Taiwan, Korea, and other local economies. In 2021, total trade between the EU and United States was approximately $1.1 trillion, on top of reciprocal investments in the trillions. These large numbers reflect America's stakes in these relationships.[52]

The Middle East, however, seems to fit the model of Central and South America's role in U.S. strategy better than it does the European and Asian one. Between the Spanish-American War and the late Cold War, the United States was preoccupied by Latin America and South America. Washington, under the twin banners of the Monroe Doctrine and anti-communism, propped up dictators, deposed governments unfriendly to American business, and battled insurgencies in a succession of covert operations and small wars. German infiltration of South America, or fear of it, was the initial spur to Roosevelt's thinking about the Nazi threat to the U.S. economy. Yet after this long and deep involvement, interest has now faded to the point where the breakdown of the Venezuelan state—a historical foreign source of oil powering the U.S. economy—and its capture by an anti-American party was largely ignored. At this remove, it is hard to see renewed intervention outside of drugs and immigration. And these concerns relate primarily to Colombia and Mexico and won't entail the large-scale use of military force. Glancing at U.S. trade with some of Latin America's larger economies, the numbers are dwarfed by the value of trade with Asia and Europe. And trade, including U.S. services and direct investment, with Brazil ($196 billion), Venezuela ($24 billion), and Mexico ($759 billion) far exceeds trade between the United States and the largest Middle Eastern economies.

The continents on the eastern and western flanks of the United States are economic powerhouses and consist of mostly close friends of the United States, the bulk of them treaty allies. The Middle East and North Africa, like Central and South America, do not reflect such deep economic ties or, compared with Europe, shared cultural traditions. During the Cold War, strategic interests engendered strong links with the Middle East, but in subsequent decades, intervention was more contingent than structural. The conditions that underpinned U.S. engagement have dissipated over time, unlike those that have perpetually reinforced U.S. interest in Asia and Europe. Numbers cannot tell the whole story, but the contrast in trade levels is revealing. Imports from Saudi Arabia in 2019 were $14.5 billion, reflecting a 39 percent drop in ten years; reciprocal investment was about the same level. Egypt had even lower numbers. Trade with the UAE, the other large regional economy, was more robust, totaling almost $25 billion, while the United States invested about $17 billion in the UAE in 2017. The vast disparity between U.S. economic interests in the Middle East, on the one hand, and Asia and Europe, on the other, is readily apparent. So are troop levels, a good indicator of strategic interest. The likelihood that the United States will hit "repeat" on its profound involvement in the Middle East between 1990 and 2011 seems about the same as that of the United States intervening in Latin America with the fervor it did during the Cold War—that is, very low.

Of course, another event such as 9/11 might wrench the United States into another long Middle Eastern war. Economics are not the only driver of U.S. policy. But the invasion of Iraq as a response to al Qaeda's attacks was, in retrospect, sui generis. The combination of factors that produced it was idiosyncratic: foolish leaders, big ideas detached from mundane reality, catastrophic failure of U.S. defenses, and false claims about a supposed Iraqi role in the attacks. It is difficult to imagine this quadruple helix of follies and blunders coming together any time soon. Twenty years later, a slender majority of Americans regard the Iraq War as a mistake.[53] And presidents of both parties have said have repudiated it.

Still, the quality of American leaders, domestic political decadence and radicalization, and the stresses of climate change and pandemics do not favor preparedness or rational response to sudden shocks. Whether the future will comply with the verdict of an epoch eclipsed is unknowable. But whatever the future holds for the United States in the Middle East, it will scarcely resemble either the past or the present.

ACKNOWLEDGMENTS

This book draws on working relationships established over many years with American scholars and officials as well as Middle Eastern ones. Some contributed their insights directly to this project, and others indirectly as teachers and well-informed friends. It's a pity that not all are still with us. It would be impractical to list all who deserve my acknowledgment because over fifty years, the numbers add up. I do need to start somewhere, however, so I'll begin by thanking Professors Alan Richards and F. Gregory Gause for their steadfast friendship and wisdom regarding the political economy and international relations of the Middle East. The late Professor Alan Shulman, a generous and larger-than-life Egyptologist who introduced me to the history of the Middle East, albeit of a different era; and the late Professor Thomas Odin Lambdin, for my formal encounter with the Near Eastern languages; Professor David Levenson, for an understanding of the broad sweep of Levantine history; and professors John Kelsay and Emmanuel Sivan for their deep knowledge of Islamic thought. I owe professor Joshua Landis, in particular, a large debt for sharing his knowledge of Syria, and Professor Toby Dodge regarding Iraq. Last, but not conclusively, I am grateful to Professor Bernard Avishai, who has been unstinting in his help regarding Israeli politics, and Dr. Ray Takeyh and Professor Ali Ansari on Iran. On the Middle East Peace Process, Professor William Quandt provided judicious guidance based on his National Security Council experience and scholarly research.

In acknowledging my debt to colleagues—and those of them who are friends—I need to be clear that many would disagree with at least some of the conclusions in this book. Ambassadors Pickering, Kurtzer, Patterson, Ratney, Feltman, Holmes, Shapiro, Tueller, Jones, Indyk, Hale, and Ross were all helpful, some obliquely, others in relation to the drafting process. Of this distinguished group, Daniel Kurtzer was especially helpful in clarifying policies and politics at crucial junctures.

Other former government colleagues followed impressive career paths that did not culminate as a chief of mission. Aaron Miller and Richard Sokolsky, who together comprised a half century of experience as policy advisers to a succession of administrations, had an outsize role in this project, refreshing memories, interpreting policies, and sharing their own judgments. Likewise, Robert Malley helped me understand the nuances of the Middle East policies of both the Clinton and Obama administrations. On the Clinton administration, Anthony Lake was candid and incisive. I only wish I could have consulted the late Samuel (Sandy) R. Berger as well, from whom I learned so much in Clinton's second term. Denis McDonough was kind enough to share his thoughts regarding Obama's first term; Philip Gordon conveyed his thoughts about Obama's second term. Gary Samore, Mark Fitzpatrick, and Joseph Marty helped me navigate the diplomatic and technical thickets of non-proliferation policy. As for the Trump administration, Jared Kushner did respond to my request for an interview, but it proved too difficult to arrange.

Outside of government and academe, my wife, Virginia Ann Liberatore, not only put up with yet another pharaonic book project but provided invaluable feedback on the text. Dana Allin and Jonathan Stevenson read portions of the draft with a critical eye, as did Duncan Moore and Robert Worth. The late John Tirman, a truly engaged intellectual, guided me through the literature on the effect of war on noncombatants. Adam Entous was especially helpful on the ins and outs of U.S., Israeli, and Iranian intelligence matters, Robert Silverman on matters Israeli and Egyptian, and George Saghir and Nir Rosen for their on-the-ground knowledge of Syria and Iraq and readiness to share it. Grant Baker, Dakota Foster, and Hayden Schmidt provided excellent research support for which I'm grateful. The professionalism of the NSC team that reviewed and cleared the manuscript for publication was also admirable.

Finally, I'm deeply grateful to Michael Carlisle of Inkwell Management for his unflagging support and shrewd counsel, to Scott Moyers of Penguin Random House for believing in the book and compelling me to make my case rather than state it, and to the inestimable Mia Council for her very adroit editing.

NOTES

PREFACE

1. Robert S. McNamara, *In Retrospect: The Tragedy and Lessons of Vietnam* (New York: Random House, 1995); and Craig McNamara, *Because Our Fathers Lied: A Memoir of Truth and Family, from Vietnam to Today* (New York: Little, Brown, 2022).

INTRODUCTION: WHAT WENT WRONG?

1. "Transcript of President Reagan's Speech on Sending Marines into Lebanon," *New York Times*, September 21, 1982, nytimes.com/1982/09/21/world/transcript-of-president-reagan-s-speech-on-sending-marines-into-lebanon.html.
2. Jeffrey Goldberg, "Obama Unhappy with Allies, Upset at Free Riders," March 10, 2016, Atlantic Council, atlanticcouncil.org/blogs/natosource/obama-unhappy-with-allies-upset-at-free-riders.
3. Tom Porter, "Trump Dubiously Takes Credit for U.S. Energy Independence from Saudi Arabia, as Oil Prices Spike after Drone Attack," *Insider,* September 16, 2019, https://www.businessinsider.com/trump-wrongly-says-us-not-dependent-saudi-oil-takes-credit-2019-9.
4. Shane Harris, Erin Cunningham, and Kareem Fahim, "Trump Stops Short of Directly Blaming Iran for Attacks on Saudi Oil Facilities," *Washington Post,* September 17, 2019, https://www.washingtonpost.com/world/yemens-houthi-rebels

-warn-of-further-attacks-on-saudi-oil-facilities/2019/09/16/e8c75a00-d859-11e9
-ac63-3016711543fe_story.html.

5. Watson Institute, Brown University, "The U.S. Budgetary Costs of Post-9/11 Wars Through FY2022: $8 Trillion," The Costs of War Project, September 1, 2021, https://watson.brown.edu/costsofwar/figures/2021/BudgetaryCosts.

6. "Chaim Weizmann . . . knowingly played on this fear (Judeo-Bolshevism) when he suggested to officials in the British Foreign Office in 1917 the possibility that Jews in Russia could turn either to Germany or to revolution if Britain did not support the Zionist cause. His message, so credible to diplomats who believed that a 'world Jewry' always acted as one, helped to generate support for the Balfour Declaration at a crucial moment in the last years of World War I." Paul Hanebrink, *A Specter Haunting Europe: The Myth of Judeo-Bolshevism* (Cambridge: Harvard University Press, 2018), 19–20.

7. Shlomo Avineri, "Britain's True Motivation behind the Balfour Declaration," *Haaretz*, November 2, 2017, https://www.haaretz.com/opinion/.premium-britain-s-true-motivation-behind-the-balfour-declaration-1.5462518.

8. Robert Jervis, *Why Intelligence Fails: Lessons from the Iranian Revolution and the Iraq War* (Ithaca: Cornell University Press, 2010), chapter 2.

9. Warren Bass, *Support Any Friend: Kennedy's Middle East and the Making of the U.S.-Israel Alliance*, Oxford University Press, 2004.

10. Ray Takeyh, "The Coup That Wasn't: Jimmy Carter and Iran," *Survival* 64, no. 4 (2022): 137–50.

11. Paul Gewirtz, "On 'I Know It When I See It,'" *Yale Law Journal* 105, no. 4 (January 1996): 1023–47, https://doi.org/10.2307/797245.

CHAPTER ONE: JIMMY CARTER: OPENING ACT

1. Maxwell Tani, "Jimmy Carter: I Have One Big Regret from My Time as President," *Business Insider*, August 20, 2015, https://www.businessinsider.com/jimmy-carter-iranian-hostage-crisis-2015-8.

2. From John Winthrop's 1630 sermon to the pilgrims aboard the *Arbella,* paraphrasing the Gospel of Matthew (5:14), "You are the light of the world. A city that is set on a hill cannot be hidden."

3. "Eagle Claw Debacle in the Desert," *Washington Post*, November 6, 1983, https://www.washingtonpost.com/archive/entertainment/books/1983/11/06/eagle-claw-debacle-in-the-desert/ddadc4d0-ccb0-45ad-ae82-c2d634791d43/.

4. Edward T. Russell, "Crisis in Iran: Operation Eagle Claw," in *Short of War: Major USAF Contingency Operations 1947–1997*, ed. A. Timothy Warnock (Air University Press, 2000), https://media.defense.gov/2010/Oct/27/2001330212/-1/-1/0/AFD-101027-044.pdf.

5. Naval History and Heritage Command, *Iran Hostage Rescue Mission Report* (Washington, DC, 1980), https://www.history.navy.mil/research/library/online

-reading-room/title-list-alphabetically/i/iran-hostage-rescue-mission-report
.html.

6. Kai Bird, *The Outlier: The Unfinished Presidency of Jimmy Carter* (New York: Crown, 2021), 552.

CHAPTER TWO: RONALD REAGAN: EMPATHY AND INDECISION

1. Alan Bock, "Reagan's Wisdom on the Middle East: Leave," *Orange County Register*, July 21, 2006, https://www.ocregister.com/2006/07/21/reagans-wisdom-on-the-middle-east-leave/.

2. Lou Cannon, "Reagan Acknowledges Arms-for-Hostages Swap," *Washington Post*, March 5, 1987, https://www.washingtonpost.com/archive/politics/1987/03/05/reagan-acknowledges-arms-for-hostages-swap/7a5cd7cc-a112-4283-94bd-7f730ad81901/.

3. David K. Shipler, "Israel Links Truce to Deep Pullback by Forces of P.L.O.," *New York Times,* July 22, 1981, https://www.nytimes.com/1981/07/22/world/israel-links-truce-to-deep-pullback-by-forces-of-plo.html.

4. UPI, "Begin Compares Arafat to Hitler," August 5, 1982, https://www.upi.com/Archives/1982/08/05/Begin-compares-Arafat-to-Hitler/2671397368000/.

5. UPI, "Begin Says Reagan Used Word 'Holocaust,'" August 29, 1982, https://www.upi.com/Archives/1982/08/29/Begin-says-Reagan-used-word-holocaust/3133399441600/.

6. United Nations, United States of America and Lebanon: Exchange of Notes Constituting an Agreement on United States Participation in a Multinational Force in Beirut (with annex), vol. 1751, no. 30567, August 18 and 20, 1982, https://treaties.un.org/doc/Publication/UNTS/Volume%201751/volume-1751-I-30567-English.pdf.

7. Colin Campbell, "Gemayel of Lebanon Is Killed in Bomb Blast at Party Offices," *New York Times*, September 15, 1982, https://www.nytimes.com/1982/09/15/world/gemayel-of-lebanon-is-killed-in-bomb-blast-at-party-offices.html; and cf. Loren Jenkins and *Washington Post* Foreign Service, "Phalangist Ties to Massacre Detailed," *Washington Post*, September 30, 1982, https://www.washingtonpost.com/archive/politics/1982/09/30/phalangist-ties-to-massacre-detailed/f90f79a4-797b-402c-a3c5-92636a67baf7/.

8. Neil A. Lewis, "U.S. Links Men in Bomb Case to Lebanon Terrorist Group," *New York Times,* May 18, 1988, https://www.nytimes.com/1988/05/18/world/us-links-men-in-bomb-case-to-lebanon-terrorist-group.html.

9. Israel Ministry of Foreign Affairs, *104. Report of the Commission of Inquiry into the Events at the Refugee Camps in Beirut, 8 February 1983* (Tel Aviv, 1983), https://usiraq.procon.org/sourcefiles/1983-Kahan-Commission-Report.pdf.

10. Robert C. McFarlane, *Special Trust* (London: Cadell & Davis, 1994), 210.

11. Charles F. Brower IV, "Stranger in a Dangerous Land: Reagan and Lebanon,

1981–1984," in *Reagan and the World: Leadership and National Security, 1981–1989,* ed. Bradley Lynn Coleman and Kyle Longley (Lexington: University Press of Kentucky, 2017), 12:268.

12. "Transcript of President Reagan's Speech on Sending Marines into Lebanon," *New York Times,* September 21, 1982, https://www.nytimes.com/1982/09/21 /world/transcript-of-president-reagan-s-speech-on-sending-marines-into-lebanon .html.

13. United Nations, United States of America and Lebanon, "Exchange of Notes Constituting an Agreement on United States Participation in a Multinational Force in Beirut," vol. 1777, no. 31022, Beirut, September 25, 1982, https://treaties.un .org/doc/Publication/UNTS/Volume%201777/volume-1777-I-31022-English.pdf.

14. Ronald Reagan, "Address to the Nation on United States Policy for Peace in the Middle East," Ronald Reagan Presidential Library and Museum, September 1, 1982, https://www.reaganlibrary.gov/archives/speech/address-nation-united -states-policy-peace-middle-east.

15. Central Intelligence Agency, "NSDD-64: Next Steps on Lebanon," The Reagan Library, https://www.reaganlibrary.gov/public/archives/reference/scanned-nsdds /nsdd64.pdf.

16. National Security Decision Directive Number 64, "Next Steps in Lebanon," October 28, 1982, reaganlibrary.gov/public/archives/reference/scanned-nsdds /nsdd64.pdf.

17. Central Intelligence Agency, "Lebanon: Possible Israeli and Syrian Withdrawals," Freedom of Information Act Electronic Reading Room, October 7, 1982, https:// www.cia.gov/readingroom/document/cia-rdp84b00049r001403480025-0.

18. The conventional estimate is 2,000 pounds, but the internal CIA estimate was 500. Central Intelligence Agency, "Chronology of Anti-U.S. Terrorist Attacks for Iran or Iranian Supported Groups (1979–1985)," Freedom of Information Act Electronic Reading Room, June 26, 1985, https://www.cia.gov/readingroom /document/cia-rdp09-00438r000605820002-7.

19. Thomas L. Friedman, "U.S. Beirut Embassy Bombed; 33 Reported Killed, 80 Hurt; Pro-Iran Sect Admits Action," *New York Times,* April 19, 1983, https:// www.nytimes.com/1983/04/19/world/us-beirut-embassy-bombed-33-reported -killed-80-hurt-pro-iran-sect-admits-action.html.

20. Central Intelligence Agency, "Accelerating the Withdrawal of Foreign Forces from Lebanon," Freedom of Information Act Electronic Reading Room, April 27, 1983, https://www.cia.gov/readingroom/document/cia-rdp10m00666r000300 960003-1.

21. Benjamin B. Fischer, *A Cold War Conundrum: The 1983 Soviet War Scare* (Langley, VA: CIA Center for the Study of Intelligence, 1997), https://www.google.com /url?sa=t&rct=j&q=&esrc=s&source=web&cd=&ved=2ahUKEwissOulzdz1A hWrLTQIHW6aDRwQFnoECAUQAQ&url=https%3A%2F%2Fwww.cia.gov

%2Freadingroom%2Fdocs%2F19970901.pdf&usg=AOvVaw0CEC76bTgt7d
T7uxgJv8qG.

22. Central Intelligence Agency, "Soviet Policy in Lebanon: What Next?," Freedom of Information Act Electronic Reading Room, March 21, 1984, https://www.cia .gov/readingroom/document/cia-rdp85t00287r001400520001-1.

23. Flora Lewis, "Syria's Ambitions May Not Leave Room for Moscow's," *New York Times,* October 30, 1983, https://www.nytimes.com/1983/10/30/weekinreview /syria-s-ambitions-may-not-leave-room-for-moscow-s.html.

24. David M. Kennedy, "The Reagan Administration and Lebanon," Harvard Kennedy School, January 1, 1988, https://case.hks.harvard.edu/the-reagan-administration -and-lebanon/.

25. R. McFarlane, *Special Trust.*

26. Central Intelligence Agency, "McFarlane/Fairbanks Mission: Worst Case Strategy for Lebanon," Freedom of Information Act Electronic Reading Room, September 9, 1983, https://www.cia.gov/readingroom/document/cia-rdp85m00363r0003006 50012-9.

27. Central Intelligence Agency, "Worst Case Strategies for Lebanon," Freedom of Information Act Electronic Reading Room, November 2, 2010, https://www.cia .gov/readingroom/document/cia-rdp85m00363r000300650014-7.

28. "Diary Entry—Sunday, September 11, 1983," Ronald Reagan Presidential Foundation and Library, accessed November 5, 2022, https://www.reaganfoundation .org/ronald-reagan/white-house-diaries/diary-entry-09111983.

29. Ronald Reagan, *An American Life: The Autobiography* (New York: Simon & Shuster, 1990), 446.

30. Karim Pakradouni, *Le Piege* (Paris: Grasset, 1991), 76, quoted in RAND Conference Proceedings, CF-129, chapter 6, "Lebanon: 1982–1984," by John H. Kelly (citation translated by the author), accessed at https://www.rand.org/pubs/conf _proceedings/CF129/CF-129-chapter6.html.

31. "Monday, October 24, 1983, Bombings in Beirut," *New York Times*, October 24, 1983, https://www.nytimes.com/1983/10/24/nyregion/monday-october-24-1983 -bombings-in-beirut.html.

32. The White House, "NSDD-111: Next Steps Toward Progress in Lebanon and the Middle East," The Reagan Files, October 28, 1983, http://www.thereaganfiles .com/nsdd-111-version2009.pdf.

33. Bernard E. Trainor, "'83 Strike on Lebanon: Hard Lessons for U.S.," *New York Times,* August 6, 1989, https://www.nytimes.com/1989/08/06/world/83-strike-on -lebanon-hard-lessons-for-us.html.

34. Ronald Smothers, "Jackson Is Off to Syria to Seek Flier's Release," *New York Times,* December 30, 1983, https://www.nytimes.com/1983/12/30/world/jackson -is-off-to-syria-to-seek-flier-s-release.html.

35. Lou Cannon, *President Reagan: Role of a Lifetime* (New York: PublicAffairs, 1991).

36. Central Intelligence Agency, "NSPG Meeting on the Lebanon Situation," Freedom of Information Act Electronic Reading Room, Washington, DC, September 3, 1983, https://www.cia.gov/readingroom/document/cia-rdp85m00363r0003 00630018-5.

37. The White House, "NSDD-117: Lebanon," December 5, 1983, The Reagan Presidential Library and Museum, https://www.reaganlibrary.gov/public/archives /reference/scanned-nsdds/nsdd117.pdf.

38. Central Intelligence Agency, Freedom of Information Act Electronic Reading Room, "National Security Decision on Our Response to the Lebanon Crisis," Freedom of Information Act Electronic Reading Room, October 24, 1983, https://www .cia.gov/readingroom/document/cia-rdp10m00666r000200510001-3.

39. Central Intelligence Agency, "Retaliation for Beirut Bombing," Freedom of Information Act Electronic Reading Room, October 28, 1983, https://www.cia.gov /readingroom/document/cia-rdp88b00443r001404090006-1.

40. Micah Zenko, "When America Attacked Syria," *Council on Foreign Relations* (blog post), February 13, 2012, https://www.cfr.org/blog/when-america-attacked-syria; David C. Wills, *The First War on Terrorism: Counter-terrorism Policy during the Reagan Administration* (Lanham, MD: Rowman & Littlefield, 2003), 71–80.

41. Patrick Tyler, *A World of Trouble: The White House and the Middle East—from the Cold War to the War on Terror* (New York: Farrar, Straus and Giroux, 2010), 299.

42. Tim Naftali, *Blind Spot: The Secret History of American Counterterrorism* (New York: Basic Books, 2005), 131.

43. R. McFarlane, *Special Trust,* 172.

44. Reagan, *An American Life,* 463–64.

45. Interview with David Ivry, Tel Aviv, January 2019.

46. Leslie Maitland Werner, "American Gets Life for Giving Secrets to Israel," New York Times, March 5, 1987, A1, https://www.nytimes.com/1987/03/05/us /american-gets-life-for-giving-secrets-to-israel.html?searchResultPosition=3.

47. Eric Hooglund, "Reagan's Iran," *Middle East Report* 151 (March/April 1988), https://merip.org/1988/03/reagans-iran/.

48. The White House, "NSDD-99: United States Security Strategy for the Near East and South Asia," The Regan Files July 12, 1983, https://www.thereaganfiles.com /nsdd-99.pdf.

49. Central Intelligence Agency, "Soviet Strategy and Capabilities for Multitheater War: National Intelligence Estimate," NIE 11-19-85/D, Freedom of Information Act Electronic Reading Room, June 1985, http://www.foia.cia.gov/sites/default /files/document_conversions/1700321/1985-06-01a.pdf.

50. Graham Fuller, "Toward a Policy on Iran," National Intelligence Council, May 17, 1985, https://pt35b.files.wordpress.com/2015/04/memorandum_1985_gfuller .pdf.

51. Timothy Appleby, "A Man Who Will Fight to the End?" *The Globe and Mail* (To-

ronto), February 7, 2003, https://www.theglobeandmail.com/news/world/a-man
-who-will-fight-to-the-end/article1010551/.

52. Theodore Draper, *A Very Thin Line: The Iran-Contra Affairs*, Hill and Wang, 1991, 142; Malcolm Byrne, *Iran-Contra: Reagan's Scandal and the Unchecked Abuse of Presidential Power*, University Press of Kansas, 67.

53. National Security Council memorandum from Dan Fortier and Howard H. Teicher to Robert C. McFarlane, "U.S. Policy Toward Iran," The Reagan Files, June 11, 1985, https://thereaganfiles.com/draft-nsdd-on-iran-june.pdf.

54. U.S. Congress, *Report of the Congressional Committees Investigating the Iran-Contra Affair* (Washington, DC: U.S. Senate Select Committee on Secret Military Assistance to Iran and the Nicaraguan Opposition, 1987), 166, https://catalog .hathitrust.org/Record/000847584.

55. United States Court of Appeals for the District of Columbia Circuit, Final Report of the Independent Counsel for Iran/Contra Matters, Lawrence E. Walsh, Independent Council, Washington, DC, August 4, 1993, https://irp.fas.org/offdocs /walsh/chap_08.htm.

56. "'Big Strong President Reagan' Encourages Sale of Weapons to Iran," citing Caspar W. Weinberger, diary entry for December 7, 1985, The National Security Archive, https://shec.ashp.cuny.edu/items/show/1657.

57. Hunter S. Thompson, "Fear and Loathing at the Super Bowl," *Rolling Stone*, February 28, 1974, https://www.rollingstone.com/feature/fear-and-loathing-at-the -super-bowl-37345/.

58. Maureen Dowd, "The White House Crisis; McFarlane Suicide Attempt 'What Drove Me to Despair,'" *New York Times*, March 2, 1987, https://www.nytimes.com /1987/03/02/world/the-white-house-crisis-mcfarlane-suicide-attempt-what-drove -me-to-despair.html.

59. Hayns Johnson, "The Buck Reaches the Top," *Washington Post*, December 17, 1986, https://www.washingtonpost.com/archive/politics/1986/12/17/the-buck-reaches -the-top/1fcb8133-2dca-4525-8509-ba533ffdff06/.

60. Maureen Dowd, "The White House Crisis; McFarlane Suicide Attempt: 'What Drove Me to Despair,'" *New York Times,* March 2, 1987, https://www.nytimes.com /1987/03/02/world/the-white-house-crisis-mcfarlane-suicide-attempt-what -drove-me-to-despair.html.

61. David B. Crist, "Joint Special Operations in Support of Earnest Will," *Joint Force Quarterly* (Autumn/Winter 2001–02): 15–22, https://apps.dtic.mil/sti/citations /ADA403506.

62. David Crist, *The Twilight War: The Secret History of America's Thirty-Year Conflict with Iran* (New York: Penguin Books, 2013), 255–309.

63. Louis B. Sohn, John Noyes, Erik Franckx, Kristen Juras, *Cases and Materials on the Law of the Sea*, Second Edition, Martinus Nijhoff Publishers, 2014, 101.

64. Robert Pear, "Khomeini Accepts 'Poison' of Ending the War with Iraq; U.N. Sending Mission," *New York Times*, July 21, 1988, https://www.nytimes.com/1988

/07/21/us/khomeini-accepts-poison-of-ending-the-war-with-iraq-un-sending
-mission.html.

65. Cf. https://www.state.gov/about-us-bureau-of-counterterrorism/; and Larry C. Johnson, "Terrorism: Why the Numbers Matter," Global Security (undated), https://www.globalsecurity.org/security/library/congress/2005_h/050512-johnson.pdf.

66. Bob Woodward, "Don't Make the Libya Problem Worse," *Washington Post*, February 2, 1986, https://www.washingtonpost.com/archive/opinions/1986/02/02/dont-make-the-libya-problem-worse/0634dc4a-af32-4431-a3eb-5dbbde3bb0c1/.

67. David C. Wills, *The First War on Terrorism: Counter-Terrorism Policy during the Reagan Administration* (Lanham, MD: Rowman & Littlefield, 2004), 169.

68. Douglas Little, "To the Shores of Tripoli: America, Qaddafi, and Libyan Revolution 1969–89," *International History Review* 35, no. 1 (2013): 70–99, http://www.jstor.org/stable/24701340.

69. Little, "To the Shores of Tripoli."

CHAPTER THREE: GEORGE H. W. BUSH: THE OLD NEW WORLD ORDER

1. Author interview with Aaron Miller, September 19, 2020.

2. Andrew Rosenthal, "The World; What the U.S. Wants to Happen in Iraq Remains Unclear," *New York Times,* March 24, 1991, https://www.nytimes.com/1991/03/24/weekinreview/the-world-what-the-us-wants-to-happen-in-iraq-remains-unclear.html.

3. Michael R. Gordon and General Bernard E. Trainor, *The Generals' War: The Inside Story of the Conflict in the Gulf* (Boston: Little, Brown, 1995), 461.

4. Author's recollection.

5. For an assessment of the U.S. government's response to Saddam's use of chemical weapons in this instance, see Jeffrey Goldberg, "The Great Terror," *New Yorker*, March 17, 2002, https://www.newyorker.com/contributors/jeffrey-goldberg.

6. "The Banca Nazionale del Lavoro (BNL) Scandal and the Department of Agriculture's Commodity Credit Corporation (CCC) Program for Iraq," Hearing before the Committee on Banking, Finance, and Urban Affairs, House of Representatives, 102nd Cong., 2d Sess. Session (Washington, DC: U.S. Government Printing Office, 1993).

7. NSD 26 can be accessed at https://bush41library.tamu.edu/files/nsd/nsd26.pdf.

8. John F. Burns, "MIDEAST TENSIONS; Iraqi President Renews Threat to Attack Israel," *New York Times*, October 10, 1990, https://www.nytimes.com/1990/10/10/world/mideast-tensions-iraqi-president-renews-threat-to-attack-israel.html.

9. Paul A. Gigot, "A Great American Screw-Up: The U.S. and Iraq, 1980–1990," *National Interest*, no. 22 (Winter 1990–91): 3–10, http://www.jstor.org/stable/42894705.

10. R. Jeffrey Smith, "Saddam's Beef with the Press," *Washington Post*, September 30,

1990, https://www.washingtonpost.com/archive/opinions/1990/09/30/saddams
-beef-with-the-press/a8cb8c5a-ca68-484c-9dcf-3ee2efdf2b79/.

11. F. Gregory Gause III, "Iraq's Decisions to Go to War, 1980 and 1990," *Middle East Journal* 56, no. 1 (Winter 2002): 47–70.

12. "Confrontation in the Gulf; Excerpts from Iraqi Document on Meeting with U.S. Envoy," *New York Times*, September 23, 1990, https://www.nytimes.com/1990/09/23/world/confrontation-in-the-gulf-excerpts-from-iraqi-document-on-meeting-with-us-envoy.html.

13. Michael R. Gordon, "Bush Sends U.S. Force to Saudi Arabia as Kingdom Agrees to Confront Iraq; Bush's Aims: Deter Attack, Send a Signal," *New York Times*, August 8, 1990, https://www.nytimes.com/1990/08/08/world/bush-sends-us-force-saudi-arabia-kingdom-agrees-confront-iraq-bush-s-aim-s-deter.html.

14. Joseph Sassoon and Alissa Walter, "The Iraqi Occupation of Kuwait: New Historical Perspectives," *Middle East Journal* 71, no. 4 (Autumn 2017): 607–28, https://www.jstor.org/stable/90016498.

15. "Bush 'Out of These Troubled Times . . . a New World Order,'" *Washington Post*, September 9, 1990, https://www.washingtonpost.com/archive/politics/1990/09/12/bush-out-of-these-troubled-times-a-new-world-order/b93b5cf1-e389-4e6a-84b0-85f71bf4c946/.

16. George H. W. Bush and Brent Scowcroft, *A World Transformed* (New York: Vintage, 1999), 383.

17. Robert A. Divine, "Review: The Persian Gulf War Revisited: Tactical Victory, Strategic Failure," *Diplomatic History*, Vol. 24, No. 1 (Winter 2000), 129–138, https://www.jstor.org/stable/24914159.

18. Dan Balz and Rick Atkinson, "Powell Vows to Isolate Iraqi Army and 'Kill It,'" *Washington Post*, January 24, 1991, https://www.washingtonpost.com/archive/politics/1991/01/24/powell-vows-to-isolate-iraqi-army-and-kill-it/cfe3f2cd-4ef2-40d1-9176-841171c278f3/.

19. Central Intelligence Agency, "Iraq: Impact of Sanctions," Freedom of Information Act Electronic Reading Room, October 23, 1990, https://www.cia.gov/readingroom/docs/DOC_0000453183.pdf.

20. UN Security Council, Resolution 678, S/RES/678 (November 29, 1990), http://unscr.com/files/1990/00678.pdf.

21. "Confrontation in the Gulf: Text of Letter from Bush to Hussein," *New York Times*, January 13, 1991, https://www.nytimes.com/1991/01/13/world/confrontation-in-the-gulf-text-of-letter-from-bush-to-hussein.html.

22. David Hoffman, "Bush's Letter Left on Conference Table 6 ½ Hours," *Washington Post*, January 11, 1991, https://www.washingtonpost.com/archive/politics/1991/01/11/bushs-letter-left-on-conference-table-6-12-hours/5cb5eaf7-5afe-4b20-964d-4fdc278e1f47/.

23. Author's personal recollection.

24. Eric Schmitt, "Air Force Chief Is Dismissed for Remarks on Gulf Plan; Cheney Cites Bad Judgment," *New York Times,* September 18, 1990, https://www.nytimes.com/1990/09/18/world/confrontation-gulf-air-force-chief-dismissed-for-remarks-gulf-plan-cheney-cites.html.

25. John M. Broder, "U.S. War Plane in Iraq: 'Decapitate' Leadership: Strategy the Joint Chiefs Believe the Best Way to Oust the Iraqis Would Be Air Strikes Designed to Kill Hussein," *Los Angeles Times*, September 16, 1990, https://www.latimes.com/archives/la-xpm-1990-09-16-mn-1221-story.html.

26. Adam Clymer, "Confrontation in the Gulf: Congress Acts to Authorize War in Gulf," *New York Times*, January 13, 1991, https://www.nytimes.com/1991/01/13/world/confrontation-gulf-congress-acts-authorize-war-gulf-margins-are-5-votes-senate.html.

27. Michael Ross, "Ex-Joint Chiefs Back Gulf Delay: Mideast Crisis: Adm. Crowe and Gen. Jones Tell a Congressional Committee That Sanctions against Iraq Should Be Given More Time. Bush May Call Special Session," *Los Angeles Times*, November 29, 1990, https://www.latimes.com/archives/la-xpm-1990-11-29-mn-7442-story.html.

28. James M. Lindsay, "TWE Remembers: Congress's Vote to Authorize the Gulf War, *Council on Foreign Relations* (blog post), January 12, 2011, https://www.cfr.org/blog/twe-remembers-congresss-vote-authorize-gulf-war.

29. Rick Atkinson, "Chapter One: First Night," in *Crusade: The Untold Story of the Persian Gulf War* (New York: Houghton Mifflin, 1993), https://www.washingtonpost.com/wp-srv/inatl/longterm/fogofwar/index/crusade.htm.

30. Richard L. Bernard, "The Defense Special Missile and Astronautics Center," National Security Agency, https://www.nsa.gov/Portals/70/documents/news-features/declassified-documents/cryptologic-spectrum/desfmac.pdf.

31. Israel Ministry of Foreign Affairs, Historical Documents, "No. 180 Press Conference with Foreign Ministers Levy and Genscher—24 January 1991," January 24, 1991, https://mfa.gov.il/MFA/ForeignPolicy/MFADocuments/Yearbook8/Pages/180%20Press%20Conference%20with%20Foreign%20Ministers%20Levy%20a.aspx.

32. Avi Shlaim, "Israel and the Conflict," in *International Perspectives on the Gulf Conflict, 1990–91*, ed. Alex Danchev and Dan Keohane (London: St Martin's Press, 1994), 59–79.

33. Richard H. P. Sia and Karen Hosler, "Bush Disputes Schwarzkopf over End of Gulf War," *Baltimore Sun*, March 28, 1991, https://www.baltimoresun.com/news/bs-xpm-1991-03-28-1991087061-story.html.

34. Tracy Wilkinson, "U.S. Says It Won't Fire on Copters: Cease-fire: The Iraqi Aircraft Are Safe as Long as They Don't Threaten Allied Forces, Schwarzkopf Vows," *Los Angeles Times*, March 24, 1991, https://www.latimes.com/archives/la-xpm-1991-03-24-mn-1397-story.html.

35. Reuters, "Excerpts from 2 Statements by Bush on Iraq's Proposal for Ending Conflict," *New York Times*, February 16, 1991, https://www.nytimes.com/1991/02/16/world/war-gulf-bush-statement-excerpts-2-statements-bush-iraq-s-proposal-for-ending.html.

36. Colin L. Powell and Joseph E. Persico, *My American Journey* (New York: Ballantine Books, 2003), 531.

37. Al Kamen and R. Jeffrey Smith, "U.S., Arabs Fear Breakup or Fundamentalist Takeover of Iraq," *Washington Post,* March 8, 1991, https://www.washingtonpost.com/archive/politics/1991/03/08/us-arabs-fear-breakup-or-fundamentalist-takeover-of-iraq/66ebc839-ee88-4985-977d-fb91e194c905/.

38. Micah L. Sifry and Christopher Cerf, eds., *The Gulf War Reader: History, Documents, Opinions* (New York: Atria Books, 2003), 123.

39. Margaret Tutwiler, "U.S. State Department Daily Briefing #53, Regional/Civil Unrest, Development/Relief Aid, Refugees, Security Assistance and Sales," U.S. State Department, April 2, 1991, https://web.archive.org/web/20080724223052/http://dosfan.lib.uic.edu/ERC/briefing/daily_briefings/1991/9104/053.html.

40. George H. W. Bush and Toshiki Kaifu, "The President's News Conference with Prime Minister Toshiki Kaifu of Japan in Newport Beach, California," in *Public Papers of the Presidents of the United States: George H. W. Bush (1991, Book I)* (Washington, DC: U.S. Government Publishing Office, 1991), https://www.govinfo.gov/content/pkg/PPP-1991-book1/html/PPP-1991-book1-doc-pg326.htm.

41. Caryle Murphy, "Remaining U.S. Troops Wait Out 'Operation Desert Calm,'" *Washington Post,* June 8, 1991, https://www.washingtonpost.com/archive/politics/1991/06/08/remaining-us-troops-wait-out-operation-desert-calm/1420e1ca-3ee0-4dd3-876b-b266598fc55f/.

42. F. Gregory Gause III, *The International Relations of the Persian Gulf* (Cambridge: Cambridge University Press, 2010), 136–83.

43. Osama bin Laden, "Jihad against Jews and Crusaders," published in *FAS*, February 23, 1998, https://fas.org/irp/world/para/docs/980223-fatwa.htm.

44. Peter L. Bergen, *Holy War, Inc.: Inside the Secret World of Osama bin Laden* (New York: Simon & Schuster, 2002), 100–101.

45. Bergen, *Holy War,* 22, 98.

46. Anonymous, *Through Our Enemies' Eyes: Osama bin Laden, Radical Islam, and the Future of America* (Washington, DC: Brassey's, 2002), 53.

47. "Transcript of President's State of the Union Message to Nation," *New York Times*, January 30, 1991, https://www.nytimes.com/1991/01/30/us/state-union-transcript-president-s-state-union-message-nation.html.

48. Thomas L. Friedman, "Baker, in a Middle East Blueprint, Asks Israel to Reach Out to Arabs," *New York Times*, May 23, 1989, https://www.nytimes.com/1989/05/23/world/baker-in-a-middle-east-blueprint-asks-israel-to-reach-out-to-arabs.html.

49. Amir Tibon, "Did James Baker Really Say 'F*** the Jews'?," *Haaretz*, September 29, 2020, https://www.haaretz.com/us-news/.premium-did-james-baker-really-say-f-the-jews-new-book-clarifies-infamous-quote-1.9194779.

50. John M. Goshko, "Baker Bars Israeli Loan Aid Unless Settlements Are Halted," *Washington Post*, February 25, 1992, https://www.washingtonpost.com/archive politics/1992/02/25/baker-bars-israeli-loan-aid-unless-settlements-are-halted /e7311eea-e6d3-493b-8880-a3b98e0830a1/.

CHAPTER FOUR: WILLIAM J. CLINTON: ENLARGEMENT AND CONTAINMENT

1. When I asked Fukuyama about this, he averred that his "end of history" thesis had no influence at all on the Clinton administration.

2. Jacob Heilbrunn, "Lake Inferior: The Pedigree of Anthony Lake," *New Republic* 27 (September 1993), 29–35.

3. Martin Indyk, "The Clinton Administration's Approach to the Middle East," Washington Institute for Near East Policy, May 18, 1993, https://www.washingtoninstitute.org/pdf/view/10374/en.

4. Anthony Lake, "Confronting Backlash States," Foreign Affairs, March/April 1994, https://www.foreignaffairs.com/articles/iran/1994-03-01/confronting-backlash-states.

5. The key documents include "Iraq's Ground Forces: An Assessment," May 1991, https://www.cia.gov/readingroom/docs/DOC_0001261414.pdf; "Iraq: Saddam Likely to Hang On," June 1992, https://nsarchive2.gwu.edu/NSAEBB/NSAEBB167/10.pdf; "Prospects for Iraq: Saddam and Beyond," December 1993, https://www.cia.gov/readingroom/docs/DOC_0001188931.pdf; and "Iraq: Regime under Greater Stress," March 1995, https://www.cia.gov/readingroom/docs/DOC_0001219431.pdf.

6. "Iraq's Ground Forces: An Assessment."

7. "Iraq: Saddam Likely to Hang On."

8. "No Rest for Iraq's Weary," June 20, 1995, https://www.cia.gov/readingroom/docs/DOC_0001435821.pdf.

9. "Prospects for Iraq: Saddam and Beyond."

10. "Iraq: Saddam Likely to Hang On."

11. World Health Organization, *The Health Conditions of the Population in Iraq Since the Gulf Crisis* (Geneva: World Health Organization, 1996), http://apps.who.int /iris/bitstream/handle/10665/59845/WHO_EHA_96.1.pdf;jsessionid =0D3128381710D7F184A86AF3024F8082?sequence=1.

12. Mohamed M. Ali and Iqbal H. Shah, "Sanctions and Childhood Mortality in Iraq," *The Lancet* 355, no. 9218 (May 2000): 1851–57, https://www.thelancet.com /pdfs/journals/lancet/PIIS0140673600022893.pdf.

13. George A. Lopez and David Cortright, "Containing Iraq: Sanctions Worked,"

Foreign Affairs, July/August 2004, https://www.foreignaffairs.com/articles/iraq /2004-07-01/containing-iraq-sanctions-worked.

14. Lopez and Cortright, "Containing Iraq."

15. Jon Jackson, "Watch: Madeleine Albright Saying Iraqi Kids' Deaths 'Worth It,'" *Newsweek*, March 23, 2022, https://www.newsweek.com/watch-madeleine-albright -saying-iraqi-kids-deaths-worth-it-resurfaces-1691193.

16. Joy Gordon, "A Peaceful, Silent, Deadly Remedy: The Ethics of Economic Sanctions," *Ethics & International Affairs* 13 (March 1999): 123–42, https://doi.org /10.1111/j.1747-7093.1999.tb00330.x.

17. Washington Institute for Near East Policy, "Evolution of U.S. Policy on Iraq, the Iraqi Opposition, and Northern Iraq: Between Humanitarian and Strategic Interests," September 19, 1996, https://www.washingtoninstitute.org/policy-analysis /evolution-us-policy-iraq-iraqi-opposition-and-northern-iraq-between -humanitarian.

18. The White House, "President Clinton Announces End of Operation Desert Fox," Office of the Press Secretary, December 19, 1998, https://clintonwhitehouse5 .archives.gov/WH/New/html/19981219-2655.html.

19. Anthony H. Cordesman, *The Lessons of Desert Fox: A Preliminary Analysis* (Washington, DC: Center for Strategic & International Studies, February 16, 1999), https://www.csis.org/analysis/lessons-desert-fox-preliminary-analysis.

20. William Safire, "Roth Plot II," *New York Times*, December 20, 2004, https:// www.nytimes.com/2004/12/20/opinion/roth-plot-ii.html.

21. "Memorandum of Telephone Conversation—Prime Minister Tony Blair of the United Kingdom," Clinton Digital Library, December 18, 1998, https://clinton .presidentiallibraries.us/items/browse?tags=Boris+Yeltsin&output=omeka-xml.

22. Charles Duelfer, "The Inevitable Failure Of Inspections in Iraq," *Arms Control Today*, September 2002, Vol. 32, No. 7 (September 2002), pp. 8–11, https://www .jstor.org/stable/23626551.

23. William J. Clinton Presidential History Project, *Interview 2 with Anthony Lake* (Charlottesville: UVA Miller Center, 2004), https://s3.amazonaws.com/web.poh .transcripts/ohp_2004_1106_lake.pdf; Evan Thomas, "The Rise and Fall of Chalabi: Bush's Mr. Wrong," *Newsweek*, May 30, 2004, https://www.newsweek .com/rise-and-fall-chalabi-bushs-mr-wrong-127615; "The Theory of Knots," *The Economist*, November 18, 2015, https://www.economist.com/obituary/2015/11/18 /the-theory-of-knots.

24. Jim Hoagland, "How CIA's Secret War on Saddam Collapsed," *Washington Post*, June 26, 1997, https://www.washingtonpost.com/archive/politics/1997/06/26 /how-cias-secret-war-on-saddam-collapsed/b83592cb-0117-4c3c-a101-9550 e29c94a3/.

25. Todd S. Purdum, "Clinton to Order a Trade Embargo against Teheran," *New York Times*, May 1, 1995, https://www.nytimes.com/1995/05/01/world/clinton-to-order -a-trade-embargo-against-teheran.html.

26. President Bill Clinton, "Prohibiting Certain Transactions with Respect to Iran," *Federal Register* 60, no. 89, May 9, 1995, https://www.federalregister.gov/docu ments/1995/05/09/95-11694/prohibiting-certain-transactions-with-respect -to-iran.

27. Daniel Southerl and Ann Devroy, "Clinton Bars U.S. Oil Pacts with Iran," *Washington Post*, March 15, 1995, https://www.washingtonpost.com/archive/politics /1995/03/15/clinton-bars-us-oil-pacts-with-iran/f91c1de0-3f7c-4660-a732 -ee8c38513651/.

28. David E. Sanger, "Conoco Told U.S. Years Ago of Oil Negotiations with Iran," *New York Times*, March 17, 1995, https://www.nytimes.com/1995/03/17/us/conoco -told-us-years-ago-of-oil-negotiations-with-iran.html.

29. Elaine Sciolino, "Iranian Leader Says U.S. Move on Oil Deal Wrecked Chance to Improve Ties," *New York Times*, May 16, 1995, https://www.nytimes.com/1995 /05/16/world/iranian-leader-says-us-move-on-oil-deal-wrecked-chance-to -improve-ties.html.

30. Sciolino, "Iranian Leader Says."

31. Humans naturally prioritize evidence that confirms what they already believe to be true and discount new information that runs counter to their beliefs. This confirmation bias is a significant hurdle for would-be signalers.

32. Mark D. Silinsky, "Iran's Islamic Revolutionary Guard Corps: Its Foreign Policy and Foreign Legion," *Expeditions with MCUP* (September 2019): 5–6, https://doi .org/10.36304/ExpwMCUP.2019.01.

33. U.S. Department of Justice, "Attorney General Statement," June 21, 2001, https://www.justice.gov/archive/opa/pr/2001/June/275ag.htm.

34. United States District Court, Eastern District of Virginia, Alexandria Division, Indictment, "U.S. v. Ahmed Al-Mughassil, aka "Abu Omran," Ali Al-Houri, Hani Al-Sayegh, Ibrahim Al-Yacoub, Abdel Karim Al-Nasser, Mustafa Al-Qassab, Sa'ed Al-Bahar, Abdallah Al-Jarash, Hussein Al-Mughis, Ali Al-Marhoun, Saleh Ramadan, Mustafa Al-Mu'alem, Fadel Al-Alawe, Criminal No: 01-228-A John Doe," https://nsarchive2.gwu.edu/NSAEBB/NSAEBB318/doc05.pdf.

35. David B. Ottaway and Brian Duffy, "Iranian Aide Linked to Bombing Suspect," *Washington Post*, April 13, 1997, https://www.washingtonpost.com/archive/politics /1997/04/13/iranian-aide-linked-to-bombing-suspect/65c5ce9f-e122-4f0b -845e-77d8b8165627/.

36. Bruce Riedel, "Remembering the Khobar Towers Bombing," Brookings Institution, June 21, 2021, https://www.brookings.edu/blog/order-from-chaos/2021/06 /21/remembering-the-khobar-towers-bombing/.

37. Patrick Seale, "Special Report: Worldwide Angers Erupts over D'Amato-Kennedy Act," *Washington Report on Middle East Affairs*, October 1996, https://www.wrmea .org/1996-october/worldwide-angers-erupts-over-d-amato-kennedy-act.html.

38. "Message to President Khatami from President Clinton," William J. Clinton

Presidential Library, https://nsarchive2.gwu.edu/NSAEBB/NSAEBB318/doc02
.pdf.

39. "Message from President Khatami to President Clinton."

40. Secretary of State Madeleine K. Albright, "Remarks before the American-Iranian Council" (speech, Washington, DC, March 17, 2000), U.S. Department of State Archive, https://1997-2001.state.gov/statements/2000/000317.html.

41. Martin S. Indyk, "United States Policy toward the Middle East," testimony, House International Relations Committee, June 8, 1999 (Washington, DC: U.S. Department of State, 1999), https://1997-2001.state.gov/policy_remarks/1999 /990608_indyk_mepolicy.html; "Thus, in November of last year, President Clinton announced a new policy with regard to Iraq: henceforth, we would contain Saddam Hussein while we sought a new regime to govern in Baghdad."

42. C. Ross Anthony et al., *The Costs of the Palestinian-Israeli Conflict* (Santa Monica, CA: RAND Corporation, 2015).

43. "Peace in the Middle East," George W. Bush Presidential Library, accessed November 5, 2022, https://georgewbush-whitehouse.archives.gov/infocus/mideast /archive.html.

44. Raphael Cohen-Almagor, "Israel-PLO Peace Process: Interview with Ambassador Daniel Kurtzer," *Israel Studies* 24, no. 3 (2019): 127–56.

45. See Robert Malley and Hussein Agha, "Camp David the Tragedy of Errors," *New York Review of Books*, https://www.nybooks.com/articles/2001/08/09/camp-david -the-tragedy-of-errors/; and Dennis Ross, Gidi Grinstein, Hussein Agha, and Robert Malley, "Camp David: An Exchange," *New York Review of Books*, https:// www.nybooks.com/articles/2001/09/20/camp-david-an-exchange/.

46. National Security Archive, "Documenting Iran-U.S. Relations, 1978–2015," December 29, 2019, https://nsarchive.gwu.edu/briefing-book/iran/2019-12-19 /documenting-iran-us-relations-1978-2015.

CHAPTER FIVE: GEORGE W. BUSH: WRONG MAN, WRONG TIME

1. Bryan Pietsch, "George W. Bush Called Iraq War 'Unjustified and Brutal.' He Meant Ukraine," *Washington Post*, May 19, 2022, https://www.washingtonpost .com/politics/2022/05/19/george-bush-iraq-ukraine-war-speech/.

2. Nicholas D. Kristof, "Bush and the Texas Land Grab," *New York Times*, July 16, 2002, https://www.nytimes.com/2002/07/16/opinion/bush-and-the-texas-land -grab.html.

3. Condoleezza Rice, "Campaign 2000: Promoting the National Interest," *Foreign Affairs*, January/February 2000.

4. Kenneth Katzman, "Iraq: U.S. Regime Change Efforts and the Iraqi Opposition," *CRS*, February 10, 2003, https://www.everycrsreport.com/files/20030210 _RL31339_8714e3b55291f450b9620f06725034a31ec7a99c.pdf.

5. Elaine Sciolino, "Bush's Foreign Policy Tutor: An Academic in the Public Eye," *New York Times*, June 16, 2000, https://www.nytimes.com/2000/06/16/world/2000-campaign-advisor-bush-s-foreign-policy-tutor-academic-public-eye.html.

6. Mark Oliver, "Rice: Bush Understood al-Qaida threat," *The Guardian,* April 8, 2004, https://www.theguardian.com/world/2004/apr/08/september11.usa2.

7. Kevin Bohn, "Dramatic new details released of Bush, Cheney dealing with 9/11 attacks," ABC News, November 11, 2022, https://abcnews.go.com/Politics/dramatic-details-released-bush-cheney-dealing-911-attacks/story?id=93083567.

8. Daniel Benjamin and Steven Simon, "The New Face of Terrorism," *New York Times*, January 4, 2000, https://www.nytimes.com/2000/01/04/opinion/the-new-face-of-terrorism.html.

9. Bruce Riedel, *Kings and Presidents: Saudi Arabia and the United States since FDR* (Washington, DC: Brookings Institution Press, 2017).

10. Dana Lesemann and Michael Jacobson, "Workplan: Issues Relating to the FBI Informant with Whom 9/11 Hijackers Nawaf al-Hazmi and Khalid al-Mihdhar Resided," Federal Bureau of Investigation, June 6, 2003, https://www.archives.gov/files/declassification/iscap/pdf/2012-048-doc17.pdf.

11. Central Intelligence Agency, "The System Was Blinking Red," *The 9/11 Commission Report*, 2004, 254 and 533, https://www.cia.gov/library/abbottabad-compound/0B/0B72A302B86EECAD443BBCDCDC76A5B1_911Report.pdf.

12. Lawrence Freedman, *The Revolution in Strategic Affairs* (London: Routledge, 1998).

13. Stephen Van Evera, "The Cult of the Offensive and the Origins of the First World War," *International Security* 9, no. 1 (Summer 1984): 58–107.

14. James Curry, "From Blitzkrieg to Airland Battle: the United States army, the Wehrmacht, and the German origins of modern American military doctrine" (master's thesis, UWA, 2015), https://api.research-repository.uwa.edu.au/ws/portalfiles/portal/4865111/Curry_James_2015.pdf.

15. George W. Bush, "President Bush Delivers Graduation Speech at West Point," (speech, West Point, NY, June 1, 2002), The White House, https://georgewbush-whitehouse.archives.gov/news/releases/2002/06/print/20020601-3.html.

16. Michael R. Gordon and Judith Miller, "U.S. Says Hussein Intensifies Quest for A-Bomb Parts," *New York Times*, September 8, 2002, https://www.nytimes.com/2002/09/08/world/threats-responses-iraqis-us-says-hussein-intensifies-quest-for-bomb-parts.html.

17. See also "The National Security Strategy," September 2002: "The security environment confronting the United States today is radically different from what we have faced before. . . . The greater the threat, the greater is the risk of inaction—and the more compelling the case for taking anticipatory action to defend ourselves, even if uncertainty remains as to the time and place of the enemy's attack. . . . To forestall or prevent such hostile acts by our adversaries, the United States will, if necessary, act preemptively in exercising our inherent right of self-defense," https://georgewbush-whitehouse.archives.gov/nsc/nss/2002/.

18. Ron Suskind, *The One Percent Doctrine: Deep Inside America's Pursuit of Its Enemies Since 9/11* (New York: Simon & Schuster, 2007), 175.

19. Dick Cheney, interviewed by Tim Russert, "The Vice President Appears on 'Meet the Press' with Tim Russert," *Meet the Press*, September 8, 2002, https:// georgewbush-whitehouse.archives.gov/vicepresident/news-speeches/speeches/ vp20010916.html.

20. Robert Draper, *To Start a War: How the Bush Administration Took America into Iraq* (New York: Penguin Press, 2020), 27.

21. Pew Research Center, "Public Attitudes toward the War in Iraq: 2003–2008," March 19, 2008, https://www.pewresearch.org/2008/03/19/public-attitudes -toward-the-war-in-iraq-20032008/.

22. Wikiwand, "White House Iraq Group," https://www.wikiwand.com/en/White _House_Iraq_Group.

23. Florian Huber, *"Promise Me You'll Shoot Yourself": The Mass Suicide of Ordinary Germans in 1945* (New York: Little, Brown Spark, 2020).

24. Central Intelligence Agency, *National Intelligence Estimate: Iraq's Continuing Programs for Weapons of Mass Destruction*, approved for release April 2004, https:// fas.org/irp/cia/product/iraq-wmd-nie.pdf.

25. Jamie Gaskarth, "How the Iraq War Led to a Legacy of Public Mistrust in Intelligence," The British Academy, February 24, 2020, https://www.thebritishacademy .ac.uk/blog/how-iraq-war-led-legacy-public-mistrust-intelligence/.

26. Bob Woodward, *Plan of Attack: The Definitive Account of the Decision to Invade Iraq* (New York: Simon & Schuster, 2004), 281.

27. Dick Cheney, interviewed by Tim Russert, "Interview of the Vice President by Tim Russert, NBC News, Meet the Press," *Meet the Press* September 10, 2006, https://georgewbush-whitehouse.archives.gov/news/releases/2006/09/text /20060910.html.

28. UN Security Council, Resolution 1441, S/RES/1441 (2002), adopted by the Security Council at its 4644th meeting, November 8, 2002, http://unscr.com/files /2002/01441.pdf.

29. Douglas Jehl, "Wary Powell Said to Have Warned Bush on War," *New York Times*, April 17, 2004, https://www.nytimes.com/2004/04/17/world/the-struggle-for -iraq-policy-wary-powell-said-to-have-warned-bush-on-war.html.

30. Robert Draper, "Colin Powell Still Wants Answers," *New York Times*, July 16, 2020, https://www.nytimes.com/2020/07/16/magazine/colin-powell-iraq-war .html.

31. David Barstow, William J. Broad, and Jeff Gerth, "A Special Report: How White House Embraced Suspect Iraq Arms Intelligence," *New York Times*, October 3, 2004, https://www.nytimes.com/2004/10/03/washington/us/the-nuclear-card -the-aluminum-tube-story-a-special-report-how.html.

32. Jon Schwarz, "Lie after Lie: What Colin Powell Knew about Iraq 15 years Ago and What He Told the U.N.," *The Intercept,* February 6, 2018, https://theinter

cept.com/2018/02/06/lie-after-lie-what-colin-powell-knew-about-iraq-fifteen
-years-ago-and-what-he-told-the-un/.

33. Rebecca Leung, "The Man Who Knew," CBS News, October 14, 2003, https://
www.cbsnews.com/news/the-man-who-knew-14-10-2003/.

34. "Statement by France to Security Council," *New York Times*, February 14, 2003,
https://www.nytimes.com/2003/02/14/international/middleeast/statement-by
-france-to-security-council.html.

35. "Germany to Oppose Iraq War in U.N.," Deutsche Welle, January 22, 2003,
https://www.dw.com/en/germanyto oppose-iraq-war-in-un/a-761326.

36. Ewen MacAskill and Julian Borger, "Iraq War Was Illegal and Breached UN Char-
ter, Says Annan," *The Guardian*, September 16, 2004, https://www.theguardian
.com/world/2004/sep/16/iraq.iraq.

37. Sean D. Murphy, "Assessing the Legality of Invading Iraq," *92 Georgetown Law
Review*, no. 4 (2004), https://scholarship.law.gwu.edu/cgi/viewcontent.cgi?article
=1898&context=faculty_publications.

38. Elisabeth Zoller, "The Law Applicable to the Preemption Doctrine," *Proceedings
of the ASIL Annual Meeting* 98 (March 31–April 3, 2004): 333–37, https://www
.jstor.org/stable/25659947.

39. John C. Yoo, "International Law and the War in Iraq," *American Journal of International Law* 97, no. 3 (July 2003): 563–76, https://escholarship.org/uc/item
/5xf8q46x.; and William H. Taft IV and Todd F. Buchwald, "Preemption, Iraq,
and International Law," *American Journal of International Law* 97, no. 3 (July
2003): 557–63, https://doi.org/10.2307/3109840.

40. Antonio Gramsci, *Selections from the Prison Notebooks*, eds. Quintin Hoare and
Geoffrey Nowell Smith (London: Lawrence and Wishart, 1971), 52: "The historical unity of the ruling classes is realized in the state." Startling evidence for
this observation can be found in viral internet photos of George W. Bush embraced by Michelle Obama and Ellen DeGeneres.

41. David E. Sanger and John F. Burns, "Bush Orders Start of War on Iraq: Missiles
Apparently Miss Hussein," *New York Times*, March 20, 2003, https://www
.nytimes.com/2003/03/20/world/threats-responses-white-house-bush-orders
-start-war-iraq-missiles-apparently.html.

42. George W. Bush, "President Bush Addresses the Nation" (speech, Washington,
DC, March 19, 2003), https://georgewbush-whitehouse.archives.gov/news/releases
/2003/03/20030319-17.html.

43. Lisa Schiffren, "Hey, Flyboy," *Wall Street Journal*, May 9, 2003, https://www.wsj
.com/articles/SB105244292810654300.

44. George W. Bush, "President Bush Announces Major Combat Operations in
Iraq Have Ended" (speech, Washington, DC, May 1, 2003), https://georgewbush
-whitehouse.archives.gov/news/releases/2003/05/20030501-15.html.

45. General George S. Patton, Jr., *War as I Knew It* (Boston: Houghton Mifflin, 1947),
269.

46. Dwight D. Eisenhower, "The Mission of This Allied Force Was Fulfilled at 0241, Local Time, May 7th, 1945," Dwight D. Eisenhower Library, https://www.archives .gov/publications/prologue/2015/summer/war-message.html.

47. A British scholar of Iraq, Professor Toby Dodge, was told this by Aziz in a 2002 interview in Baghdad.

48. Stephen T. Hosmer, *Why the Iraqi Resistance to the Coalition Invasion Was So Weak*, Project Air Force (Santa Monica, CA: RAND Corporation, 2007), 77.

49. Rajiv Chandrasekaran, *Imperial Life in the Emerald City: Inside Iraq's Green Zone* (New York: Vintage Books, 2007), 103.

50. Toby Dodge, "Tracing the Rise of Sectarianism in Iraq after 2003," London School of Economics Middle East Centre, June 29, 2018, https://blogs.lse.ac.uk /mec/2018/09/13/tracing-the-rise-of-sectarianism-in-iraq-after-2003/.

51. Toby Dodge, "The Causes of U.S. Failure in Iraq," *Survival* 49, no. 1 (Spring 2007): 85–106, https://www.tandfonline.com/doi/abs/10.1080/00396330701 254545?journalCode=tsur20.

52. Michael R. Gordon, "Fateful Choice on Iraq Army Bypassed Debate," *New York Times*, March 17, 2008, https://www.nytimes.com/2008/03/17/world/middleeast /17bremer.html.

53. James P. Pfiffner, "U.S. Blunders in Iraq: De-Baathification and Disbanding the Army," *Intelligence and National Security* 25, no. 1 (February 2010): 76–85, http:// pfiffner.gmu.edu/files/pdfs/Articles/CPA%20Orders,%20Iraq%20PDF.pdf.

54. Michael R. Gordon, "Fateful Choice on Iraq Army Bypassed Debate," *New York Times*, March 17, 2008, https://www.nytimes.com/2008/03/17/world/middleeast /17bremer.html.

55. Gordon, "Fateful Choice."

56. The White House, "National Security Presidential Directive/NSPD-24," January 20, 2003, https://fas.org/irp/offdocs/nspd/nspd-24.pdf. The Bush administration as-signed the Pentagon the task of postwar planning and overall management of the U.S. occupation.

57. Neta C. Crawford, "Civilian Death and Injury in the Iraq War, 2003–2013: Costs of War, March 2013," https://watson.brown.edu/costsofwar/files/cow/imce /papers/2013/Civilian%20Death%20and%20Injury%20in%20the%20Iraq %20War%2C%202003-2013.pdf; Neta C. Crawford and Catherine Lutz, "Human Cost of Post-9/11 Wars: Direct War Deaths in Major War Zones, Afghanistan and Pakistan (October 2001–October 2019), Iraq (March 2003–October 2019), Syria (September 2014–October 2019), Yemen (October 2002–October 2019), and Other," November 13, 2019, https://watson.brown.edu/costsofwar/files/cow/imce /papers/2019/Direct%20War%20Deaths%20COW%20Estimate%20November %2013%202019%20FINAL.pdf.

58. U.S. Department of Defense, "U.S. Military Casualties—Operation Iraqi Free-dom, as of September 23, 2022," https://dcas.dmdc.osd.mil/dcas/app/conflict Casualties/oif/byMonth.

59. Rebecca Leung, "Abuse of Iraqi POWs by GIs Probed," CBS News, April 27, 2004, https://www.cbsnews.com/news/abuse-of-iraqi-pows-by-gis-probed/.

60. Seymour M. Hersh, "Torture at Abu Ghraib," *New Yorker*, May 10, 2004, https://www.newyorker.com/magazine/2004/05/10/torture-at-abu-ghraib.

61. Charlie Savage and Elisabeth Bumiller, "An Iraqi Massacre, a Light Sentence and a Question of Military Justice," *New York Times*, January 27, 2012, https://www.nytimes.com/2012/01/28/us/an-iraqi-massacre-a-light-sentence-and-a-question-of-military-justice.html.

62. James A. Baker III and Lee H. Hamilton, co-chairs, et al., *Iraq Study Group Report: A Way Forward, a New Approach* (New York: Vintage Books, 2006), 3.

63. Everett S. P. Spain, J. D. Mohundro, and Bernard B. Banks, "Intellectual Capital: A Case for Cultural Change," *Parameters* 45, no. 2 (2015): 77–91, https://press.armywarcollege.edu/parameters/vol45/iss2/9.

64. David Petraeus, "How We Won in Iraq," *Foreign Policy*, October 29, 2013, https://foreignpolicy.com/2013/10/29/how-we-won-in-iraq/.

65. Thom Shanker and Eric Schmitt, "A Nation at War: The Pentagon; Rumsfeld Says Iraq Is Collapsing, Lists 8 Objectives of War," *New York Times*, March 22, 2003, https://www.nytimes.com/2003/03/22/world/nation-war-pentagon-rumsfeld-says-iraq-collapsing-lists-8-objectives-war.html.

66. Toby Dodge, *From War to a New Authoritarianism* (London: International Institute for Strategic Studies, 2012), 147–80.

67. Office of the Press Secretary, The White House, "President Bush Discusses Freedom in Iraq and Middle East," November 6, 2003, https://georgewbush-whitehouse.archives.gov/news/releases/2003/11/20031106-2.html.

68. U.S. State Department, "Remarks at the American University in Cairo" (speech, Secretary Condoleezza Rice, June 20, 2005), https://2001-2009.state.gov/secretary/rm/2005/48328.htm.

69. Michele Dunne, "The Baby, the Bathwater, and the Freedom Agenda in the Middle East," *Washington Quarterly* 32, no. 1 (January 2009): 129–41, https://carnegieendowment.org/files/09jan_Dunne.pdf.

70. Shibley Telhami, "America in Arab Eyes," *Survival* 49, no. 1 (Spring 2007): 107–22.

71. Eva Bellin, "The Robustness of Authoritarianism in the Middle East: Exceptionalism in Comparative Perspective," *Comparative Politics* 36, no. 2 (January 2004): 139–57, https://doi.org/10.2307/4150140.

72. "Transcript: Bush Discusses War on Terrorism," *Washington Post*, October 6, 2005, https://www.washingtonpost.com/wp-srv/politics/administration/bushtext_100605.html.

73. Jenny Gross, "Far-Right Groups Are behind Most U.S. Terrorist Attacks, Report Finds," *New York Times*, October 24, 2020, https://www.nytimes.com/2020/10/24/us/domestic-terrorist-groups.html.

74. F. Gregory Gause III, "Can Democracy Stop Terrorism?," *Foreign Affairs*, Septem-

ber/October 2005, https://www.foreignaffairs.com/articles/middle-east/2005-09
-01/can-democracy-stop-terrorism.

75. Robert A. Pape, "The Strategic Logic of Suicide Terrorism," *American Political Science Review* 97, no. 3 (August 2003): 343–61, https://www.jstor.org/stable /3117613.

76. Jeremy Pressman, "Power without Influence: The Bush Administration's Foreign Policy Failure in the Middle East," *International Security* 33, no. 4 (Spring 2009): 149–79, http://www.jstor.org/stable/40207155.

77. David Morgan, "'Democracy Isn't the Objective': Republican U.S. Senator Draws Democrats' Ire," Reuters, October 8, 2020, https://www.reuters.com/article/us -usa-election-lee-democracy/democracy-isnt-the-objective-republican-u-s -senator-draws-democrats-ire-idUSKBN26T2YX.

78. Apoorva Mandavilli, "The Price for Not Wearing Masks: Perhaps 130,000 Lives," *New York Times*, October 23, 2020, https://www.nytimes.com/2020/10/23/health /covid-deaths.html.

79. Elizabeth Dias, "Biden and Trump Say They're Fighting for America's 'Soul.' What Does That Mean?," *New York Times*, October 17, 2020, https://www.nytimes .com/2020/10/17/us/biden-trump-soul-nation-country.html?action=click &module=Top%20Stories&pgtype=Homepage.

80. Joel Brinkley, "Rice Calls Off Mideast Visit after Arrest of Egyptian," *New York Times*, February 26, 2005, https://www.nytimes.com/2005/02/26/politics/rice-calls -off-mideast-visit-after-arrest-of-egyptian.html?searchResultPosition=4.

81. Abeer Allam, "A Political Rival of Mubarak Loses His Seat in Parliament," *New York Times,* November 11, 2005, https://www.nytimes.com/2005/11/11/world /africa/a-political-rival-of-mubarak-loses-his-seat-in-parliament.html?search ResultPosition=2.

82. George W. Bush, "President Bush Calls for New Palestinian Leadership" (speech, Washington, DC, June 24, 2002), https://georgewbush-whitehouse.archives.gov /news/releases/2002/06/20020624-3.html.

83. "Salah Shehadeh—Special Investigatory Commission," Israel Ministry of Foreign Affairs, February 27, 2011, https://www.gov.il/en/Departments/news/spokesh chade270211.

84. United Nations Security Council, "Letter dated 7 May 2003 from the Secretary-Genreal addressed to the President of the Security Council," United Nations Digital Library, May 7, 2003, https://digitallibrary.un.org/record/494137.

85. Steven Erlanger, "Hamas Seizes Broad Control in Gaza Strip," *New York Times*, June 14, 2007, https://www.nytimes.com/2007/06/14/world/middleeast/14mid east.html.

86. Reuters Staff, "Israeli PM 'Google-bombed' As 'Miserable Failure,'" Reuters, January 21, 2007, https://www.reuters.com/article/idUSL21663647.

87. Bernard Avishai, "A Plan for Peace That Still Could Be," *New York Times*, Febru-

ary 7, 2011, https://www.nytimes.com/2011/02/13/magazine/13Israel-t.html ?referringSource=articleShare.

88. Nazila Fathi, "Wipe Israel 'off the Map' Iranian Says," *New York Times*, October 27, 2005, https://www.nytimes.com/2005/10/27/world/africa/wipe-israel-off -the-map-iranian-says.html; Greg Myre, "In a Slip, Israel's Leader Seems to Confirm Its Nuclear Arsenal," *New York Times*, December 12, 2006, https:// www.nytimes.com/2006/12/12/world/middleeast/12olmert.html.

89. Isabel Kershner, "Former Israeli Prime Minister Is Indicted," *New York Times*, August 30, 2009, https://www.nytimes.com/2009/08/31/world/middleeast/31israel .html.

90. Al Jazeera Investigations, "The Palestine Papers," January 2011, http://transparency .aljazeera.net/en/projects/thepalestinepapers/.

91. Daniel C. Kurtzer et al., *The Peace Puzzle: America's Quest for Arab-Israeli Peace, 1989–2011* (Ithaca: Cornell University Press, 2013), 239–40.

92. Matthew Cooper, "A Saddam Souvenir," *Time*, May 29, 2004, http://content.time .com/time/magazine/article/0,9171,644112,00.html.

93. Karl Marx, *The Eighteenth Brumaire of Louis Bonaparte* (New York: Die Revolution, 1852).

CHAPTER SIX: BARACK H. OBAMA: LIVE AND LEARN

1. Mark Landler, "Obama Warns U.S. Faces Diffuse Terrorism Threats," *New York Times*, May 28, 2014, https://www.nytimes.com/2014/05/29/us/politics/obama -foreign-policy-west-point-speech.html.

2. Matthew Yglesias, "Interview with Barack Obama," *Vox*, January 2015, https:// www.vox.com/a/barack-obama-interview-vox-conversation/obama-foreign -policy-transcript.

3. "Black Man Given Nation's Worst Job, *The Onion*, November 4, 2008, https:// www.theonion.com/black-man-given-nations-worst-job-1819570341.

4. Robert Rich, "The Great Recession: December 2007–June 2009," *Federal Reserve History*, November 22, 2013, https://www.federalreservehistory.org/essays/great -recession-of-200709.

5. Andy Barr, "The GOP's No-Compromise Pledge," *Politico*, October 28, 2010, https:// www.politico.com/story/2010/10/the-gops-no-compromise-pledge-044311.

6. CBS News, "Obama and Clinton: The 60 Minutes Interview," January 27, 2013, https://www.cbsnews.com/news/obama-and-clinton-the-60-minutes -interview/.

7. Peter Baker and Jeff Zeleny, "Emanuel Wields Power Freely, and Faces the Risks," New York Times, August 15, 2009, https://www.nytimes.com/2009/08/16/us /politics/16emanuel.html.

8. John Heilemann, "The Tsuris," *New York Magazine*, September 16, 2011, https:// nymag.com/news/politics/israel-2011-9/.

9. Tovah Lazaroff, "Settler Population Rose 4.9% in 2009," *Jerusalem Post*, March 10, 2010, https://www.jpost.com/israel/settler-population-rose-49-percent-in-2009; and Josef Federman, "Israeli Settlements Have Grown during the Obama Years," AP News, September 16, 2016, https://apnews.com/article/93e1597c5da7493ea49c29260f7f8004.

10. International Crisis Group, "The Israeli-Palestinian Roadmap: What a Settlement Freeze Means and Why It Matters," Report 16, July 25, 2003, https://www.crisisgroup.org/middle-east-north-africa/eastern-mediterranean/israelpalestine/israeli-palestinian-roadmap-what-settlement-freeze-means-and-why-it-matters.

11. Interview with participant who requested anonymity.

12. "Text: Obama's Speech in Cairo," *New York Times*, June 4, 2009, https://www.nytimes.com/2009/06/04/us/politics/04obama.text.html.

13. Dana Allin and Steven Simon, *Our Separate Ways: The Struggle for the Future of the U.S.- Israel Alliance* (New York: Public Affairs, 2016), 86.

14. Adam Entous and Mohammed Assadi, "Biden Scolds Israel Over Settlement Plan," Reuters, March 9, 2010, https://www.reuters.com/article/us-usa-israel-biden/biden-scolds-israel-over-settlement-plan-idUSTRE6271YE20100310.

15. Akiva Eldar, "U.S. Gave Israel Green Light for East Jerusalem Construction," *Haaretz*, March 12, 2010, https://www.haaretz.com/2010-03-12/ty-article/u-s-gave-israel-green-light-for-east-jerusalem-construction/0000017f-f07f-d497-a1ff-f2ff32560000.

16. Barak Ravid, "Identity of Secret Mediator in Israeli-Palestinians Talks Revealed," *Haaretz*, Nov 27, 2014, https://www.haaretz.com/2014-11-27/ty-article/.premium/identity-of-secret-mediator-revealed/0000017f-e89b-da9b-a1ff-ecff88710000.

17. Allin and Simon, *Our Separate Ways*, 92.

18. "U.S. Official Calls Netanyahu a 'Chickenshit Prime Minister,'" *Haaretz*, October 28, 2014, https://www.haaretz.com/2014-10-28/ty-article/.premium/u-s-official-calls-netanyahu-chickenshit/0000017f-efe3-dc28-a17f-fff73f9b0000; and Jonathan Topaz, "Obama, Bibi 'Chickensh—' Uproar," *Politico*, October 29, 2014, https://www.politico.com/story/2014/10/benjamin-netanyahu-chickenshit-112303.

19. Allin and Simon, *Our Separate Ways*, 110.

20. Samuel P. Huntington, *Political Order in Changing Societies* (New Haven: Yale University Press, 1968), 177.

21. Marcus Baram, "'The Revolution Will Not Be Televised'—Gil Scott-Heron (1970)," https://www.loc.gov/static/programs/national-recording-preservation-board/documents/TheRevolutionWillNotBeTelevised.pdf.

22. Peter Baker, "The Return of Pushing Democracy," *New York Times*, February 12, 2011, https://www.nytimes.com/2011/02/13/weekinreview/13baker.html.

23. Helene Cooper, Mark Landler, and David E. Sanger, "In U.S. Signals to Egypt,

Obama Straddled a Rift," *New York Times*, February 12, 2011, https://www
.nytimes.com/2011/02/13/world/middleeast/13diplomacy.html.

24. Mark Landler, "Obama Cautions Embattled Ally against Violence," *New York
Times*, January 28, 2011, https://www.nytimes.com/2011/01/29/world/middlee
ast/29diplo.html.

25. Karen DeYoung, "Obama Presses Mubarak to Move 'Now,'" *Washington Post*,
February 2, 2011, https://www.washingtonpost.com/national/obama-presses
-for-move-now/2011/02/01/AB3hHbE_story.html.

26. Barack Obama, *A Promised Land* (New York: Crown, 2020), 648.

27. Douglas Hamilton, "Israel Shocked by Obama's 'Betrayal' of Mubarak," Reuters,
January 2011, https://www.reuters.com/article/us-egypt-israel-usa/israel-shocked
-by-obamas-betrayal-of-mubarak-idUSTRE70U53720110131.

28. Mark Memmott, "Gadhafi Blames 'Rats' and Foreign 'Agents'; Says He Will Be a
'Martyr,'" NPR, February 22, 2011, https://www.npr.org/sections/thetwo-way
/2011/02/22/133960871/gadhafi-blames-rats-and-foreign-agents-says-he
-will-be-a-martyr.

29. Edward Wyatt, "Security Council Calls for War Crimes Inquiry in Libya," *New
York Times*, February 26, 2011, https://www.nytimes.com/2011/02/27/world/africa
/27nations.html.

30. UN Security Council, Resolution 1973, S/RES/1973 (March 17, 2011), https://
www.un.org/press/en/2011/sc10200.doc.htm#Resolution.

31. Barack Obama, *A Promised Land* (New York: Crown, 2020), 657.

32. Philip H. Gordon, *Losing the Long Game: The False Promise of Regime Change in the
Middle East* (St Martin's Press, 2020), 106.

33. BBC, "President Obama: Libya Aftermath 'Worst Mistake' of Presidency," April
11, 2016, https://www.bbc.com/news/world-us-canada-36013703.

34. Jay Solomon and Dion Nissenbaum, "Security Cut before Libya Raid," *Wall
Street Journal*, October 10, 2012, https://www.wsj.com/articles/SB10000872396
390444799904578048344154761294.

35. Khaled Yacoub Oweis, "U.S. Officials Find 'Common Ground' in Syria," Reuters,
March 7, 2009, https://www.reuters.com/article/idINIndia-38397720090308.

36. Isabel Kershner, "Secret Israel-Syria Peace Talks Involved Golan Heights Exit,"
New York Times, October 12, 2012, https://www.nytimes.com/2012/10/13/world
/middleeast/secret-israel-syria-peace-talks-involved-golan-heights-exit.html.

37. Mariam Karouny, "Syria to Send in Army after 120 Troops Killed," Reuters, June
6, 2011, https://www.reuters.com/article/topNews/idCATRE7553AI20110606
?edition-redirect=ca.

38. Barack Obama, "Statement by President Obama on the Situation in Syria" (speech,
Washington, DC, August 18, 2011), https://obamawhitehouse.archives.gov/the
-press-office/2011/08/18/statement-president-obama-situation-syria.

39. Anthony Shadid, "Syrian Leader Vows 'Iron Fist' to Crush 'Conspiracy,'" *New
York Times,* January 10, 2012, https://www.nytimes.com/2012/01/11/world

/middleeast/syrian-leader-vows-to-crush-conspiracy.html; Nada Bakri, "In Rare Public Appearance, Assad Addresses Rally in Syria," *New York Times*, January 11, 2012, https://www.nytimes.com/2012/01/12/world/middleeast/president-assad -makes-rare-public-speech-in-syria.html.

40. Neil MacFarquhar, "Syrian Rebels Land Deadly Blow to Assad's Inner Circle," *New York Times*, July 18, 2012, https://www.nytimes.com/2012/07/19/world /middleeast/suicide-attack-reported-in-damascus-as-more-generals-flee.html.

41. Mark Mazzetti, "C.I.A. Study of Covert Aid Fueled Skepticism about Helping Syrian Rebels," *New York Times*, October 14, 2014, https://www.nytimes.com /2014/10/15/us/politics/cia-study-says-arming-rebels-seldom-works.html.

42. Ben Hubbard and Hwaida Saad, "Images of Death in Syria, but No Proof of Chemical Attack," *New York Times*, August 21, 2013, https://www.nytimes.com /2013/08/22/world/middleeast/syria.html.

43. Shawna Thomas, "Obama Draws a 'Red Line' for Syria on Chemical and Biological Weapons," NBC News, August 20, 2012, https://www.nbcnews.com/news /world/obama-draws-red-line-syria-chemical-biological-weapons-flna954570.

44. "Syria Crisis: Cameron Loses Commons Vote on Syria Action," BBC, August 30, 2013, https://www.bbc.com/news/uk-politics-23892783.

45. The proposal to be voted on was narrowly cast: "prevent or deter the use or proliferation" of chemical or biological weapons "within, to or from Syria" and to "protect the United States and its allies and partners against the threat posed by such weapons." See: Peter Baker and Jonathan Weisman, "Obama Seeks Approval by Congress for Strike in Syria," *New York Times*, August 31, 2013, https:// www.nytimes.com/2013/09/01/world/middleeast/syria.html.

46. Scott Shane, "Weren't Syria's Chemical Weapons Destroyed? It's Complicated," *New York Times*, April 7, 2017, https://www.nytimes.com/2017/04/07/world /middleeast/werent-syrias-chemical-weapons-destroyed-its-complicated.html.

47. Ben Rhodes, "Inside the White House during the Syrian 'Red Line' Crisis," *The Atlantic*, June 3, 2018, https://www.theatlantic.com/international/archive/2018 /06/inside-the-white-house-during-the-syrian-red-line-crisis/561887/.

48. Adam Goldman and Ellen Nakashima, "CIA and Mossad Killed Senior Hezbollah Figure in Car Bombing," *Washington Post*, January 30, 2015, https://www .washingtonpost.com/world/national-security/cia-and-mossad-killed-senior -hezbollah-figure-in-car-bombing/2015/01/30/ebb88682-968a-11e4-8005 -1924ede3e54a_story.html.

49. Aaron Maté, "Ex-Obama Official: We Fueled the Syria War Rather Than Stopping It," *Real News Network*, August 23, 2018, https://therealnews.com/ex-obama-official -we-fueled-the-syria-war-rather-than-stopping-it.

50. Alex Johnson, "Obama Says U.S. Knew Russian Military Planned to Intervene in Syria," NBC News, October 11, 2015, https://www.nbcnews.com/storyline /isis-terror/obama-says-u-s-knew-russian-military-planned-intervene-syria -n442596.

51. David Ignatius, "Russia and the 'Facts on the Ground' in Syria," *Washington Post*, October 1, 2015, https://www.washingtonpost.com/opinions/russias-facts-on-the-ground-in-syria/2015/10/01/45fe3bb2-687e-11e5-8325-a42b5a459b1e_story.html.

52. U.S. Department of State, "Defense Cooperation Agreement between the United States of America and Iraq, Signed at Baghdad November 17, 2008," Treaties and Other International Acts Series 09-101.1, https://www.state.gov/wp-content/uploads/2019/02/09-101.1-Iraq-Defense-Coop.pdf.

53. Erik Gustafson, "Obama's Legacy in Iraq," *The Hill*, January 20, 2017, https://thehill.com/blogs/congress-blog/foreign-policy/315247-obamas-legacy-in-iraq.

54. Peter Beinart, "Obama's Disastrous Iraq Policy: An Autopsy," *The Atlantic*, June 23, 2014, https://www.theatlantic.com/international/archive/2014/06/obamas-disastrous-iraq-policy-an-autopsy/373225/.

55. U.S. Senate, Committee on Armed Services Hearing, *Security Issues Relating to Iraq*, 112th Cong., 1st Sess., November 15, 2011, 7–65, https://www.govinfo.gov/content/pkg/CHRG–112shrg74867/html/CHRG–112shrg74867.htm.

56. Agence France-Presse, "Republicans Are Bashing Obama for Pulling Troops Out of Iraq," *Insider,* January 10, 2014, https://www.businessinsider.com/republicans-are-bashing-obama-for-pulling-troops-out-of-iraq-2014-1.

57. James Traub, "The Mess Obama Left Behind in Iraq," *Foreign Policy*, October 7, 2016, https://foreignpolicy.com/2016/10/07/the-mess-obama-left-behind-in-iraq-surge-debate/.

58. "Leon Panetta: U.S. Mistakes Helped Create 'Vacuum' That Spawned ISIS," NBC News, October 7, 2014, https://www.nbcnews.com/storyline/isis-terror/leon-panetta-u-s-mistakes-helped-create-vacuum-spawned-isis-n220586.

59. James Franklin Jeffrey, "Behind the U.S. Withdrawal from Iraq," *Wall Street Journal*, November 2, 2014, https://www.wsj.com/articles/james-franklin-jeffrey-behind-the-u-s-withdrawal-from-iraq-1414972705.

60. Peter Baker and Eric Schmitt, "Many Missteps in Assessment of ISIS Threat," *New York Times*, September 29, 2014, https://www.nytimes.com/2014/09/30/world/middleeast/obama-fault-is-shared-in-misjudging-of-isis-threat.html.

61. "Obama: U.S. Underestimated Rise of ISIS in Iraq and Syria," CBS News, September 28, 2014, https://www.cbsnews.com/news/obama-u-s-underestimated-rise-of-isis-in-iraq-and-syria/.

62. Richard Esposito, "Intel Officials Take Issue with Obama on 'Underestimate' of ISIS Threat," NBC News, September 29, 2014, https://www.nbcnews.com/storyline/isis-terror/intel-officials-take-issue-obama-underestimate-isis-threat-n214376.

63. Alice Fordham, "Fact Check: Did Obama Withdraw from Iraq Too Soon, Allowing ISIS to Grow?," *Morning Edition*, December 19, 2015, https://www.npr.org/2015/12/19/459850716/fact-check-did-obama-withdraw-from-iraq-too-soon-allowing-isis-to-grow.

64. Mark Mazzetti and Matt Apuzzo, "Inquiry Weighs Whether ISIS Analysis Was Distorted," *New York Times*, August 25, 2015, https://www.nytimes.com/2015/08/26/world/middleeast/pentagon-investigates-allegations-of-skewed-intelligence-reports-on-isis.html.

65. James Kitfield, "How Mike Flynn Became America's Angriest General," *Politico Magazine*, October 16, 2016, https://www.politico.com/magazine/story/2016/10/how-mike-flynn-became-americas-angriest-general-214362.

66. Rick Brennan, "Withdrawal Symptoms: The Bungling of the Iraq Exit," *Foreign Affairs*, November/December 2014, https://www.foreignaffairs.com/articles/united-states/withdrawal-symptoms; Lawrence J. Korb and Rick Brennan, "Exit Music: Did Obama Bungle the Iraq Withdrawal?," *Foreign Affairs*, January/February 2015, https://www.foreignaffairs.com/articles/middle-east/2014-12-03/exit-music.

67. Jeffrey M. Jones, "Three in Four Americans Back Obama on Iraq Withdrawal," Gallup, November 2, 2011, https://news.gallup.com/poll/150497/three-four-americans-back-obama-iraq-withdrawal.aspx.

68. Margaret MacMillan, *War: How Conflict Shaped Us* (New York: Random House, 2020), 206.

69. The standard account has been challenged on the basis of new archival material: Simon Miles, "The War Scare That Wasn't: Able Archer 83 and the Myths of the Second Cold War," *Journal of Cold War Studies* 22, no. 3 (Summer 2020): 86–118, https://doi.org/10.1162/jcws_a_00952.

70. National Security Archive, *Special National Intelligence Estimate: Prospects for Further Proliferation of Nuclear Weapons*, George Washington University, August 23, 1974, https://nsarchive2.gwu.edu//NSAEBB/NSAEBB240/snie.pdf.

71. Peter Oborne and David Morrison, "U.S. Scuppered Deal with Iran in 2005, Says Then British Foreign Minister," openDemocracy, September 23, 2013, https://www.opendemocracy.net/en/us-scuppered-deal-with-iran-in-2005-says-then-british-foreign-minister/.

72. National Intelligence Council, "Iran: Nuclear Intentions and Capabilities," National Intelligence Estimate, Office of the Director of National Intelligence, November 2007, https://www.dni.gov/files/documents/Newsroom/Reports%20and%20Pubs/20071203_release.pdf.

73. Henry A. Kissinger, "Misreading the Iran Report," *Washington Post*, December 13, 2007, https://www.henryakissinger.com/articles/misreading-the-iran-report/; Eli Lake, "Review: Iran Never Halted Nuke Work in '03," *Washington Times*, January 19, 2010, http://www.washingtontimes.com/news/2010/jan/19/review-says-iran-never-halted-nuke-work-in-2003/.

74. James Risen, "U.S. Faces a Tricky Task in Assessment of Data on Iran," *New York Times*, March 17, 2012, https://www.nytimes.com/2012/03/18/world/middleeast/iran-intelligence-crisis-showed-difficulty-of-assessing-nuclear-data.html.

75. Risen, "U.S. Faces."

76. Although the United States has not officially acknowledged Israel's nuclear weapons status, two Israeli prime ministers, Ehud Olmert and Yair Lapid, have both referred to it publicly, if inadvertently. In 1986, Mordechai Vanunu, an employee in Israel's weapons program, disclosed to the London *Times* detailed information and photographic evidence of Israel's stockpile. The United States has declassified at least one intelligence estimate that refers to Israel's nuclear weapons program.

77. Reuters staff, "Saudi Crown Prince Says Will Develop Nuclear Bomb If Iran Does: CBS TV," Reuters, March 15, 2018, https://www.reuters.com/article/us-saudi -iran-nuclear/saudi-crown-prince-says-will-develop-nuclear-bomb-if-iran -does-cbs-tv-idUSKCN1GR1MN.

78. Office of the Press Secretary, The White House, "Remarks of President Barack Obama—Address to Joint Session of Congress, February 24, 2009," https://obama whitehouse.archives.gov/the-press-office/remarks-president-barack-obama -address-joint-session-congress.

79. Ewen MacAskill, "Obama Sent Letter to Khamenei before the Election, Report Says," *The Guardian*, June 24, 2009, https://www.theguardian.com/world/2009 /jun/24/khamenei-obama-letter.

80. Helene Cooper and David E. Sanger, "Obama's Message to Iran Is Opening Bid in Diplomatic Drive," *New York Times*, March 20, 2009, https://www.nytimes.com /2009/03/21/world/middleeast/21iran.html.

81. Cooper and Sanger, "Obama's Message to Iran."

82. Associated Press, "Iran's Supreme Leader Rebuffs Obama Message," *New York Times*, March 21, 2009, https://www.nytimes.com/2009/03/22/world/middlee ast/22iran.html.

83. "Iran: Report of Second Letter from Obama to Tehran [Updated], *Los Angeles Times*, September 2, 2009, https://latimesblogs.latimes.com/babylonbeyond /2009/09/iran-report-of-secret-letter-from-obama-to-tehran.html.

84. Ron Kampeas, "Donilon Talks Iran with Israeli Counterpart," *Jewish Telegraphic Agency*, November 12, 2012, https://www.jta.org/2012/11/12/united-states/donilon -talks-iran-with-israeli-counterpart.

85. Barak Ravid, "Barak Hints U.S. Military Preparations May Eliminate Israel's Need for Iran Strike," *Haaretz*, September 7, 2012, https://www.haaretz.com/2012 -09-07/ty-article/barak-gets-dovish-on-iran/0000017f-e62b-da9b-a1ff -ee6f2e5d0000.

86. Michael B Kelley, "Israel Is Set to Receive 5,000 U.S. Bunker Buster Bombs after Delaying Its Attack on Iran," *Business Insider*, December 13, 2012, https://www .businessinsider.com/the-us-sale-of-5000-bunker-buster-bombs-to-israel -israel-bunker-busters-in-exchange-for-not-striking-iran-2012-12; David Deptula and Michael Makovsky, "Sending a Bunker-Buster Message to Iran," *Wall Street Journal*, April 7, 2014, https://www.wsj.com/articles/SB100014240527023 04418404579462970629373280; Dennis Ross and David H. Petraeus, "How to

Put Some Teeth into the Nuclear Deal with Iran," *Washington Post*, August 25, 2015, https://www.washingtonpost.com/opinions/how-to-put-some-teeth-into-the-nuclear-deal-with-iran/2015/08/25/6f3db43c-4b35-11e5-bfb9-9736d04fc8e4_story.html; David S. Cloud, "Israel Will Be First to Receive V-22 Osprey Aircraft from U.S.," *Los Angeles Times*, October 31, 2013, https://www.latimes.com/world/worldnow/la-fg-wn-israel-v22-osprey-us-20131031-story.html.

87. Adam Entous and Julian E. Barnes, "Pentagon Seeks Mightier Bomb vs. Iran," *Wall Street Journal*, January 28, 2012, https://www.wsj.com/articles/SB10001424052970203363504577187420287098692?mod=WSJ_WSJ_News_BlogsModule.

88. David E. Sanger, "U.S. Rejected Aid for Israeli Raid on Iranian Nuclear Site, *New York Times*, January 10, 2009, https://www.nytimes.com/2009/01/11/washington/11iran.html?scp=1&sq=january%202009%20sanger%20bush%20natanz&st=cse.

89. Ellen Nakashima and Joby Warrick, "Stuxnet Was Work of U.S. and Israeli Experts, Officials Say," *Washington Post*, June 2, 2012, https://www.washingtonpost.com/world/national-security/stuxnet-was-work-of-us-and-israeli-experts-officials-say/2012/06/01/gJQAInEy6U_story.html.

90. For an exceptionally well-informed study of the Stuxnet episode and the strengths and weaknesses of such weapons, see David E. Sanger, *The Perfect Weapon: War, Sabotage, and Fear in the Cyber Age* (New York: Crown, 2018).

91. "Stuxnet: Computer Worm Opens New Era of Warfare," CBS News, June 4, 2012, https://www.cbsnews.com/news/stuxnet-computer-worm-opens-new-era-of-warfare-04-06-2012/; and Jesse Emspak, "Why We Soon Won't See Another Stuxnet Attack," NBC News, July 25, 2011, https://www.nbcnews.com/id/wbna43888006.

92. James Long, "Stuxnet: A Digital Staff Ride," Modern War Institute at West Point, March 8, 2019, https://mwi.usma.edu/stuxnet-digital-staff-ride/.

93. Ronen Bergman, "When Israel Hatched a Secret Plan to Assassinate Iranian Scientists," *Politico Magazine*, March 5, 2018, https://www.politico.com/magazine/story/2018/03/05/israel-assassination-iranian-scientists-217223/.

94. Mehdi Jedinia, "History of Assassinations of Iran's Top Nuclear Scientists," VOA News, December 3, 2020, https://www.voanews.com/extremism-watch/history-assassinations-irans-top-nuclear-scientists.

95. Ethan Bronner, "Israel Says Iran Is Behind Bomb," *New York Times*, February 13, 2012, https://www.nytimes.com/2012/02/14/world/middleeast/israeli-embassy-officials-attacked-in-india-and-georgia.html.

96. Adam Entous, "Spy vs. Spy: Inside the Fraying U.S.-Israel Ties," *Wall Street Journal*, October 22, 2015, https://www.wsj.com/articles/spy-vs-spy-inside-the-fraying-u-s-israel-ties-1445562074.

97. Adam Entous, "Israel Spied on Iran Nuclear Talks with U.S.," *Wall Street Journal*, March 23, 2015, https://www.wsj.com/articles/israel-spied-on-iran-talks-1427164201.

98. David E. Sanger, "Fear of Israeli Leaks Fuels Distrust over U.S. Talks with Iran," *New York Times*, February 17, 2015, https://www.nytimes.com/2015/02/18/world /fear-of-israeli-leaks-fuels-distrust-as-us-and-iran-hold-nuclear-talks.html.

99. Entous, "Israel Spied on Iran."

100. David Ignatius, "Is Israel Preparing to Attack Iran?," *Washington Post*, February 2, 2012, https://www.washingtonpost.com/opinions/is-israel-preparing-to-attack -iran/2012/02/02/gIQANjfTkQ_story.html.

101. TOI Staff, "Barak: Netanyahu Wanted Strike Iran in 2010 and 2011, but Colleagues Blocked Him," *Times of Israel*, August 21, 2015, https://www.timesofisrael.com /barak-netanyahu-wanted-to-strike-iran-in-2010-and-2011-but-colleagues -blocked-him/.

102. David Ignatius, "Is Israel Preparing to Attack Iran?," *Washington Post*, February 2, 2012, https://www.washingtonpost.com/opinions/is-israel-preparing-to-attack -iran/2012/02/02/gIQANjfTkQ_story.html.

103. Jeffrey Goldberg, "The Crisis in U.S.-Israel Relations Is Officially Here," *The Atlantic*, October 2014, https://www.theatlantic.com/international/archive/2014/10 /the-crisis-in-us-israel-relations-is-officially-here/382031/.

104. TOI Staff, "Kerry Phones Netanyahu, Apologizes for 'Chickenshit' Comment," *Times of Israel*, October 31, 2014, https://www.timesofisrael.com/kerry-phones -netanyahu-apologizes-for-chickenshit-comment/.

105. "IAEA Director General Comments on Cooperation Framework with Iran," press release, IAEA, November 11, 2013, https://www.iaea.org/newscenter/pressreleases /iaea-director-general-comments-cooperation-framework-iran.

106. Farnaz Fassihi, "Iran's Foreign Minister, in Leaked Tape, Says Revolutionary Guards Set Policies," *New York Times*, April 25, 2021, https://www.nytimes.com /search?query=Iran%27s+foreign+minister%2C+in+leaked+tape.

107. Ishaan Tharoor, "The Historic Nuclear Deal with Iran: How It Works," *Washington Post*, July 14, 2015, https://www.washingtonpost.com/news/worldviews/wp /2015/07/14/the-historic-nuclear-deal-with-iran-how-it-works/.

108. Peter Baker, "G.O.P. Senators' Letter to Iran about Nuclear Deal Angers White House," *New York Times*, March 9, 2015, https://www.nytimes.com/2015/03/10 /world/asia/white-house-faults-gop-senators-letter-to-irans-leaders.html.

109. Jonathan Weisman and Peter Baker, "Obama Yields, Allowing Congress Say on Iran Nuclear Deal," *New York Times*, April 14, 2015, https://www.nytimes.com /2015/04/15/us/senators-reach-deal-on-iran-nuclear-talks.html.

110. "An Act to Provide for Congressional Review and Oversight of Agreements Relating to Iran's Nuclear Program, and for Other Purposes, Public Law 114-17," *U.S. Statutes at Large* 42 (2015): 201–12, https://www.congress.gov/114/plaws/publ17 /PLAW-114publ17.pdf.

111. Elizabeth Drew, "How They Failed to Block the Iran Deal," *New York Review of Books*, October 22, 2015, https://www.nybooks.com/articles/2015/10/22/how -they-failed-block-iran-deal/.

112. Jeffrey Goldberg, "The Obama Doctrine," *The Atlantic*, April 15, 2016, https://www.theatlantic.com/magazine/archive/2016/04/the-obama-doctrine/471525/.

113. Javier Blas, "Saudi Arabia's Chief Oil Whisperer Spills Some of His Secrets," Bloomberg, June 1, 2022, https://www.bloomberg.com/opinion/articles/2022-06-01/-oil-leaders-review-saudi-arabia-s-chief-oil-whisperer-spills-his-secrets.

114. Lucy Madison, "Mitt Romney Accuses Obama of Throwing Israel 'under the Bus,'" CBS News, May 19, 2011, https://www.cbsnews.com/news/mitt-romney-accuses-obama-of-throwing-israel-under-the-bus/.

CHAPTER SEVEN: DONALD J. TRUMP: THE DEAL OF THE CENTURY

1. "ABC News anchor David Muir interviews President Trump," ABC News, January 25, 2017, https://abcnews.go.com/Politics/transcript-abc-news-anchor-david-muir-interviews-president/story?id=45047602.

2. Rosalind S. Helderman, "Trump Attacks American Jews, Posting They Must 'Get Their Act Together' on Israel," *Washington Post*, October 16, 2022, https://www.washingtonpost.com/politics/2022/10/16/trump-jews-israel.

3. Reuters Staff, "Trump: I Told Saudi King He Wouldn't Last without U.S. Support," Reuters, October 2, 2018, https://www.reuters.com/article/us-usa-trump-saudi/trump-i-told-saudi-king-he-wouldnt-last-without-u-s-support-idUSKCN1MD066.

4. Katie Bo Williams, "Outgoing Syria Envoy Admits Hiding U.S. Troop Numbers; Praises Trump's Mideast Record," *Defense One*, November 12, 2020, https://www.defenseone.com/threats/2020/11/outgoing-syria-envoy-admits-hiding-us-troop-numbers-praises-trumps-mideast-record/170012/.

5. Eric Schmitt, "U.S. to Reduce Troop Levels in Iraq to 3,000," *New York Times*, September 9, 2020, https://www.nytimes.com/2020/09/09/us/politics/iraq-troops-trump.html.

6. Steven Simon, "The Middle East: Trump Blunders In," *New York Review of Books*, February 13, 2020, https://www.nybooks.com/articles/2020/02/13/middle-east-trump-blunders-in/.

7. "Joint Comprehensive Plan of Action," U.S. Department of State, July 14, 2015, https://2009-2017.state.gov/e/eb/tfs/spi/iran/jcpoa/index.htm.

8. Mark Landler, "Trump Abandons Iran Nuclear Deal He Long Scorned," *New York Times*, May 8, 2018, https://www.nytimes.com/2018/05/08/world/middleeast/trump-iran-nuclear-deal.html.

9. International Crisis Group, *On Thin Ice: The Iran Nuclear Deal at Three* (Brussels: ICG, 2019), https://d2071andvip0wj.cloudfront.net/195-on-thin-ice.pdf.

10. Robert Einhorn and Richard Nephew, "The Iran Nuclear Deal: Prelude to Proliferation in the Middle East?," Brookings Institution, May 2016, https://www.brookings.edu/research/the-iran-nuclear-deal-prelude-to-proliferation-in-the-middle-east/.

11. Ben Hubbard, "Saudi Crown Prince Likens Iran's Supreme Leader to Hitler," *New York Times*, March 15, 2018, https://www.nytimes.com/2018/03/15/world /middleeast/mohammed-bin-salman-iran-hitler.html.

12. Ben Hubbard, Palko Karasz, and Stanley Reed, "Two Major Saudi Oil Installa- tions Hit by Drone Strike, and U.S. Blames Iran," *New York Times*, September 15, 2019, https://www.nytimes.com/2019/09/14/world/middleeast/saudi-arabia -refineries-drone-attack.html.

13. Lara Seligman, "Pentagon Chief Kept Tight Circle on Suleimani Strike," *Foreign Policy*, January 5, 2020, https://foreignpolicy.com/2020/01/05/pentagon-chief -kept-tight-circle-on-suleimani-strike/: "'The usual approval process, the decision -making process, did not occur,' said one defense official, speaking on condition of anonymity to discuss sensitive issues. Even among the small group of officials who were in the loop, there was dissent about whether killing Soleimani was a wise deci- sion, said a former senior administration official with knowledge of the discussions. 'The DoD was not all in agreement that killing the second most popular person in Iran at an international airport in Iraq was a good idea,' the former official said."

14. Reuters staff, "Inside the Plot by Iran's Soleimani to Attack U.S. Forces in Iraq," Reuters, January 3, 2020, https://www.reuters.com/article/us-iraq-security -soleimani-insight/inside-the-plot-by-irans-soleimani-to-attack-u-s-forces-in -iraq-idUSKBN1Z301Z.

15. Eric Schmitt et al., "Trump Sought Options for Attacking Iran to Stop Its Grow- ing Nuclear Program," *New York Times*, November 16, 2020, https://www.nytimes .com/2020/11/16/us/politics/trump-iran-nuclear.html.

16. "Avenging the Murder of General Soleimani Is Certain," Khamenei.Ir, December 16, 2020, https://english.khamenei.ir/news/8181/Avenging-the-murder-of-General -Soleimani-is-certain.

17. Barbara Starr, "U.S. Says Iranian-Backed Militias 'Almost Certainly' behind Re- cent Rocket Attack Near U.S. Embassy in Baghdad," CNN, December 23, 2020, https://www.cnn.com/2020/12/23/politics/centcom-iran-baghdad-embassy /index.html.

18. "Top U.S. Officials Discuss 'Range of Options' to Protect Americans in Iraq from Iran Attacks—Senior U.S. Official," Reuters, December 23, 2020, https://news.trust .org/item/20201223181516-vebph/.

19. Helene Cooper, "Trump Warns Iran of Retaliation after Attacks on U.S. Embassy in Baghdad," *New York Times*, December 23, 2020, https://www.nytimes.com /2020/12/23/us/politics/trump-iran.html?action=click&module=Well&pgtype =Homepage&section=Politics.

20. Falih Hassan, Tim Arango, and Alissa J. Rubin, "A Shocked Iraq Reconsiders Its Relationship with the U.S.," *New York Times*, January 3, 2020, https://www .nytimes.com/2020/01/03/world/middleeast/us-iraq.html?fbclid=IwAR1k1 AHNQoMlAeVPv2qNteXq2kmFHENwotAd39JnqNWKfkU6BVkDPqxKWqE.

21. Steven Simon and Jonathan Stevenson, "Iran: The Case against War," *New York*

Review, August 15, 2019, https://www.nybooks.com/articles/2019/08/15/iran
-case-against-war/.

22. Eric Schmitt, "To Deter Iranian Attacks on U.S. Troops, Pentagon Orders B-52 Flights to Middle East," *New York Times*, December 10, 2020, https://www.nytimes.com/2020/12/10/world/middleeast/bombers-iran-deterrence.html.

23. Shira Rubin, "Israel Deploys Submarine to Persian Gulf in Message of Deterrence to Iran," *Washington Post*, December 23, 2020, https://www.washingtonpost.com/world/middle_east/iran-israel-fakhrizadeh-nuclear-assassination/2020/12/23/fca9e0fe-44e8-11eb-ac2a-3ac0f2b8ceeb_story.html.

24. Barbara Slavin, "Why Was Iran's Top Nuclear Scientist Killed?," *New York Times*, November 28, 2020, https://www.nytimes.com/2020/11/28/opinion/iran-nuclear-scientist-killed.html; David E. Sanger et al., "Gunmen Assassinate Iran's Top Nuclear Scientist in Ambush, Provoking New Crisis," *New York Times*, November 27, 2020, https://www.nytimes.com/2020/11/27/world/middleeast/iran-nuclear-scientist-killed.html.

25. HaMaaracha ben HaMilchamot in Hebrew.

26. "Transnational Threats Project Database on Israeli Strikes," Center for Strategic and International Studies, unpublished; Isabel Kershner, "Israel, in Rare Admission, Confirms Strike on Iranian Targets in Syria," *New York Times*, January 13, 2019, https://www.nytimes.com/2019/01/13/world/middleeast/israel-iran-strike-syria-tunnels.html?module=inline; Judah Ari Gross, "IDF Reveals 'Operation Chess,' Its Efforts to Keep Iranian Reprisals in Check," *Times of Israel*, May 11, 2018, https://www.timesofisrael.com/idf-reveals-operation-chess-its-effort-to-thwart-iranian-reprisals-from-syria/.

27. Judah Ari Gross, "IDF Says It Has Bombed over 200 Iranian Targets in Syria since 2017," *Times of Israel*, September 4, 2018, https://www.timesofisrael.com/idf-says-it-has-carried-out-over-200-strikes-in-syria-since-2017/.

28. Liz Sly and Suzan Haidamous, "Another Suspected Israeli Strike in Lebanon as War Fears Intensify," *Washington Post*, August 26, 2019, https://www.washingtonpost.com/world/war-fears-intensify-as-israel-strikes-lebanon/2019/08/26/22840d86-c835-11e9-9615-8f1a32962e04_story.html.

29. Alissa J. Rubin and Ronen Bergman, "Israeli Airstrike Hits Weapons Depot in Iraq," *New York Times*, August 22, 2019, https://www.nytimes.com/2019/08/22/world/middleeast/israel-iraq-iran-airstrike.html.

30. Amos Yadlin and Assaf Orion, "The Campaign between Wars: Faster, Higher, Fiercer?," *INSS Insight* no. 1209, August 30, 2019, Institute for National Security Studies, Tel Aviv University, https://www.inss.org.il/publication/the-campaign-between-wars-faster-higher-fiercer/.

31. Michael Crowley, "Israel, U.A.E., and Bahrain Sign Accords, with an Eager Trump Playing Host," *New York Times*, September 15, 2020, https://www.nytimes.com/2020/09/15/us/politics/trump-israel-peace-emirates-bahrain.html.

32. Peter Baker et al., "Israel and United Arab Emirates Strike Major Diplomatic

Agreement," *New York Times*, August 13, 2020, https://www.nytimes.com /2020/08/13/us/politics/trump-israel-united-arab-emirates-uae.html.

33. TOI Staff, "Israel Said to Estimate UAE Deal Worth Hundreds of Millions in Trade a Year," *Times of Israel*, August 16, 2020, https://www.timesofisrael.com /israel-said-to-estimate-uae-deal-worth-hundreds-of-millions-in-trade-a-year/.

34. Hagai Amit, "The Real Deal for Israel and the UAE Is Weapons," *Haaretz*, August 17, 2020, https://www.haaretz.com/israel-news/business/.premium-the-real-deal -for-israel-and-the-uae-is-weapons-1.9077725.

35. "United States-Israel Strategic Partnership Act of 2014, Public Law 113-296," *U.S. Statutes at Large* 128 (2014): 4075–81, https://www.congress.gov/113/plaws /publ296/PLAW-113publ296.pdf; Jeremy M. Sharp et al., *Israel's Qualitative Military Edge and Possible U.S. Arms Sales to the United Arab Emirates* (Washington, DC: Congressional Research Service, 2020), https://crsreports.congress.gov/product /pdf/R/R46580.

36. Mark Mazzetti, Edward Long, and Michael LaForgia, "Netanyahu Privately Condoned U.S. Plan to Sell Arms to U.A.E., Officials Say," *New York Times*, September 3, 2020, https://www.nytimes.com/2020/09/03/us/politics/israel-uae -weapons.html.

37. Rina Bassist, "Gantz, Netanyahu Split Again over U.S. F-35 Sale to UAE," *Al-Monitor*, October 26, 2020, https://www.al-monitor.com/pulse/originals/2020 /10/israel-us-uae-benjamin-netanyahu-benny-gantz-f-35-stealth.html.

38. Ishaan Tharoor, "Trump's Parting Gift to Morocco," *Washington Post*, December 14, 2020, https://www.washingtonpost.com/world/2020/12/14/trumps-parting -gift-morocco/.

39. Dion Nissenbaum, Jared Malsin, and Felicia Schwartz, "Israel and Morocco Agree to Normalize Ties, Trump and Netanyahu," *Wall Street Journal*, December 10, 2020, https://www.wsj.com/articles/trump-says-morocco-will-establish-full -diplomatic-relations-with-israel-11607617872.

40. Adela Suliman and Charlene Gubash, "Sudan Formally Recognizes Israel in U.S.-brokered Deal," NBC News, October 23, 2020, https://www.nbcnews.com /news/world/sudan-formally-recognizes-israel-u-s-brokered-deal-n1240839.

41. On-the-record press call by National Security Adviser, Ambassador Robert O'Brien on recent actions in Iraq, via telephone, 5:20 p.m. January 3, 2020, https:// macenews.com/white-house-briefing-on-killing-of-iran-quds-force-chief/.

42. Hassan, Arango, and Rubin, "A Shocked Iraq Reconsiders," *New York Times*, January 3, 2020, https://www.nytimes.com/2020/01/03/world/middleeast/us -iraq.html?fbclid=IwAR1k1AHNQoMlAeVPv2qNteXq2kmFHENwotAd39Jn qNWKfkU6BVkDPqxKWqE.

43. Isabel Coles and Catherine Lucey, "Trump Pushes Iraq, Threatens Sanctions after Vote to Expel U.S. Troops," *Wall Street Journal*, January 6, 2020, https://www.wsj .com/articles/iraqi-parliament-votes-in-favor-of-expelling-u-s-troops-11578236473.

44. The Iraq Body Count project (IBC) figure of documented civilian deaths from violence is 183,535–206,107 through April 2019, https:// www.iraqbodycount .org/. This includes reported civilian deaths due to coalition and insurgent military action, sectarian violence, and increased criminal violence.

45. Coles and Lucey, "Trump Pushes Iraq."

46. Chelsea Bailey and Erik Ortiz, "Syria Airstrike: Trump Declares 'Mission Accomplished' after Chemical Weapons Targets Hit," NBC News, April 14, 2018, https://www.nbcnews.com/politics/donald-trump/syria-airstrikes-trump -declares-mission-accomplished-after-hitting-weapons-targets-n866001.

47. Linda Qiu, "Fact-Checking Trump on Syria, Erdogan and the Kurds," *New York Times*, October 16, 2019, https://www.nytimes.com/2019/10/16/us/politics /factcheck-trump-syria-kurds.html.

48. White House, "Statement from the Press Secretary," press release, October 6, 2019, https://trumpwhitehouse.archives.gov/briefings-statements/statement-press -secretary-85/.

49. Jason Motlagh, "The Betrayal of the Kurds," *Rolling Stone,* December 18, 2019, https://www.rollingstone.com/politics/politics-features/trump-betrayal-of-the -kurds-927545/.

50. Julian Borger, "Trump Contradicts Aides and Says Troops in Syria 'Only for Oil,'" *The Guardian,* November 13, 2019, https://www.theguardian.com/us-news/2019 /nov/13/donald-trump-syria-oil-us-troops-isis-turkey.

51. Lauren Hirsch, "Trump Wants to Make a Deal with Exxon or Others to Tap Syrian Oil: 'We Should Be Able to Take Some,'" CNBC, October 27, 2019, https:// www.cnbc.com/2019/10/27/trump-wants-to-make-a-deal-with-exxon-or -others-to-tap-syrian-oil.html.

52. Lara Seligman and Ben Lefebvre, "Little-Known U.S. Firm Secures Deal for Syrian Oil," *Politico,* August 3, 2020, https://www.politico.com/news/2020/08/03 /delta-crescent-energy-syrian-oil-391033.

53. Ellen Nakashima, Adam Entous, and Greg Miller, "Russian Ambassador Told Moscow That Kushner Wanted Secret Communications Channel with Kremlin," *Washington Post*, May 26, 2017, https://www.washingtonpost.com/world/national -security/russian-ambassador-told-moscow-that-kushner-wanted-secret-com munications-channel-with-kremlin/2017/05/26/520a14b4-422d-11e7-9869 -bac8b446820a_story.html?tid=sm_fb&utm_term=.7fb4395f2b1a.

54. Alexandra Petri, "I Have Just Read 25 Books and Am Here to Perform Your Open-Heart Surgery," *Washington Post*, January 29, 2020, https://www.washing tonpost.com/opinions/2020/01/29/i-have-just-read-25-books-am-here-perform -your-open-heart-surgery/.

55. CNN (@cnn), "Jared Kushner, senior adviser to the President, says the White House's Middle East plan is 'a great deal' and if Palestinians reject it, 'they're going to screw up another opportunity, like they've screwed up every other

opportunity that they've ever had in their existence,'" Twitter, January 28, 2020, https://twitter.com/CNN/status/1222267596210343940.

56. Personal interview with Saeb Erekat, Jericho, West Bank, January 15, 2019. When asked about this, the NSC official familiar with the issue confirmed Erekat's statement.

57. Aaron Rupar (@atrupar), "JARED KUSHNER tries to sell his Middle East Peace Plan on Fox & Friends: 'Past proposals have been 2 to 3 pages—this is an over 80-page proposal with a map. Never been done before,'" Twitter, January 29, 2020, https://twitter.com/atrupar/status/1222516374427316224.

58. David D. Kirkpatrick and Kate Kelly, "Before Giving Billions to Jared Kushner, Saudi Investment Fund Had Big Doubts," *New York Times*, April 10, 2022, https://www.nytimes.com/2022/04/10/us/jared-kushner-saudi-investment-fund.html.

CHAPTER EIGHT: JOSEPH BIDEN: BACK TO THE FUTURE?

1. Kate Sullivan, Betsy Klein and Kaitlan Collins, "Biden Tries to Turn the Page on U.S.-Saudi Relations but Khashoggi Murder Looms over Meetings," CNN, July 15, 2022, https://www.cnn.com/2022/07/15/politics/biden-west-bank-saudi-arabia-day-3/index.html.

2. Associated Press, "Biden says U.S. 'Will Not Walk Away' from Middle East," *Politico*, July 16, 2022, https://www.politico.com/news/2022/07/16/biden-says-u-s-will-not-walk-away-from-middle-east-00046204.

3. "Joe Biden Compares Plight of Palestinians under Israel to That of Irish Catholics under Britain," *Irish Times*, July 15, 2022, https://www.irishtimes.com/world/middle-east/2022/07/15/joe-biden-compares-plight-palestinians-under-israel-to-that-of-irish-catholics-under-britain/.

4. Derek Brower and Myles McCormick, "ExxonMobil Slashes Capex and Will Write Off up to $20bn in Assets," *Financial Times*, November 30, 2020, https://www.ft.com/content/145765b3-2385-4d2f-a71b-82d9b81e85da.

5. McKinsey & Company, "Global Oil Outlook to 2040," *Energy Insights by McKinsey*, February 2021, https://www.mckinsey.com/~/media/mckinsey/industries/oil%20and%20gas/our%20insights/global%20oil%20supply%20and%20demand%20outlook%20to%202040/global-oil-supply-and-demand-outlook-to-2040-online-summary.pdf.

6. Hiroko Tabuchi, "Inside the Saudi Strategy to keep the World Hooked on Oil," *New York Times*, Nov. 21, 2022, https://www.nytimes.com/2022/11/21/climate/saudi-arabia-aramco-oil-solar-climate.html.

7. Karen DeYoung, "Trump Pardons Blackwater Contractors Convicted in Deaths of 14 Iraqi Civilians," *Washington Post*, December 22, 2020, https://www.washingtonpost.com/national-security/trump-pardon-blackwater-contractors-iraq/2020/12/22/603da1f4-44b8-11eb-a277-49a6d1f9dff1_story.html.

8. Lara Seligman and Ben Lefebvre, "Little-Known U.S. Firm Secures Deal for

Syrian Oil," *Politico*, August 3, 2020, https://www.politico.com/news/2020/08/03/delta-crescent-energy-syrian-oil-391033.

9. Kelsey Davenport, "IAEA Reports Signal Escalating Nuclear Crisis with Iran," Arms Control Association, Arms Control Now, June 1, 2022, https://www.armscontrol.org/blog/2022-06-01/iaea-reports-signal-escalating-nuclear-crisis-with-Iran.

10. Ned Price, "Department Press Briefing—March 31, 2022," U.S. Department of State, March 31, 2022, https://www.state.gov/briefings/department-press-briefing-march-31-2022/#post-330423-IsrealIran.

11. Joshua Landis and Steven Simon, "The Pointless Cruelty of Trump's New Syria Sanctions," *Foreign Affairs*, August 17, 2020, https://www.foreignaffairs.com/articles/syria/2020-08-17/pointless-cruelty-trumps-new-syria-sanctions.

12. Alana Abramson, "Saudi Lobbying in the U.S. Has Tripled Since Trump Took Office," *Time*, October 18, 2018, https://time.com/5426499/jamal-khashoggi-saudi-influence-lobbying/.

13. Anna Massoglia, "Saudi Arabia Ramped Up Multi-Million Foreign Influence Operation after Khashoggi's Death," Open Secrets, October 2, 2019, https://www.opensecrets.org/news/2019/10/saudi-arabia-ramped-up-foreign-influence-after-khashoggi/.

14. Ben Rhodes and Jake Sullivan, "How to Check Trump and Repair America's Image," *New York Times*, November 25, 2018, https://www.nytimes.com/2018/11/25/opinion/a-chance-to-repair-americas-image-abroad.html.

15. Julian E. Barnes and David E. Sanger, "Saudi Crown Prince Is Held Responsible for Khashoggi Killing in U.S. Report," *New York Times*, February 26, 2021, https://www.nytimes.com/2021/02/26/us/politics/jamal-khashoggi-killing-cia-report.html.

16. Barnes and Sanger, "Saudi Crown Prince."

17. Joe Biden, "Remarks by President Biden on America's Place in the World" (speech, Washington, DC, February 4, 2021), https://www.whitehouse.gov/briefing-room/speeches-remarks/2021/02/04/remarks-by-president-biden-on-americas-place-in-the-world/.

18. The Fix staff, "Transcript: The November Democratic Debate," *Washington Post*, November 21, 2019, https://www.washingtonpost.com/politics/2019/11/21/transcript-november-democratic-debate/.

19. Stephen Kalin, Summer Said, and Warren P. Strobel, "CIA Chief Met Saudi Crown Prince Last Month in Push to Mend Ties," *Wall Street Journal*, May 3, 2022, https://www.wsj.com/articles/cia-chief-met-saudi-crown-prince-last-month-in-push-to-mend-ties-11651588201.

20. Aamer Madhani and Ellen Knickmeyer, "As Gas Prices Soar, Biden Leans toward Visiting Saudi Arabia," Associated Press, June 2, 2022, https://apnews.com/article/russia-ukraine-biden-boris-johnson-africa-8a1ec9511650906c8a65afd80e3f90e5.

21. Arshad Mohammed, "Biden Should Not Visit Saudi, Meet Crown Prince, Democratic Rep. Schiff Says," Reuters, June 5, 2022, https://www.reuters.com/world

/middle-east/biden-should-not-visit-saudi-meet-crown-prince-democratic-rep
-schiff-says-2022-06-05.

22. "Biden Delays Possible Trip to Saudi Arabia, Israel, Reports Say," Agence France-Presse, June 4, 2022, https://www.voanews.com/author/agence-france-presse
/vv-yt.

23. "The North Atlantic Treaty, Washington D.C.—4 April 1949," Article 5, NATO,
last updated April 10, 2019, https://www.nato.int/cps/en/natolive/official_texts
_17120.htm.

24. "Fact Sheet: Results of Bilateral Meeting between the United States and the King-dom of Saudi Arabia," The White House, July 15, 2022, https://www.presidency
.ucsb.edu/documents/fact-sheet-results-bilateral-meeting-between-the-united
-states-and-the-kingdom-saudi.

25. Stanley Reed, "OPEC Plus Agrees to Cut Production by 100,000 Barrels a Day,"
New York Times, September 5, 2022, https://www.nytimes.com/2022/09/05
/business/opec-plus-meeting.html.

26. "Readout of President Joseph R. Biden, Jr. Call with Prime Minister Benjamin
Netanyahu of Israel," The White House, February 17, 2021, https://www.white
house.gov/briefing-room/statements-releases/2021/02/17/readout-of-president
-joseph-r-biden-jr-call-with-prime-minister-benjamin-netanyahu-of-israel/.

27. David M. Halbfinger, "Biden's Win Means a Demotion for Netanyahu and Less
Focus on Israel, *New York Times*, November 9, 2020, https://www.nytimes.com
/2020/11/09/world/middleeast/biden-israel.html?action=click&module=Related
Links&pgtype=Article.

28. Michael Crowley, "Biden Will Restore U.S. Relations with Palestinians, Revers-ing Trump Cutoff," *New York Times*, January 26, 2021, https://www.nytimes.com
/2021/01/26/world/middleeast/biden-palestinians-israel.html; "F-22 and GBU-57 in Tel-Aviv? America Could Soon Sell Israel the World's Stealthiest Fighter
and the Biggest Bunker Buster Bomb," *Military Watch*, November 1, 2020, https://
militarywatchmagazine.com/article/f-22-and-gbu-57-in-tel-aviv-america
-could-soon-sell-israel-the-world-s-stealthiest-fighter-and-the-biggest-bunker
-buster-bomb.

29. Arie Egozi, "Israel Seeks $8B Arms Deal at White House: F-35s, V-22s, KC-46s,"
Breaking Defense, September 15, 2020, https://breakingdefense.com/2020/09
/israel-seeks-8b-arms-deal-at-white-house-f-35s-v-22s-kc-46s/.

30. Jacob Magid and Judah Ari Gross, "Bipartisan House Bill Will Encourage U.S. to
Sell Bunker Buster Bombs to Israel," *Times of Israel*, October 27, 2020, https://
www.timesofisrael.com/bipartisan-house-bill-will-encourage-us-to-sell-bunker
-buster-bombs-to-israel/.

31. TOI Staff and AP, "Netanyahu Warns against Reengaging with Iran, in Apparent
Message to Biden," *Times of Israel*, November 22, 2020, https://www.timesofisrael
.com/netanyahu-warns-against-reengaging-with-iran-in-apparent-message-to
-biden/.

32. David Brennan, "Israel Will Stop Iran Nuclear Program 'with or without' Joe Biden Deal, Benjamin Netanyahu Warns," *Newsweek*, February 23, 2021, https://www.newsweek.com/israel-stop-iran-nuclear-program-without-joe-biden-deal-benjamin-netanyahu-warns-1571301.

33. Richard Pérez-Peña, "Israel's Parliament Approves New Government, Ousting Netanyahu," *New York Times*, June 13, 2021, https://www.nytimes.com/live/2021/06/13/world/israel-knesset-bennett-lapid-netanyahu.

34. Jonathan Hessen and Erin Viner, "Lapid: Israel Not Bound by JCPOA," TV7 Israel News, August 23, 2022, https://www.tv7israelnews.com/lapid-israel-not-bound-by-jcpoa/.

35. Sheri Walsh, "Israel Urges West to Reject 'Bad' Nuclear Deal with Iran," UPI, August 24, 2022, https://www.upi.com/top_news/world-news/2022/08/24/yair-lapid-us-eu-iran-nuclear-deal/6751661368327/.

36. Idrees Ali and Phil Stewart, "U.S. Air Strikes in Syria Target Iranian-Backed Militia—Pentagon," Reuters, February 25, 2021, https://www.reuters.com/article/us-usa-syria-strike-exclusive/u-s-carries-out-airstrikes-against-iranian-backed-militia-facilities-in-syria-pentagon-idUSKBN2AP33D.

37. Helene Cooper and Eric Schmitt, "U.S. Airstrikes in Syria Target Iran-Backed Militias That Rocketed American Troops in Iraq," *New York Times*, February 25, 2021, https://www.nytimes.com/2021/02/25/us/politics/biden-syria-airstrike-iran.html.

38. James Inhofe, "Congress Will Make It Tough for Biden on Iran," *Foreign Policy*, February 1, 2021, https://www.inhofe.senate.gov/inhofe-in-foreign-policy-congress-will-make-it-tough-for-biden-on-iran.

39. Matthew Lee, "Iran Deal Tantalizingly Close, but U.S. Faces New Hurdles," Associated Press, August 19, 2022, https://apnews.com/article/salman-rushdie-iran-nuclear-indictments-nationalsecurity-104e765471526318f26d7c66ca00309f. Also, Spencer Bokat-Lindell, "After the Rushdie Attack, Can the Iran Nuclear Deal Be Saved?," *New York Times*, August 17, 2022, https://www.nytimes.com/2022/08/17/opinion/rushdieiran-nuclear-deal.html.

40. Stephanie Liechtenstein, "Iran Nuclear Talks Head into Deep Freeze Ahead of Midterms," *Politico*, September 13, 2022, https://www.politico.com/news/2022/09/13/iran-nuclear-talks-midterms-00056312.

41. Ben Samuels, "AIPAC-backed Republicans at Center of New Capitol Riot Revelations," *Haaretz*, June 16, 2022, https://www.haaretz.com/us-news/2022-06-16/ty-article/.highlight/aipac-backed-republicans-at-center-of-new-capitol-riot-revelations/00000181-6ce9-d9d1-a395-ecebd8ef0000.

42. Chris McGreal, "'Morally Bankrupt': Outrage after Pro-Israel Group Backs Insurrectionist Republicans," *The Guardian*, March 23, 2022, https://www.theguardian.com/us-news/2022/mar/23/aipac-pro-israel-group-backs-insurrectionist-republicans.

43. Steven Simon, "Course Correction: Preventing State Collapse in Syria," Quincy

Institute for Responsible Statecraft, Quincy Paper no. 3, August 2020, https://quincyinst.org/2020/08/11/course-correction-preventing-state-collapse-in-syria/.

44. Ambassador Tom Nides (@USAmbIsrael), Twitter, May 17, 2020, https://twitter.com/usambisrael/status/1262024480005726209.

45. Robert Burns, "Milley Urges 'Relook' at Permanent Overseas Basing of Troops," Associated Press, December 3, 2020, https://apnews.com/article/persian-gulf-tensions-south-korea-united-states-5949185a8cbf2843eac27535a599d022.

46. Michael R. Auslin, "The Sino-American War of 2025: A Future History," *Spectator World* magazine, February 19, 2021, https://spectator.us/topic/sino-american-war-2025-future-history/.

47. Jim Sciutto, Ryan Browne, and Deirdre Walsh, "Congress Releases Secret '28 Pages' on Alleged Saudi 9/11 Ties," CNN, July 15, 2016, https://www.cnn.com/2016/07/15/politics/congress-releases-28-pages-saudis-9-11.

48. The state of Palestinian politics, shaped by the reciprocal effects of occupation and internal dynamics—what the historian Rashid Khalidi described as a "striking absence of realism and clarity as to their objectives" and a "popular demobilization and rigorous suppression of dissent"—contributed to the eclipse of the peace process. Rashid Khalidi, "The Crisis of the Palestinian Political System," *Politique Étrangère*, issue 3, 2009, 651–62, https://www.cairn-int.info/journal-politique-etrangere-2009-3-page-651.htm.

49. Jeremy M. Sharp et al., *U.S. Foreign Assistance to the Middle East: Historical Background, Recent Trends, and the FY2021 Request* (Washington, DC: Congressional Research Service, 2020), https://crsreports.congress.gov/product/pdf/R/R46344/3.

50. Timothy Gardner, "Trump Says U.S. Does Not Need Middle East Oil, but Cargoes Keep Coming," Reuters, September 16, 2019, https://www.reuters.com/article/us-saudi-aramco-attacks-trump/trump-says-u-s-does-not-need-middle-east-oil-but-cargoes-keep-coming-idUSKBN1W12RO.

51. On the link between America's post-9/11 wars and the financial and economic crisis that started in 2008, see: Dana H. Allin and Erik Jones, *Weary Policeman: American Power in an Age of Austerity* (New York and Abingdon, UK: Routledge, 2012), 71–72, 160–63.

52. In 2020, U.S. trade with Japan was over $250 billion, including services provided by the United States; trade with Taiwan was over $90 billion; with Korea, over $127 billion. In 2021, the United States had invested $2.4 trillion in the EU, which in turn invested $2.0 trillion in the United States. All trade figures in this section can be accessed at https://ustr.gov/countries-regions.

53. J. Baxter Oliphant, "The Iraq War Continues to Divide the U.S. Public, 15 Years after It Began," Pew Research, March 19, 2008, https://www.pewresearch.org/fact-tank/2018/03/19/iraq-war-continues-to-divide-u-s-public-15-years-after-it-began/.

INDEX